PRICE THEORY

Other Macmillan books by D. W. Pearce

Cost–Benefit Analysis

Cost–Benefit Analysis: Theory and Practice
(with Ajit K. Dasgupta)

Capital Investment Appraisal
(with C. J. Hawkins)

The Economics of Natural Resource Depletion
(editor)

PRICE THEORY

W. J. L. RYAN
Professor of Political Economy, University of Dublin, Eire

REVISED BY
D. W. PEARCE
*Professor of Political Economy
University of Aberdeen*

REVISED EDITION

© W. J. L. Ryan 1958

Revised edition © W. J. L. Ryan and D. W. Pearce 1977

All rights reserved. No part of this publication may be reproduced or transmitted, in any form or by any means, without permission.

First edition 1958
Reprinted 1960, 1961, 1962, 1964 (twice),
1965, 1966, 1967, 1969
Revised edition 1977

Published by
THE MACMILLAN PRESS LTD
London and Basingstoke
Associated companies in New York Dublin
Melbourne Johannesburg and Delhi

ISBN 0 333 17912 9 (hard cover)
     0 333 17913 7 (paper cover)

Text set in 10/12 pt Photon Baskerville, printed by photolithography, and bound in Great Britain at The Pitman Press, Bath

This book is sold subject to the standard conditions of the Net Book Agreement.

The paperback edition of this book is sold subject to the condition that it shall not, by way of trade or otherwise, be lent, resold, hired out, or otherwise circulated without the publisher's prior consent, in any form of binding or cover other than that in which it is published and without a similar condition including this condition being imposed on the subsequent purchaser.

CONTENTS

Preface to the Revised Edition   xi

Preface to the First Edition   xiv

1   *Preferences and Consumer Equilibrium*   1

1.0	The Household and the Consumer	1
1.1	Preference and Indifference	2
1.2	Commodity Space	5
1.3	General Axioms of Choice	7
1.4	Deriving the Indifference Map of a Consumer	9
1.5	A Digression: Lexicographic Orderings	12
1.6	Convex Preferences	14
1.7	Some Properties of Indifference Curves	17
1.8	The Consumer's Budget Set	19
1.9	Consumer Equilibrium	20
1.10	Some 'Pathological' Cases	21
1.11	The Utility Function	28

2   *Demand Functions*   31

2.0	Income–Consumption Relationship	31
2.1	Income Elasticity of Demand	34
2.2	Price–Consumption Relationship	36
2.3	The Demand Curve	38
2.4	Price Elasticity of Demand	42
2.5	Price Elasticity and Total Revenue	44
2.6	Income and Substitution Effects	46
	(a) The Hicks Approach	47
	(b) The Slutsky Approach	49
2.7	Redefining 'Normal', 'Inferior' and 'Giffen' Goods	51

2.8	On Various Demand Curves	52
2.9	Substitutes and Complements	56
2.10	Revealed Preference	58
2.11	Some 'Pathological' Demand Curves	62
2.12	Market Demand	65
2.13	Market Demand: Aggregation Problems	66

3	*Short-Run Sales Plan of the Firm: The Production Function*	70
3.0	Purchase and Sales Plans	70
3.1	Firms' Objectives	71
3.2	Planning Periods	72
3.3	The Production Function: Linear Case	73
3.4	The Production Function: Smooth Case	79
3.5	The Convexity of Isoproduct Curves	80
3.6	The Law of Non-Proportional Returns	82
3.7	Linearity and Product Curves	86

4	*Short-Run Sales Plan of the Firm: Cost Functions and Equilibrium*	88
4.0	Cost Minimisation	88
4.1	Changes in Relative Input Prices	89
4.2	Cost Functions	92
4.3	Output and Substitution Effects	97
4.4	Equilibrium of the Firm	99
4.5	The Response of Sales Plans to Changes in Product Price	104
4.6	Market Supply	105
4.7	Price-Elasticity of Supply	106
4.8	Changes in Supply	107

5	*Long-Run Sales Plan of the Firm: Production, Cost and Supply Functions*	109
5.0	The Long Run	109
5.1	Returns to Scale	110
5.2	The Cobb–Douglas Production Function	112
5.3	Indivisibilities	113
5.4	Long-Run Production Possibilities	114
5.5	Long-Run Costs	116
5.6	Choice of a Sales Plan	118

5.7	The Intermediate Period	119
5.8	The Multiproduct Firm	121

6 The Determination of Relative Product Prices — 123

6.0	Supply and Demand	123
6.1	Price Determination: Short-Run	124
6.2	Short-Run Price Determination: A Simple Algebraic Approach	130
6.3	Short-Run Demand and Supply Analysis: Applications to Price Control and Taxation	132
6.4	Price Determination: Long-Run	139
6.5	Long-Run Demand and Supply Analysis: Applications	144
6.6	Long-Run Supply: Changing Input Prices	148
6.7	Short-Run and Long-Run Demand	150

7 The Purchase Plan of the Firm — 154

7.0	Introduction	154
7.1	Short-Run Demand for One Variable Input	154
7.2	Input Price-Elasticity	158
7.3	The Effects of Parameter Changes	159
7.4	The Short-Run Demand Curve: Two Variable Inputs	160
7.5	The Long-Run Demand Curve	164
7.6	The Total Demand Curve for an Input	165
7.7	The Firm's Demand for a Durable Good	168

8 The Sales Plan of the Consumer: The Supply of Effort — 172

8.0	Consumption Time and Work Time	172
8.1	Optimal Allocation of Time	173
8.2	The Supply Curve of Labour	175
8.3	Income and Substitution Effects	178
8.4	The Effort-Demand for Labour	180
8.5	Long-Run Supply	183
8.6	The Sales Plan for the Services of Land	186

9 The Sales Plan of the Consumer: Saving and Savings — 188

9.0	The Saving Plan	188
9.1	The Savings Plan: Money and Bonds	204
9.2	The Savings Plan: Wider Portfolio Choice	209

10	*The Determination of Relative Input Prices*	216
10.0	Relative Wage-Rates	216
10.1	The Determination of the Relative Price of a Durable Good	222
10.2	The Pricing of the Services of Durable Goods	224
10.3	Classifying Inputs: A Note on Human Capital	226
10.4	A Note on Differences in Efficiency between Units of the 'Same' Input	228
10.5	A Note on 'Economic Rent'	230
10.6	The Rate of Interest	233
11	*The Determination of Relative Prices: General Equilibrium*	246
11.0	General and Partial Analysis	246
11.1	The General Consequences of an Economic Event	248
11.2	The Uses of General Analysis	249
11.3	A Formal Approach to General Equilibrium	251
11.4	The Existence of General Equilibrium Prices	254
11.5	The Stability of General Equilibrium Prices	256
12	*Market Behaviour and Market Morphology*	259
12.0	The Methodology of Market Models	259
12.1	Pure Competition	261
12.2	Perfect Competition	264
12.3	A Classification of Markets	272
13	*Monopoly*	276
13.0	The Nature of Monopoly	276
13.1	The Equilibrium of the Monopolist	276
13.2	The Objectives of the Monopolist	280
13.3	Monopolistic Price Discrimination	282
13.4	Advertising	285
13.5	Potential New Entrants	287
13.6	Long-Run Decreasing Costs	289
13.7	Genesis of Monopoly and Maintenance of Monopoly	290
14	*Monopolistic Competition*	294
14.0	The Nature of Monopolistic Competition	294

14.1	Short-Run Equilibrium under Monopolistic Competition	295
14.2	Long-Run Equilibrium under Monopolistic Competition	296
14.3	Full-Cost or Average-Cost Pricing	298

15 *Monopsony and Monopsonistic Competition* — 302

15.0	Monopsonistic Markets	302
15.1	Equilibrium under Monopsony	303

16 *Oligopoly* — 307

16.0	The Nature of Oligopoly	307
16.1	The Cournot Model	308
16.2	Leadership Models	316
16.3	The Kinked Oligopoly Demand Curve	325
16.4	Collusive Oligopoly	329
16.5	Game Theory and Oligopoly	339

17 *Bilateral Monopoly* — 344

17.0	Price-Taker Context	344
17.1	Price-Maker Context	347

18 *Normative Price Theory* — 354

18.0	Introduction	354
18.1	Consumer's Surplus: The Concept	355
18.2	Consumer's Surplus: The Marshallian Approach	356
18.3	Hicks's Four Measures of Consumer's Surplus	362
18.4	Compensation Tests	368
18.5	Pareto Optimal Allocations	371
18.6	The Optimality of Perfect Competition	376
18.7	The Problem of Second Best	378
18.8	Public Goods	381
18.9	External Effects	385

Index — 389

PREFACE TO THE REVISED EDITION

In the preface to the first edition of *Price Theory* (1958) Professor Ryan remarked that he had used 'only the traditional tools of analysis', and that 'were this book being written five or ten years later the emphasis given to the various tools would have to be completely reversed'. Fifteen years later the tools of analysis have certainly changed as far as the professional economist is concerned. Linear and non-linear programming, game theory, linear algebra and the traditional weapons of the calculus now play a very much larger role in research and in teaching than they did some years ago. The modern university and polytechnic student is expected to accommodate at least some of these techniques, but it seems right to say that the average student is still largely non-numerate and is likely to remain so for some time, although standards are clearly rising. The modern author does therefore have a choice. He can write for the numerate and reach only a small proportion of the student audience, perhaps hoping that the increasing preponderance of numerate textbooks will give the non-numerate more incentive to learn some mathematics. Or he can write for the non-numerate, gain the larger audience, but at the cost of some rigour, some elegance and the omission of topics which can best be treated mathematically.

I have, in this revised edition of Professor Ryan's justly famous work, tried to steer a middle path. What I have done is to use *some* mathematical *language* in the belief that the biggest obstacle to learning numerate economics is the jargon and not the mathematical manipulation of equations. What I have not done, except occasionally – and only then where a non-mathematical approach has also been used – is to *operate* with mathematics. In this way I hope the reader will gain some of the flavour of modern approaches without being faced with the impenetrable barrier of mathematical limitation.

The actual process of revising the first edition turned out to be far more complex than I imagined. Both Professor Ryan and the publishers merit my apologies and indebtedness for being so patient with me. The problem lay in the fact that Professor Ryan's original treatment was almost 100 per cent self-contained. It had a logical sequence which, though I strived not to, I fear I have broken. On the other hand, it was difficult to see how *any* change from the original edition could preserve the unique features of that edition. The only real loose ends in the original edition were contained in Chapter 12 entitled 'Some Further Problems'. The topics in that chapter are now integrated in the main body of the text.

In making other changes I have been deliberately subjective and there is no question that I shall be criticised for having included some things, elaborated on others, and omitted still others. The biggest issue was whether to include a substantial section on 'new' theories of the firm. Had I done this the book would have been longer than it is now, and my feeling was that (*a*) it would have departed even further from Professor Ryan's original aims, and (*b*) it would have been redundant in face of some excellent recent volumes which have concentrated on this issue. In consequence, the main changes have been to introduce linearity into the chapters on consumer theory and on cost and production theory; to extend the general equilibrium chapter; to 'update' chapters where I have felt this expedient; and to add a new chapter on the normative uses of price theory – that is, welfare economics. While this is a small list, the result has been a substantial change, although I have done little to change Professor Ryan's meticulous treatment of firm equilibrium under various market forms. The chapters have also been rearranged slightly, although here again it was Professor Ryan's careful juxtaposition of chapters in logical sequence that was a dominant feature of the original edition. I can only hope that some of the logical rigour and value of Professor Ryan's original approach, which I cannot hope to emulate, remains.

Lastly, I have written for the market, and this has sometimes meant that I have taken a fairly neutral approach to issues on which I have, in fact, the most decided opinions. In particular I have recorded the conventional approach to the 'efficiency' of market systems, although reference to some of my other work will show that I find this notion of efficiency very unattractive. There is nothing novel in the content of the revised edition: it has all been said before. I can only hope that the arrangement of the material and the exposition will appeal. My debts are therefore fairly obvious and include all writers on economic issues.

A special debt is owed to Christopher Nash of Southampton University who read many of the new sections and commented in his usual invaluable way. And, of course, I owe an immense debt to Professor Ryan for his assistance and advice during the preparation of this manuscript. As always, my greatest debt is to my family. None of these people, least of all my family, bear any responsibility for the errors which no doubt remain.

D. W. P.

University of Leicester
April 1976

PREFACE TO THE FIRST EDITION

It is tempting to begin by defining the scope of economics and describing the methods by which economic truths are customarily pursued in academic circles. The temptation is acute for an economist, for the fascination of economics with its own scope and method verges on neurosis. It is with reluctance, therefore, that we do not deal with these topics explicitly. We shall not prejudice their importance, however, if we define economics as the kinds of thing that economists habitually talk about, and its methodology as the way in which they customarily do so.

Economists generally describe certain decisions that are taken by individuals who are acting on their own behalf, or as agents, in a free society, and attempt to explore some of their effects. The kinds of decision that interest economists are those which lead to a purchase or to a sale. In the Western world, those who decide to buy and sell may be classified roughly into households, firms and the various agencies of government. Each household decides what commodities and services to buy and when, where and in what quantities to buy them. These decisions make up the *purchase plan* of the household. Each household will also have a *sales plan* setting out the things that its members have decided to sell and the quantities, prices and places at which they will be sold. The sales and purchase plans of the household will be related to one another, for the sums of money that the members of the household get from selling their labour or lending their savings or renting their land generally constitute the fund out of which they buy the goods and services of everyday consumption.

Similarly, each firm in the economy must decide what goods to produce and sell and when, where and the quantities in which to sell them. All these decisions make up the *sales plan* of the firm. In addition, each firm must decide what things to use in making its products, and when, where, how, and in what quantities to use them. All decisions of this kind are summarised in its *purchase plan*.

The purchase and sales plans of the firms are not independent of one another, for firms buy in order to sell. The sums of money that they earn by selling the goods they produce are used directly or indirectly to pay for the things they require to assist in their production and sale. We would expect, too, some relation between the plans of households and those of firms. The things that firms plan to sell must be similar to those which households plan to buy, and the things that firms plan to buy must be more or less the same as the things that households or other firms are planning to sell.

In a free world the implementation and revision of these plans affect almost all facets of human life and endeavour. As economists, however, we are primarily interested in how these plans determine both relative prices and price levels. As firms and households act on the plans they have made, the relationship between prices may alter: butter may become more expensive than nails or bread less dear as compared with jam. And almost all prices might rise as they have done since 1939, or fall as they did in the early 1930's. These twin effects are inextricably and indistinguishably linked together, but if we are to grasp their nature we must examine each in isolation. In this book we are primarily concerned with the determination of the relationship between the prices of the things that are bought and sold.

This book is intended as a text-book for students who are planning to specialise in economics. I have tried to state all the assumptions explicitly and to keep the analysis rigorous. The analysis may occasionally seem to be a trifle self-conscious, for I believe that it is important for students to learn not only what economists do but why and how they do it. There are frequent summaries of the analyses, and I hope that these will be more helpful than they are tedious. I do not think that there is anything that is original in the contents of this book, but there may be some originality in the form in which they are presented.

In elaborating the theory of relative prices, I have used only the traditional tools of analysis. While these tools are suffering a rapid obsolescence, they still do a better job than the prototypes of the tools which may soon supplant them and which are briefly described in the final chapter. It is not improbable, however, that were this book being written five or ten years later, the emphasis given to the various tools would have to be completely reversed.

I am deeply indebted, either directly or indirectly, to all economists who have written on the theory of price. If I make no attempt to acknowledge my debts in detail, it is because they are too numerous and because I have forgotten the transactions in which many of them originated. I wish to express my gratitude to Professor G. A. Duncan, Professor A. T. Peacock, Professor G. L. S. Shackle, Dr. A. W. H. Phillips, Mr. Jack Wiseman and Mr. F. P. R. Brechling who read the manuscript and made many valuable suggestions and criticisms, and to the students in the London School of Economics and Political Science and in the University of Dublin who forced me to strive after clarity both in thought and expression.

W. J. L. RYAN

TRINITY COLLEGE
DUBLIN

1

Preferences and Consumer Equilibrium

1.0 The Household and the Consumer

Microeconomic theory tends to assume that *individuals* are the economic agents exercising the act of consumption, the decision to purchase goods and services. The way in which this decision is exercised is the subject matter of this chapter.

In practice, however, the individual consumer does not often act independently of the other members of his or her household. In other words, it is not just the tastes and preferences of the individual that determine which commodities he or she buys. In buying the weekly shopping Mrs A has to consider what her husband and her children like. It is convenient, then, to distinguish

(*a*) the individual
(*b*) the family or household

as *consuming units*.

The essential distinctions between the two units in terms of behaviour are:

(i) that households may not have the same objectives as individuals: parents frequently judge on behalf of the 'junior' members of the family;

(ii) that the purchases of one individual in a family unit may affect the 'welfare' of other individuals in the unit – there are 'external effects' (see Chapter 18) which limit the preferences of the individual;

(iii) that a given money income may be shared between several individuals so that the preferences of all the individuals in the household tend to determine the final 'mix' or 'bundle' of commodities purchased, even though the income might derive from only one member of the family;

(iv) some commodities are 'collectively consumed' by the family:

the benefits of central heating, for example, if made available to one member of the family, are made available to all members. Other examples might include television programmes and lighting. In other words, some family commodities are jointly supplied to various members of the family.

For these reasons it seems likely that family behaviour will differ from the behaviour of an individual in isolation. The theory of behaviour applicable to an individual may not, therefore, be used without modification for the family or household. In general, individual preferences are constrained by family objectives, and, in many respects, the family or 'household' is analogous to the economic behaviour of society as a whole. We shall henceforth call the basic consuming unit the *consumer,* acknowledging that on some occasions the consumer is an individual, and on others the family, or household.

1.1 Preference and Indifference

Consumers are assumed to select commodities according to their *preferences*. It is tempting to investigate this notion more deeply: whether preferences are 'real' or manipulated by advertising, for example. The position taken here, however, is that preferences, however determined, are the basic data for the study of the consumer.

Preferences assume significance in the context of *choice*. Indeed, it is the choice context that defines the area of economic study. If all goods were free, there would be no problem of selecting between alternatives. But goods are not free, neither at the national macroeconomic level nor at the microeconomic level of the consumer's weekly budget.

Hence we can establish a very general proposition which must be investigated further: *consumer preferences determine which commodity bundles are purchased*. And we shall assume that the notion of a preference requires no further elaboration.[1] Notice that the object of the choice made by a consumer is some 'mix' of commodities. These com-

---

[1] This statement should not be taken to imply that an investigation into the nature of preferences is unimportant. The basic assumption of most economic theory is that of 'consumers' sovereignty', which means (a) that the consumer knows best what serves his own welfare, and (b) that his preferences *should* determine the allocation of resources and goods in an economy. Few governments would ever permit consumers' sovereignty to reign supreme: preferences are frequently based on ignorance or are determined by the 'hidden persuaders' of the advertising industry. In consequence, we can all argue about the extent to which economic democracy should be advanced. But, fascinating and important though such problems are, they lie outside the scope of a text which is predominantly 'positive' in content.

modities, the quantities of which can be measured, are the *choice variables* of the consumer.

Consumers express preferences for goods and services – which we group together as *commodities*. Later, we shall have occasion to note that consumers also express the opposite of a preference – a 'dispreference' – for 'bads' and disservices such as noise, air pollution, fouled beaches, and so on. The preference may be expressed as between two or more individual commodities, or between two or more *bundles* of commodities. It is convenient to work with commodity bundles, for reasons that will be clear shortly. Hence we introduce some notation:

$$X = \{x_1, x_2\}.$$

The first expression refers to a commodity bundle X, comprising two elements, or components – an amount x_1 of good 1 and an amount x_2 of good 2. We can summarise this by saying that X is a *two-component vector*.

For the sake of diagrammatic exposition, it is very convenient to work with commodity bundles that have only two goods as components. The reason is simply that diagrams are most easily drawn in two dimensions. Three-dimensional diagrams can, of course, be drawn, but much is lost in a confusion of lines and perspective. But, in practice, consumers exercise their preferences over many commodities and many commodity bundles. There is nothing we can do about representing such a situation diagrammatically, but the symbolic expression above is not limited in this way. If there are n commodities (where n is any number), for example, we can write

$$X = \{x_1, x_2, x_3, \ldots, x_n\}.$$

The technical way of expressing this is to say that each commodity bundle X is an *n-component vector*.

Given two bundles, X and Y, say, the consumer can either prefer X to Y, prefer Y to X, or be indifferent between X and Y. Hence there are two basic relations between commodity bundles as far as the consumer is concerned: preference and indifference. Once again, it is convenient to have some notation to express these relationships. We introduce the notation P for 'is preferred to' and I for 'is indifferent to'. The possible relationships between X and Y are therefore summarised as

XPY which means 'X is preferred to Y';
YPX which means 'Y is preferred to X';
XIY which means 'X is indifferent to Y'.

In fact, the relationship of indifference is not an *extra* notion over and above that of preference. For to say that XIY is to say only that it is *not* the case that XPY and it is *not* the case that YPX. We have just one 'primitive notion', that of preference. The relationship of indifference can be derived from it.

The reader may have noted that the sentence beginning 'For to say ...' above was a clumsy one. Some further notation would assist in providing some rigour and brevity to expressions of this kind. We introduce some further symbols:

- & which means, simply, 'and';
- − which means 'it is not the case that';
- → which means 'logically implies', or 'if . . . then';
- ↔ which means that the first expression logically implies the second, and the second implies the first, or, more conveniently, 'if and only if'.

As an example of the use to which these symbols can be put, consider again the sentence: 'To say that XIY is to say that it is not the case that XPY and it is not the case that XPX.' This can be translated into our formal language as

$$XIY \leftrightarrow -(XPY) \& -(YPX)$$

or, in words again, XIY if, and only if, neither XPY nor YPX is the case. These expressions may look daunting at first, but they are essentially very simple, and exceedingly useful as a shorthand with which to express statements that would otherwise be very involved.

In saying that XPY, the consumer is *ranking* or *ordering* X and Y. This is equivalent to listing the alternatives and placing the most preferred one at the top of the list. Thus, if X is placed first, Y second, Z third, A fourth, B fifth, we could write, XPY, YPZ, ZPA, APB. If the relationships between the alternatives are all of the type 'preferred to' – i.e. if indifference does not enter the picture – the consumer's ordering is referred to as a *strict ordering* or *strong ordering*. If, however, the ordering included indifference between any pair, say Y and Z, with the other relationships being of the preference kind, the ordering would be a *weak ordering*.

Although the notion of a preference is the basic one and its importance emerges again shortly, it is useful to begin with the notion of indifference. The indifference relationship possesses three attributes without which it would not be possible to establish the theory of consumer behaviour that follows in the subsequent chapters. These attributes are:

(i) TRANSITIVITY. (XIY) & $(YIZ) \leftrightarrow (XIZ)$

This condition simply says that if the consumer is indifferent between X and Y, and is indifferent between Y and Z, then he is indifferent between X and Z. This condition certainly appears reasonable. Notice that it applies even more forcefully to the preference relationship. If XPY and YPZ, then it is natural to infer that XPZ.[1]

(ii) REFLEXIVENESS. XIX

This is an unexceptionable condition, declaring that X must be indifferent to itself. Notice that preference is irreflexive however.

(iii) SYMMETRY. $(XIY) \rightarrow (YIX)$

Again, a harmless enough assumption which simply declares that if X is indifferent to Y, then Y is indifferent to X.

These three attributes characterise the indifference relation. It is sometimes summarised by saying that indifference is an 'equivalence' relationship (hint: apply the same analysis to the symbol $=$; this, too, is an equivalence relationship, whereas inequalities such as $>$ or $<$ are not).[2]

1.2 Commodity Space

The individual consumer exercises his preferences by choosing between commodity bundles. In two dimensions we can measure the amount of each of two commodities, x_1 and x_2, along the horizontal and vertical axes, as shown in Figure 1.2.1. In general, we confine

---

[1] Transitivity is a crucial attribute of the theory of consumer behaviour. Unfortunately, experiments tend to suggest that individuals do not obey this axiom in practice: they might express a preference for X over Y, for Y over Z, but faced with the choice between X and Z they choose Z. However, they also tend to acknowledge their 'irrationality' when the results are pointed out to them. In accepting the transitivity of indifference we also ignore that body of thought which declares indifference to be intransitive. See W. Armstrong, 'Utility and the Theory of Welfare', *Oxford Economic Papers,* Oct. 1951, and the discussion in T. Majumdar, *The Measurement of Utility* (Macmillan, London, 1958) and J. Rothenberg, *The Measurement of Social Welfare* (Prentice-Hall, New Jersey, 1961).

[2] To some extent the reader must take it on trust that these conditions are necessary to establish the subsequent theory. The technical reason is that equivalence relationships enable us to divide up (partition) the commodity space (all the possible combinations of goods) into non-overlapping classes.

ourselves to the right-hand quadrant of the figure, the axes of which show positive amounts of both goods 1 and 2. The left-hand quadrant shows positive amounts of good 2 and *negative* amounts of good 1. Use of this quadrant can be made when we consider goods that can be held in negative quantities – such as financial securities – or in analysing 'bads' – such as pollution. But we concentrate on the right-hand quadrant, which we term *commodity space*.

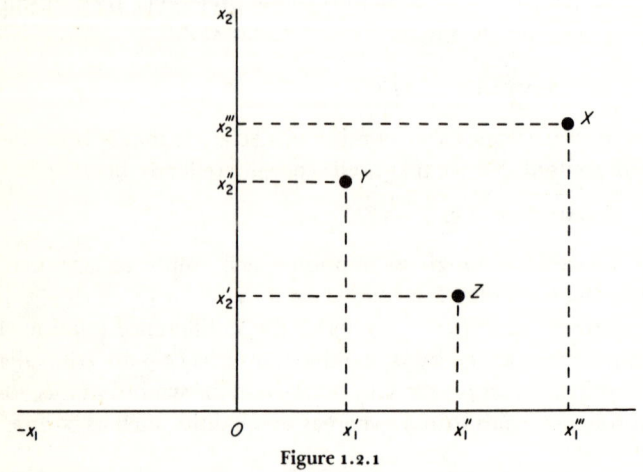

Figure 1.2.1

In the figure, we have $Y = \{x_1', x_2''\}$, $X = \{x_1''', x_2'''\}$ and $Z = \{x_1'', x_2'\}$. That is, the points X, Y and Z are all representations of commodity bundles. The figure is in two dimensions, but it will be recalled that the analysis of consumer behaviour will be applicable to a situation where there are n commodities. Just as the commodity space in Figure 1.2.1 is shown as the positive quadrant of a two-dimensional diagram, in n dimensions we work with the positive *orthant*: the n-dimensional space that consists of positive quantities of all commodities.

Now it is customary to think of the goods being measured along the axes x_1 and x_2 in terms of apples and oranges, or wheat and wine. The characteristics of such goods are that they are highly divisible – we can have minute quantities of wine and wheat. But, of course, the sort of goods that the consumer buys includes washing machines, cars, record players, as well as food, clothing, fuel, etc. Many of these goods are *indivisible* in various degrees. If now good 2 in Figure 1.2.1 is highly divisible, but good 1 is not, it will not be possible to attach meaning to some of the points in the commodity space.

For example, if good 1 can be purchased in units of x_1' and x_1''', then a point such as Z would not have meaning since there is no 'proper' quantity of good 1 corresponding to x_1''. Thus, Z might correspond to 2 pints of beer and $1\frac{1}{4}$ washing machines. The existence of this kind of indivisibility means that there are 'holes' in the commodity space, and that points corresponding with these holes have no significance for analysis. Clearly, this is a problem that it would be very convenient to avoid. It would be better if we could assume that there are no holes in the commodity space, and this we do. We simply introduce the assumption that the commodity space is *continuously divisible*, which is sometimes stated as the *axiom of commodity space connectedness*.

The reader should not be too alarmed that we have assumed away a very real problem. We do so partly because our theory will become too complicated if we acknowledge indivisibilities at this early stage, and the aim is to build up a theory based on conditions which, while they may be restrictive, are not too unreasonable. Second, we could argue that our theory, when it is derived, is not concerned with locating *precise* points in commodity space. We shall be mainly interested in general statements about what happens when goods' prices change, when income changes, and so on. In each case, it tends to be the *direction* of change that matters, a general prediction rather than a precise forecast.

1.3 General Axioms of Choice

The consumer exercises his choices in commodity space. We have already introduced the notions of preference and indifference. We now further assume that all points in commodity space can be brought into the relationship of preference or indifference. That is, it must be possible for the consumer to *order* (i.e. rank) points such as X, Y and Z in Figure 1.2.1. This is a reasonable assumption, but it is perfectly possible to imagine situations in which the consumer knows how to rank, say, X and Z, but cannot rank Y because he has no experience of it. This will be unlikely in the case we are considering, but the reader must remember that many commodities often lie outside the experience of most individuals – holidays in South America, eating Mediterranean squid, and so on.

We formalise this assumption in the form of an *axiom*. As we shall see, various axioms will be required before we can derive a framework within which to discuss consumer theory. Hence we state the first axiom:

Axiom 1 The Axiom of Completeness.

All commodity bundles can be compared in terms of either indifference or preference. In terms of the formal symbolism introduced earlier, we can write this as

$$(X)(Y)(XRY \text{ v } YRX).$$

The X in parentheses simply means 'for all X'.[1] Similarly with Y. The symbol 'v' simply means 'or'. The R is a convenient way of saying 'preferred or indifferent' and could be translated as meaning 'at least as desirable as'. Hence, the above statement reads, 'for all X and for all Y, it is either the case that X is preferred or indifferent to Y or it is the case that Y is preferred or indifferent to X'.

If the reader refers to other literature he should take care to note that there is no standard terminology relating to these axioms. In this case, for example, the axiom of completeness is sometimes referred to as the axiom of *comparability* or *connectedness* (do not confuse this with the connectedness of commodity space).

With the idea of axioms introduced, we can now consider the other necessary axioms.

Axiom 2 The Axiom of Transitivity.

The nature of transitivity was introduced earlier in connection with indifference. We now state formally that both indifference and preference must be transitive:

$$(X)(Y)(Z)(XRY \text{ \& } YRZ \rightarrow XRZ).$$

Axiom 3 The Axiom of Selection.

We now endow the consumer with a purpose; with an aim that he tries to attain. This aim is to reach the *most preferred state*, and we refer to this as the consumer's *'objective function'*. Essentially, we require that the consumer select a point in commodity space which is most preferred, and, of course, is attainable. It is useful then to introduce the idea of a *feasible set*, or, as it is otherwise known, the *choice set*, or *attainable set*. The feasible set will simply be the points in commodity space that the consumer is able to reach. As we shall see shortly, the feasible set is usually

---

[1] The reader may also come across the 'universal quantifier', as the 'for all X' symbolism is known, in the form of the symbol $\forall$.

determined by the consumer's income since this determines what he is able to purchase. We omit the possibility that there is no limit to the feasible set: we say that it is *bounded*. The axiom of selection is therefore a compound of individual statements:

(a) if *XPY*, *X* is chosen: the consumer chooses the preferred alternative;

(b) there will be a commodity bundle such that if that bundle is feasible, it will be chosen. This merely ensures that *something* will be selected from the attainable set;

(c) The consumer will select the most preferred commodity bundle in the feasible set. If he selects *X*, then there will be another bundle *Y* such that *XIY*, but it *cannot* be the case that another bundle *Z* exists in the feasible set such that *ZPY*.

Although it looks involved, this axiom tells us that the consumer will aim to reach the most preferred state within the feasible set. The axiom of selection establishes the objective of the consumer.[1] Later on we shall have occasion to refer to this axiom in terms of the assumption that each consumer aims to *maximise his utility* (see Section 1.11).

1.4 Deriving the Indifference Map of a Consumer

So far, we have established certain conditions relating to commodity space, and to consumer preferences. What we have not done is to relate directly the consumer's preferences to the commodity space of Figure 1.2.1. This we do by introducing a further axiom:

Axiom 4 The Axiom of Dominance.

Consider points *X* and *Y* in Figure 1.2.1. *X* has more of both commodities. We say that *X dominates Y*. We now introduce a simple axiom which tells us that if *X* dominates *Y*, the consumer will prefer *X*.

$$(X)(Y)(X > Y \rightarrow XPY).$$

---

[1] In formal language, the axiom can be written

$$(X)[CX \rightarrow \exists Y(XIY \& AY) \& -\exists Z(AZ \& ZPY)].$$

The backward-facing *E* simply means 'there is an *X*' or 'there is a *Y*' as the case may be. It is the 'existential quantifier'. *CX* means '*X* is chosen' and *AX* means '*X* is feasible (attainable)'. Formulated in this way, the axiom tells us that the consumer selects from the *maximal* elements of the attainable set: a maximal element being, in our case, a commodity bundle in the feasible set which is preferred or indifferent to all other bundles. The emphasis on feasibility is essential, of course, because it may well be the case that *ZPY* and hence *ZPX*, but *Z* lies outside the feasible set.

In short, the consumer always prefers *more* of both commodities to less.[1]

We can, in fact, widen this definition a little since the axiom allows for the possibility that X has more of one commodity and the same amount of the other one. In Figure 1.4.1 below, for example, X dominates Y, as does Z. Indeed, any point in the shaded area with Y as origin dominates Y. We can conclude, therefore, that any point in the shaded area is preferred to Y. By analogous reasoning we can infer that any point in the lower – south-west – quadrant is inferior to Y since Y dominates all points in it. In this way we have begun to map the preference relationship into commodity space.

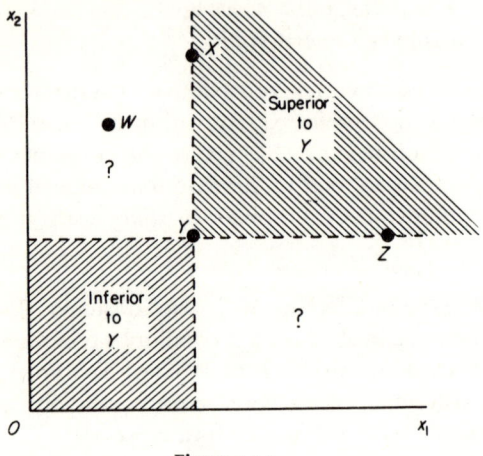

Figure 1.4.1

The axiom of dominance is also termed the axiom of *nonsatiation* or the axiom of *monotonicity*.[2] Notice that the axiom holds only for goods.

---

[1] For the moment, we can use the axiom of dominance to justify our neglect of consumer savings, i.e. our assumption that all income is spent. Since the consumer obtains more satisfaction from more goods, savings imply a sacrifice of satisfaction. This hints at the explanation of savings behaviour: some income will be saved if either (*a*) the consumer is satiated with respect to his total expenditure, or (*b*) by saving he can secure a commodity bundle in a *future* period which dominates the bundle that could have been bought (with the money otherwise saved) in the *current* period. It is convenient and not misleading to introduce the time factor when we consider savings behaviour explicitly (see Chapter 9).

[2] Recalling the definition of an equivalence relation, the reader can confirm that, since $X > Y$ provides an irreflexive, asymmetric and transitive relation between X and Y, the axiom of dominance can provide only a *partial* ordering, an equivalence relation being necessary for a complete ordering.

Preferences and Consumer Equilibrium

For 'bads' we are likely to get the opposite of dominance: less air pollution and noise will be preferred to more.

Now Figure 1.4.1 tells us remarkably little. There remain the two 'zones of ignorance' about which we have said nothing. Compared to Y, each zone contains less of one commodity and more of the other.

Point W, for example, has more of good 2 and less of good 1. The axiom of dominance does not enable us to say anything about this point, at least not without some further manipulation.

Figure 1.4.2 repeats the general structure of 1.4.1. A line from the origin is drawn to the north-west of X so that it passes through the north-west zone of ignorance, but also through the two zones which are known to be inferior and superior to X respectively. We know from

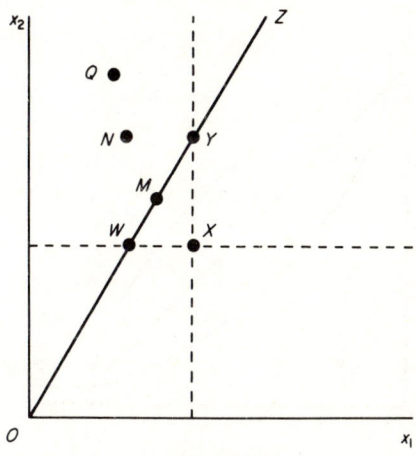

Figure 1.4.2

the axiom of dominance, that all points on the line section YZ are preferred to X, simply because YZ lies in the superior quadrant with X as origin. Similarly, all points on OW are inferior to X. But a point like Y must be preferred to W, since Y lies north-west of W: it contains more of both commodities. In other words, somewhere between W and Y there is a point which indicates a switch of preferences: up to W we know that X is preferred, whereas from Y onwards we know that each point on the ray is preferred to X. Hence there must be a point where this changeover occurs, and this point must lie on WY. As long as this preference relationship changes smoothly, we can safely assert that there is a point, say M, which is *indifferent* to X.

If we repeat this exercise but with M as the reference point, we can establish that there is likely to be point like N, such that NIM. Then, with N as reference point, we can establish Q, such that QIN, and so on. The continuous line (the 'locus') joining Q, N, M and X with similar points in the south-east quadrant is called an *indifference curve*. This curve can be thought of as a boundary line: to the right of the line we have a set of points which are preferred to the set of points to the left of the line. On the line itself, all points are indifferent to each other. Notice that we have established only that the line slopes downwards from left to right. It could have any of the shapes shown in Figure 1.4.3 (or, indeed, any combination of these shapes). After a brief digression we shall set limits on the shape of the indifference curve.

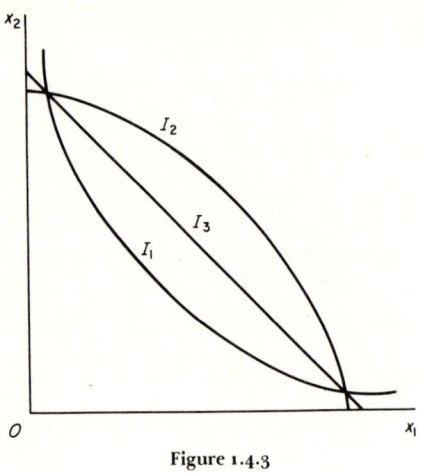

Figure 1.4.3

1.5 A Digression: Lexicographic Orderings

Although we have argued that the indifference curve is likely to have one of the shapes shown in Figure 1.4.3, it is as well to recognise that we have not proved the existence of an indifference curve. A counter-example will show that, if a consumer orders bundles of commodities in a particular way, an indifference curve does not exist. Imagine someone with a craving for cheese, like Ben Gunn in Stevenson's *Treasure Island*. It is quite likely that Ben would prefer any bundle with more cheese, regardless of the amount of the other commodity in the bundle. At the same time, if two bundles contained equal amounts of cheese we can assume that Ben prefers the bundle with more of the other commodity. This kind of ordering is shown in Figure 1.5.1.

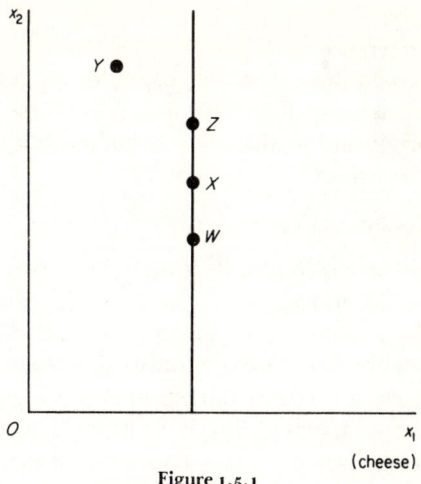

Figure 1.5.1

To the right of X, all bundles contain more cheese: hence all points to the right of X, regardless of which quadrant they are in, are preferred to X. Similarly, all points to the left of X are inferior to X. For bundles with a given amount of cheese – that is, bundles lying on the vertical line through X – those to the north are preferred to those to the south. Now consider a point like Y, the sort of point that in our previous analysis could have been a candidate for indifference to X. But Y is inferior to X because it lies to the left of it. Points like Z and W are superior and inferior respectively. In short, there are no points, other than X itself, which are indifferent to X. There is no indifference curve.

This kind of ordering is called a *lexicographic* or *lexical* ordering. To establish an indifference curve we must rule out the possibility of lexicographic orderings (which amounts, essentially, to ignoring addicts, whether it be cheese, alcohol or whatever).

In order to ensure that we have indifference curves like those in Figure 1.4.3, we had best assert that they exist. This we do with the next axiom.

Axiom 5 The Axiom of Continuity of Preferences.

There exists a set of points on a boundary dividing the commodity space into less preferred and more preferred areas such that these points are indifferent to each other.

1.6 Convex Preferences

Figure 1.4.3 showed three possible shapes for an indifference curve (there are others, as we shall see). We shall select curve I_1. This curve is convex to the origin and we shall, in fact, embody the selection of this shape in a further axiom.

Axiom 6   The Axiom of Convexity of Preferences.

The indifference curve is convex. As it happens, the word 'convex' also described curve I_3 in Figure 1.4.3. We shall shortly distinguish 'general' convexity from 'strict' convexity so that we can restrict the analysis to curves like I_1. I_1 is strictly convex; I_3 is convex.

Consider a move down the indifference curve in Figure 1.6.1 from X to Y. For Y to be indifferent to X, as it must be if it lies on the same indifference curve, the gain of x_1, shown as Δx_1 must exactly compensate the consumer for the loss of x_2, shown as $-\Delta x_2$. The ratio $-\Delta x_2/\Delta x_1$ is referred to as the *personal rate of substitution* (*PRS*) of good 1 for good 2, or sometimes as the *rate of commodity substitution* (*RCS*), or, more

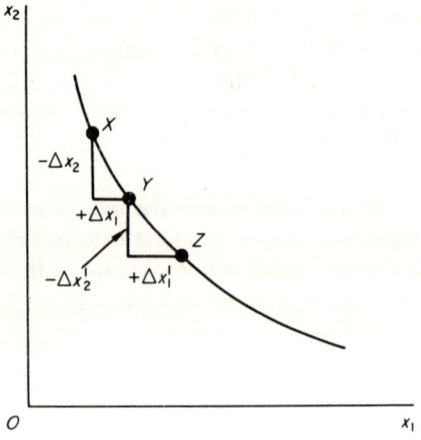

Figure 1.6.1

traditionally, the *marginal rate of substitution (MRS)*.[1]

Now consider a move from Y to Z, and let the loss of x_2 be the same as that involved in the move from X to Y – that is, $-\Delta x_2' = -\Delta x_2$. Then, because of the shape of the indifference curve, it will be noted that a larger amount of good 1 is required by the consumer to compensate him for the loss of x_2. The magnitude $-\Delta x_2/\Delta x_1$ has become smaller. With indifference curves shaped like the one in Figure 1.6.1, then, we have a *diminishing PRS* as we move down the curve (= diminishing MRS = diminishing RCS). A possible rationale for supposing that the PRS will diminish is that as the consumer has less and less of good 2, he will require successively larger and larger amounts of good 1 to compensate him for the loss of good 2. The less we have of something the more highly we tend to value the last unit possessed.[2]

As it happens, our axiom 6 is not quite rigorous enough. Simply to speak of 'convexity' does not rule out the possibility of indifference curves that are completely linear (i.e. straight lines) or indifference curves that are 'piecewise linear' (i.e. have linear segments). A piecewise linear indifference curve is shown in Figure 1.6.2. Although

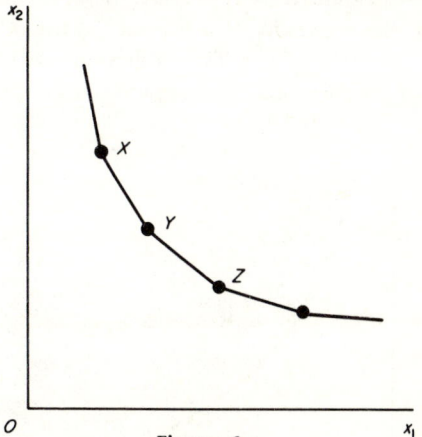

Figure 1.6.2

[1] *PRS* is the term used by Peter Newman in his excellent text *The Theory of Exchange* (Prentice-Hall, New Jersey, 1965). *RCS* is used by J. Henderson and R. Quandt, *Microeconomic Theory: a Mathematical Approach* (McGraw-Hill, New York, 1958). Both these texts are concerned to avoid the redundancy of the term 'marginal' in this context, and both terms indicate that we are interested in the rate at which the consumer substitutes commodities. Other 'rates of substitution' enter the theory later on, particularly in production theory. Hence the term *MRS*, due to Hicks, is best avoided.

[2] But convexity and the so-called 'law of diminishing marginal utility' are not necessarily related. See H. A. J. Green, *Consumer Theory* (Macmillan, London, revised edn. 1976) pp. 85–9.

the analysis is not unduly complicated by the existence of such curves, it is convenient to assume that indifference curves take on the smooth convexity of the curve in Figure 1.6.1. To ensure this, we can rephrase axiom 6 as

Axiom 6*   The Indifference Curve is Strictly Convex.

Clearly, to assume strict convexity is to place yet a further restriction on the applicability of the ensuing analysis. But it is useful to build up the theory on the basis of convenient axioms. The interested reader can then relax some of the assumptions and see what difference it makes; unless the axioms that are relaxed include transitivity, completeness or dominance, the effects are not generally drastic. Some indications of awkward results are given in Section 1.8.

We have used the terms 'convex' and 'strictly convex' and, since they will emerge again, some explanation is called for.

It will be found that the term 'convex' is used to refer to two different things. In our context we may speak of the convexity of the indifference curve itself, and of the convexity of the area to the right of the indifference curve (the shaded area in Figure 1.6.3). In the former case we are speaking of the convexity of a *function*. In the latter case we are speaking of the convexity of a *set*. The indifference curve in Figure 1.6.3 is such that both the curve and the area to the right of it are convex.

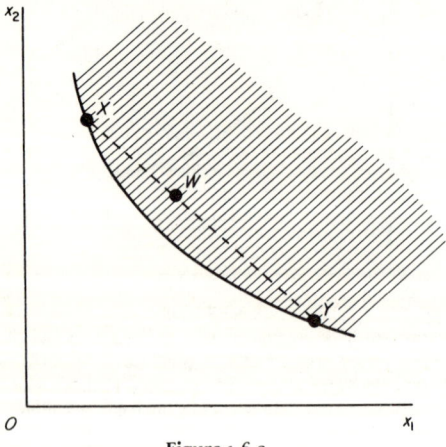

Figure 1.6.3

It is also useful to distinguish convexity from strict convexity. In Figure 1.6.3 the line *XY* joins two 'end points', *X* and *Y*. A point intermediate between *X* and *Y* is given by $W = (1-a)X + aY$, where *a* has a value between O and 1. W is seen to be preferred to X and Y. Since W is a weighted average of X and Y, the convexity axiom is sometimes stated in terms of 'preferences for means over extremes'. If W lies to the right of the indifference curve, the curve is *strictly convex*. If, however, when constructing the chord XY we find that W lies on the indifference curve, the curve is simply *convex*, without the prefix 'strictly'. In other words, the term 'convex' covers both the strictly convex case and the case where W lies on the indifference curve. The reader should confirm for himself that W will lie on the indifference curve if the curve is linear (see below, Section 1.10, where convexity is called 'weak convexity' to make a contrast with strict convexity).

The strict convexity axiom can be written

$$(1-a)X + aY > X \text{ (or } Y).$$

There is one other important implication of strict convexity: the indifference curves cannot cut the axes. If they did, the axes would become extensions of the indifference curves. But, since the axes are linear, this is inconsistent with strict convexity, although it is consistent with (weak) convexity. Hence, strict convexity rules out the possibility of indifference curves cutting the axes.

1.7 Some Properties of Indifference Curves

We shall assume that indifference curves are strictly convex. The commodity space in which the consumer expresses his preferences will then be 'filled' with indifference curves, each one lying outwards and to the right of the preceding one. Since our commodity space is, *ex hypothesi*, continuous (we ruled out indivisible commodities) we can draw as many indifference curves as we like, so close to each other that they are barely distinguishable. In practice, our figures would lose what use they have as visual aids if we drew the curves so close together. Hence we draw several curves only. All these curves make up the consumer's *indifference map*.

The indifference map illustrates the consumer's tastes or desires for the two goods, and his preferences as between different combinations of them. So long as there is no change in his tastes and preferences, the whole indifference map will remain stable. If tastes and preferences change, then the existing indifference map will be replaced by a new one. If, for example, good x_2 is aspirin and good x_1 is bread, and if the consumer develops a headache, then each of the indifference curves will sink towards the horizontal axis, as is shown in Figure 1.7.1, for now that the headache has intensified the desire for aspirin, a smaller quantity of aspirin OF can be expected to be as attractive to the consumer as the quantity of bread OG. When headaches have been cured, the indifference curves will return to their initial positions.

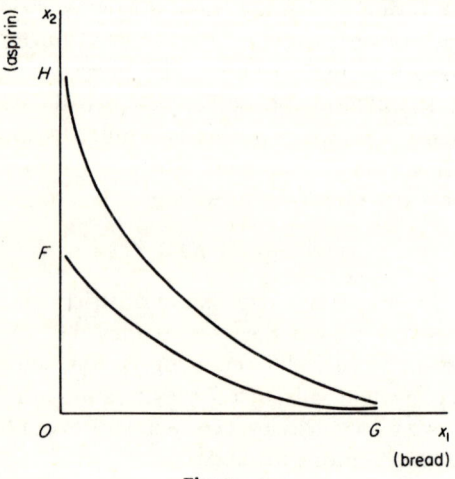

Figure 1.7.1

It is also a relatively simple matter to show that, while indifference curves need not be parallel, they cannot intersect. Consider the two curves in Figure 1.7.2. By the axiom of dominance we have TPR, but R

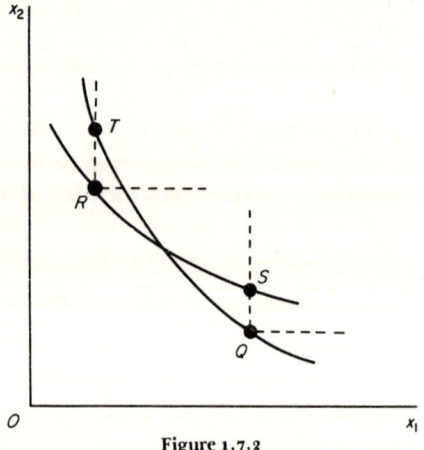

Figure 1.7.2

and S lie on the same indifference curve so that RIS. By dominance, SPQ. Hence, by the axiom of transitivity, it must be the case that TPQ. But T and Q are on the same indifference curve: hence TIQ. The results are contradictory. We can conclude therefore that intersecting indifference curves entail the violation of some of the axioms used to establish their very existence.

1.8 The Consumer's Budget Set

The consumer has a limited income, and this income can be plotted on to commodity space as shown in Figure 1.8.1. We assume, for convenience, that all the consumer's income is spent (i.e. none is saved). The line H divides the commodity space into feasible and non-feasible sets; the consumer is unable to achieve points to the right of H (–A means 'not attainable') even though his preference ordering can be expressed for points in –A. Points in set A are attainable so that we know the consumer must end up somewhere in the area A or on the line H. H is the consumer's *budget line* (sometimes called the *price line*, or *wealth constraint*), and the budget line partitions commodity space into attainable and non-attainable sets.

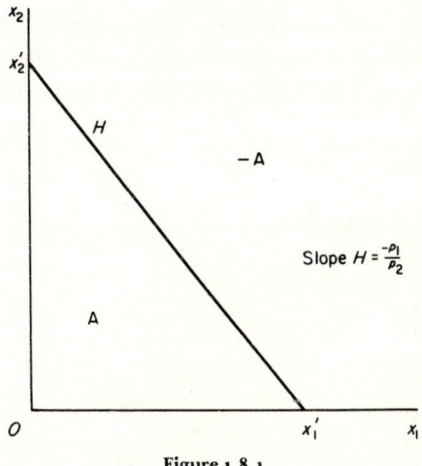

Figure 1.8.1

The location and slope of H is determined by the prices of goods 1 and 2. If all the consumer's income is spent on 2 he can buy an amount x_2'. Similarly, if all his income is spent on 1 he can buy x_1'. The various combinations of 1 and 2 that can be bought are shown by the points on H. H is drawn as a straight line because the consumer is assumed to be unable to influence the prices of the goods: prices are assumed 'given', being determined by a market mechanism over which the consumer has no control.

If the consumer spends all of his income it follows that

$$Y_c = p_1 . x_1 + p_2 . x_2$$

where Y_c is the consumer's income, and p_1 and p_2 are the prices of 1 and 2 respectively. Rearranging this budget line equation, we have

$$x_2 = \frac{Y_c}{p_2} - \frac{p_1 . x_1}{p_2}$$

which is a straight line of slope $-p_1/p_2$. In short, the budget line has a slope which is equal to the ratio of relative prices.

In two-dimensional commodity space the line H has one dimension. If there were three commodities, H would be a two-dimensional plane. Generalised to n commodities, we say that H is an *hyperplane*.

1.9 Consumer Equilibrium

With the aid of the indifference curve construction and the budget line, we can now establish which commodity bundle the consumer will purchase. Figure 1.9.1 shows the equilibrium at X, where the desired

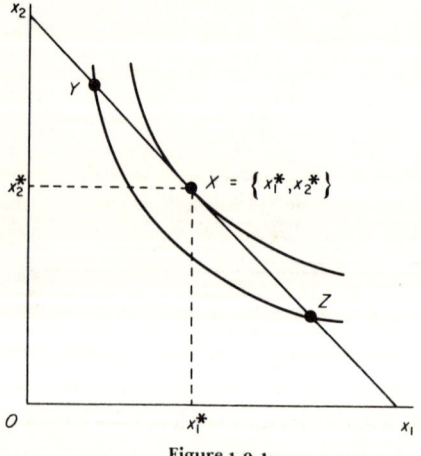

Figure 1.9.1

quantities x_1 and x_2 are purchased. X must also be an *optimum* – that is, a most preferred point. By definition of H, the consumer cannot go outside the region bounded by H. On the other hand, he aims to reach the highest indifference curve (the axiom of selection). Any point to the left of X (such as Y) places the consumer on a lower indifference curve, as does any point to the right of X, such as Z. Hence X is the optimum.

The optimum exists then when the budget line is *tangential* to the highest indifference curve. This tangency property indicates a useful result. We know that the slope of the indifference curve is the personal rate of substitution, and that the slope of the budget line is the ratio of prices. Hence at the optimum X, we have

$$\text{PRS}_{x_1, x_2} = \frac{p_1}{p_2}$$

In n dimensions, the tangency solution is summarised by saying that the budget hyperplane 'supports' the preference set. In Figure 1.9.1, for example, H is a supporting hyperplane (in two dimensions only) because it contains at least one point on the boundary of the preferred set, the boundary having already been defined as an indifference curve.

1.10 Some 'Pathological' Cases

Our theory of consumer equilibrium is now complete. We have not yet investigated how consumers will react to changes in prices and incomes: this is the subject of Chapter 2. Before looking at this aspect, however, it is interesting to observe briefly the effects of relaxing some of the strict axioms that have been introduced. A considerable amount of modern theoretical literature concerns itself with 'widening' the theory in this way in an attempt to make consumer theory more general.

(i) ALLOWING WEAK CONVEXITY

It will be recalled that weak convexity permits the indifference curve to be linear or to have linear segments. Figures 1.10.1(a) and (b) show the possibilities that arise when weak convexity is allowed. In figure (a) the budget line is seen to be coincident with a linear segment of the indifference curve. As a result, *all* the points on H between A and B are optima. By analogy, the same would be true if H coincided with the completely linear indifference curve in diagram (b). Diagram (b) illustrates the possibility that the indifference curve has a different slope to the budget line. The optimum lies at point C on the x_2 axis since any other point on H lies on a lower indifference curve. Solutions of this kind are called *'corner' solutions*.

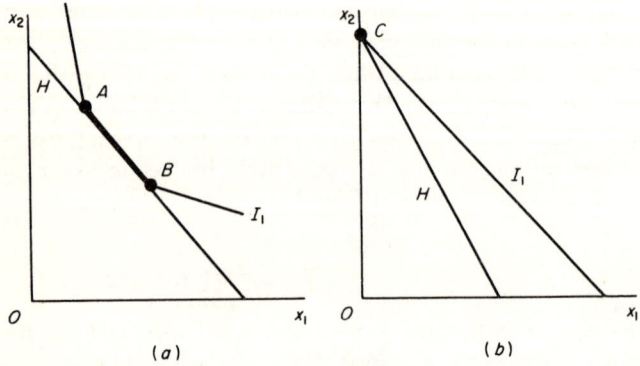

Figure 1.10.1

Are linear or piecewise linear indifference curves possible? A linear curve means that the *PRS* is constant over the whole curve: the consumer does *not* require greater amounts of good 1 to compensate him for the loss of good 2. This situation could only arise if the consumer regarded the two goods as *perfect substitutes*. Linear indifference curves therefore arise when goods are perfect substitutes. Introspection suggests that such goods are rare, so that we do not lose a great deal of generality by ignoring linear curves. A number of modern writers, however, have argued that weak convexity should be permitted, particularly as the problems generated by it are fairly easily handled with modern mathematics.

(ii) ALLOWING CONCAVITY

If the convexity axiom is relaxed altogether, we are permitted to have concave curves as in Figure 1.10.2 below. Once again, the optimum lies at a corner point Y, even though there is an apparent tangency at point X.[1]

---

[1] This case also illustrates an important mathematical principle. Applying the differential calculus to this problem would have given first-order conditions showing X to be the optimum. Only by finding the second-order conditions would we have discovered that X was not, after all, the optimum.

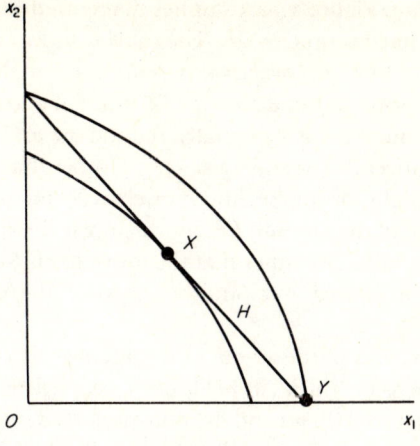

Figure 1.10.2

(iii) RELAXING THE AXIOM OF DOMINANCE

In Figure 1.10.3 the indifference curves are drawn as ⌐-shaped. This implies that a point such as B is indifferent to a point such as A, even though B contains more of one commodity and no less of the other. Permitting A and B to be indifferent amounts to relaxing the axiom of dominance. We could say that Figure 1.10.3 permits 'weak' dominance (a point such as C cannot be indifferent to A) but not 'strong' dominance.

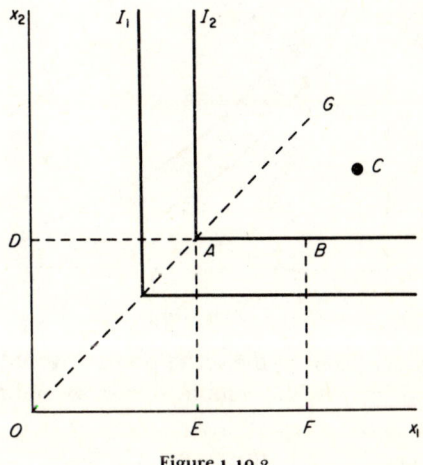

Figure 1.10.3

The situation in Figure 1.10.3 implies that commodities have to be consumed in a fixed ratio *OD/OE*. The ratio is shown by the line *OG*. The goods would be *perfect complements*. Notice that in this case, point *A* is indifferent to point *B*. But *B* absorbs *EF* more of good 1 than does *A*. Hence, the amount *EF* is essentially redundant and the consumer would have no incentive to end up at a point other than a corner point such as *A*. He might, of course, find himself at *B* and discover that it is costly to dispose of the amount *EF*, in which case he would settle at *B*. Some modern analysis assumes that the move from *B* to *A* is costless, sometimes incorporated into another axiom: the axiom of 'free disposal'.

A slight relaxation of the axiom of dominance also permits the indifference curve to be 'thick', as in Figure 1.10.4. Instead of a *boundary* between the preferred (P) set and the non-preferred set (–P), we obtain a *band*. On the analysis presented so far, a point like *B* would, by the dominance axiom, be preferred to a point like *A*. But if the indifference curve is 'thick', points inside the shaded area – more technically, points *interior* to the indifference set – are indifferent to each other. Hence, in Figure 1.10.4, we have *AIB*. The indifference curve in this case is not a boundary because points like *B* are not boundary points of the set P.

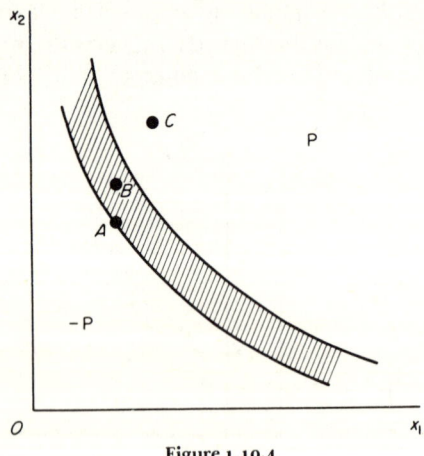

Figure 1.10.4

To be a boundary point of the set P, point *B* would have to have a neighbourhood (that is, the minute area surrounding *B*) which included a point in the set –P. But the neighbourhood of *B* lies in the thick area. Hence the thick curve is not a boundary curve.

Preferences and Consumer Equilibrium

The argument in favour of thick curves is that dominance applies only when the consumer *perceives* the difference between points like A and B in Figure 1.10.4. If it can be argued that the very small changes in the components of A and B are *not* perceived, then B cannot be declared to dominate A. Only when some 'threshold' of perception is passed — that is, when the consumer goes to the right of the outside edge of the thick indifference set — will the consumer express a preference for a point like C, in the set P. Again, however, thick indifference sets are inconvenient for further analysis.

(iv) SATIATION IN ONE COMMODITY

The axiom of dominance ruled out satiation in *all* commodities, and, in the form presented in Chapter 1, it ruled out the possibility that a point such as B in Figure 1.10.5 could be anything other than preferred to A. But this condition is unduly restrictive and we should perhaps permit the very real possibility of satiation in *one* commodity.[1] The indifference curve then takes on a 'horseshoe' shape. The point C

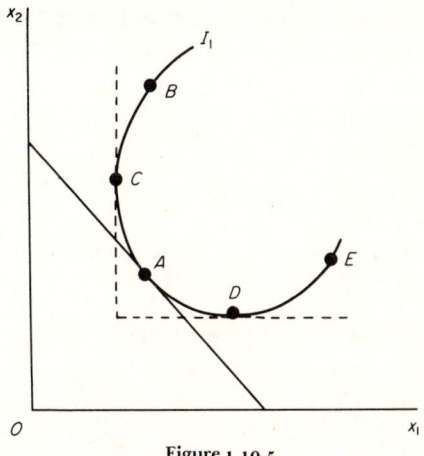

Figure 1.10.5

---

[1] Since satiation in one commodity is a likely event, it should not perhaps be treated under the heading of 'pathological' cases. However, problems of analysis arise even with satiation in one commodity, so that most current analysis omits the possibility. The brief analysis that ensues holds for satiation in *two* commodities in a three-commodity world, three in a four-commodity world, and so on. The implications of satiation are discussed in detail in G. Debreu, *Theory of Value* (Cowles, Foundation Monograph, Wiley, New York, 1959). Debreu's work is one of the major foundations of modern consumer theory, but the reader is warned that it makes use of advanced techniques.

is indifferent to A, but we also have BIC instead of BPC which is what we would normally expect from the dominance axiom. What has happened is that the consumer has reached a point of satiation in good 2, and this point is at C. From C upwards through B, the consumer requires *more* x_1 in order to tolerate *more* of good 2. Similarly, D is a point of satiation with respect to good 1 so that after D the indifference curve begins to bend upwards through E. Notice that the existence of this kind of satiation does not affect the equilibrium at A.

(v) SATIATION IN ALL COMMODITIES

If satiation exists with respect to *all* goods, the result will be as shown in Figure 1.10.6: the indifference map will be 'closed' and takes on the appearance of an archery target. The analogy is a good one since the optimum will exist in the 'bullseye', point X in the figure. What has happened here is that we not only have the 'ordinary' segment CD, and the two segments CB and DE introduced in the previous sections, but an added segment BE which closes the indifference curve making it an approximate circle. The section BE is odd in that it implies the consumer has had enough of *both* commodities: as he moves from B towards E the consumer gains an *unwanted* amount of good 1 and is indifferent to the extra amount x_1 as long as he can get rid of some of good 2.

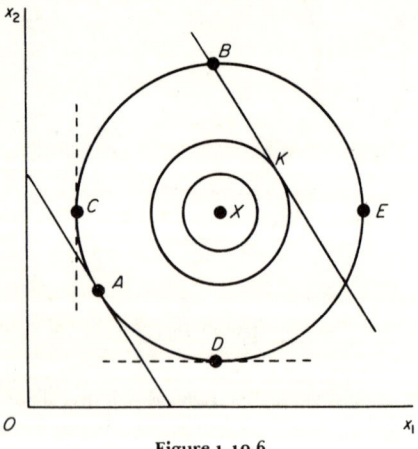

Figure 1.10.6

Notice that the indifference curve through B and E is *not* superior to the one through K. 'Higher' indifference curves lie *inside*, so that the best point is X.

Preferences and Consumer Equilibrium

This possibility does have implications for equilibrium. If the budget line is one through A, then the analysis is not upset. But if it is through K, then, although there is tangency at K, it is not an optimum. The consumer is better off not spending all his income and settling at point X, which is an *interior* point in the attainable set. Notice that the budget line could be vertical (e.g. through C in Figure 1.10.6) or horizontal (through D). The former would imply a zero price for good 2 and the latter a zero price for good 1: they would be 'free goods'. Between C and B, relative prices are negative. If we wish to restrict the domain of discussion to exclude the last possibility, we refer to situations with *non-negative prices* – that is, prices are positive or zero.

(vi) NON-LINEAR BUDGET LINES

The budget line has been drawn as a straight line because prices were taken as 'given'. In practice, consumers might be able to exert some 'monopsonistic' power – some influence over the prices of the goods. Thus, if the consumer can force the price of x_1 down by purchasing more of good 1, the ratio p_2/p_1 would increase as more of good 1 is purchased. The budget line will then be concave as in Figure 1.10.7. The theory so far developed is still applicable, as the figure shows. If, however, the budget line was to be strictly convex – that is, bent inwards as x_1 increases – we get results similar to those involved in having linear indifference curves. This implies that the consumer has to pay higher and higher prices for good 1 as he buys more. Figure 1.10.8 shows a case where numerous optima exist because the budget line and the indifference curve are, in part, coincident, and Figure 1.10.9 shows a corner solution because the budget line has a different slope to the indifference curve (strict convexity has also been relaxed since I_1 cuts the x_2 axis).

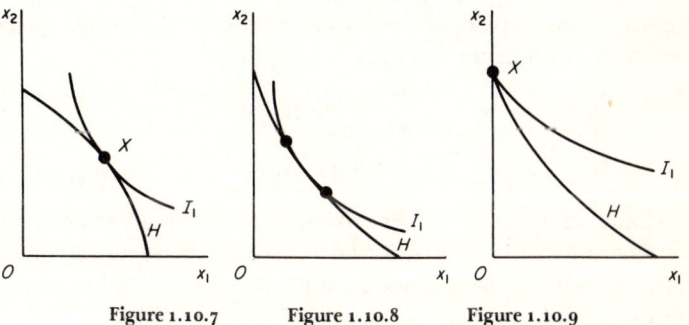

Figure 1.10.7   Figure 1.10.8   Figure 1.10.9

1.11 The Utility Function

Figure 1.11.1 shows an indifference map with an arbitrary but continuously increasing 'ray' R drawn from the origin. Then, along this ray we know that ZPY, YPX and XPW. Also, of course, AIZ. We now define a *utility* function to be any real-valued function such that

$$\begin{aligned}
&\text{if } ZPY, & U(Z) &> U(Y), \\
&\text{if } YPX, & U(Y) &> U(X), \\
&\text{if } XPW, & U(X) &> U(W), \\
&\text{if } AIZ, & U(A) &= U(Z).
\end{aligned}$$

The notation $U(Z)$ etc., simply means the utility derived from commodity bundle Z, although this tends to imply that utility is some objectively measurable entity. Rather than enter this debate, we confine ourselves to the above definition which simply tells us that we can translate our statements about preference into statements about utility. An indifference curve can be renamed an *'iso-utility'* curve, a curve showing points in commodity space which yield the consumer equal utility (i.e. between which he is indifferent). For every point in commodity space, therefore, there will correspond a utility number. The only requirement we stipulate is that utility should be held to increase as we move up a ray such as that in Figure 1.11.1. This ray is *monotonically increasing* – it does not go up and then down, although it need not be straight or without bumps. This means that *any* equation which preserves this characteristic will serve as a utility function. No significance can be attached to the distances between indifference curves along the ray.

In its most general form then, the utility function has the form

$$U = U(x_1, x_2, x_3, \ldots x_n)$$

which simply tells us that utility is a function of ('depends upon') the amounts of the individual commodities purchased. In more specific form the utility function could be

$$U = U(x_1, x_2) + C$$
$$\text{or} \quad U = U^2(x_1, x_2)$$
$$\text{or} \quad U = \log U(x_1, x_2)$$

etc. Each of these equations preserves the requirements of a monotonically increasing function. There is, therefore, no unique utility function for the individual: any order-preserving function will suffice. To put it another way, the utility index is *ordinal*.

Preferences and Consumer Equilibrium

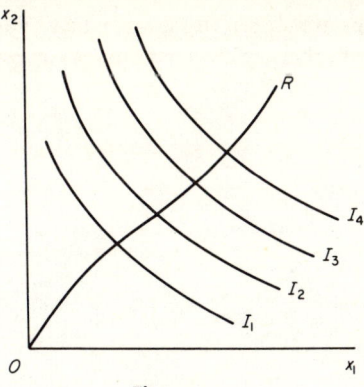

Figure 1.11.1

It may be worth using an example to show the relationship between the utility function and the indifference curve. All points on an indifference curve are points of equal utility. Thus, if we have a utility function with the general equation

$$U = f(x_1, x_2),$$

we have for any indifference curve

$$f(x_1, x_2) = \bar{U}$$

where $\bar{U}$ means 'constant utility'. Suppose, for example, that the utility function has the specific equation

$$U = 2x_1 \cdot x_2.$$

Then, to construct an indifference map corresponding to this utility function, we select arbitrary levels of utility and trace out the combinations of x_1 and x_2 that will achieve each arbitrary level. Thus, if we begin by selecting $\bar{U} = 18$, we can trace out the corresponding indifference curve by observing all values of x_1 and x_2 that satisfy $2x_1 x_2 = 18$, that is, $x_1 x_2 = 9$. Such values are, for example,

$x_1 = 9, x_2 = 1$
$x_1 = 6, x_2 = 1.5$
$x_1 = 3, x_2 = 3$
$x_1 = 1.5, x_2 = 6$
$x_1 = 1, x_2 = 9.$

These combinations are shown in Figure 1.11.2. The reader can then trace out for himself other indifference curves corresponding to other utility levels.

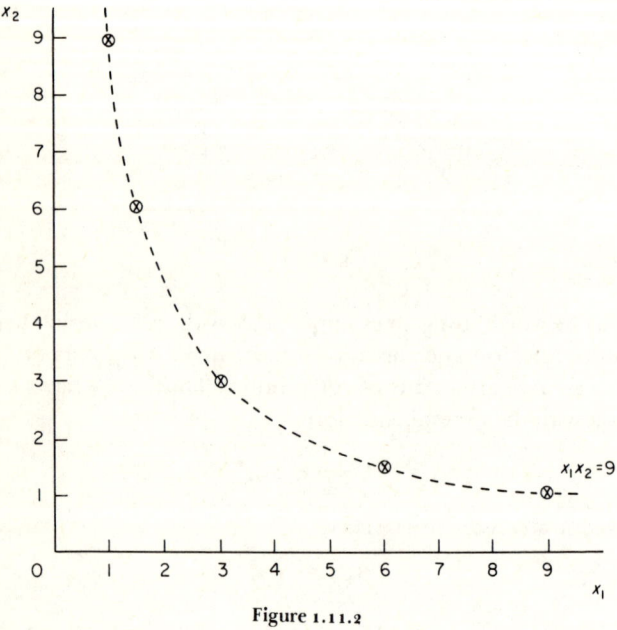

Figure 1.11.2

We can summarise the preceding discussion and this chapter by saying that our theory of consumer behaviour is based on the view that consumers aim to maximise utility subject to a budget constraint.

2

Demand Functions

2.0 Income–Consumption Relationship

The consumer's purchase plan will be revised if he experiences (*a*) a change in income; (*b*) a change in the prices of the goods; (*c*) a change in tastes, or (*d*) any combination of two or all of these. We consider first a change in income.

Figure 2.0.1 shows the consumer's indifference map. If income increases, *with relative prices remaining constant*, the consumer can buy more of both goods. Hence the budget line moves outwards in a parallel fashion. The consumer's new equilibria are plotted and the line joining the equilibria is called the *income–consumption curve* (*YCC*), or the *expenditure–consumption curve*.

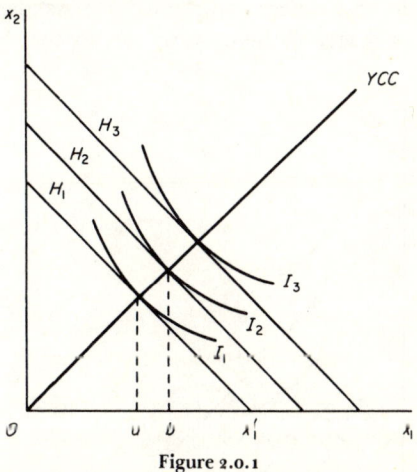

Figure 2.0.1

This curve shows the quantities of the two goods that the consumer would plan to buy at different levels of income if his tastes and preferences and the prices of these goods remain the same. In Figure 2.0.1. the income–consumption curve slopes upwards. Our general knowledge of how individuals react to an increase in their incomes or in their wealth suggests that most expenditure–consumption curves are of this shape, for the increase in expenditure is usually distributed over most of the goods that the household buys. In Figure 2.0.2 the expenditure–consumption curve begins to move towards the x_2 axis showing that, after a certain point, as expenditure rises less of good 2 is bought. In Figure 2.0.3, the curve curls towards the x_2 axis showing that, as expenditure increases, less of good 2 is ultimately bought. Expenditure–consumption curves of these shapes are not unknown. Many economists have observed that when, for any reason, a low-income household is enabled to spend more, it may buy less margarine or fewer potatoes, or a smaller number of loaves. It may choose to satisfy its hunger with goods that are more palatable and less monotonous, such as butter, vegetables, fruit and cake. Those goods of which the quantity that the consumer plans to purchase falls as income rises are called *inferior goods*. In Figure 2.0.2, good 1 is an inferior good. In Figure 2.0.3, good 2 is an inferior good.

Notice that if the prices of 1 and 2 were each cut by 50 per cent, the effect would be the same as that of doubling income. If incomes doubled and all prices doubled at the same time, the two effects would cancel out and the consumer should purchase exactly the same commodity bundle as before. If he does so, we say that he is free of the

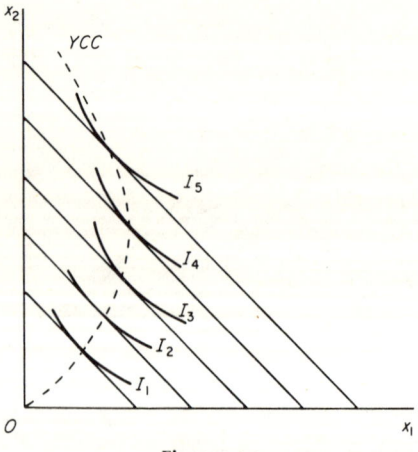

Figure 2.0.2

Demand Functions

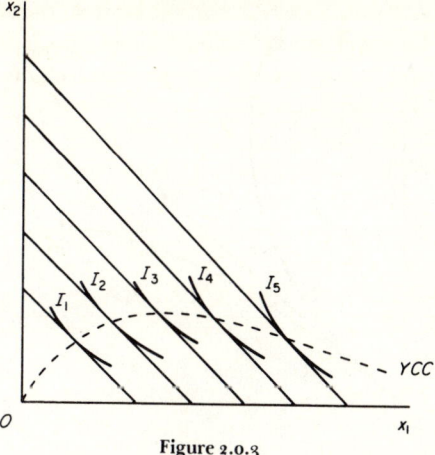

Figure 2.0.3

money illusion — he is able to observe that he is no better off in real terms, nor any worse off, so that his behaviour should not change. If, in fact, he did alter his behaviour, believing himself to be better off, he would be subject to the money illusion.

The *YCC* curves in Figures 2.0.1 to 2.0.3 can be used to derive the relationship between the demand for a commodity and the income of the consumer. The resulting relationships will look very similar (but not identical) to the *YCC* curves in the previous figures. In Figure 2.0.1, for example, we know that the consumer's income at the first budget line is equal to $p_1 . Ox'_1$ — i.e. by looking at total expenditure if only good 1 is purchased. At this level of income he buys Oa of commodity 1. Carrying out the same exercise for the next income level we see that he buys Ob of good 1, and so on. Plotting this relationship diagrammatically gives the curve E_1 in Figure 2.0.4. E_2 and E_3 show the curves corresponding to the *YCC* curves in Figures 2.0.2 and 2.0.3. These curves show how the consumer's demand for *one* commodity varies with income, and are called *Engel curves*.[1]

In general, we expect the income-quantity demanded relationship to look like the curves E_1 or E_3, since E_2 relates to the situation in which good 1 is an inferior good. (Note: E_3 shows the demand for good 1 increasing as income increases — it is good 2 that is the inferior good in this case. Shapes like E_3 do not depend on the other good being an inferior good, however.)

---

[1] Although most writers reserve the term for the income-consumption curve itself.

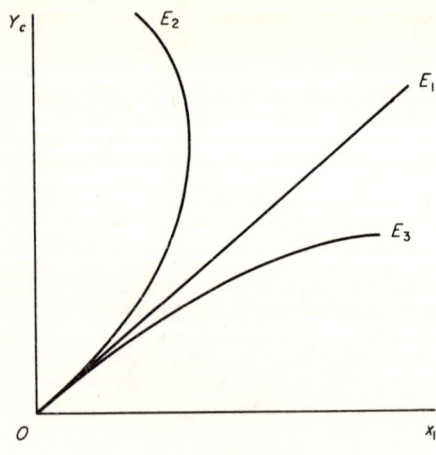

Figure 2.0.4

2.1 Income Elasticity of Demand

We know the likely *direction* of change of demand with respect to income changes. It is frequently useful to *quantify* this relationship. The measure used by economists is generally applicable to the variations in any one variable, say A, with respect to changes in another variable, say B: the relationship is called the *elasticity* of A with respect to B. In the case above we can speak of the elasticity of the demand for good 1 with respect to income Y_c. This is the *income elasticity of demand* for good 1. One essential aspect of all elasticity measures is that they are not measured in absolute units. An example will indicate the importance of this. Suppose income fell from £20 to £19 and the demand for good 1 fell by 5 units. Now suppose income is £10, falls to £9 and demand falls by 5 units. In each case there has been a fall of £1 in income and an equal change in demand. It is tempting to think that the 'responsiveness' of demand to income is the same in each case. In fact, however, the first case shows a 5 units change with respect to a 5 per cent change in income; the second shows a 5 units change with respect to a 10 per cent change in income. Similarly, we would not wish to treat each 5 units as being directly comparable if in the first case it is a change of 5 on a base of 20 and in the second a change of 5 on a base of 10. To eliminate the distortions that arise because of measurement in absolute units, we define elasticities in terms of *percentage* changes. In

Demand Functions

the most general case, then, the elasticity of A with respect to B is

$$\frac{\text{percentage change in } A}{\text{percentage change in } B}$$

In the case of income elasticity, which we symbolise by e_Y, we have

$$e_Y = \frac{\text{percentage change in demand}}{\text{percentage change in income}}$$

$$= \frac{\Delta x_1}{x_1} \div \frac{\Delta Y_c}{Y_c}$$

$$= \frac{Y_c}{x_1} \cdot \frac{\Delta x_1}{\Delta Y_c}$$

Notice that $\Delta x_1/\Delta Y_c$ is the inverse of the slope of the Engel curves in Figure 2.0.4, and that the elasticity measure should not, therefore, be confused with the gradient of any curve.

The demand for any good is said to be *income elastic* if the demand rises more than proportionately with an increase in income: curve E_3 in Figure 2.0.4 is therefore income elastic over much of its range: i.e. the value of e_Y is greater than unity for much of the curve. If the value of e_Y is unity, the good has unit income elasticity: curve E_1, in fact, has unit elasticity over its entire length.

As it happens, any linear Engel curve emanating from the origin has an income elasticity of unity over its whole range. In Figure 2.1.1

$$e_Y = \frac{Y_c}{x} \cdot \frac{\Delta x}{\Delta Y_c}.$$

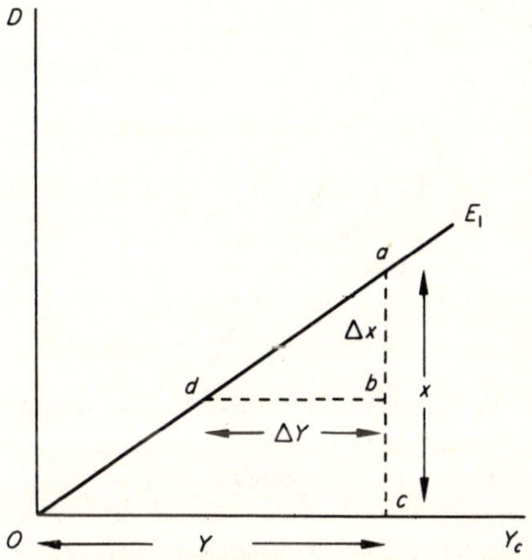

Figure 2.1.1

But abd and acO are similar triangles, hence $ab/db = ac/Oc$, or

$$\frac{\Delta x}{\Delta Y_c} = \frac{x}{Y_c},$$

which, substituted in the formula for e_Y, gives

$$e_Y = \frac{Y_c}{x} \cdot \frac{x}{Y_c} = 1.$$

If e_Y is less than 1, the good is *income inelastic*. Income elasticity will be negative for inferior goods: thus $e_Y < 0$ over the backward-sloping range of E_2. Before it bends backward, E_2 tends to illustrate income inelasticity for much of its range.[1]

2.2 Price–Consumption Relationship

Suppose, now, that the price of good 1 falls, that of 2 staying the same. The effect is to move the budget line outwards, pivoting about point L in Figure 2.2.1. Successive shifts are shown as the price of good 1 falls further. The new equilibria of the consumer are plotted, and when the points P, Q, R etc. are joined, the resulting locus is termed the *price–consumption curve* (*PCC*), or *offer curve*.

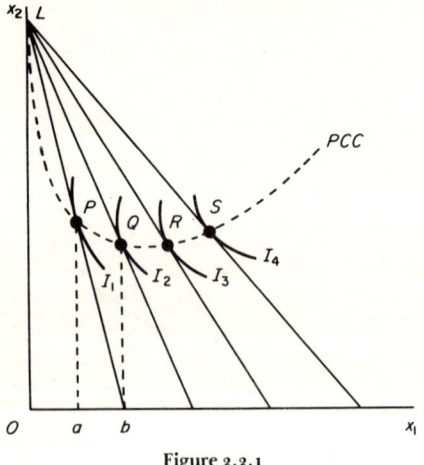

Figure 2.2.1

[1] The case of income inelasticity for food was reported in 1857 by the German statistician, Ernst Engel, after whom the curves are named.

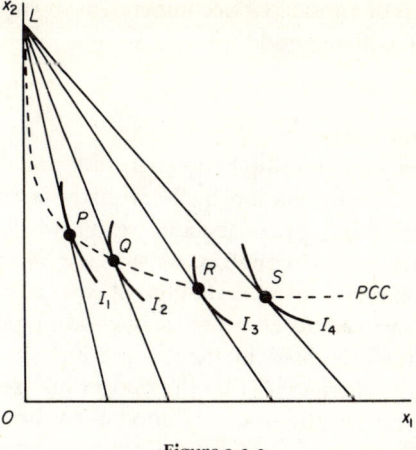

Figure 2.2.2

Some different possibilities are classified in Figures 2.2.1, 2.2.2 and 2.2.3. The first two figures show the consumer planning to increase his purchases of good 1 when its price falls. This illustrates the most common reaction to a price reduction, for we know that most consumers buy more of a good when it becomes relatively cheaper. The price–consumption curve shown in Figure 2.2.3, while not common, is possible. There, when the price of good 1 falls below a certain level, less and less of good 1 is bought. When consumers react in this way –

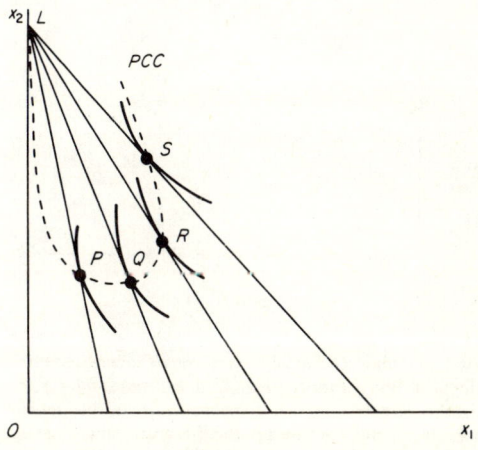

Figure 2.2.3

when they buy less of a good as it becomes relatively cheaper – we refer to that good as a 'Giffen' good.[1]

2.3 The Demand Curve

Just as we derived a relationship between income and the demand for good 1, so we can derive a relationship between the price of good 1 and demand. The resulting price–demand relationship is called the *Marshallian demand curve*, although, as we shall see, we shall have occasion to note the existence of several different types of demand curve.

In Figure 2.2.1 we can observe that Oa of good 1 is purchased at the price of good 1 represented in the budget line through P. Ob is purchased when p_1 changes so that the budget line goes through Q, and so on. By plotting the prices of good 1 on the vertical axis of Figures 2.3.1 and the quantities Oa, Ob, etc., on the horizontal axis, we obtain the consumer's demand curve D, indicating, as the PCC curve for a 'normal' good does, that demand will be greater the lower is the price. By observing the PCC curve in Figure 2.2.3, the reader can confirm that the demand curve for an inferior good will have an *upward*-sloping section.

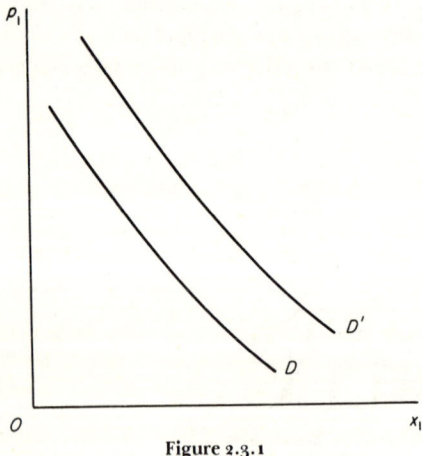

Figure 2.3.1

---

[1] So named after Sir Robert Giffen who is alleged to have observed that when the price of bread rose the poor bought more bread and less meat and less of some other more expensive foodstuffs. Notice that Giffen goods are here distinguished from inferior goods: the two are frequently confused in the literature, since the Giffen good is a particular example of an inferior good. The precise distinction is given below, p. 51.

There is an alternative method for deriving the demand curve from the *PCC* curve, but which has greater appeal in that the price of good 1 can be equated directly with the slope of the budget line. The procedure is as follows. Instead of assuming that the consumer is faced with two commodities only, we put on the vertical axis the *expenditure on all goods except good 1*. In our two-good case, this means that the vertical axis measures $p_2 \cdot x_2$ instead of x_2. On the horizontal axis we plot x_1. This may look impermissible, but it is a convenient construction that the reader will find used in many texts and articles.
We know that

$$Y_c = p_1 \cdot x_1 + m$$

where m refers to the expenditure on all goods *other* than good 1 ($m = p_2 x_2$ if there are two goods only). The equation of the budget line is then

$$m = Y_c - p_1 \cdot x_1.$$

The slope of this line is the *absolute* price of 1, namely p_1, and not a price ratio. Figure 2.3.2 shows how the demand curve is derived from this construct. Note that this is merely an alternative to the method outlined at the beginning of this section.

The demand curves in Figures 2.3.1 and 2.3.2 can be written in functional form as

$$D_1 = D(p_1)$$

which simply says that the demand for good 1 depends upon its price.

As it happens, Figure 2.3.1 is a slightly misleading diagrammatic representation of the demand function, since it shows price on the vertical axis and the amount demanded (quantity) on the horizontal axis. It is customary to place the *dependent variable* on the vertical axis and the *independent variable* on the horizontal axis. In this case, quantity depends on price, so that quantity should appear on the vertical axis and price on the horizontal axis. It is merely an oddity in the development of demand analysis that the axes have, usually, been reversed.

The demand function may also be expressed as

$$f: p \to D$$

which is the expression for a *mapping*. This notation is equivalent to the function form above, but is somewhat more frequently used today. Again, if the student wishes to be familiar with the notation used in

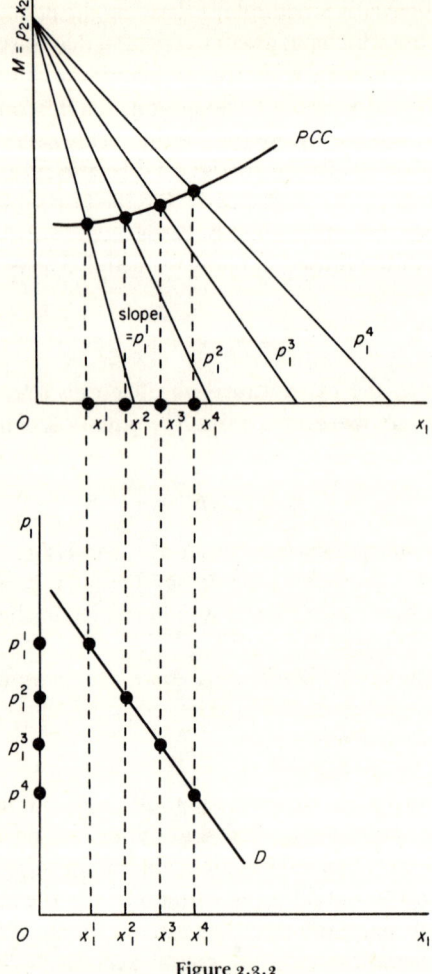

Figure 2.3.2

journals and more advanced books, he should familiarise himself with this terminology. The last expression declares that price 'maps' to quantity: for each price there corresponds some quantity. If a *unique* quantity is associated with each price, then there is a *one-to-one mapping*. The demand curve in Figure 2.3.1 is a one-to-one mapping. In some cases (see below Section 2.11) one price might be associated with more than one quantity, or several prices with one quantity (the former corresponds to situations in which parts, or all, of the demand curve as conventionally drawn is horizontal, the latter with situations in which vertical sections exist). These latter cases are not therefore one-to-one mappings. To complete this brief discussion of notation, we may observe that p is said to occupy a *domain*, and D the *counterdomain* or *range*. Given the nature of the function that 'transforms' p to D, then the value of D associated with a particular value of p is said to be the *image* of that value of p.

Hence the general form of the demand function may be summarised by saying that it maps price into quantity.

Now, we have already seen that demand depends upon income as well. Income is not indicated in Figures 2.3.1 and 2.3.2. Rather it is a *parameter* of the price–demand relationship: it fixes the position of D. A change in the *variable* p_1 would lead to a movement *along* the demand curve. A change in the *parameter* income would lead to a *shift* in the demand curve. Thus, an increase in income causes the demand curve to shift to the right, say, to D' in Figure 2.3.1. Correspondingly, a reduction in income leads to a shift to the left. The equation for the demand function can therefore be widened to

$$D_1 = D(p_1, Y_c).$$

Demand is a function of both price and income. Later, we can add other components to the demand function. Remember that, insofar as we work with the price–demand relationship of Figure 2.3.1, all the factors other than p_1 determining demand will be parameters. In practice, all the factors are likely to change at the same time. By omitting the many other variables that influence D_1 we confine ourselves to *partial demand functions*. These are convenient for our present analytical purposes, but later it becomes essential to demonstrate the essential interdependence of the economic system.

The reader will also note that the demand curve in Figure 2.3.1 is derived by observation of the *optimal consumption quantities*: the amounts x_1^1, x_1^2, x_1^3, x_1^4 etc. The optimal amount of good 1 purchased changes as the price of good 1 changes, and it is these optimal amounts that are plotted by the demand curve. Writing the optimal amount of good 1 as x_1^*, then we can express the demand equation as

$$x_1^* = D(p_1, Y_c).$$

In this form, as in the previous one, the *quantity* of good 1 is the *dependent* variable (that is, determined by price and income), and price and income are the *independent variables* – which in this case are also 'given' as data: they are *exogenous*. It is, however, quite possible to reverse the relationship between quantity and price and obtain an *inverse demand function*. Ignoring income, instead of $x_1^* = D(p_1)$, we could write $p_1 = F(x_1^*)$. In this case, the price of good 1 appears as a function of the quantities purchased. The possibility of writing the demand function for non-Giffen goods in the inverse form arises because the demand curve is *monotonically decreasing* – the curve slopes down from left to right and nowhere does a fall in price lead to a fall in the amount demanded. It is sometimes convenient in dealing with systems of demand equations to operate with the inverses rather than with the original functions.

2.4 Price Elasticity of Demand

Just as we derived income elasticity of demand, so we can express *price elasticity of demand*, e_p, as

$$e_p = \frac{\text{percentage change in demand}}{\text{percentage change in price}}$$

$$= \frac{\Delta x_1}{x_1} \div \frac{\Delta p_1}{p_1}$$

$$= \frac{p_1}{x_1} \cdot \frac{\Delta x_1}{\Delta p_1}.$$

For a price *fall*, $\Delta p_1 < O$, and $\Delta x_1 > O$, so that e_p will be a negative quantity. Similarly, for a price *rise*, $\Delta p_1 > O$ and $\Delta x_1 < O$ so that e_p will again be negative. Strictly, then, the measure of e will always have a negative sign. However, the negative sign tends to cause confusion, especially when we see how price elasticity measures are commonly used. *The usual convention, and it is no more than that, is to multiply the expression for e_p above by -1.* In what follows, then, we rewrite e_p as

$$e_p = -\frac{p_1}{x_1} \cdot \frac{\Delta x_1}{\Delta p_1}.$$

In a manner analogous to the analysis of income elasticity, we say that demand is price elastic at a particular price if $e_p > 1$ at that price, *price inelastic* if $e_p < 1$, and it has *unit price elasticity* if $e_p = 1$. We can also introduce the ideas of *perfect price elasticity* and *perfect price inelasticity*. A perfectly elastic demand curve is shown in Figure 2.4.1, and a perfectly inelastic curve in Figure 2.4.2. In the former case, a small change in price leads to an infinite reaction on the part of the consumer: essentially $\Delta x_1/\Delta p_1$ tends towards infinity, so that e_p also approaches infinity. The perfectly inelastic curve in Figure 2.4.2 shows a zero reaction in quantity bought to a price change – i.e. $\Delta x_1/\Delta p_1 = 0$. This quotient once again 'swamps' the elasticity expression so that e_p is also zero.

Both curves can be thought of as limiting cases, but the perfectly elastic demand curve has played a significant role in the development of economic theory, as we shall see.

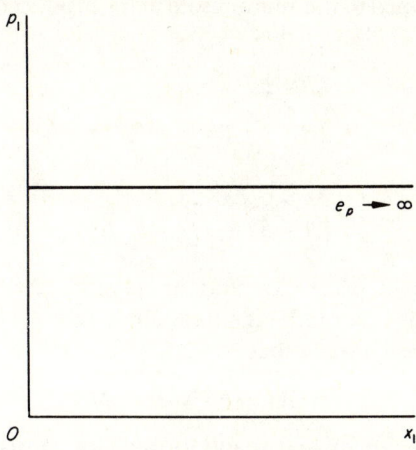

Figure 2.4.1

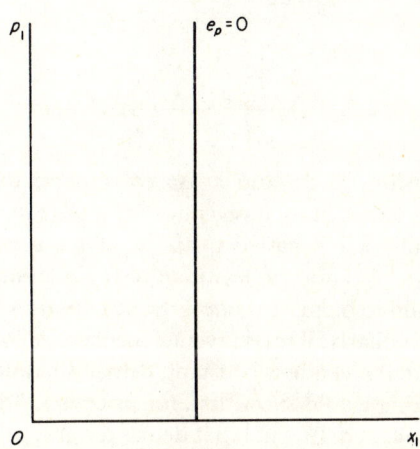

Figure 2.4.2

2.5 Price Elasticity and Total Revenue

A useful indicator of the strength of price elasticity of demand is to see whether the total expenditure on the commodity has risen or fallen after the price change. If we ignore commodity taxes, the expenditure made by the consumer on a commodity is equal to the *revenue* received by the firm selling the commodity. The direction of change in total revenue is an indicator of elasticity of demand. This can be demonstrated as follows. The total revenue (TR) from the sale of any commodity is equal to the amount sold of the product multiplied by its price. Thus,

$$TR = p \cdot x.$$

It follows that $\quad TR + \Delta TR = (p + \Delta p)(x + \Delta x).$

For a price rise, $\quad \Delta p > 0, \Delta x < 0,$
$$\therefore TR + \Delta TR = px - p \cdot \Delta x + x \cdot \Delta p - \Delta p \cdot \Delta x.$$

If the changes in price (Δp) and in quantity (Δx) are small, the magnitude of $\Delta p \cdot \Delta x$ can be ignored. Since $TR = p \cdot x$, it can be subtracted from both sides so that

$$\Delta TR = -p \cdot \Delta x + x \cdot \Delta p.$$

Now the price elasticity of demand formula for a price rise is

$$e_p = -\frac{p \cdot -\Delta x}{x \cdot \Delta p} = \frac{p \cdot \Delta x}{x \cdot \Delta p}$$

if $p \cdot \Delta x > x \cdot \Delta p$, $e_p > 1$
if $p \cdot \Delta x < x \cdot \Delta p$, $e_p < 1$
if $p \cdot \Delta x = x \cdot \Delta p$, $e_p = 1$

But the expressions $p \cdot \Delta x$ and $x \cdot \Delta p$ correspond to the two components of the change in total revenue. For a price *increase*, $\Delta x < 0$, so that $p \cdot \Delta x$ will be a negative quantity. If $p \cdot \Delta x > x \cdot \Delta p$, then $TR = -p \cdot \Delta x + x \cdot \Delta p$ must be less than zero. Conveniently, then, demand can be said to be price *elastic* if the price *increase* leads to a *fall* in total revenue. Similarly, if total revenue increases, demand is price inelastic, and if total revenue is constant, demand has unit elasticity.

Similar working would show that, for price *cuts*, TR will increase if demand is elastic, and TR will fall if demand is inelastic. We can summarise these results:

Demand Functions

Price change	TR	e_p
up	falls	elastic
up	rises	inelastic
down	rises	elastic
down	falls	inelastic
up/down	constant	unitary

One feature of most demand curves is that elasticity will *vary along the length of the curve*. Inspection of Figure 2.5.1 shows that a move from point A to point B involves an increase in total revenue (from *OfAa* to *OeBb*) as price falls. Hence points between A and B are price elastic. From B to C, however, the change in price causes a fall in total revenue. Hence demand is price inelastic between B and C. Clearly there must be a point where demand switches from being elastic to inelastic. This is the point B where elasticity is unity. In this respect, it can be misleading to speak of demand *curves* as being elastic or inelastic. It is more sensible to retain the term for reference to a *point* or to a small section of the demand curve.

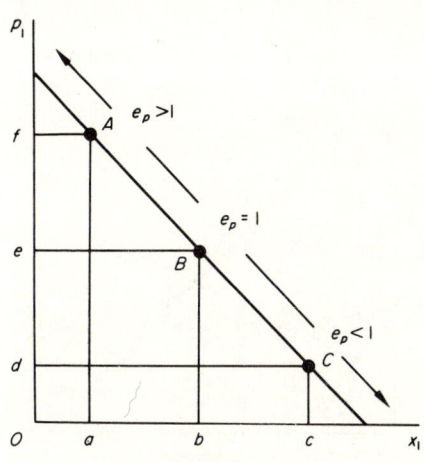

Figure 2.5.1

By looking at e_p in terms of 'small changes' in price, we have been measuring *arc elasticity*. If the change in price is very small indeed, so small in fact that the change in price is virtually negligible, we shall have a measure of e_p *at a point*. At best then, arc elasticity is an approximation of point elasticity. For the latter measure we adopt the symbol '*d*' instead of '*Δ*'. Point elasticity is then defined as

$$e_p = \frac{p \cdot dx}{x \cdot dp}$$

It is worth noting that the price elasticity of demand for good 1 can be read directly from the indifference–budget map of the consumer. Figure 2.5.2 shows such a map with *income* measured on the vertical axis and good 1 on the horizontal axis. The consumer's expenditure on good 1 can be seen directly by observing distances such as *AB*. Thus, if the consumer purchases $\bar{x}_1$ of good 1, his expenditure on good 1 is shown as the distance *AB*. But we know that price elasticity of good 1 is indicated by the change in total expenditure on good 1. A move from *A* to *D*, for example, involves a *reduction* in expenditure, since the distance from *D* to the line from *C* through *B* is smaller than the distance *AB*. Hence, if the *PCC* curve is like PCC_1, good 1 must be price *inelastic* over that range. By similar reasoning PCC_3 is relevant to the section of a demand curve which is price elastic, and PCC_2 to a section with unit price elasticity.

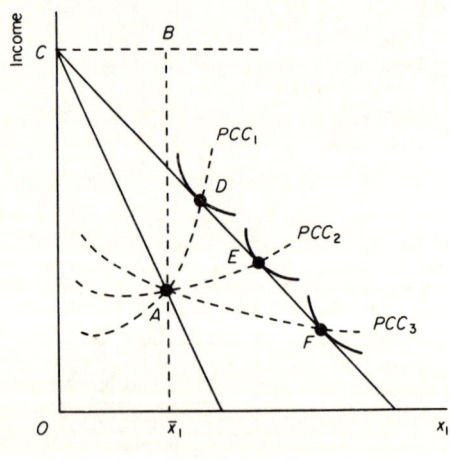

Figure 2.5.2

2.6 Income and Substitution Effects

We return now to the indifference map diagram of Section 2.2. The move from one point on the *PCC* curve to another can be analysed into two component moves.

The first of these components is the feeling of 'better-offness' that a consumer experiences when the price of even one of the things that he buys falls. With his given planned consumption expenditure, he can now buy the same quantity of each good as he did before the fall in the price of one of them, and have some money left over. It is as if all prices had remained unchanged and the consumer had been enabled to increase his planned expenditure. Clearly, for any given fall in the prices of any good, the size of this 'gain' will be the greater, the larger does the good figure in the household's purchase plan. We can, therefore, think of this first force as operating along the income–consumption curve. It is called the *income effect*, because the increase in the purchasing power of the consumer that follows a relative fall in the price of one of the goods that he buys is as if his income has risen and all prices have remained at the same levels.

The second component consists of the consumer's reaction to the change in the relative attractiveness of the cheaper good. He will tend to buy more of the cheaper good, substituting it for the good that is now relatively more expensive. This effect is called the *substitution effect*.

These notional components of the move from one point on the *PCC* curve to another can be illustrated in two different ways.

2.6(a) THE HICKS APPROACH

The first approach to differentiating the income and substitution effects is due to Hicks, although the method chronologically succeeds the Slutsky approach.[1] The *YCC* and *PCC* curves are shown in Figure 2.6.1, and a fall in the price of good 1 is indicated by the shifting budget line pivoting about the point L. In addition, a budget line H_3 parallel to the new budget line H_2 and tangential to the original indifference curve I_1 is drawn. By the definitions in the previous sections, a price–consumption curve joins X to Y, the actual move made by the consumer, and an income–consumption curve joins Z to Y, Z being the point of tangency between the constructed budget line and the original indifference curve. The point of the construction H_3 is to illustrate what would happen if the consumer's *real income* was held constant whilst permitting the relative price change. The way in which Hicks defines real income is important here: real income is held to be constant if the consumer stays on his original indifference curve (i.e. his utility has not increased). The line H_3 achieves this since it is drawn tangential to I_1: the consumer remains on the same indifference curve.

[1] J. R. Hicks, 'A Reconsideration of the Theory of Value', *Economica*, Feb. 1934.

We imagine some hypothetical tax which achieves this constant real income.

The consumer has nonetheless altered his equilibrium in this hypothetical situation: he has moved down I_1 to point Z. The notional move from X to Z is called the *substitution effect*. In terms of the x_1 axis it is measured as the distance ab. Notice that with a *reduction* in the price of good 1, the substitution effect shows an *increase* in the amount purchased of good 1, 'real income' being held constant. This result, which should be obvious from the fact that indifference curves slope downwards, is summarised by saying that the *substitution effect is negative*. If the price of good 1 was to increase, less of good 1 would be purchased, real income being held constant.

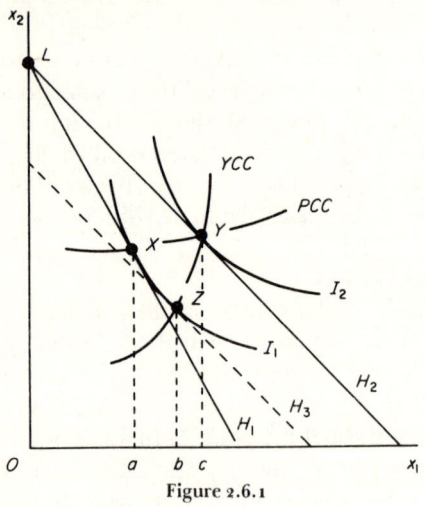

Figure 2.6.1

Now the consumer actually moves from X to Y, involving an increase in the consumption of good 1 equal to ac on the x_1 axis. The 'residual' amount left over after the substitution effect has been calculated is the *income effect*. In terms of the notional movements, it comprises the move along the YCC curve from Z to Y. The amount bc measures the income effect. The two effects combine to form the *price effect*. Hence we can always write

$$\text{Price Effect} = \text{Substitution Effect} + \text{Income Effect}.$$

This general equation is known as the '*Slutsky Equation*' and provides a cornerstone of modern demand theory.

Demand Functions

Notice that the income effect in this case is *positive* with respect to the income change – an increase in real income is associated with an increase in the amount of good 1 purchased. It will be *negative* with respect to the price change: the *fall* in the price of good 1 leads, via the income effect, to an *increase* in the amount of x purchased. As we shall see, however, although the substitution effect is *always* negative, the income effect (with respect to a price change) can be either negative or positive. It will be negative for a normal (or 'superior') good, and positive for an inferior good.[1]

2.6(*b*) THE SLUTSKY APPROACH

The general equation for the component parts of a price effect was given the name 'Slutsky equation' after the Italian economist, Slutsky, who first defined the distinction in 1915.[2] However, Slutsky's original approach was slightly different to that of Hicks.

Whereas in the Hicks approach the hypothetical budget line H_3 was drawn parallel to H_2 and tangential to I_1, in the Slutsky approach H_3 is drawn parallel to H_2 such that *it passes through the original commodity bundle X in Figure 2.6.1*. The Slutsky H_3 is shown in Figure 2.6.2. Drawn in this way, H_3 is a budget line illustrating the effect of an imaginary tax that takes some of the consumer's real income away so that he can buy the *same* commodity bundle *after* the tax as he did before. For Slutsky, then, holding 'real income' constant does not mean staying on the same indifference curve, for, given that the slope of H_3 is not the same as the slope of H_1, the consumer will be able to reach a higher indifference curve with H_3 than with H_1. This result is shown in Figure 2.6.2, the hypothetical budget line H_3 enabling the consumer to reach point Z compared to point X. In the Slutsky analysis, the price effect from X to Y is made up of the substitution effect, which consists of the move from X to Z, and the 'residual' income effect, which is a move from Z to Y along the income–consumption curve.

---

[1] It is worth emphasising a terminological distinction here. If more of good 1 is purchased as real income increases, the income effect is *positive with respect to the income change*. For normal goods, the income effect is *negative with respect to the price change*, since a fall in price leads to more of good 1 being purchased. Simply to speak of income effects as being 'positive' or 'negative' can therefore be confusing. The rule adopted here is to refer to the income effect with respect to a *price* change.

[2] E. Slutsky, 'On the Theory of the Budget of the Consumer', *Giornale degli Economisti* (English translation of the original title), 1915. Reprinted in English in American Economic Association, *Readings in Price Theory*, ed. J. Viner *et al.* (Allen & Unwin, London, 1953).

The Slutsky substitution effect could therefore be measured as *ac* in Figure 2.6.2, and the income effect as *cd*. In order to compare this with the Hicks approach we can observe the point *W* lying on the budget line parallel to H_2 and tangential to I_1. The hypothetical move from *X* to *W* is the Hicks substitution effect, measured along the x_1 axis as *ab*. The difference in the Hicks and Stutsky approaches is the amount *bc*. As it happens, if the change in the price of good 1 is very small, this difference *bc* will be negligible, so that the two approaches do not differ substantially.

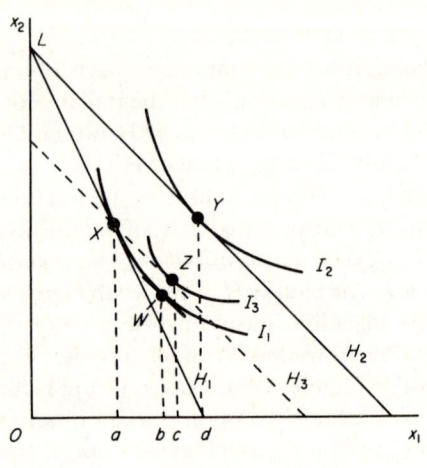

Figure 2.6.2

Which is the better approach, the Hicks or the Slutsky analysis? Part of the answer to this question must depend on which definition of 'constant real income' is to be preferred. In the Hicks case it means constant utility – i.e. staying on the same indifference curve. In the Slutsky case it means being able to buy the same *commodity bundle* as before. Since relative prices have, *ex hypothesi*, changed, however, the Slutsky approach enables the consumer to move down the budget line to a point of tangency with a higher indifference curve. The Slutsky-type consumer is 'overcompensated', in the Hicks sense, since he can reach a higher indifference curve: the Hicks type consumer is 'under-compensated', in the Slutsky sense, since, on H_2, he cannot buy his original commodity bundle. Arguments of this kind are not fruitful, however, since they reduce to quarrels about definitions. More important is the empirical measurability of the effects. In the Hicks case, it is not possible to compute the substitution effect (and hence the income effect since that is estimated as a residual) because it is difficult to devise a test which enables us to say that a particular amount of compensation leaves the consumer with the same *utility*. The Slutsky approach, however, is testable since the compensating variation in the hypothetical tax is such as to enable the consumer to buy the original commodity bundle, an observable entity. In short, it is difficult to say in practice where point W in Figure 2.6.2 would be; but it would be possible to identify point Z. On the 'testability' count, the Slutsky approach is to be preferred.

As it happens, the distance bc in Figure 2.6.2 tends to zero as the rate of change in p_1 gets smaller. In other words, for small enough price changes, the Hicks and Slutsky approaches produce near-identical results.

2.7 Re-defining 'Normal', 'Inferior' and 'Giffen' Goods

The concepts of income and substitution effects enable us to look a little more rigorously at the concept of an inferior good. Both the income and substitution effects were seen to be negative for 'normal' goods: that is, a *fall* in price led, on both counts, to an *increase* in the amount of the good bought. Figure 2.7.1 shows the indifference and budget map for various goods. For diagrammatic simplicity we adopt

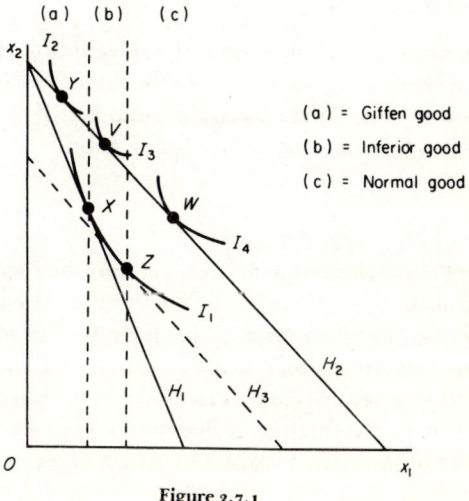

Figure 2.7.1

the Hicks approach to income and substitution effects. The price effect consists of the move from X to Y in the case of I_2, X to V in the case of I_3 and X to W in the case of I_4. The substitution effect in each case is shown as the move along I_1 from X to Z, so that this effect is, as always, negative with respect to the price change. In cases I_2 and I_3, the income effect is positive with respect to the price change. In case I_4, the income effect is negative.

The good for which I_3 is the indifference curve is *inferior* since the income effect is positive. The overal price effect remains negative, however – that is, the overall move from X to V involves more of good 1 being purchased after the price fall. The good for which I_2 is the indifference curve, however, has a positive overall price effect, which implies that it is a *Giffen* good. The positive income effect has, in this case, outweighed the negative substitution effect.

It may be useful to tabulate these results:

Income effect (with respect to price) (y)	Substitution effect (s)	Relation between y and s	Price effect	Type of good
–	–	$\|y\| \lessgtr \|s\|$	–	normal
+	–	$\|y\| < \|s\|$	–	inferior
+	–	$\|y\| > \|s\|$	+	Giffen

These three cases are exclusive since the substitution effect cannot be positive. The three cases correspond to the three 'zones' distinguished in Figure 2.7.1. Thus, if the new equilibrium is at W, the good is normal; if at V it is inferior; and at Y, a Giffen good.

2.8 On Various Demand Curves

The demand curve derived in Section 2.3 was obtained directly from the price–consumption curve. Armed with the Hicks and Slutsky approaches to income and substitution effects, we can now analyse the assumptions underlying that demand curve and show that other, frequently more relevant, curves can be derived from the consumer's indifference map. The analysis is shown in Figure 2.8.1, which looks slightly forbidding at first sight but which is essentially straightforward.

Demand Functions 53

The top diagram repeats Figure 2.6.2 and shows the various income and substitution effects associated with the Hicks and Slutsky analysis. The various quantities of good 1 are mapped directly on to an identical horizontal axis in the lower diagram. On this lower part, however, the price of good 1 is shown on the vertical axis. We saw earlier that there was no direct way of observing the price of good 1 from the general indifference map diagram unless 'all other goods' were shown on the vertical axis. In Figure 2.8.1, we have simply selected an arbitrary point on the vertical axis of the lower diagram and called this p_1^1: this price

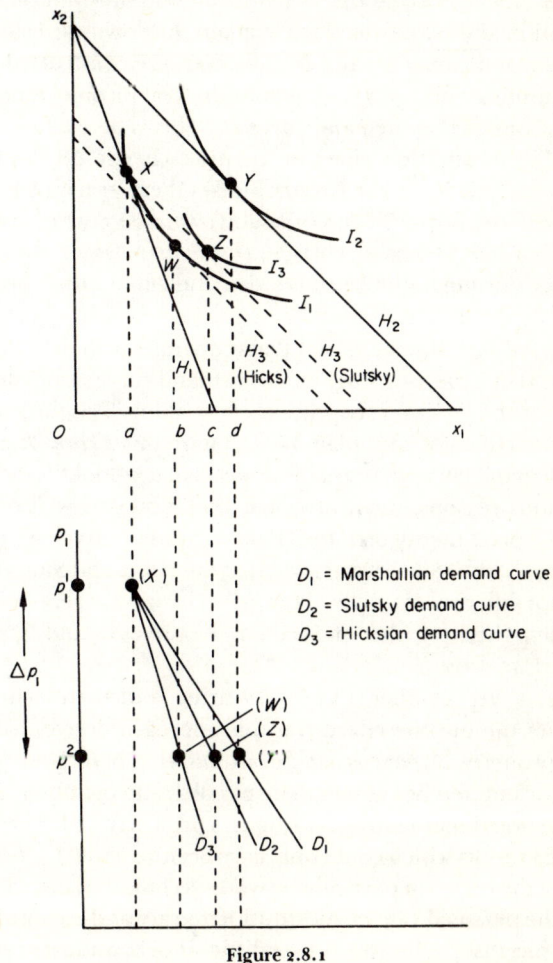

Figure 2.8.1

corresponds to the price of good 1 when the budget line is H_1 in the upper part of the figure. The change in p_1, reflected in the swing from H_1 to H_2, is shown as Δp_1 in the lower part, i.e. the move from p_1^1 to p_1^2. By drawing the horizontal line from p_1^2 into the quadrant of the lower part of the figure, we can observe various demand curves.

The move from X to Y, for example, the 'price effect', is shown as lying on demand curve D_1, which is the same demand curve as was derived in Section 2.3. This is the 'Marshallian' demand curve. The significant point about the demand curve D_1 is that, as we move down it, real income is *not* constant: both income and substitution effects are in operation and both, therefore, explain the downward slope of D_1.

The demand curves D_2 and D_3, however, are constructed such that the substitution effect *only* is in operation: 'real income' is not allowed to vary. Consider the demand curve D_2. This is derived by observing the Slutsky substitution effect of the price change Δp_1 — that is, the move from H_1 to H_2. In the sense of Slutsky then, 'real income' does *not* vary as we move down D_2. D_2 slopes downward because of the substitution effect alone. Hence we christen D_2 a *Slutsky demand curve*. In terms of Slutsky's original phrase: it is a demand curve with 'apparent real income' held constant.

The curve D_3 is similar except that it operates with the Hicks definition of real income. Once again, this demand curve slopes downwards because of the (Hicks) substitution effect alone. The income effect is not allowed to come into play. We can term this a *Hicks demand curve*.

The demand curve that usually appears in textbooks is the curve D_1. For various reasons, most of which would take us well beyond the scope of a price theory text, the Hicks or Slutsky curves are preferable in many contexts. Since we argued that the Hicks and Slutsky analyses would not differ substantially if the price change was very small, we can safely lump them together and refer to the curves D_2 and D_3 as *'compensated' demand curves*.

There is yet another way of securing a demand curve which eliminates the income effect, but this approach derives from a particular property of *parallel indifference curves*. There is no particular reason for indifference curves to be parallel, and the observant reader will have noted that many of the figures presented so far have, in fact, produced results which could only have been achieved by 'twisting' the shapes of the curves in particular ways. In technical terms, we have permitted the personal rate of substitution to vary as the consumer's real income increases. This much is realistic since consumers certainly do

Demand Functions

vary their rates of substitution as income rises: they do not continue to buy goods in the same proportion. However, as a limiting case, suppose that the *PRS* is constant as we move from one parallel budget line to another along a vertical line. This is shown in the upper part of Figure 2.8.2. The *PRS* is the same at *X*, *Y* and *Z*. The vertical line is, in fact, an income–consumption curve, but the same amount of good 1 is purchased at each equilibrium. In short, the income effect is zero.

Now consider a price change in good 1 such that the budget line shifts from H_1 to H_2. On the Hicks analysis we construct the

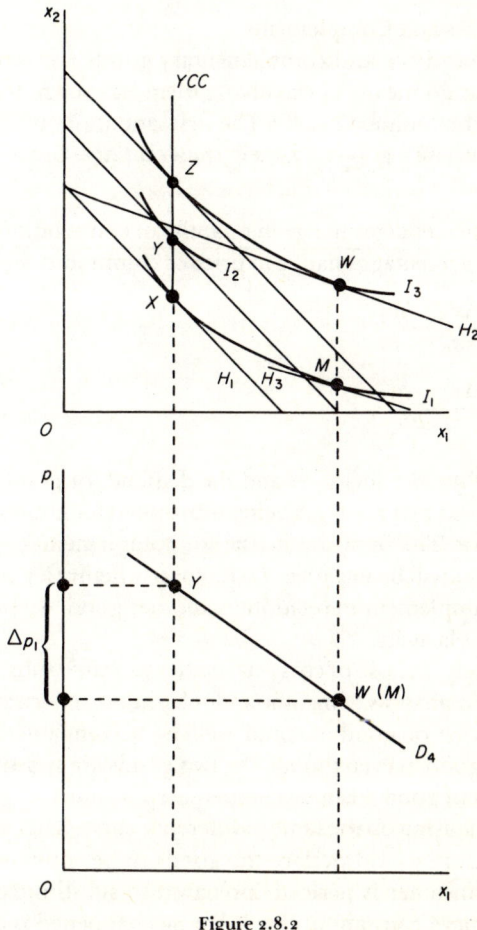

Figure 2.8.2

hypothetical budget line H_3 with tangency at M. The move from X to W is the price effect, and the move from X to M is the substitution effect.

But, by virtue of the vertical parallelism of the indifference curves, point M is directly below point W. The income effect is zero. Hence the demand curve D_4 in the lower part of the figure slopes downward because of the substitution effect alone. The problem with D_4 is that it requires a further axiom of consumer behaviour that it is difficult to admit – that is, that as income increases the consumer will continue to purchase commodities in the same proportion.

2.9 Substitutes and Complements

The idea of substitute and complementary goods was introduced in Chapter 1, but no means of classifying them was suggested. Two approaches will be outlined briefly. The first, and more traditional, approach is to classify goods by their *cross–elasticity*. Cross elasticity is defined as

$$e_C = \frac{\text{percentage change in quantity of commodity 1}}{\text{percentage change in price of commodity 2}}$$

$$= \frac{\Delta x_1}{x_1} \div \frac{\Delta p_2}{p_2}$$

$$= \frac{\Delta x_1}{x_1} \cdot \frac{p_2}{\Delta p_2}.$$

If the price of good 2 increases and the demand for good 1 increases also, this suggests that good 1 is being substituted for good 2. Hence, e_C will be positive. The opposite is true for complementary goods: the magnitude of e_C will be negative. To discover whether a good is a substitute or a complement in relation to another good, we simply compute the cross elasticity.

Unfortunately, the use of cross elasticities to define substitutes is inadequate as our analysis of income and substitution effects can show. A rise in the price of good 1 could well be accompanied by *smaller* purchases of good 2, even though the two goods are substitutes in the sense that less of good 1 can be compensated by more of good 2 with the consumer staying on the same indifference curve. That is, the cross-elasticity measure would declare the goods to be complements even though the consumer is perfectly prepared to substitute one for the other and achieve constant utility. What has happened is that the income effect of the increased price of good 1 has caused a reduction in x_1 and x_2, and has outweighed the substitution effect. This hints that a proper definition would be in terms of substitution effects alone. This indeed was the approach adopted by Hicks, although the analysis must be extended to at least *three* goods. The reason is simply that two goods invariably bear a substitute relationship to each other, in the sense that indifference curves have negative slopes. Hence we assume three goods: 1, 2 and 'all other goods' (*M*).

The Hicks definitions are.[1]

(*a*) Good 1 is a *substitute* for good 2, if the *PRS* of 1 for *M* falls as good 2 is substituted for *M* such that the consumer stays on the same indifference plane;

(*b*) Good 1 is a *complement* of good 2, if the *PRS* of 1 for *M* increases as good 2 is substituted for *M* such that the consumer stays on the same indifference plane.

We avoid a diagrammatic presentation of these points since it would involve three-dimensional figures (hence the reference to an indifference 'plane' rather than curve). The final part of the definitions reminds us that we are trying to abstract from the income effects which, as we saw, upset our first definition.

The terms *gross substitute* and *gross complement* are reserved for goods in situations where the income effect has *not* been eliminated. The terms *substitute* and *complement* are reserved for situations where the income effect has been allowed for.

Returning to two commodities, with the above definitions in mind, we can say that if, after a hypothetical tax has constrained the consumer to his original indifference curve (held his 'real income' constant in the Hicks sense), a fall in p_1 leads to a fall in x_2, then good 1 is a substitute for good 2. If a fall in p_1 leads to a rise in x_2, then goods 1 and 2 are complements.

Notice that, with the idea of substitute and complementary goods introduced, our expression for the demand function must now be expanded further. It now reads

$$D_1 = D(p_1, Y_c, p_2, p_3)$$

where good 2 is the only substitute good and good 3 is the only com-

---

[1] J. R. Hicks, *Value and Capital* (Oxford University Press, London, 1964). Hicks did not use the term 'personal rate of substitution'.

plementary good. The price p_1 is frequently referred to as the 'own price' to distinguish it from the prices of other goods.

2.10 Revealed Preference

The theory of consumer behaviour so far developed has been based on a set of axioms, the aim of which was to establish the consumer's preference ordering over the commodity bundles in commodity space. The axiom system led us to establish the existence of indifference curves and through them to derive a number of useful statements about consumer demand. It is possible, due to Samuelson,[1] to obtain the same results by an alternative axiomatic approach: the *revealed preference* approach. No more than the basic ideas of revealed preference are presented here. Any greater detail would over-extend the text, and the final theorems are the same as those we have already obtained. Nonetheless, the reader should be aware of the existence of this parallel approach. The essence of the revealed preference approach is that a model of consumer behaviour, equivalent in almost every way to the model already established, is obtained by observing *actual choices*.

The axiom system for the revealed preference approach can be presented as follows:

Axiom 1 Each consumer is faced by a price/income context and he cannot influence prices by his own actions.[2]

This axiom amounts to saying no more than that the consumer has a given income, which he can change – e.g. by increasing the supply of his own labour – and is faced by given prices which he cannot influence. The latter assumption enables us to make the budget line linear.

Axiom 2 In any price/income context the consumer always chooses a commodity bundle.

This axiom merely ensures that, faced with a particular budget line, the

---

[1] P. Samuelson, *Foundations of Economic Analysis* (Harvard University Press, 1947), although the core of the theory was developed earlier. See also P. Samuelson, 'Consumption Theorems in Terms of Overcompensation Rather than Indifference Comparisons', *Economica,* 1953. Undoubtedly the most thorough comparison of the two approaches is by Newman, op. cit. chapter 6. Newman refers to the two approaches as 'preference theory' – i.e. the approach followed up to this section – and 'choice theory' – i.e. revealed preference.

[2] Newman, op. cit., refers to the price/income context as a *situation*.

Demand Functions

consumer will choose *something*. It is therefore entirely analagous to the similar guarantee encompassed by the axiom of selection in the preference axiom system.

Axiom 3 The consumer spends all his income.

As before, this axiom precludes us from worrying about savings.

Axiom 4 For every commodity bundle, X, there exists at least one price/income context such that the consumer selects X.

This axiom ensures that each point in commodity space can be chosen.

Axiom 5 The Weak Axiom of Revealed Preference.

If X is chosen from a context that includes Y as an available alternative (i.e. if XCY), then if Y is chosen, X must not be available. Violation of this axiom implies inconsistency on the part of the consumer; indeed the axiom is sometimes called an axiom of 'consistent choice'. To see why this is so, we can analyse each statement in terms of prices and quantities. If XCY then X and Y must lie on the same budget line, or Y must lie inside the attainable set with X on the boundary, as is the case in Figure 2.10.1 with context 1. We can therefore say

$$XCY \rightarrow p^1.X \geqslant p^1.Y$$

where $p^1 X$ is interpreted as the bundle X at prices in context 1.

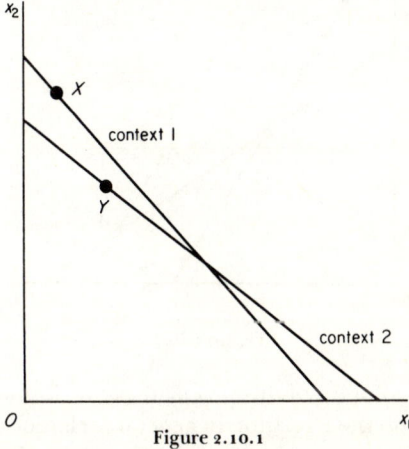

Figure 2.10.1

Now suppose context 2 rules. Our axiom requires that if Y is chosen, X should not be available. This is so in Figure 2.10.1, and we can write

$$-YCX \rightarrow p^2.X > p^2.Y$$

since X is now 'too expensive' to be bought in context 2. Our axiom therefore becomes

$$(p^1X \geqslant p^1Y) \to (p^2 . X > p^2Y).$$

All that is being said is that the choice of X (when Y is available) 'reveals' a preference for X over Y, while the purchase of Y at a new set of prices implies that he must be unable to afford X at the new prices.

Axiom 6 The Strong Axiom of Revealed Preference.

The set of axioms 1 to 5 are still not adequate for us to derive a theory of consumer behaviour. Consider Figure 2.10.2. We cannot, in this case, write XCY since Y is not available when X is chosen $(p^1Y > p^1X)$. But we cannot write YCX either, because if Y is chosen, X is not available $(p^2 . Y < p^2 . X)$. We simply cannot apply the weak axiom. X and Y are said to be 'non-comparable' and, in consequence, we are unable to order the consumer's preferences over the various states simply by looking at his revealed choices. Although we have been able to develop an axiom system based on the C relation, it fails to fulfil the purpose of such a system.

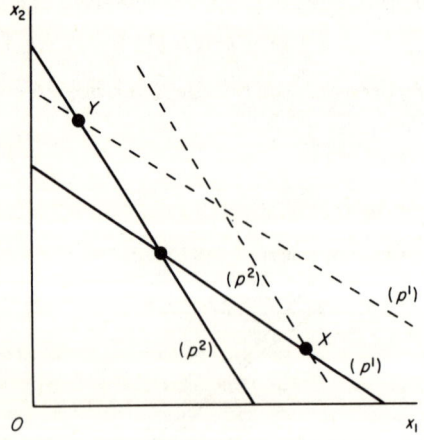

Figure 2.10.2

A clue to the solution of this problem can be found if we compare the C relation with the P relation in general preference theory. A brief table shows that P is transitive (XPY & $YPZ \to XPZ$), asymmetric ($XPY \to -YPX$), and irreflexive ($-XPX$). A similar analysis of C, however, shows that it is

Demand Functions

asymmetric and irreflexive, but *intransitive*.

P	C
transitive	intransitive
asymmetric	asymmetric
irreflexive	irreflexive

To overcome this intransitivity we introduce the *strong axiom* of revealed preference. To do this we require the concept of 'indirectly preferred to', which, following Newman,[1] we symbolise as Q. The essential idea is to compare a *sequence* of points which can be directly compared. Then, if XCX^1, X^1CX^2, ..., $X^{n-1}CX^n$, and X^nCY, we have XQY. By finding a 'chain' of indirect preferences, most of the points in commodity space will be ranked with respect to a particular point, say Y. When no sequence can be found[2], the point is *unranked* with respect to Y and it is possible to show that the locus of these unranked points is convex to the origin – just like an indifference curve. Technically, however, this locus is not an indifference curve since it shows only *unranked points*, not points where we have explicit evidence of indifference.

The requirement for indirect preference is that if YQX, then X must never be indirectly chosen over Y: i.e.

$$YQX \to -XQY$$

which is the *strong axiom of revealed preference*. In this case, Y has been ranked with respect to X. If, on the other hand, no sequence of this kind is found, Y and X would lie on the locus of 'unranked' points. This locus partitions the commodity space in the same way as the indifference curve partitions the space into preferred and non-preferred sets.

We can briefly show how concepts analogous to the income and substitution effect can be illustrated.

In Figure 2.10.3 the consumer chooses X in a context defined by H_1. The price of x_1 falls to that H_2 now operates, and we suppose the consumer chooses Z. We draw H_3, parallel to H_2, through X, so that H_3 is equivalent to a Slutsky compensated budget line. If the consumer faces H_3 he has an attainable set Oab. When he faced H_1, it was Ocd. The

---

[1] Newman, op. cit. Newman refers to the relation Q as 'sequentially chosen' for reasons that will be obvious. More advanced readers may come to the strong axiom in terms of guaranteeing 'integrability' conditions.

[2] Points for which no sequence can be found are referred to by Newman as being 'inaccessible' to each other.

shaded area is common to both sets. With H_3 the area aXc is ruled out, but Xdb is attainable. Hence, the consumer facing H_3 has only two options – he can stay at X, or move to a point like Y. Since H_3 is constructed to eliminate the income effect of the price change, any move from X to Y must be (some kind of) a substitution effect. It has been given various titles: the 'quasi substitution effect', and confusingly, an 'overcompensation effect.' By analogy, the move from Y to Z would be a sort of income effect.

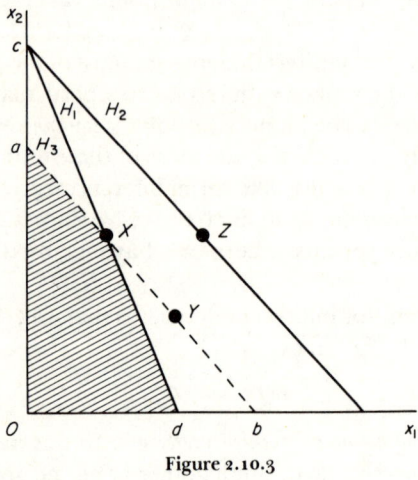

Figure 2.10.3

The main point is that the substitution effect in this analysis is either negative (with respect to price) or zero (the consumer could stay at X). But if the substitution effect is zero, our goods will not obey the basic 'law' of demand (the downward-sloping demand curve) unless the income effect is positive with respect to income. In short, normal goods will ensure the downward slope of the demand curve.

2.11 Some 'Pathological' Demand Curves
The 'normal' demand curve slopes downwards from left to right. The demand curve for 'Giffen' goods will contain a 'kink' such that, after a point, the demand for the good will *rise* with price. The (unlikely) case of a Giffen good is shown in Figure 2.11.1.

Other 'pathological' cases are possible, deriving from possible relaxations of the axiom system presented in Chapter 1. Thus, if the in-

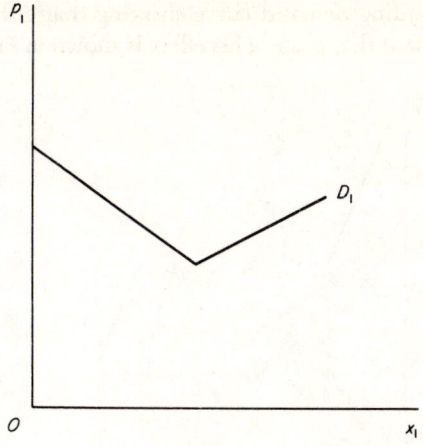

Figure 2.11.1

difference curve is convex for part of its length and concave elsewhere, the equilibrium situation will appear as in Figure 2.11.2. Given H_1 the consumer cannot do better than reach A or B, but on H_2 he will not settle at C (on the 'old' indifference curve) because he can move to D on I_2. Thus each budget line is tangential to *two* indifference curves: at a concave section of the lower one, and at *two* convex sections of the higher one. For the price of good 1 relevant to H_1, then, there is a discontinuity

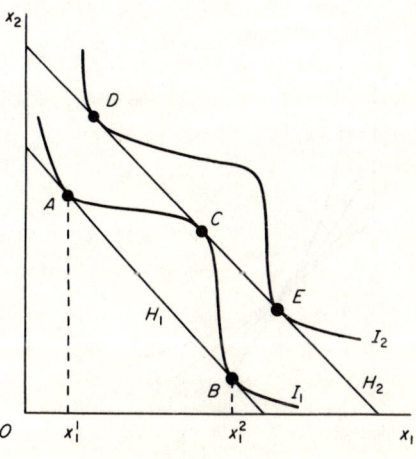

Figure 2.11.2

in the corresponding demand curve showing that either x_1^1 or x_1^2 of good 1 is bought at that price. This effect is shown in Figure 2.11.3.

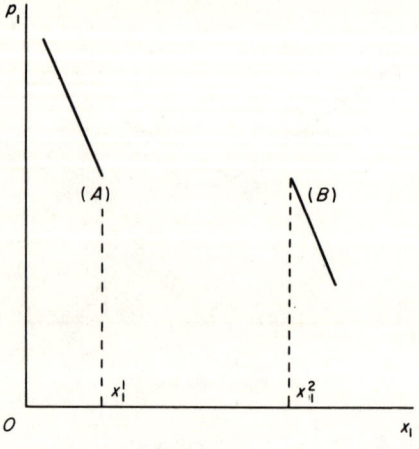

Figure 2.11.3

A similar effect, but this time producing a complete vertical section in D_1 is obtained if the indifference curve has any 'sharp' corners such as A in Figure 2.11.4. Any array of prices of good 1, corresponding to H_1, H_2, H_3 etc. in Figure 2.11.4, will secure equilibrium at A: the limits of these prices being set by the slopes of the indifference curve to the left and right of A respectively. The effect is shown in Figure 2.11.5.

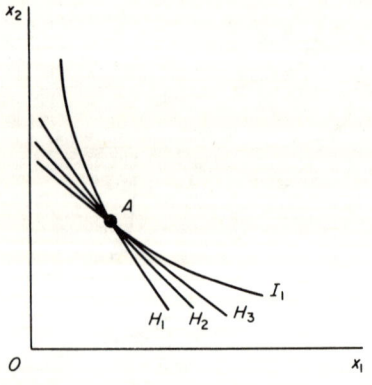

Figure 2.11.4

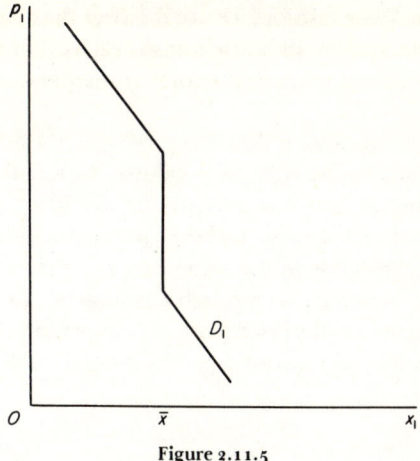

Figure 2.11.5

The 'pathological' case shown in Figure 2.11.3 would, of course, not be possible with an axiom system requiring (weak) convexity of indifference curves: i.e. the concave sections of the indifference curves could not exist. The case in Figure 2.11.5 *could* however exist in the context of *strong* convexity, which was generally assumed in Chapter 1. Strong convexity ruled out *linear segments* but not 'kinks'. For all further analytical purposes, however, we ignore demand curves with vertical segments.

2.12 Market Demand

The consumer whose demand for good 1 is illustrated in Figure 2.5.1 is not the only purchaser of that good. We can, however, derive the demand for good 1 of each other consumer that is a potential purchaser of good 1 in precisely the same way. The total or market demand for good 1 is obtained by adding together the demands for good 1 of all the consumers that are planning to buy it. The way in which this summation is effected is illustrated in Figure 2.12.1. The first three diagrams show the demand curves for good 1 of three separate and independent consumers. We get the total demand curve by adding together the quantities of good 1 that each consumer plans to buy at each price. Thus at the price $\bar{p}_1$, consumer A plans to buy a_1, B plans to buy b_1, and C plans to buy c_1. The total quantity that all consumers plan to buy at the price p_1 is therefore a_1 plus b_1 plus c_1, and this quantity is plotted against the price p_1 in the diagram on the extreme right of the figure. In the same fashion, we can discover the quantity of good 1 that will be demanded by all households at each other price. When all these points are joined we have the total or market demand curve for X.

It is very rarely that a total demand curve will not slope downwards and monotonically to the right. A good may be a Giffen good for an individual consumer, but it is seldom that any given good will be a Giffen good for all consumers. And even if it is, it is unlikely that it will be so for each consumer in the same range of prices. In both these cases, there will generally be enough consumers who increase their planned purchases as the price falls to compensate for those consumers who buy less because for them the good is a Giffen good in that range of prices.

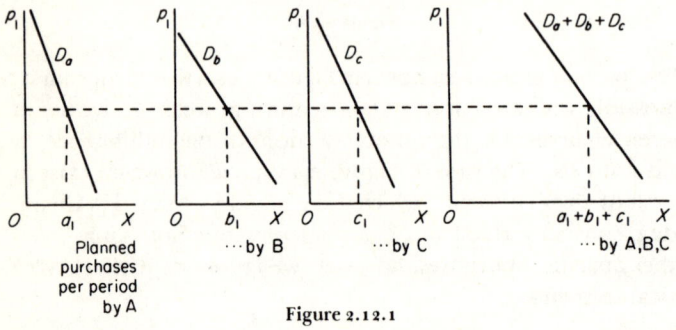

Figure 2.12.1

We have assumed that each consumer in planning his purchases faces given prices for the goods that he plans to buy. In doing this, we have not been unrealistic, for in any period each consumer's purchases of any good constitute only a very small proportion of the total quantity of that good that is currently being bought by all consumers. While each consumer plans on the assumption that each price is given and beyond his control, the total effect of *all* consumers implementing their purchase plans is to assist in the determination of the relations between the prices of things that they buy. The price-determining role of the purchase plans of consumers is summarised in the total demand curve for each of the goods that they buy.

2.13 Market Demand: Aggregation Problems

Figure 2.13.1 assumes that it is perfectly legitimate to total individuals' demand curves to obtain the market demand curve. But suppose that the demand curves are not independent: suppose, for example, that B's purchases depend on A's purchases, either because B 'envies' A and follows him in order to be like him ('keeping up with the Joneses'), or because B's income depends in some way upon A's purchases. If this kind of taste or income interdependence exists, then we cannot simply add up the demand curves of individuals to form the market demand curve. We must observe how a shift in A's demand curve affects the demand of B, C, etc. We have an *aggregation problem*. The most convenient 'solution' to this problem is to assume that it does not exist. Indeed, most 'pure theory' proceeds on just this assumption, embodied sometimes in a formal axiom:

Supplementary Axiom Consumers' Preferences are 'Selfish'.

By this axiom we assume that each consumer's preferences are not influenced by the purchase of others, nor does anyone judge quality by price (i.e. buy more at higher prices because higher prices are thought to mean higher quality). Simple observation and introspection suggests that this axiom is severely restrictive. Most of the axioms presented so far have involved simplifications, but the selfishness axiom implies a substantial departure from reality. It is important, then, to see whether these interdependencies entail major corrections to our theory of consumer behaviour. To do this we relax the selfishness axiom.

Leibenstein has presented a convenient taxonomy for the interdependencies which generate the aggregation problem. He has also analysed their effects on the market demand curve.[1] Only a brief outline of the general results is given here.

A 'bandwagon effect' is said to exist if any individual purchases goods in order to behave like other members of his social group. If their demand for a good increases, so will his, since he wishes to identify with them. In Figure 2.13.1 an ordinary market demand curve D_A is shown. The effect of a fall in price from P_1 to P_2 is to increase the amount purchased from Q_1 to Q_2. But the bandwagon effect will mean that more consumers will enter the market for this good, extending demand to, say, Q_3. Hence the 'true' demand curve connects points a and b. Bandwagon effects therefore have the general result of making market demand curves more elastic.

A 'snob' effect exists if the consumer attempts to differentiate himself from his social group by purchasing commodities which they

---

[1] H. Leibenstein, 'Bandwagon, Snob and Veblen Effects in the Theory of Consumers' Demand', *Quarterly Journal of Economics*, May 1950.

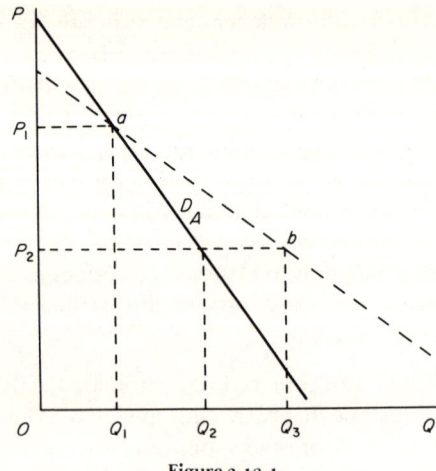

Figure 2.13.1

do not purchase, and, conversely, reducing his purchases of commodities which they purchase. Hence, when their demand increases, his will fall. In Figure 2.13.2, for example, the fall in price leads to an expected increase in demand along the ordinary market demand curve. But, as the amount purchased by the group increases, the amount purchased by the snob consumer will fall, reducing demand to a point to the left of the market demand curve. Hence the 'true' demand curve is shown as the dashed line through a and b in Figure 2.13.2. A snob effect makes the market demand curve more inelastic.

A 'Veblen' effect exists when the individual judges quality by price.[1] In Figure 2.13.3, the ordinary total price effect is shown as a move down the market demand curve from a to b. But now that price has fallen, some consumers will disappear from the market, regarding the fall in price as indicative of a fall in quality. Hence the quantity purchased will move from Q_2 to Q_3, say, or even Q_4. The 'true' market demand curve is therefore more inelastic than the market demand curve, or may even be positively sloped.

How far these interdependencies imply divergencies between true and ordinary demand curves will depend on the strength of the effects for any one consumer and, more important, on the number of consumers subject to such effects. There is, of course, no reason to sup-

---

[1] The term derives from Thorstein Veblen, *The Theory of the Leisure Class* (1932 ed.) although, as Leibenstein points out, the 'Veblen effect' was noted by various social observers much earlier than Veblen.

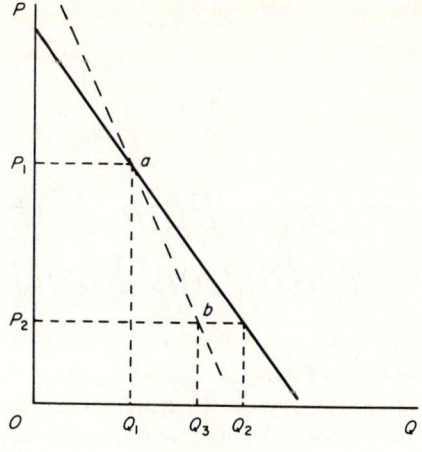

Figure 2.13.2

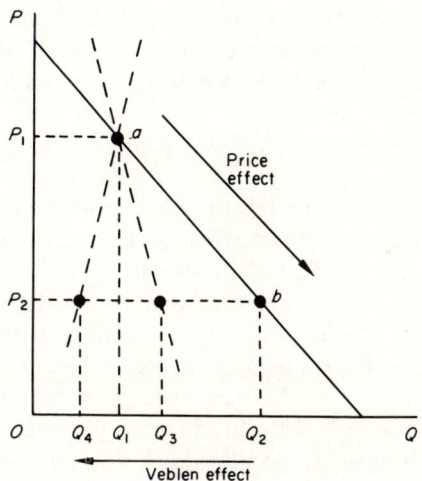

Figure 2.13.3

pose that the market is composed of people subject to just one of the effects: bandwagon, snob and Veblen effects could well all be acting together alongside 'normal' consumer behaviour.

3

Short-run Sales Plan of the Firm: The Production Function

3.0 Purchase and Sales Plans

The previous chapters derived the fundamental concepts of a demand curve. Demand is obviously demand *for* something, a good, and that something is provided by a *productive enterprise*. Hereafter, any productive enterprise will be called a *firm*. In this respect firms need not be typified by private enterprise companies: the National Health Service provides 'health', universities and schools provide 'education', pop artists may provide free 'entertainment'. Firms are not therefore defined in terms of any institutional characteristics or in terms of motives for their behaviour. All that matters is that they provide a good.

Even this is not precise enough, however, since the phrase 'provision of a good' can encompass transferring commodities from places where they are not wanted to places where they are, transforming goods in a fashion so as to make them acceptable to, or more desired by, consumers, and so on. It is convenient to follow modern terminology and refer to a firm as any agent involved in the deliberate *transformation* of one state of nature into another state. In this way, 'transformation' can be used interchangeably with 'production' so as to encompass the spatial redistribution of goods, their storage over time, their refashioning (packaging, advertising) and physical transformations of resources into usable goods.

In engaging in the process of transformation or production, firms transform *inputs* into *outputs*. In the typical case, the cabinet-maker transforms a raw material, wood, into furniture, using his own, and perhaps others', labour and capital equipment. The capital equipment is likely to be the output of another firm, but to the cabinet-maker it is an input. Equally, the health service transforms resources into 'health' and the pop artist transforms his own energy and capital equipment into 'entertainment'.

For firms that sell their products, then, there will be a *sales plan* consisting of the planned selling quantity (x_i) of each type of output it produces and the associated expected prices. The sum of these individual expected sales is the firm's *expected revenue*:

$$R_E = p_1 \cdot x_1 + p_2 \cdot x_2 + p_3 \cdot x_3 + \ldots + p_n \cdot x_n.$$

This is the equation for a multi-product firm. The analysis is easier if we assume that the firm has only one product to sell, that is,

$$R_E = p_1 \cdot x_1.$$

Few firms use only one input, however, so that there will be a corresponding *purchase plan* for inputs (n_i), the total expenditure on which will be the firm's costs,

$$C = f_1 \cdot n_1 + f_2 \cdot n_2 + f_3 \cdot n_3 + \ldots f_m \cdot n_m$$

where f_i is the price of an input.

3.1 Firms' Objectives

Obviously the sales and purchase plans of a firm will depend on what the firm aims to do. There are numerous hypotheses about how firms behave. For the moment we can mention just the main ones:

(*a*) maximise $R_E - C$. This hypothesis tells us that firms aim to maximise profits, and it underlies much of the traditional theory of the firm;

(*b*) maximise R_E. This tells us that the firm places more emphasis on *sales* than on profits, although it is unlikely that the firm would be indifferent to profits. We might expect firms to maximise R_E subject to some minimum acceptable level of profits;

(*c*) maximise managerial utility. This suggests that managers have utility functions, dependent perhaps on the firm's profits, prestige and size of labour force. The maximisation of these utility functions need not coincide with maximising profits.

Clearly, the choice of an objective function will determine the sales and purchase plans of the firm. If size of labour force is a prestige indicator, for example, more labour may be employed than is consistent with maximising profits. Indeed, it may be inconsistent with the further idea of minimising costs for a given level of output.

We need to assume something about firms' behaviour in order to establish a model of the firm. We adopt the conventional view that firms aim to

(i) *maximise profits*: i.e. select the output level that makes the difference between R_E and C as large as possible;

(ii) *minimise costs for a given output level*: that is, produce each level of output in the most efficient way.

Clearly, these are not different objectives; the activity of minimising costs for each output level is a precondition for maximising profits. These objectives are not both relevant to important institutions, such as hospitals and schools, which do not aim to maximise profits; but minimising costs for given output levels is relevant to any firm.

3.2 Planning Periods

If we are given the objective of the firm, the range of sales and purchase plans from which it may choose will depend on the period of time for which it is planning. In general, the shorter the period of time to which the sales and purchase plans are related, the narrower will be the range of choice, and vice versa. The length of the planning period affects the contents of the purchase plan in two ways: it affects the physical quantities of the different inputs that the firm might use, and it in part determines the sums of money that the firm must disburse for their use. Thus, if a firm hires its operative labour and buys its raw materials in weekly contracts, and its other inputs on contracts with a longer time period, then for periods shorter than one week the firm cannot reduce the quantities of inputs at its disposal. It might be able to buy more of some of them, but even here the limits are narrow for it may take some time to find suitable labour to hire, and to seek out new sources of more raw materials. The firm need not, of course, use all the inputs at its disposal – but even if it uses none of them, its costs will be the same, for while the contracts run, labour, etc., must be paid. For such very short periods of time, therefore, all the firm's costs might be *fixed costs*. If the planning period is longer – say, one month – then the firm's range of choice will be wider, for during a month the quantities of all inputs that are hired on contracts of less than one month can be increased or decreased. Time, however, exerts its influence not only through the possibility of making, modifying or renewing contracts, but also because time is needed in which to produce the new inputs that the firm may require. Thus, it might take twelve months to build a new factory: for planning periods of less than one year, the input 'factory-space' must be taken as fixed.

The influence of time on the number and scope of the different plans from which a firm may choose will be explored more fully later. For the moment, we conclude that the range of choice open to the firm varies directly with time: for very short periods, the range of choice may be virtually zero; for very long periods, it may be virtually infinite. While this relationship between time and the number of alternative decisions that a firm might make is a continuous one, it is customary to explore the role of time by taking three discrete periods: the *instantaneous or market period*, the *short period* (or short-run), and the *long period* (or long-run). In the instantaneous period, the sales and purchase plans are data. In the short-run, the quantities of some of the inputs that the firm uses can be increased or decreased: it is usually assumed that operative labour and raw materials are variable while the quantities and qualities of the plant, machinery and managerial labour are fixed. In the long-run, the quantities and qualities of all the inputs that the firm might use can be varied. In this chapter, we concentrate on the alternative sales and purchase plans that might be made for the short period, and in the next chapter, on the range of choice open to the firm in the long-run.

3.3 The Production Function: Linear Case

We concentrate now on the firm's purchase plan. Figure 3.3.1(*a*) shows two inputs L and K (say, labour and capital, measured as man-days and machine-days) measured on the axes. Some combination of L and K produces 1000 units, another produces 1500 and another 3000, and so on. Strictly, we require a three-dimensional diagram since we have two inputs and one output to show. Figure 3.3.1(*b*) shows what this may look like: Figure 3.3.1(*a*) is then best thought of as a bird's-eye view of some of the points in Figure 3.3.1(*b*): i.e. a view from the top of the x axis looking down at the other two axes. Figure 3.3.1(*b*) assumes that inputs L and K can be combined in virtually any fashion, and that output can be varied continuously.

The relationship between inputs and output is summarised conveniently in the form

$$x_1 = X_1(L, K).$$

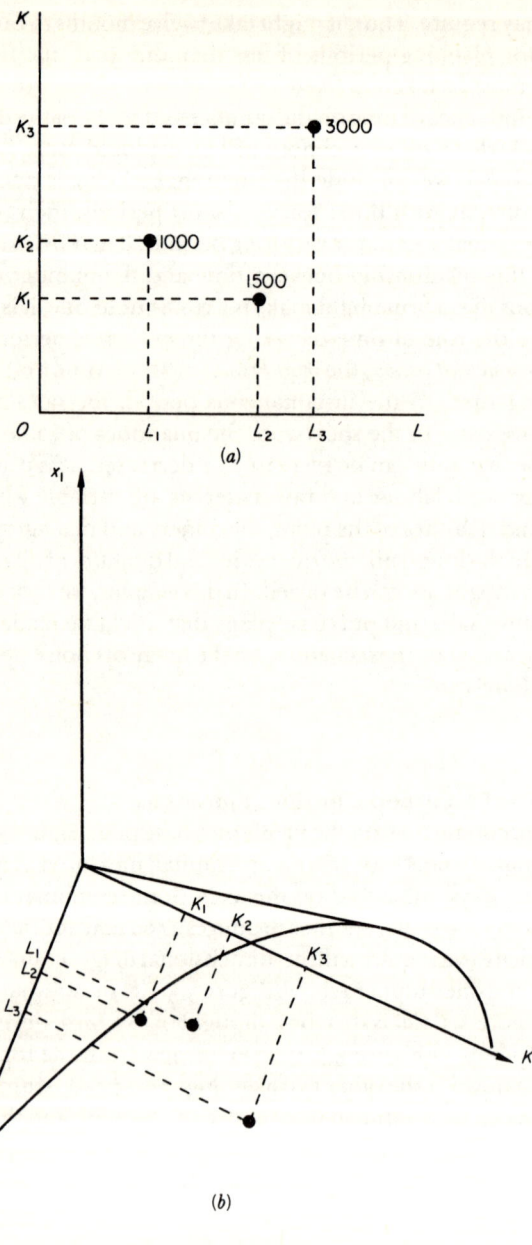

Figure 3.3.1

The Production Function

This is an equation of the firm's *production function*. As it stands, it is a very general equation telling us only that the output of good 1 depends on the quantities of the inputs K and L.

Referring back to Figure 3.3.1(*a*), consider the inputs of K and L necessary to produce 1000 units of output. Various combinations of K and L may be capable of producing this level of output, as is implied in Figure 3.3.1(*b*). The range of combinations will depend on the technology of the particular industry in question. It may take a team of men to work with one unit of capital – a blast furnace, say, – so that there is not a continuous range of input combinations available for producing a given output. The range of combinations is finite. This 'lumpiness' of production is illustrated in Figure 3.3.2 where the combinations are shown as points (each point is called a *vertex*) which are then connected to each other by straight lines, such as line *AB*. Lines *OA, OB* etc. will be explained shortly.

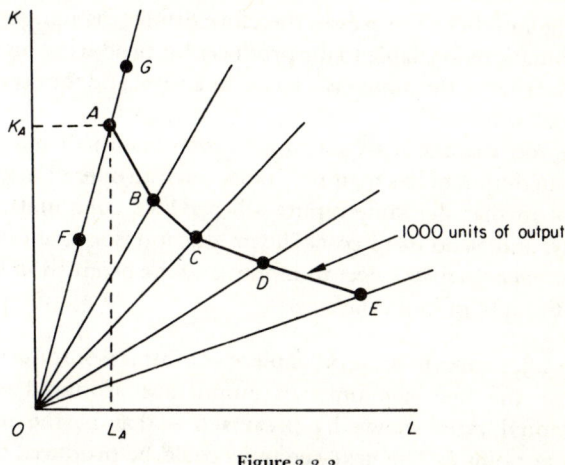

Figure 3.3.2

This illustration enables us to introduce some important terminology:

(*a*) the firm can produce 1000 units of output with an 'input-mix' as shown at *A*, or *B*, or *C*, or *D*, or *E*. As we shall see, the firm will also be able to produce at points on the lines *AB, BC*, etc. The lines *AB, BC, CD* and *DE* are called *facets*, or *line segments*. They are, of course, part of the overall piecewise linear curve *AE*, and this curve is called an *isoproduct* curve or contour. Isoproduct simply means 'equal product', so that all points on an isoproduct contour yield equal output. If it helps, the reader can draw the analogy between isoproduct curves and consumer indifference curves. Indeed, isoproduct curves are sometimes called 'producer indifference curves'. Still another, more popular, title is *production isoquant*;

(b) if the firm produces at A, it has an input combination of K_A of capital and L_A of labour. This can be expressed as a *labour/capital ratio* equal to (L_A/K_A). This ratio is the same along the entire length of the ray OA. The ratio at B is different, and is the same as the ratio along OB. If the firm can produce 1000 units at the ratio L_A/K_A, it must surely be able to produce a smaller output, while maintaining the same ratio, simply by scaling down the total quantity of inputs. Similarly, a scaling up process would increase output, and still maintain the ratio L_A/K_A. It follows that the firm is able to produce anywhere along the ray OA: points below A, like F, will mean *less* output.[1] The reasoning is equally applicable to the rays OB, OC, etc. These rays are called *processes* or *activities*. The number of processes therefore defines the options for input combinations available to the producer for producing his output. Notice that the ray through A is 'capital-intensive' and the ray through E is 'labour-intensive'.

Notice, too, that the firm could use the combination of inputs at A to produce an output of less than 1000 units. Such an operation would be inefficient in that the same inputs will produce 1000 units, if used efficiently, and at no extra cost. The production isoquant, therefore, relates *maximum possible output* to inputs, and the production function must be thought of in this fashion.

Figure 3.3.3 traces in some other piecewise linear isoproduct curves.

Suppose the first 500 units of output are produced with the labour/capital ratio shown by process C – that is, the producer operates at point F. The next 500 units could be produced with any process: suppose process B is chosen. Then we travel along a new segment of ray FG *parallel* to OB. Essentially what is happening is that *two* processes, B and C, are being combined to produce 1000 units, and the producer operates at point G on a facet of the 1000 units isoproduct contour. Just to illustrate the point again, suppose the next 500 units are produced with process A: the producer moves along GH, parallel

---

[1] We are assuming output can be increased by very small amounts. There may of course be 'lumpiness' in output, too, which means that a point like G, say, may not be achievable.

to *OA*, to produce at *H*. At this point *three* processes are being combined.

In our examples, production at *G* is the result of a *linear combination* of processes *A*, *B* and *C*. To produce 1000 units of output the producer can select a point like *A*, *B*, *C*, *D* or *E*, or a point like *H* which is a linear combination of processes. Notice that the shaded areas in Figure 3.3.3 are non-feasible – there exists no sensible combination of inputs outside the outer processes *OA* and *OE*.[1] The area encompassed by *OA*, *OE* and the relevant isoproduct curve therefore represents the feasible region for production as long as there are limited processes. This region is the *production set*. When available processes are limited, the production set is sometimes called a *finite cone*.

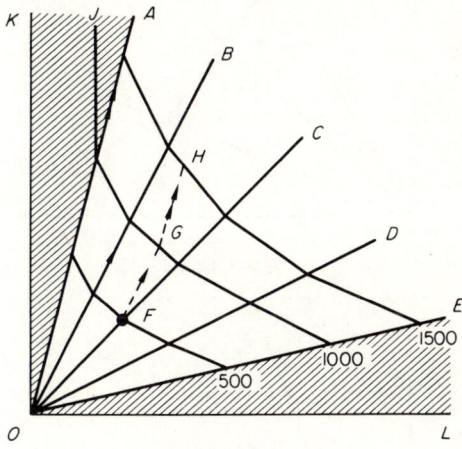

Figure 3.3.3

Lastly, note that process combination is only efficient if *adjacent* processes are combined. In Figure 3.3.4, for example, a combination of *A* and *C* produces facet *AC*, points on which show input combinations necessary to produce 1000 units of output. But a combination of *A* and *B*, or *B* and *C* would produce the same output with less *L* and *K*. In Section 3.1 we assumed that any firm would want to minimise costs for a given level of output. Hence, the combination of *A* and *C* is *inefficient*. In Figure 3.3.5 we illustrate another kind of inefficiency. Three processes are shown and the heavy line facets *DE* and

---

[1] Technically, he *could* produce at a point like *J* where the amount *JK* of capital is employed in a redundant fashion, since output at *J* is the same as output at *K*.

EF indicate equal output levels. Notice that the facets have been drawn so as to slope away from *D* and *F*, contrary to the figures previously shown. But, if *DEF* defines an isoquant, process *B* must be totally inefficient for we can combine processes *A* and *C* to secure a facet *DF* with output levels equal to output at *D* and *F*. This means that output at *G* equals output at *D*, and, in turn, output at *E*. But *E* is clearly inefficient when compared to *G* because *G* uses less of *both* inputs. Hence process *B* is inefficient.

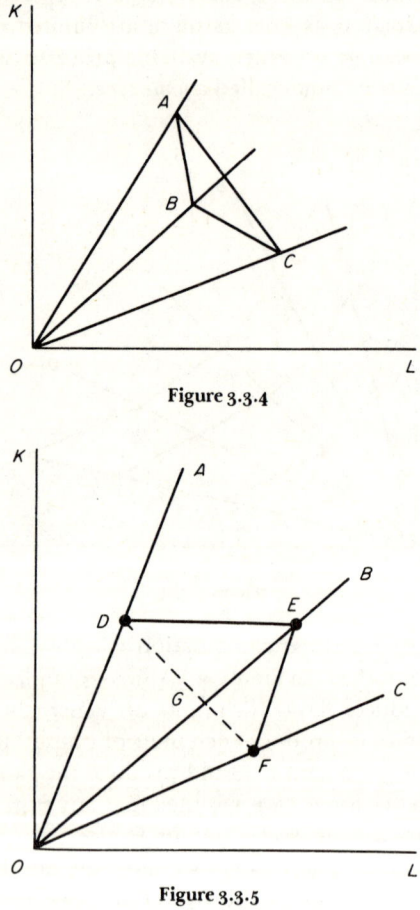

Figure 3.3.4

Figure 3.3.5

Notice that we have yet to establish criteria for exactly *where* on the isoproduct curve the producer will settle. This is the subject matter of Chapter 4.

3.4 The Production Function: Smooth Case

Imagine now that the range of processes open to the producer is large: there will then be a large number of process lines emanating from the origin in Figure 3.3.2, and the lengths of the corresponding facets will be small. If we increase the number of processes still further, the facets will get even smaller. In the limit, when the range of processes is *infinite*, the facets will become points and the isoproduct curves will appear smooth, as in Figure 3.4.1. It is worth noting that no producer would produce above points like A: to do so would mean increasing the amount of *both inputs* (e.g. to a point like E) to secure the same output as at A. The section AE (and onwards) is therefore inoperative. Similarly, points north-east of B on the next isoquant are inoperative. The irrelevant areas are eliminated by 'ridge lines' which enclose the producer's choice set.

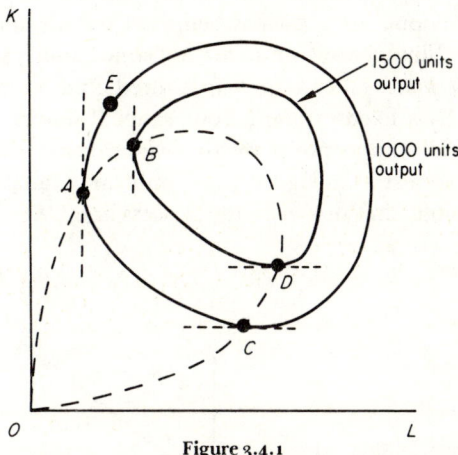

Figure 3.4.1

In Figure 3.4.1 the production isoquants beyond the ridge lines join up to form complete circles. Only the (heavily lined) parts of these isoquants are assumed relevant. To use the formal language, we assume strict convexity of the isoquants (on convexity and strict convexity, see Section 1.6). As we have seen, there is no need to appeal to observation of production functions to justify this assumption: instead, we argue that, for purposes of decision making, firms will be interested only in the strictly convex part of the production isoquants.

The attentive reader may note that the isoquants in Figure 3.4.1 bend backwards outside the ridge lines, whereas those outside the finite cone in Figure 3.3.3 moved parallel to the axes. The difference reflects only different assumptions in the 'modern' and 'neoclassical' approaches. In the 'modern', linear version, a move from K to J (Figure 3.3.3) merely involves a redundant amount of capital. That redundant amount of input does not interfere with production – i.e. it does not get in the way so as to cause output to be affected. This in turn reflects an axiom of modern production theory – the 'axiom of free disposal'.[1] This simply states that redundant inputs can be disposed of without cost. In this respect the modern theory is far less realistic than the old, since the isoquants in Figure 3.4.1 bend back precisely because the extra inputs do 'get in the way'.

3.5 The Convexity of Isoproduct Curves

The first observation to be made about the 'smooth' isoproduct curve is that the two inputs are shown as being *substitutable* in a continuous fashion. In the 'linear' case, inputs are not continuously substitutable. In fact, only *processes* can be substituted and each process is characterised by a fixed capital/labour ratio. If inputs could not be substituted at all (inputs are perfectly *complementary*), the isoproduct curves would appear as in Figure 3.5.1: only one capital/labour ratio would be possible, that shown by the process line L/K.

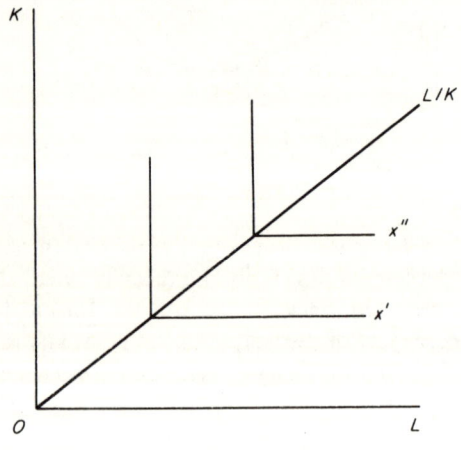

Figure 3.5.1

[1] G. Debreu, *Theory of Value* (New York, 1959) p. 42.

The relevant section of the isoproduct curve in Figure 3.4.1 is strictly convex. The piecewise linear curves of Section 3.3 are convex, but not strictly convex.

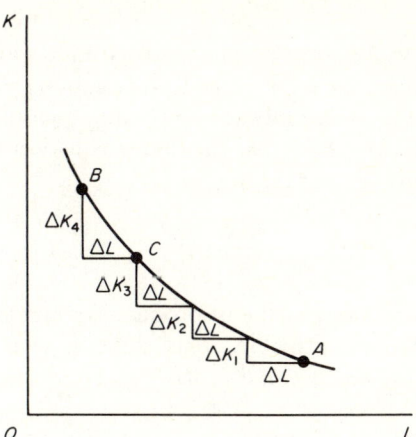

Figure 3.5.2

In each case, convexity arises because of the possibilities of substitution. If isoproduct curves were concave, for example, it would be possible to combine adjacent processes to produce the same output but with less of both inputs. This was demonstrated in Section 3.3 for the case of limited processes. It is equally true of the smooth production function case.

Figure 3.5.2 shows a magnified section of a smooth production isoquant. Consider the move from A to B. As we reduce the labour input (ΔL), the increase in $K(\Delta K)$ necessary to sustain a given output and compensate for the reduced labour gets larger and larger ($\Delta K_4 > \Delta K_3 > \Delta K_2 > \Delta K_1$). Now, the move from A to B means that some output will be gained as capital is increased, but some will be lost as labour is reduced. We shall define the *extra amount of output due to an increase in an input* as the *marginal* product of that input.

We define the marginal product concepts as

$$\text{Marginal Product of Capital} = MP_K = \frac{\Delta x}{\Delta K}$$

$$\text{Marginal Product of Labour} = MP_L = \frac{\Delta x}{\Delta L}$$

where the Δs remind us that, for the moment, we are operating with fairly noticeable changes in x, L and K. Now consider the segment CB of the isoquant in Figure 3.5.2. Then,

$$+ \Delta K \cdot MP_K + \Delta L \cdot MP_L = O.$$

That is, the net gain in output, as we move from C to B, must be zero since C and B are on the same isoquant. The gain is given by $\Delta K \cdot MP_K$ and the loss by $\Delta L \cdot MP_L$. Substitution of the equations for marginal product will quickly show that the above equation is correct. The equation can now be rearranged:

$$- \frac{\Delta K}{\Delta L} = \frac{MP_L}{MP_K}.$$

But $-\Delta K/\Delta L$ is the slope of the isoproduct curve, reflecting the substitution possibilities available. This slope is referred to as the (*marginal*) *rate of technical substitution*, $MRTS_{L,K}$. Hence, we derive a useful result:

$$MRTS_{L,K} = MP_L/MP_K.$$

3.6 The Law of Non-Proportional Returns

In the short-run, as we have seen, one or more inputs is likely to be fixed in supply. Hence we write the production function as

$$x_1 = x_1 (L, \bar{K})$$

where $\bar{K}$ reminds us that capital is fixed. Such a production function in the short-run is said to obey the *law of non-proportional returns*, a law which relates specifically to a situation in which at least one input is fixed and the others are variable. As such, the law fits neatly into the context of the short-run when it is not possible for the firm to vary all inputs. The law says that, with a given method of production, the application of further units of any variable input (say, L) to a fixed combination of other inputs will, until a certain point is reached, yield more than proportional increases in output, and thereafter less than proportional increases in output. The law is more commonly known as *the law of diminishing returns*. Since the law refers to *increases* in output, it relates to marginal product. Figure 3.6.1 shows how the law is implied by the production isoquant figures we have already used. We use the smooth isoquants, but the analysis is the same for the piecewise

The Production Function

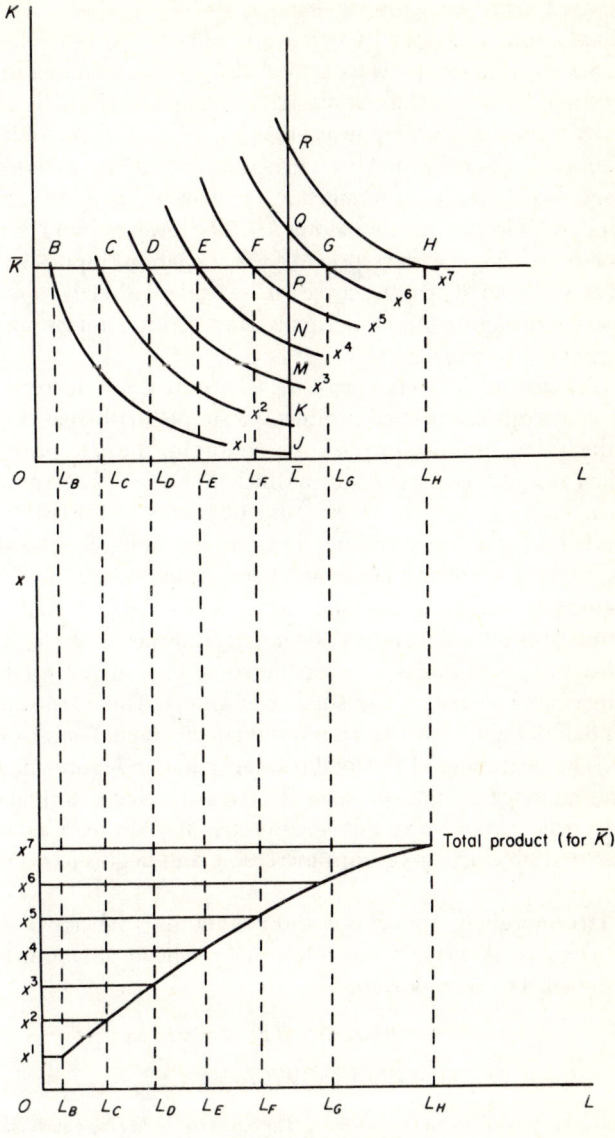

Figure 3.6.1

linear ones (except that the resulting product curves will themselves be piecewise linear, see below). Let $x^2 - x^1 = x^3 - x^2 = x^4 - x^3$, and so on, so that output increases by equal amounts as we move from one isoquant to another.[1] Now fix capital at $\bar{K}$ so that increases in output are secured by varying labour along the linear $\bar{K}H$. It will be observed that $GH > FG > EF$, which means that bigger and bigger additions to the labour force are needed to secure equal increments in output. Obviously, this is the law of diminishing returns 'on its head': marginal product is falling as we move along $\bar{K}H$. The lower half of Figure 3.6.1 shows total product with respect to a varying labour input – i.e. with K fixed at $\bar{K}$. The total product curve can be read off directly from the upper part of the figure. A parallel analysis applies to $\bar{L}R$ if labour is fixed and capital is free to vary.

Notice that the law relates to *marginal* product. But the relationship between marginal and total product is a simple mathematical one, so that the law of diminishing returns accounts for the behaviour of total product as well. The precise way in which output is affected can now be shown, but it is important to recognise the context of the law. It applies only when (a) at least one input is fixed; (b) technology can be assumed constant; and (c) substitutability between inputs exists.

Figure 3.6.1 suggests that total output (x_i) can be increased by equal amounts only by adding larger and larger amounts of labour. To put it another way, if labour is increased in equal increments, total output will increase by smaller and smaller amounts. This is shown in the lower half of Figure 3.6.1 and is repeated in the upper section of Figure 3.6.2. The beginning of the total product curve in Figure 3.6.2 shows increasing marginal returns, since the law states that marginal returns will decrease *eventually*. In this case they begin to decrease as the slope of the total product curve stops increasing and begins to decrease, at L^*.

In fact, marginal product is nothing other than the *slope* of the total product curve. Average product (output per head of labour force) is also shown. The relationships are

$$\text{TOTAL PRODUCT } (TP): x = x(L, \bar{K})$$

$$\text{MARGINAL PRODUCT } (MP): \frac{\partial x}{\partial L}$$

[1] This is not just a matter of convenience. The figure has been drawn such that x^2 is the same distance from x^1 as x^3 is from x^2, assuming these measurements are made along a diagonal from O. To borrow concepts from a later chapter, we are in fact assuming *constant* returns to scale. If, however, returns are *increasing*, the distance along the diagonal between x^3 and x^2 would be smaller, and between x^4 and x^3 smaller still.

where '∂' means 'rate of change in', so that $\partial x/\partial L$ means the rate of change in x with respect to a change in L.[1]

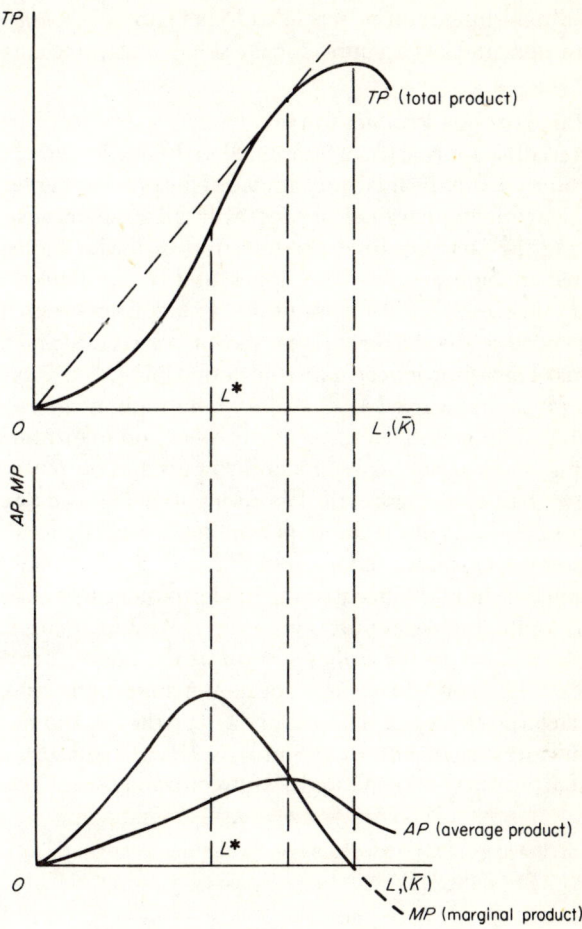

Figure 3.6.2

---

[1] Notice that MP_L is now expressed as $\frac{\partial x}{\partial L}$ where before it was expressed as $\frac{\Delta x}{\Delta L}$. The Δ notation referred to 'a change in' whereas ∂ relates only to 'very small changes in'. Technically, it is small changes we are interested in. ∂ also makes it clear that it is a small change in x with respect to a small change in L: *the rate of change in x with respect to other inputs being held constant* (∂ is the partial derivative sign).

AVERAGE PRODUCT $(AP): \dfrac{x}{L}$

The MP curve will always cut AP at the latter's highest point.[1] The law of diminishing returns 'sets in' at L^* in Figure 3.6.2, *before* AP falls. The law none the less accounts for the slope of all three curves.

3.7 Linearity and Product Curves

The preceding approach can be applied to the linear segmented curves of Section 3.3, but the final appearance of the product curves is not the same. Essentially, marginal product will fall in a 'stepwise' fashion, reflecting the fact that total product rises in linear segments, as illustrated in Figure 3.7.1. The upper part of the figure shows the familiar process/output relationship. For convenience, the 'cone' which encompasses the three rays is shown with vertical and horizontal sections of the isoproduct curves (the dotted lines), as discussed in Section 3.3.[2] Capital is fixed at $\bar{K}$. As the labour input is changed from L_A to L_B then output rises from 100 to 200 units, and so on along $\bar{K}F$. The resulting relationship between labour inputs and output is shown in the lower half of the figure, the labour inputs being read directly from the horizontal axis of the upper part of the figure. The left-hand scale measures total product and it is seen that total product rises in a linear segmented fashion. Notice that the total product curve changes slope at B, D and F, but *not* at points in between. As it happens, B, D and F occur at vertices in the upper section of the figure. Between those vertices, total product rises in a constant manner. The reason is that, between B and D, for example, the line $\bar{K}F$ cuts the isoproduct curves at a constant rate such that $BC = CD$. Similarly, $\bar{K}A = AB$ and $DE = EF$. Hence marginal product between $\bar{K}$ and B, between B and D and between D and

---

[1] Proof: Leaving out $\bar{K}$, we have have $x = x(L)$, and average product is therefore $x(L)/L$. Average product is maximised when

$$\frac{\partial \dfrac{x(L)}{L}}{\partial L} = 0 = \frac{\partial x}{\partial L}/L - \frac{x}{L^2}.$$

Hence, for average product to be a maximum,

$$\frac{\partial x}{\partial L}/L = \frac{x}{L^2}, \text{ hence } \frac{\partial x}{\partial L} = \frac{x \cdot L}{L^2} = \frac{x}{L}.$$

But $\partial x/\partial L$ is marginal product, and x/L is average product. Hence the two are equal when average product is at a maximum.

[2] Note that $\bar{K}$ would not be used for output level 100 because A is inefficient.

The Production Function

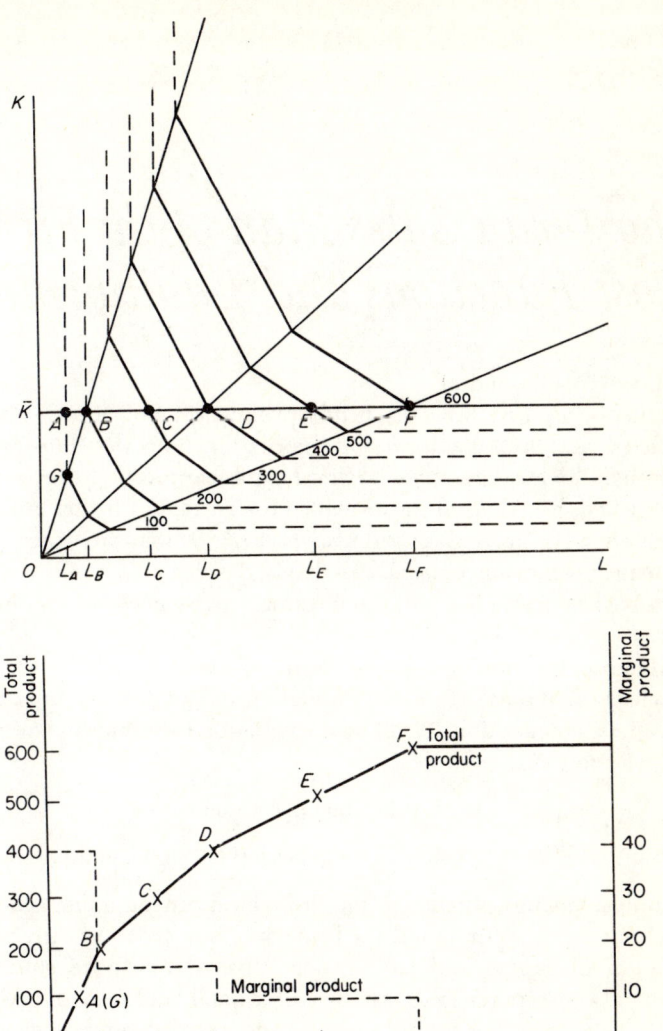

Figure 3.7.1

F, does not change; marginal product being just the slope of the total product curve. It can be seen that marginal product only changes when a new vertex along $\bar{K}F$ is reached.

4

Short-run Sales Plan of the Firm: Cost Functions and Equilibrium

4.0 Cost Minimisation

Chapter 3 showed how the firm's production function could be depicted, and both the linear and smooth functions were illustrated. Although the idea of *technically efficient* combinations of processes was introduced, no criterion was provided for deciding whether any one point on the isoquant was *economically more efficient* than any other. This is the problem of *cost minimisation* – that is, the idea of minimising costs for any given level of output. To illustrate this we need to know input prices.

Suppose the firm has a fixed sum of money available for the purchase of inputs, say £1m. Capital costs £50,000 per unit, and labour £2,000 per unit. Then, by the equation introduced in Section 3.0, we know that

$$£1\text{m.} = £50{,}000\,K + £2{,}000\,L$$

or
$$500 = 25K + L \text{ (with the £ signs omitted)}.$$

If capital *only* was purchased, the firm could buy 20 units (500/25). If labour *only* was purchased, the firm could buy 500 units. Any combination of capital and labour that satisfies the above equation could also be purchased: say, 10 of capital and 250 of labour ($500 = 25 \times 10 + 1 \times 250$), or 5 capital and 375 of labour. A general form of the previous equation is therefore

$$C = f_K \cdot K + f_L \cdot L$$

where, in our example, $C = 500$, $f_K =$ the price of capital $= 25$, and $f_L =$ the price of labour $= 1$. The equation can be rearranged as

$$K = \frac{C}{f_K} - \frac{f_L}{f_K} \cdot L.$$

This equation is depicted by line *a* in Figure 4.0.1 where the axes are the same as for the production isoquants. Line *a* is an *isocost line: it shows all the combinations of K and L which can be bought with the fixed sum C.* The shaded area is therefore the *feasible region* for the firm.

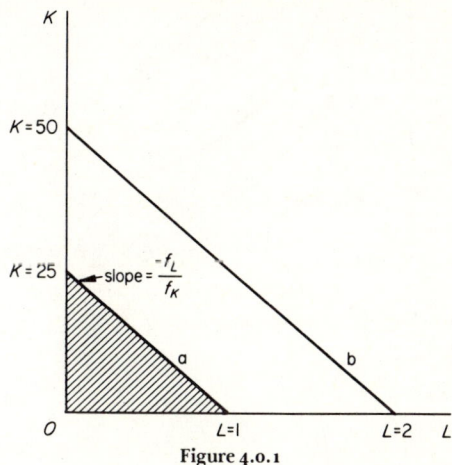
Figure 4.0.1

The construction of an isocost line is entirely analogous to that for a budget line in Chapter 1. If C increases, with f_L and f_K staying constant, the isocost line shifts to b (where the sum available has increased to $2C$). Note, too, that the *slope* of the isocost line is the ratio of relative input prices, $-f_L/f_K$. Drawing on the consumer analogy even further, we now place production isoquants on the isocost diagram, showing, respectively, the smooth and linear cases.

In Figure 4.0.2 the cost-minimising position is, for the first isoquant, A. For higher isoquants it is B, C and D. The line joining A, B, C, D ... is the firm's cost-minimising *expansion path*. Notice that, for a cost level C_A, the firm *could* produce at E which is on the boundary of the feasible region, like A, but it would secure a lower output. Equally, the firm *cannot* produce at F since this lies outside the feasible region. A is therefore the optimal position.

In Figure 4.0.3 the optimum occurs at A, at a vertex on the isoquant. The expansion path in this case is along the process ray $OABC$.

4.1 Changes in Relative Input Prices

Just as the consumer was observed to respond to changes in the relative prices of the commodities he purchased, so the firm responds to

90   Price Theory

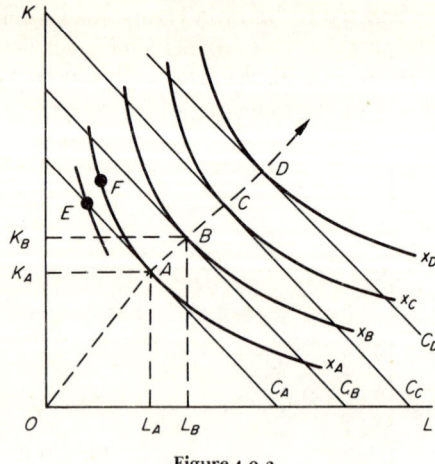

Figure 4.0.2

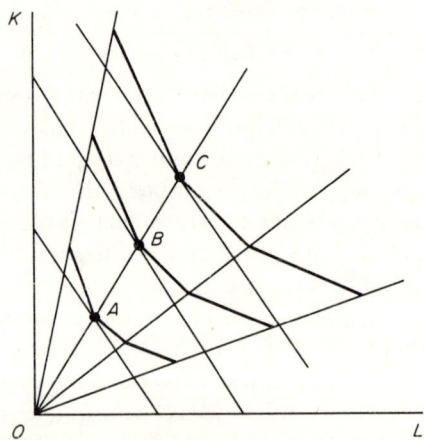

Figure 4.0.3

changes in input prices. In Figure 4.1.1 the isocost line C_A changes to C, reflecting a fall in the price of labour relative to capital. For illustrative purposes we show the change in such a way that the firm stays on its original production isoquant. The change in price causes the firm to move from A to B, substituting labour for capital, which is what we would expect now that labour is cheaper relative to capital. Note that at A and B the slope of the relevant isocost line is equal to the slope of the production isoquant. This enables us to write

$$\frac{f_L}{f_K} = \frac{-MP_L}{MP_K},$$

that is, price of labour/price of capital = marginal rate of technical substitution, or,

$$\frac{MP_L}{f_L} = \frac{MP_K}{f_K}.$$

This equivalence holds for all points on the firm's expansion path.

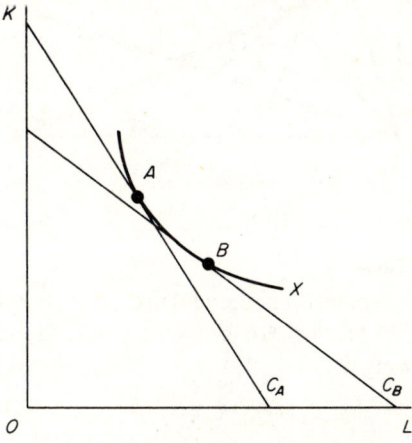

Figure 4.1.1

In Figure 4.1.2 isocost line C_A produces an equilibrium at A, which is a vertex of the isoquant ABC. A shift in the isocost line to C_B means that the optimum is at B, another vertex but this time using process 2 (P_2) compared to the previous use of process 1. Of course the idea of a process should now be sufficiently familiar for us to realise that we are only saying in technical language that it is now better to substitute some labour for capital. But it is important to observe that the substitution would not have taken place at all if C_A had changed its slope only slightly such that the optimum was still at A. This is the essential difference between the 'smooth' and 'linear' approaches: in the former case the smallest change in relative prices will lead to input substitution, whereas in the latter case it requires a significant change in relative prices to bring about substitution.[1] Notice, too, that a move to isocost line C_C in Figure 4.1.2 produces a situation where any point on the facet BC is optimal.

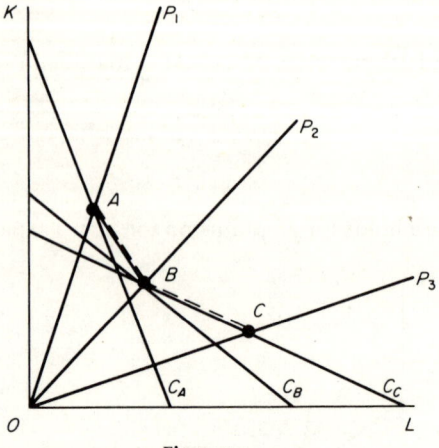

Figure 4.1.2

4.2 Cost Functions

Look again at the expansion path in Figure 4.0.2. At A the firm uses K_A of capital and L_A of labour. Hence its total expenditure on inputs to produce output x_A is

$$C_A = f_K \cdot K_A = f_L \cdot L_A.$$

If we move up the expansion path we observe that

$$C_B = f_K \cdot K_B + f_L \cdot L_B,$$

and so on for C_C, C_D, etc. Notice that we assume *input prices do not change*. This should enable us to map total expenditure on inputs – or *total cost* as we shall now call it – to output. From the above equations we know that

output x_A costs C_A to produce
output x_B costs C_B to produce

and so on.

[1] The smaller the number of processes, in general, the larger the price shift necessary to induce substitution.

Cost Functions and Equilibrium

However, the expansion path shown in Figure 4.0.2 will indicate total cost for each level of output assuming *both inputs are variable*. This is correct for the long-run, but not the short-run. The expansion path is therefore a long-run concept. In the short-run we observed that one input at least, usually some form of capital, is fixed. If we are interested in short-run cost functions for the moment, we need to map short-run output levels to short-run costs. To see how this is done refer to Figure 4.2.1, which shows the 'smooth' production function case.

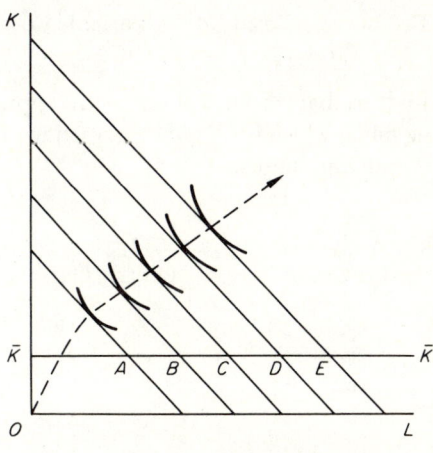

Figure 4.2.1

As before, capital is fixed at $\bar{K}$, but it is important to ask what this means. The reason capital is fixed is that we are interested, for the moment, in short-run analysis and hence the use of capital K cannot be *exceeded* (that is the region above line $\bar{K}\bar{K}$ in Figure 4.2.1 is non-attainable). But it is also the case that some capital will be necessary to produce *at all*[1] – i.e. certain equipment must be installed before even one unit of output can be produced. The costs of such equipment are *fixed costs*. This may be some amount less than $\bar{K}$, but if we interpret the short-run very strictly, we can safely assume that whatever equipment is installed in order to begin, production is also the maximum amount of equipment that can be used in the short-run. This is certainly convenient for analysis since it means that production in the short-run

---

[1] Making *all* of capital fixed in the short-run is obviously unrealistic. It is shown this way because readily comprehensible figures require only two inputs, 'labour' and 'capital' in our case. Effectively what is fixed in the short-run, however, is *plant size*, with other forms of 'capital', such as raw materials and working capital, being variable.

must take place along the line $\bar{K}\bar{K}$ in Figure 4.2.1.[1] The expansion path in the short-run is $ABCDE$.

Confining the analysis to the short-run it is obvious that diminishing returns will affect costs and diminishing returns will set in along $\bar{K}\bar{K}$. Along $\bar{K}\bar{K}$, then, we have two types of cost. The cost of capital equipment, which is fixed at $f_K \cdot \bar{K}$, and the cost of labour, the variable input, which is $f_L \cdot L$, where L varies with output. These latter costs are *variable costs*. Hence

$$\text{Total Cost} = \text{Fixed Cost} + \text{Variable Costs}$$
$$C = f_K \cdot \bar{K} + f_L \cdot L(x)$$

where $L(x)$ reminds us that labour will vary with output.

The following table, which fits Figure 4.2.1, shows how these costs will vary with output and inputs.

x	$\bar{K}$	f_K	$\bar{K}\cdot f_K$ (TFC)	L	f_L	$L \cdot f_L$ (TVC)	C (TC)	C/x (AC)	$\Delta C/\Delta x$ (MC)
10	5	2	10	2	3	6	16	1.60	—
20	5	2	10	4	3	12	22	1.10	0.6
30	5	2	10	7	3	21	31	1.03	0.9
40	5	2	10	11	3	33	43	1.07	1.2
50	5	2	10	16	3	48	58	1.16	1.5
60	5	2	10	24	3	72	82	1.35	2.4

The final columns show *average cost* – i.e. total cost divided by total output – and *marginal cost* – i.e. the change in total costs due to an extra discrete change in output. Since output changes in discrete amounts of 10 units, we retain the use of the Δ notation. If we recorded the change in cost due to a change in output of only *one unit*, we would use the more correct notation ∂. In other words, marginal cost $= \partial C/\partial x$ for small changes. The column headed $L \cdot f_L$ shows the total cost of the labour force employed at various outputs. Since labour is the only variable input, this column can be thought of as *total variable cost* (TVC).

If we were to map costs to output we would get a picture like the one shown in Figure 4.2.2.

---

[1] It also means that $\bar{K}$ is the minimum capital required to engage in production in any period. Technically, therefore, the long-run expansion path cannot appear as we have shown it in the figures in the text. The figure is not altered in substance, however. All that happens is that the horizontal L axis effectively becomes the $\bar{K}\bar{K}$ line.

Notice that the shape of the total cost curve is determined by the shape of the variable cost curve and that this, in turn, is largely determined by the fact of diminishing returns as we move along *ABCDE* in Figure 4.2.1. The relationships between marginal, average and total concepts, noted in Chapter 3, are again present with cost curves. As soon as diminishing returns set in, marginal cost rises, as Figure 4.2.3 shows. Average cost continues to fall even though marginal cost rises, mainly because fixed costs are being distributed over a larger and larger output even though variable costs are rising.

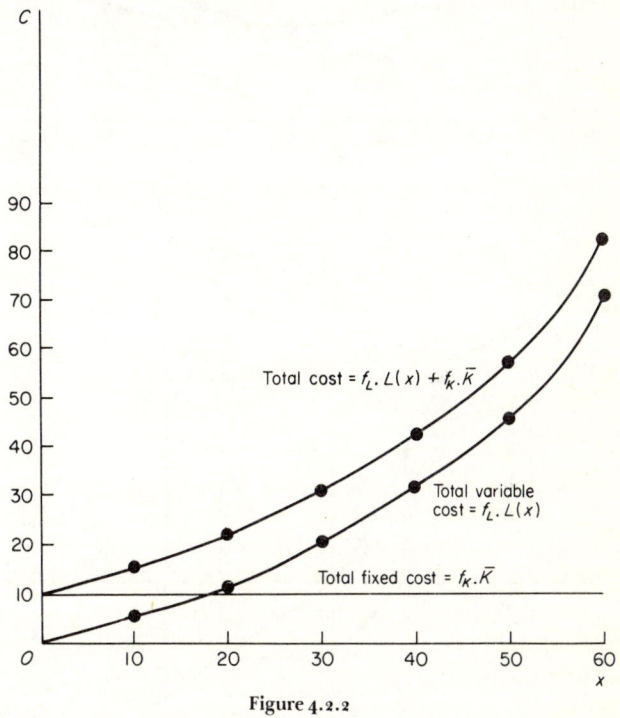

Figure 4.2.2

The preceding analysis applies to the 'smooth' production function case. In fact, the cost curves in Figure 4.2.3 can be derived directly from the product curves. Figure 4.2.4 illustrates this for the total variable cost curve. The total product curve is shown in the north-east quadrant. The south-east quadrant measures total variable cost against labour inputs, giving a straight line the slope of which is the

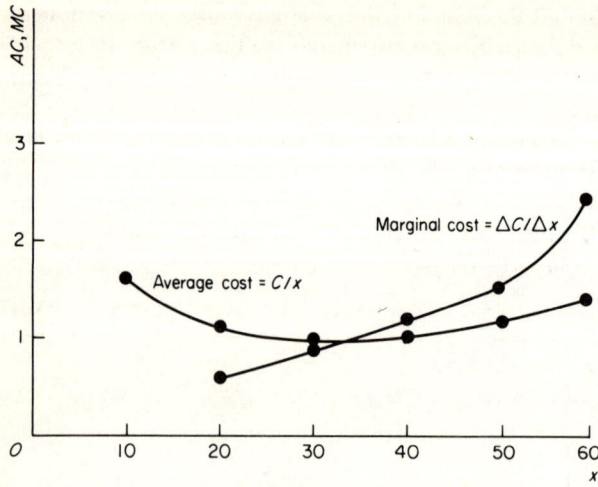

Figure 4.2.3

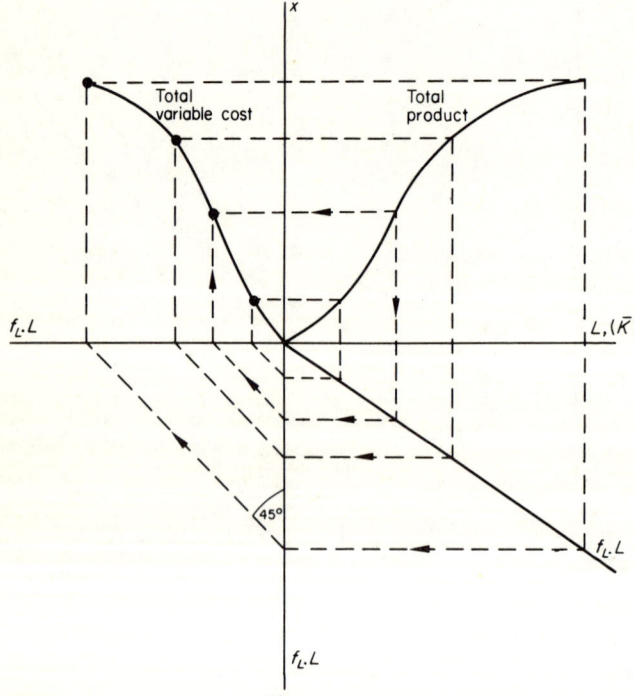

Figure 4.2.4

wage rate, f_L. Points on the total product curve are projected leftwards to the north-west quadrant and then down to the $f_L \cdot L$ space. The south-west quadrant is a 'dummy' quadrant containing $f_L \cdot L$ measured against itself: hence points on the vertical $f_L \cdot L$ axis are simply transferred to the horizontal $f_L \cdot L$ axis by 45° lines. These points are then projected up to intersect with the horizontal lines from the total product curve.

These intersections define the locus for the total variable cost curve which has to be viewed by looking from the right-hand side of the page. The curve is a 'mirror image' of the total product curve, but the image will be slightly squashed or elongated, depending on the slope of the $f_L \cdot L$ line in the south-east quadrant, that is, on f_L.[1]

If the isoquants are in linear segments, the relevant cost curves are as shown in Figure 4.2.5. The reasoning is identical to that for plotting the linear product curves in Chapter 3, as it must be if cost curves are only 'mirror images' of product curves.

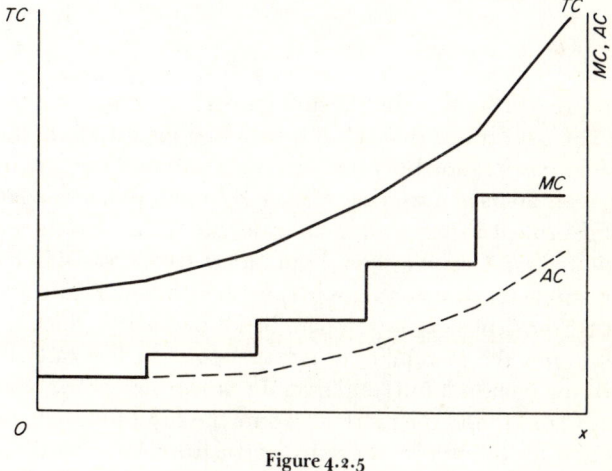

Figure 4.2.5

4.3 Output and Substitution Effects

Just as the consumer's reaction to a price change could be analysed into income and substitution effects, so can the reaction of a

[1] It will only be an *exact* mirror image if $f_L \cdot L$ is at 45° to the horizontal.

producer to changes in relative *input* prices. This time we show the effect in terms of moving to a different isoquant.

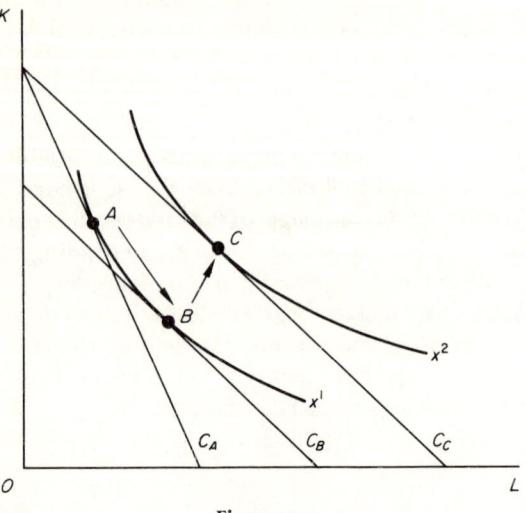

Figure 4.3.1

As the price of labour falls, the firm moves from position A to position C. The isocost line through B is such that the firm faces the new relative input price ratio but produces its old output. The move from A to B, then, is an *input substitution effect*, and from B to C an *output effect* (sometimes called an 'expansion' or 'scale' effect). In the former case L is substituted for K. In the latter, both inputs are increased in use.

It is possible that the isoquants may be shaped as in Figure 4.3.2, in which case the firm's expansion path bends backwards. Such a situation illustrates the possibility of *inferior inputs*. In this case, labour would be the inferior input: the larger the firm grows the less it favours the use of labour and the more it favours the substitution of capital. The input substitution effect leads to a move from A to B, so that more labour is used. But the output effect, the move from B to C, leads to less labour being used, and the output effect outweighs the substitution effect.

The slope of the isoproduct curve measures the marginal rate of technical substitution. The fact that the isoquant is convex indicates that the inputs K and L are not perfect substitutes: if they were the isoquant would be linear. It is frequently useful to measure the degree of substitutability between inputs by the *elasticity of input substitution*.

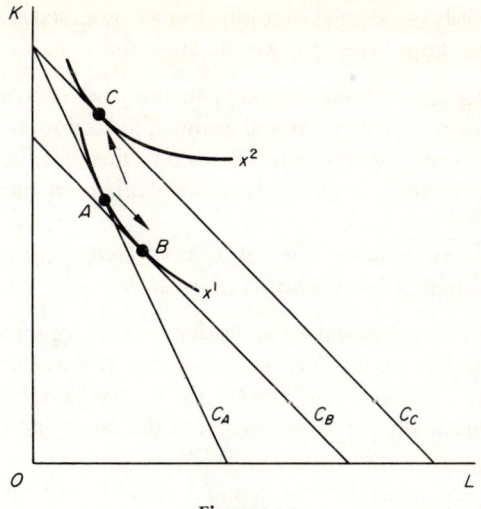

Figure 4.3.2

This elasticity, e_i, is measured as the percentage change in factor proportions divided by the percentage changes in relative input prices. The percentage change in input proportions is, now for a very small change,

$$\frac{d(K/L)}{K/L},$$

and the percentage change in input prices is

$$\frac{d(f_K/f_L)}{f_K/f_L}.$$

Now, at equilibrium, the slope of the isocost line is equal to the slope of the isoquant, Hence, at equilibrium,

$$e_i = \frac{d(K/L)}{K/L} \cdot \frac{dK/dL}{d(dK/dL)}$$

If $e_i = 0$, the two inputs are perfect complements – they must be used in fixed proportion. If $e_i = -\infty$, the two inputs are perfect substitutes.

4.4 Equilibrium of the Firm

With the aid of the cost curves of Section 4.2 we can show how the firm selects its output. But first we revise the concept of *revenue*. Total revenue is simply price times quantity, but we observed that price may well change as output changed. We distinguish two cases:

(a) *a price-taker context* where price does *not* change as output varies. This means the firm can sell as much as it chooses at the going price without worrying about its effects on other producers. We call this *perfect competition*, a term which we explain in more detail in Chapter 12;

(b) *a price-maker context* where price is affected by the firm's output decision. We shall call this *imperfect competition*.

Demand curves for price-takers and price-makers are shown in Figure 4.4.1. Also shown are the corresponding *total revenue* curves and the slopes of the total revenue curves, or *marginal revenue*. Marginal revenue is simply the extra revenue from the sale of an extra unit of output.

Now, for the *price-taker* the demand curve facing the firm is the ruling price curve, $\bar{p}$, where the ruling price is set by the market forces of total supply and total demand. Hence we have

$$\text{Total Revenue} = TR = \bar{p} \cdot x.$$

If the price-taker sells 10 units of output, his total revenue will be

$$TR_{10} = 10 \cdot \bar{p},$$

and if he sells 11 units we have

$$TR_{11} = 11 \cdot \bar{p}.$$

Hence, the *marginal revenue* from the eleventh unit is

$$TR_{11} - TR_{10} = 11 \cdot \bar{p} - 10 \cdot \bar{p} = \bar{p}(11 - 10) = \bar{p}.$$

In short, for the price-taker, marginal revenue and price are identical. This is obvious on reflection since, if price does not change, the sale of an extra unit of output must add revenue equal to the ruling price.

It is as well to contrast this result with that which would be obtained in a *price-maker* context. In this case, extra sales affect the price of the product, making it fall. But since all units of output must (generally) be sold at the same price, total revenue after the price fall will be affected by the fact that all the previous output must now be sold at the new, reduced price. If we write total revenue *before* the price fall as $TR_0 = p_0 \cdot x_0$, and *after* the price fall as $TR_1 = p_1 \cdot x_1$, we have

$$MR = TR_1 - TR_0 = p_1 \cdot x_1 - p_0 \cdot x_0.$$

Cost Functions and Equilibrium

Let $x_1 = x_0 + 1$, so that

$$MR = TR_1 - TR_0 = p_1(x_0 + 1) - p_0 \cdot x_0 - p_1 \cdot x_0 + p_1 - p_0 \cdot x_0$$
$$= x_0 \cdot (p_1 - p_0) + p_1.$$

Now $p_1 - p_0$ is in fact negative since $p_1 < p_0$. Hence $x_0 (p_1 - p_0)$ is

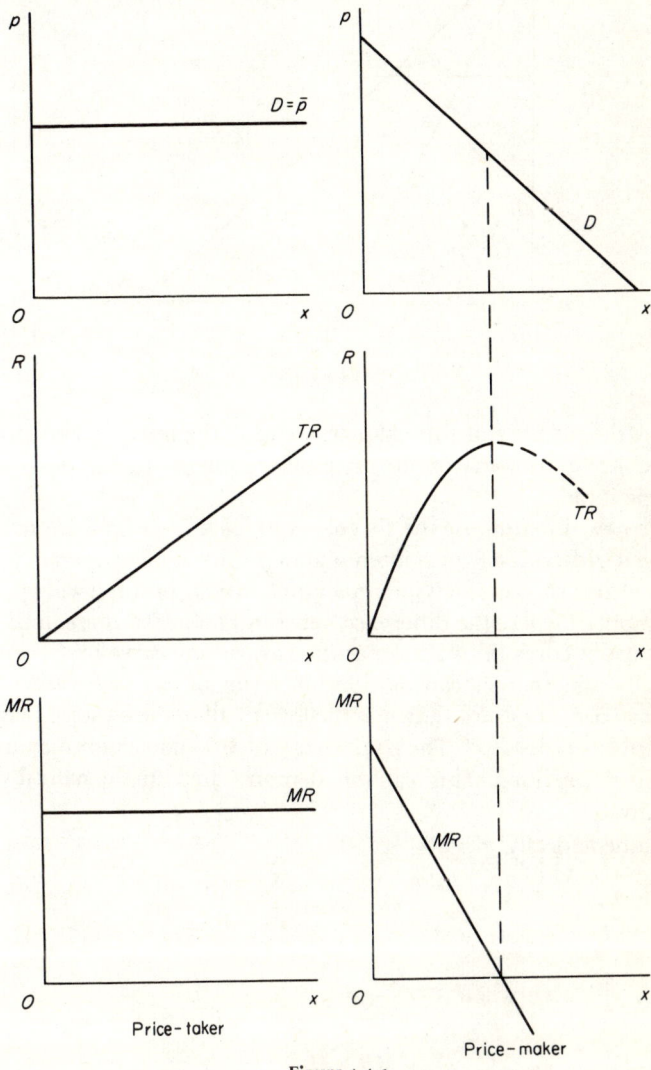

Figure 4.4.1

negative. The whole expression for MR, then, must be less than p_1. In short, MR lies below the demand curve, as is shown in Figure 4.4.2.

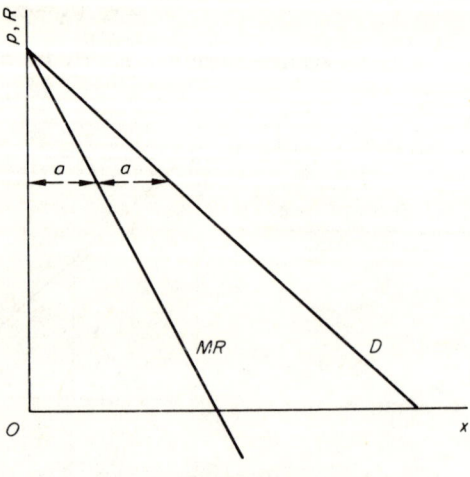

Figure 4.4.2

For the purpose of this chapter, we omit the price-maker context and concentrate solely on the price-taker context – that is, on 'perfect competition'.

We now superimpose the TR curve of Figure 4.4.1 on the total cost derived earlier. If a firm is interested in profits, it must operate in the shaded area shown. If it is interested in *maximising* profits it will operate at output x^* where the difference between TR and TC is greatest. The total profit curve (π) is shown as the dashed line curve in the figure. Equally, the analysis can be done in terms of *marginal revenue* and *marginal cost*. These are shown in the lower half of the figure. Their intersection occurs at x^*. The equivalence of MC and MR for maximum profits is obvious. This can be demonstrated mathematically or intuitively.

Mathematically, $\pi = R(x) - C(x)$

$$\therefore \quad \pi_{max} \text{ occurs when } \frac{\partial R}{\partial x} - \frac{\partial C}{\partial x} = 0$$

i.e. when $\quad \dfrac{\partial R}{\partial x} = \dfrac{\partial C}{\partial x}$

i.e. when $MR = MC$.

Cost Functions and Equilibrium

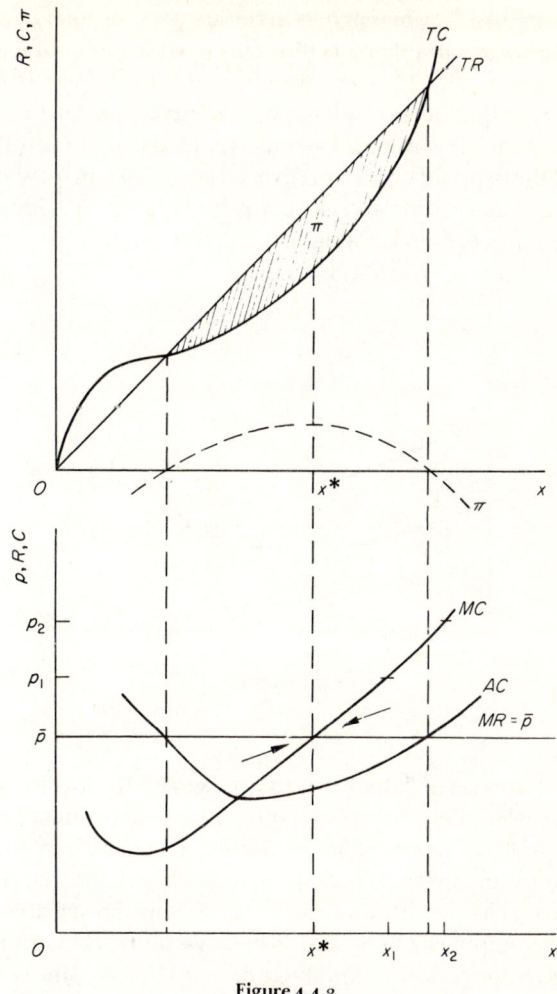

Figure 4.4.3

Intuitively, if $MR > MC$, more is being added to revenue than costs. Hence it is worthwhile expanding output (see the direction of the arrows in Figure 4.4.3). If $MC > MR$, the last units of output yield more costs than revenue. Hence output has been expanded too far and should be reduced. Only when $MR = MC$ can profits be at a maximum.

It is worth noting that, in the short-run, a firm may operate at a price which fails to cover total cost. In terms of Figure 4.4.4, the firm may accept a price like p_1, whereas p_2 is necessary to cover total costs. Price p_1 covers average variable costs, but fails to contribute sufficiently to covering fixed costs. However, since the firm must meet fixed costs whatever its output, it may well pay to continue in production as long as variable costs are covered. Eventually, market conditions may improve and the firm will be able to cover all costs. Even in the short-run, however, it is not worth accepting a price below p_3 in Figure 4.4.4, since, at this price, even variable costs are not covered.

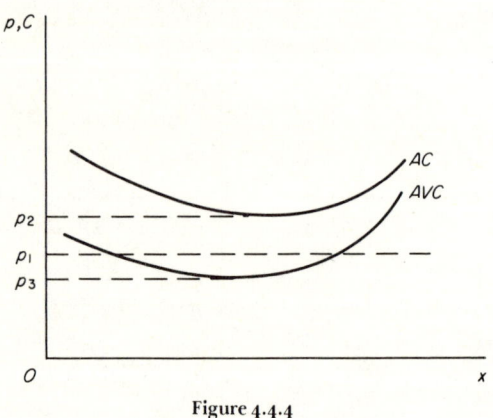

Figure 4.4.4

4.5 The Response of Sales Plans to Changes in Product Price

To observe how sales plans respond to changes in product prices, we vary the price of the product in Figure 4.4.3 and see what new equilibrium is obtained. It is simplest to work with the marginal cost curve. If price changes from $\bar{p}$ to p_1, profits are maximised at output x_1. If price is p_2, output will be x_2, and so on. If we plot each output against each expected price, we obtain the firm's *supply curve*. Since each new equilibrium is a point on the firm's marginal cost curve, the supply curve in Figure 4.5.1 turns out to be identical with the firm's marginal cost curve. It must be emphasised that Figure 4.5.1 is to be preferred to Figure 4.4.3 even though the relationships in it are derived from data portrayed in the latter. The chief danger in using the derived relationships is that frequently they seem to be interpreted behaviouristically. Thus, the sales plan which the firm chooses is commonly described as that which will equate marginal cost and expected selling price. This, however, is merely an alternative way of putting our assumption that the firm aims to make its expected profits as great as possible. While to try to equate marginal cost and price is to try to maximise profits, it is best not to state the firm's objective in this way, for if we do we risk interpreting, or seeming to interpret, the cost and revenue lines in Figure 4.4.3 behaviouristically.

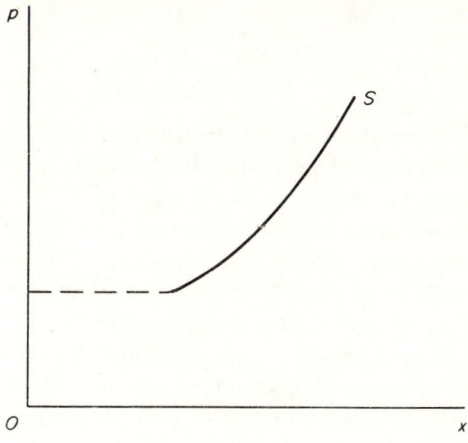

Figure 4.5.1

4.6 Market Supply

The firm whose supply curve is illustrated in Figure 4.5.1 may not be the only supplier of x. We can, however, derive the supply of x of each other existing firm that is a potential supplier in a precisely similar way. If the prices of the variable inputs are data for all the firms, then the total or market supply may be obtained simply by adding together the supplies of the firms that are planning to produce and sell. The way in which this summation is effected is illustrated in Figure 4.6.1. (a), (b) and (c) show the supply curves of three separate and independent firms. We get the total supply curve by adding together the quantities that each firm would plan to sell at each expected selling price. Thus, at the price p_1, firm A plans to sell a_1, B plans to sell b_1, and C, c_1. The total quantity that all the firms plan to sell at p_1 is therefore $a_1 + b_1 + c_1$, and this is plotted against the price p_1 in (d). In the same way we can discover the quantity that will be supplied by all these firms at each other's expected selling price. When all these points are joined together in (d) we have the total or market supply curve.

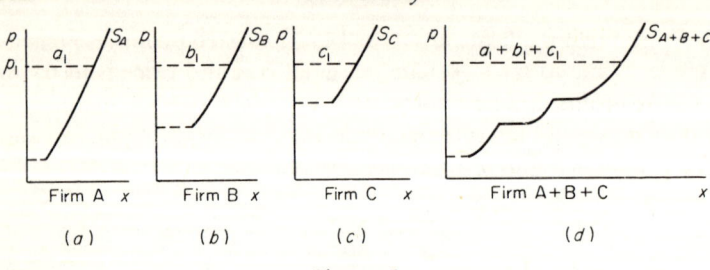

Figure 4.6.1

In Figure 4.6.1 it is assumed that the firms A, B and C have different supply curves. We would expect this to be generally the case, for there will be differences between firms in the quantity, kind and quality of the inputs they are using. Different firms may have different production possibilities open to them in the short-run because they made different decisions in the past about the size of plant and the quantity and kind of equipment and machinery to use. There may be differences in the qualities of the variable inputs they use: if each must pay the same time-rate of wages, and if C, for example, because of its location or past behaviour, can employ only the less efficient labour, then C's costs will be relatively higher, and the quantities it plans to sell at each price relatively less, than those of its competitors.

We have assumed that each firm in making its sales plan expects the selling price of its product to be beyond its control. While each firm may plan on this assumption, the total effect of all firms implementing their sales plans is to assist in the determination of the relations between the prices of the things they sell. The price-determining role of these sales plans is summarised in the total or market supply curve for each product. The manner in which this role is played will be described at some length in Chapter 6.

4.7 Price-Elasticity of Supply

Just as we observed price elasticity of demand, so we can calculate price elasticity of supply. Elasticity of supply, e_s, is measured as the percentage change in output with respect to a percentage change in price.

$$e_s = \frac{\Delta x_s}{x_s} \bigg/ \frac{\Delta p}{p}$$

$$= \frac{\Delta x_s \cdot p}{\Delta p \cdot x_s}$$

where x_s reminds us that it is quantity *supplied* that is relevant here.

In this case we are not troubled by negatives in the expression for e_s since price and supply move together. When $e_s = 0$, the supply curve is perfectly inelastic; when $e_s = \infty$, the supply curve is perfectly elastic. Measured at a point, e_s is more strictly calculated as

$$e_s = \frac{dx_s \cdot p}{dp \cdot x_s}$$

4.8 Changes in supply

The relationship that we have called 'supply' shows us the sales plan that the firm, in our example, would choose at each expected selling price, when its production possibilities, its objective, its contractual obligations, and the prices it expects to have to pay for its variable inputs, all remain unchanged. We must now examine what will happen to supply when there is any alteration in one or other of these.

First, the effects of a change in the production possibilities. The production possibilities may be altered by the firm choosing a new method of production, or by extending or contracting its existing buildings and plant while maintaining its existing method. In either case, the isoquant map will be replaced by a new one. If the firm's objective and the prices of its inputs remain unchanged, there will be a new supply curve which may bear almost any relationship to the old one. In general, if a firm expands its potential outputs, the new supply curve will usually lie south and east of the old, indicating that the firm will plan to produce and sell more per time period at each expected selling price than before.

Second, the effects of a revision in the firm's contractual arrangements with its 'fixed' inputs. If these revisions occur at the same time as the firm chooses a new method of production or decides to exploit its existing method differently, then the effects on supply will be those described in the previous paragraph. The only kind of contractual revision that will not alter the range of production possibilities is one which affects only the payments to the firm's existing 'fixed' inputs. Revisions of this kind will have no effect whatsoever on the firm's supply: provided the quantity and quality of the 'fixed' inputs at the firm's disposal remain unchanged, its supply is in no way affected by its fixed costs. A change in fixed costs arising solely from a change in the prices paid to the fixed inputs will, however, alter the length of time for which the firm's existing supply will be maintained. Thus, if the fixed costs were reduced to zero, the firm, if it chose, could produce indefinitely at prices above minimum average variable cost.

Third, the effects on supply of a change in the firm's objective. These will depend on what new objective is chosen. The supply, in our example, is what it is because we have assumed, *inter alia*, that the firm wished to earn maximum profits in each period. If the firm wished merely to cover its total costs of production, then its supply curve would be the rising part of its average total cost curve in Figure 4.4.3. If its aim were to earn a constant profit, then its supply curve would be a curve lying directly above the rising part of its average cost curve, and asymptotically approaching it as planned output increases.

Fourth, the effect of a change in the price of one or more of the firm's variable inputs. We may ascertain this by repeating step-by-step the argument of this chapter. If the price of K falls while the price of L remains the same, then each output can be produced with less expenditure on variable inputs: the expansion path in Figure 4.0.2 will swing towards the vertical axis, and the variable and total cost curves, the average total cost, average variable cost and marginal cost curves, and the supply curve, will all shift southwards and eastwards, for the cost of each output will now be lower. Conversely, if the price of one or other of the variable inputs should rise, the supply curve would shift northwards and westwards: the firm would plan to produce and sell less at each expected selling price than before.

5

Long-Run Sales Plan of the Firm: Production, Cost and Supply Functions

5.0 The Long-Run
We have generally assumed in the preceding chapters that the firm's current behaviour was circumscribed by past commitments. Some time in the past, the firm built, bought or leased factory buildings of given size and design, installed in them a number of machines and certain quantities of other equipment, and hired managerial and executive labour. While these past decisions still bind it (i.e in the short-run), the firm is limited in each production period to the alternative outputs that these 'fixed' inputs can produce with the aid of certain variable inputs. From the range of possible outputs, the firm, in the light of its expectations about the prices of its products and of its variable inputs, chooses that which promises, when produced and sold, to achieve its objective. In the last chapter, we showed also how the going firm would revise its sales plan in response to changes in the expected selling price of its product: the locus of these revisions was the firm's short-run supply curve.

In this chapter, we look at long-period planning. We shall assume that no past commitments bind the firm: the range of production possibilities and of sales possibilities open to the firm is no longer circumscribed by any fixed inputs: the quantities and qualities of all inputs can be varied. We shall first delineate the range of production possibilities open to the firm in this position; next, we shall describe the patterns that have been, or might be, discerned amongst them; and lastly, we shall illustrate the firm's choice of a sales plan, given the expected prices of the product and of the inputs.

5.1 Returns to Scale

In the long-run the firm will follow the expansion path of Figure 4.0.2 in Chapter 4. It is now important, however, to investigate the meaning of the distances between isoquants measured along a process ray. Figure 5.1.1 shows three possibilities: the isoquants are equally spaced, diagram (a); become closer together as we move up a ray, (b); and, lastly, become further and further away, (c).

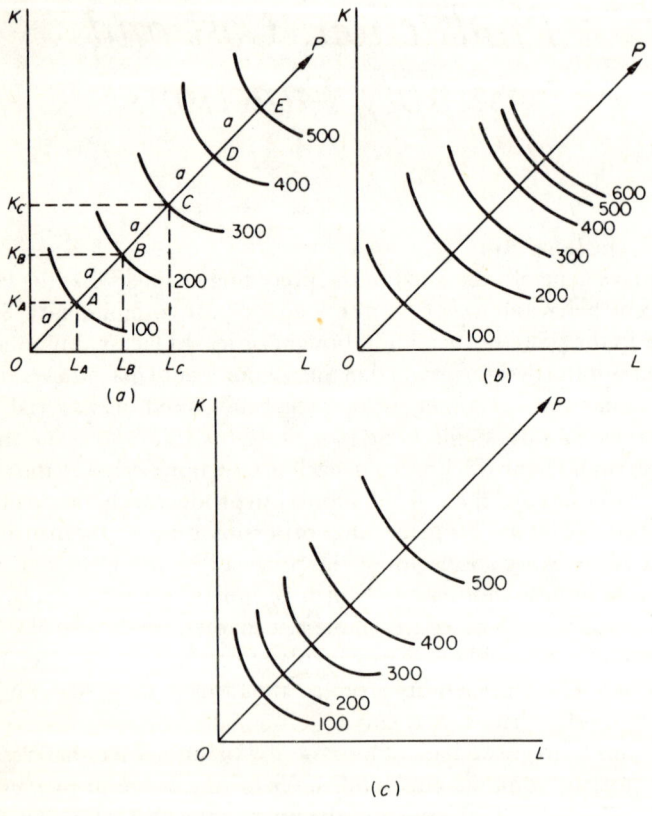

Figure 5.1.1

Consider case (a) first. The diagram is drawn so that the distance between isoquants along OP is the same. Hence, in this diagram, 100 units correspond to distance a along OP. 200 units correspond to a, and so on. It follows that if we plot the input combinations for each of the points $A, B, C \ldots$ each input will rise by a constant amount. It follows that:

$$300 \text{ units require } K_C + L_C = 3K_A + 3L_A$$
$$200 \text{ units require } K_B + L_B = 2K_A + 2L_A$$
$$100 \text{ units require } K_A + L_A = 1K_A + 1L_A.$$

There is a clear pattern: for output to double, inputs each double. For output to treble, inputs each treble.

A production function exhibiting this characteristic is called *homogeneous of degree one*. If, for example, the production function has the form

$$x = x(L, K),$$

and we multiply each input by the same multiple, say m, the new level of output (x') will be m times the old one,[1] that is,

$$x' = x(mL, mK) = m \cdot x(L,K).$$

A less technical way of saying the same thing is that there are *constant returns to scale*. 'Scale' in this case refers to the fact that *all* inputs are now variable. Constant returns therefore means that if we double (the physical quantity of) inputs, we double output.

Diagram (b) shows a situation in which the proportionate increases in combined inputs grown progressively less as equal increments in output are secured. This can only mean that the productivity of inputs must be increasing as we move along OP. This is a situation of *increasing returns to scale*. In this case, the production function is *homogeneous of degree greater than one*, provided the process lines are linear.[2]

Diagram (c) shows a situation where progressively larger proportionate increases in inputs are required to secure equal increments in output. The production function has *decreasing returns to scale*; or, in the context we analyse, is *homogeneous of degree less than one*.

Which is the correct assumption – constant, increasing or decreasing returns? Analysis is certainly easier if we assume constant or decreasing returns. But evidence from many studies suggests that

---

[1] *Homogeneity* means that $x' = m^a \cdot x$ where a can have any value. *Degree one* means that a takes on a value of unity, that is, $x' = m \cdot x$. *Degree zero* would mean $a = 0$, so that $m^a = m^0 = 1$ and $x' = x$, which is clearly not relevant here. *Degree greater than one* would mean $a > 1$, and *degree less than one* would mean $a < 1$.

[2] In other words, we could have increasing (or decreasing returns) *without* homogeneity. It is fairly safe to proceed on the assumption that, for our purposes, production functions are homogeneous.

increasing returns are important. Accordingly, we must bear in mind that all the previous contexts are possible. Indeed, we must also allow for other possibilities – e.g. increasing returns at first and then decreasing returns, increasing returns followed by constant returns, and constant followed by increasing returns.

5.2 The Cobb–Douglas Production Function

Although a number of equations 'fit' the smooth production function of the kind shown in Figure 5.1.1 and in Chapter 4, one particular function is used widely in theoretical and empirical work. This is the Cobb–Douglas function,[1] which has the following form:

$$x = A \cdot L^a \cdot K^b$$

where a, b and A are parameters. Essentially, the equation says that output depends directly on K and L, and that part of output which cannot be explained by labour and capital inputs is explained by the 'residual' A. This residual is often, rather misleadingly, called 'technical change'. But suffice it to say for our purposes that A is a 'catch-all' which accounts for output not explained by labour and capital inputs.

The Cobb–Douglas function is homogeneous. If we multiply each input by a factor m, we obtain

$$x' = A \cdot mL^a \cdot mK^b = A \cdot m^{a+b} \cdot L^a K^b = m^{a+b} \cdot x.$$

From this result we can observe that if $a + b = 1$, the function is homogeneous of degree one – i.e. it exhibits constant returns to scale. If $a + b > 1$ we have increasing returns, and if $a + b < 1$ we have decreasing returns.

If we plotted the isoproduct contours for a Cobb–Douglas function, we would get a smooth function very much like the ones already illustrated. As it happens, however, the contours cannot touch either axis – they approach the axes and get closer and closer but never actually intersect. To use the technical language, they approach the axes *asymptotically*.

Another interesting aspect of Cobb–Douglas functions is that a and

---

[1] The function is named after Paul Douglas and C. W. Cobb. The original article (there are a number) is C. W. Cobb and P. H. Douglas, 'A Theory of Production', *American Economic Review*, Mar. 1928.

b correspond to the marginal products of labour and capital respectively in the constant returns to scale case.[1]

5.3 Indivisibilities

Section 5.1 suggested that all possibilities – increasing, decreasing and constant returns to scale – should be acknowledged when analysing the firm's long-run sales plans. It is frequently argued, however, that, in the long-run, at least one input will be fixed: 'managerial ability'. Basically, the suggestion is that the larger a firm grows, the more responsibility devolves on to a few men, the so-called 'top managers'. The ability of these men to maintain detailed knowledge of the working of the firm may become impaired as the firm grows larger. If this is so, management could be thought of as a 'fixed input' in the long-run. The law of diminishing returns would apply and the analysis of Chapters 3 and 4 would be appropriate.

Management, however, is not the only input that may be incapable of continuous variation. Thus, if a firm uses one motor lorry, it cannot increase the number of lorries at its disposal by less than 100 per cent; if it uses two typewriters, it cannot increase the quantity of this input by less than 50 per cent, or reduce it by less than 50 per cent, for a typewriter must be a certain minimum size if it is to do its job properly; and if the firm is employing one accountant, it cannot do less than employ another whole accountant. Inputs such as these, the quantity of which cannot be varied continuously with output, are usually called 'indivisible' or 'lumpy' inputs. Top management, or co-ordination, is clearly an extreme example of indivisibility or lumpiness. Another extreme example of indivisibility is the amalgam of fixed inputs that the firm has at its disposal during the short-run. The technical consequence of indivisibility is that as more of the other and divisible inputs are combined with the indivisible inputs, output follows the pattern described by the Law of Non-Proportional Returns.

Most inputs that a firm uses are indivisible to some extent. The quantity of the input may be incapable of continuous variation for technical reasons, as with typewriters and lorries, for each of these must be of a certain minimum size if it is to do the work for which it was designed. The indivisibility might arise for reasons that are partly technical and partly institutional: thus, the firm might not be able to

---

[1] For a detailed analysis of this function and others, and for derivations of the characteristics concerning marginal product, see D. F. Heathfield, *Production Functions* (Macmillan, London, 1971).

hire labour in units of less than one hour or one week. Whether or not the degree of indivisibility merits the adjective 'indivisible' depends mainly on the number of units of that input that the firm is using. If a firm is engaged in road haulage and if it is already operating 200 lorries, then the degree of indivisibility in the input lorries is unlikely to be important. If the firm is a small wholesaler owning only one lorry, then the degree of indivisibility will be significant.

The notion of indivisibility depends also on the units in which we measure inputs. The input 'transport' may be measured in number of lorries or in ton-miles: indivisibility is more likely to be significant if we use the former than if we use the latter. The input 'typing services' may be measured in numbers of typewriters or in words typed per hour: the degree of indivisibility may be less notable if we use the latter units. In general, with durable goods (like lorries, machines or buildings which yield their services over many production periods), indivisibility will appear more important if we measure inputs in terms of the number of such goods rather than in terms of the services which they render. This choice of units is rather more than a linguistic quibble: a firm cannot have one-half of a lorry for one week, but if a lorry gives 100,000 ton-miles per week, a firm can have 50,000 ton-miles of input by hiring a lorry for three days, or it may procure the same quantity of input by having another firm transport its goods. If a firm has more work than one accountant can cope with but less than two could do, then it may hire accounting services from a specialist firm.

We conclude that indivisibilities are not particularly important in so far as our expectations of *decreasing* returns are concerned. But as a firm grows it has more and more opportunity to overcome the effects of some kinds of indivisibility. The apparent fixity of management can also be avoided by delegation and the reorganisation of the company into semi-autonomous units with the top managers being responsible for only major decisions and avoiding all the day-to-day decisions.

5.4 Long-Run Production Possibilities

In the short-run the firm must 'make do' with whatever inputs are fixed and must change output by varying the remaining, variable inputs. In the long-run the firm will be able to travel along its least-cost expansion path. Before the firm makes its choice, all (or almost all) inputs are potentially variable. After the firm has made its choice, however, some are fixed and some remain variable. In delineating the

Long-Run Sales Plan of the Firm

production possibilities, we use 'fixed' to mean those inputs that would be fixed, and 'variable' to mean those inputs that would remain variable, were the firm to make that particular choice.

Suppose the firm is faced with the production isoquants shown in Figure 5.4.1. Suppose the short-run situation is characterised by a fixed capital input $\bar{K}_1$. Then x_1 is produced with the combination K_1, L_1. But if the firm decides to produce x_2 in the short-run, it will have to use L_4 labour instead of combining K_2 with L_2 which is what it would have done had the option been open. Similarly, if the firm operates with a fixed capital of $\bar{K}_2$ it can only produce x_3 by using L_5 labour, instead of using K_3 and L_3 which would have been optimal if the short-run capital constraint did not exist.

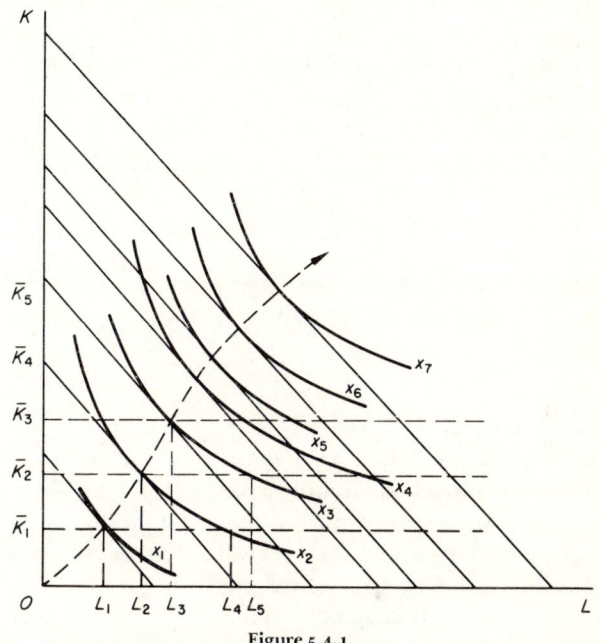

Figure 5.4.1

If we were to plot the various short-run product curves, each one corresponding to the various fixed amounts of capital, $\bar{K}_1$, $\bar{K}_2$, $\bar{K}_3$, etc., we would get a picture like that shown in Figure 5.4.2. The short-run total product curves, traced out by each of the horizontal lines through $\bar{K}_1$, $\bar{K}_2$, etc., would overlap in the manner shown. Indeed, if we varied the capital constraint very gradually, so that K_2 was only slightly larger than K_1, and so on, the curves would overlap to the extent that their outer points would form an 'envelope' curve like that shown. This curve is effectively the firm's *long-run total product curve*.

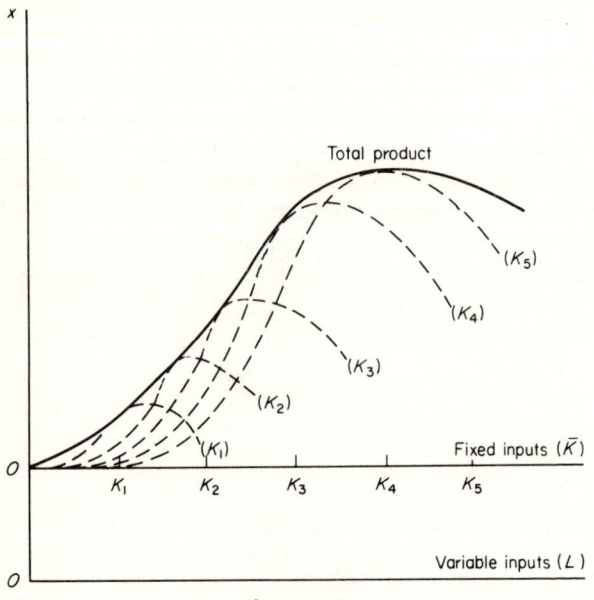

Figure 5.4.2

5.5 Long-Run Costs

The expansion path in Figure 5.4.1 shows the locus of *least total cost* combinations of inputs as output expands. We also observed in Chapter 4 that cost curves are 'mirror images' of product curves. Not surprisingly, then, long-run cost curves will be mirror images of long-run product curves. Figure 5.4.2, transformed into costs, will appear as a total cost curve entirely analogous to the short-run total cost curve. Note that we again assume input prices are invariant with output. Figure 5.5.1 shows the transformation but in terms of *average* costs. Note that the average cost curve in the long-run ($LRAC$) is a locus of the minimum points of the short-run average cost curves ($SRAC$s) that make it up. Our figure shows a $LRAC$ falling and then rising – that is, returns to scale are at first increasing and then decreasing. How reasonable such a pattern is depends on whether inputs, such as management, really are 'fixed' in the long-run. For the moment,

Long-Run Sales Plan of the Firm

however, we are interested in justifying the notion that the *LRAC* is the locus of all the minimum points of the *SRAC* curves.

Suppose the firm wishes to produce x_1 units in Figure 5.5.1. It could do this by operating either with input combinations denoted by $SRAC_1$ or by $SRAC_2$. The first curve corresponds to the fixed capital input K_1 in Figure 5.4.1, the second to K_2. But production with $SRAC_2$ clearly involves higher average costs than production with $SRAC_1$ (point a is above $SRAC_1$). If the firm is interested in profits, which is our assumption to date, it will obviously choose $SRAC_1$. We again emphasise that this choice of selecting which *SRAC* curve to operate with is a long-run decision. If the firm is constrained by having capital K_1, it will in fact have no option but to operate with $SRAC_1$. This is no problem as far as producing x_1 is concerned, but it will not be efficient if output is x_3, when $SRAC_2$ is to be preferred. Output x_2 can be produced with either the first or second plant and both have equal average costs. We would therefore expect the producer to be indifferent between plants for this output. It follows from a comparison of outputs x_1, x_2 and x_3 that points on the segments ab and bcd are inefficient. Accordingly, they can be eliminated, leaving only the points on the locus of the minimum points of the curve.

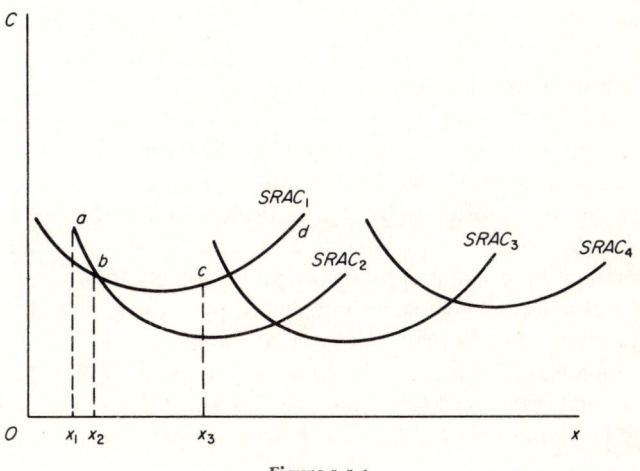

Figure 5.5.1

Figure 5.5.1 shows the *LRAC* curve with only a few alternative *SRAC* curves. If we vary the capital constraint in Figure 5.4.1 very gradually, the *SRAC* curves will overlap each other more and more closely. The result will be that the *LRAC* curve will get smoother and smoother as the number of *SRAC* curves increases.

The *LRAC* curve in Figure 5.5.1 corresponds to the cost implicit in a movement along the firm's expansion path, as in Figure 5.4.1. This movement may encompass switching processes as output expands. The main point is that the *LRAC* curve is not only the locus of the *SRAC* curves shown, it is also, by definition, the locus of all *possible* minimum average cost points.

To conclude this section, two major assumptions must be borne in mind. They need re-emphasising.

(i) The *LRAC* curve so far constructed assumes constant input prices. If the reader is in any doubt of this, it should only be necessary to remind him that the *LRAC* curve was derived from the isoquant map in Figure 5.4.1. The isocost lines were drawn parallel to indicate that relative input prices stayed the same as output expands.

(ii) The *LRAC* curve in Figure 5.5.1 slopes down at first and then rises. This reflects an assumption that there is a combination of increasing and then decreasing returns to scale. It should be remembered that there is nothing 'sacred' about this result: costs might well be constant over the whole range of output, or they might fall continually, or even rise without stop.

5.6 Choice of a Sales Plan

Given his *LRAC* curve, the producer will select that output which maximises his profit, or so we assume for the moment. If we confine our attention to the price-taker (perfect competition) context, the chosen output will be given by x^* in Figure 5.6.1 where demand (price) and marginal revenue equal marginal cost. Notice that this figure incorporates a long-run marginal cost curve, entirely analogous to the short-run marginal cost curve introduced previously. The optimum output occurs, for the price-taker, where *LRMC* = price. In the price-taker context, *LRMC* is the firm's long-run supply curve. The proof of this is exactly the same as the proof which showed short-run marginal cost to be identical with the firm's short-run supply curve.

The objective of maximising profits determines which output is chosen, and which output is chosen determines which plant is used: in this case $SRAC_3$ is used. The shaded area shows total profits. Figure 5.6.2 magnifies the actual point of equilibrium. Note that price equals *LRMC and SRMC*.

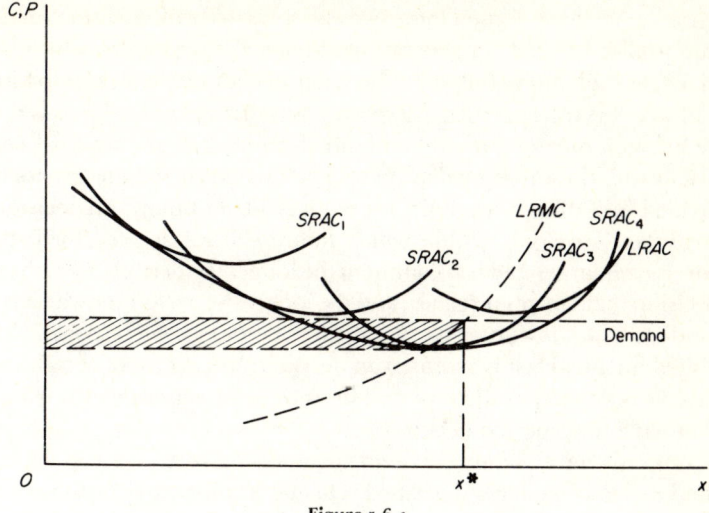

Figure 5.6.1

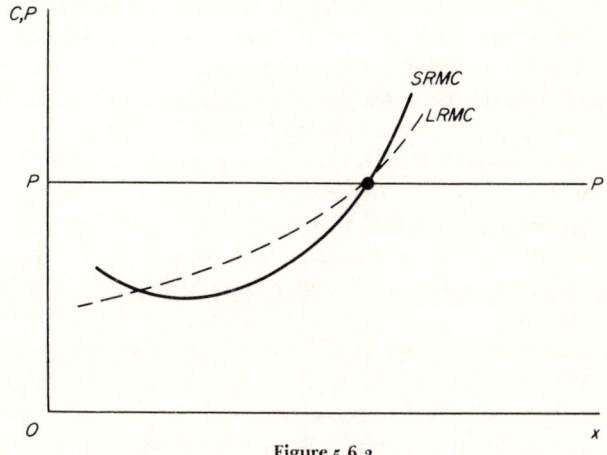

Figure 5.6.2

5.7 The Intermediate Period

So far we have assumed that the manager, in making his plans, is bound by no past commitments whatever.

In the previous chapter his range of choice was so drastically restricted by past commitments that only a few inputs remained variable. We have chosen these two extremes to focus attention on the importance of time: in general, the longer the period for which the manager is planning the wider the range of choice that is open to him, and vice versa. In practice, however, many firms plan for periods that lie between our long period and our short period, and we shall deal briefly with these intermediate period plans. For a firm, time cannot be divided into discrete periods: rather, it is a continuum. All decisions create an 'envelope' within which future choices are confined; the envelope is larger and less confining the longer the period to which the decision that creates it relates, and the longer the period for which it is binding. Thus, in our terminology, whether the egg will be poached or boiled for breakfast is a short-run decision; the choice of curtains or carpets is an intermediate-period decision, and marriage or buying a house is a long-period decision.

It is only infrequently that a manager will make a long-run plan of the kind that we have described. Having implemented it, however, some revisions may still be possible. A firm, for example, may have chosen the group of inputs that promise a particular *SRAC* curve. Soon after this choice has been made there may be a new invention which shifts the minimum range of the planning curve south-westwards. If this had been known when the firm was making its original choice, it would have chosen differently. What the firm will do depends on the relation between the costs per period it now has, and those it could have had were it now free to choose. If expected profits with the latter exceeds the 'fixed' costs plus the profits in each period with the existing method, then it may scrap the existing plant, etc., and start anew. New developments, however, seldom have such drastic effects. They are frequently such that they can be used in existing plants and offer some reduction in costs per period – though smaller reductions than would have been achieved if the plant had been initially designed to make use of them. When a firm is deciding whether or not to install improved machines, for example, its choice can be illustrated in a manner similar to that described above. We could delineate the range of production possibilities open to the firm when it is planning for the intermediate period: this will be narrower in the short-run than in the long-run for some inputs are now fixed, but wider than in the short-run for more inputs are now variable. When the expected prices of inputs are given, these production possibilities can be translated into alternative short-run cost curves that the firm might choose, and it will decide on that which promises the greatest profit per period. If the firm decides to install new machines, then its new average total cost curve will lie neither on the old planning curve nor on the new one, but somewhere between the two.

5.8 The Multiproduct Firm

Few firms produce a single product. In addition to the previous decision problems then, the firm may well have to decide how much of each alternative product to produce. Suppose the firm has just two products, x_1 and x_2, and that it is free to produce only x_1, only x_2, or some combination of x_1 and x_2. Suppose only one input is involved, say labour, and its total quantity is fixed. Then there are two production functions:

$$x_1 = x_1(L_1)$$
$$x_2 = x_2(L_2) = x_2(\bar{L} - L_1)$$
and
$$L_1 + L_2 = \bar{L}$$

where L_1 is labour used in producing x_1, L_2 is labour used in producing x_2 and $\bar{L}$ is the overall supply of labour to the firm. Possible combinations of x_1 and x_2 are shown in Figure 5.8.1 which illustrates the *production possibility frontier*.

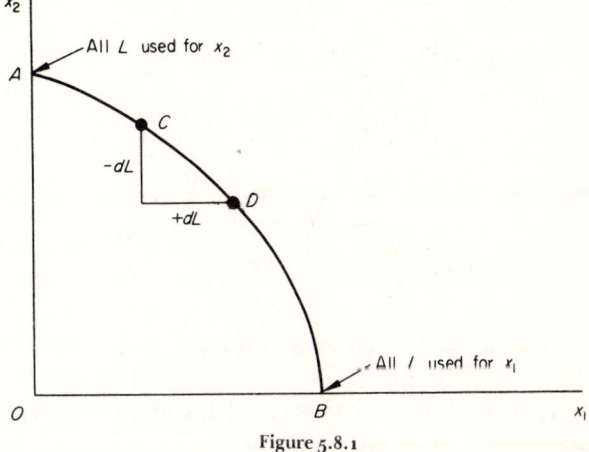

Figure 5.8.1

The slope of curve AB is the *rate of product transformation*, written

$$\frac{-dx_2}{dx_1}$$

and the figure is drawn with a concave line AB to indicate the likelihood that surrendering some of x_2 when $x_1 = O$ (marginal product of x_2 low) will result in fairly noticeable increases in x_1 (marginal product high).

Now the price of labour, f_L, is constant for both outputs. Hence x_1 will cost $f_{L_1} \cdot x_1$ and x_2 will cost $f_{L_2} \cdot x_2$. Points A and B in Figure 5.8.1 must be equally costly since total cost in both cases is $f_L \cdot \bar{L}$. But all the points on AB use up the entire labour force: hence all points are equally costly. AB can therefore be construed as an equal cost curve. We can now add lines showing the revenue that would be obtained from each combination of outputs. If we again confine our attention to price-takers, these 'isorevenue' contours will have the equation

$$R = p_1 x_1 + p_2 x_2$$

and will appear as the lines in Figure 5.8.2.

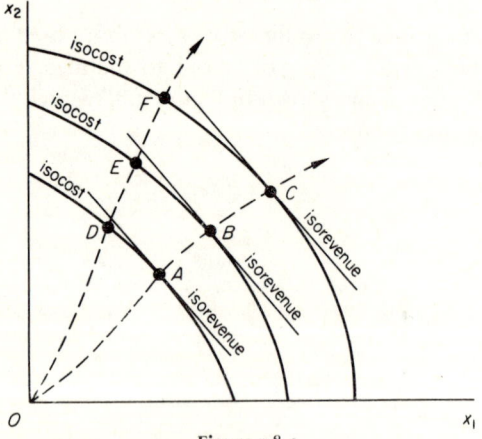

Figure 5.8.2

Optimal combinations of x_1 and x_2 are therefore shown by the points of tangency A, B, C, etc. The firm's 'expansion path' lies along ABC, with successive contours getting closer and closer together as diminishing returns set in. Changes in relative goods' prices will show up in changed slopes of the isorevenue curves, which will have the effect of making some other combination of x_1 and x_2 more profitable, thus shifting the expansion path ABC to another path, say, DEF in Figure 5.8.2.

6

The Determination of Relative Product Prices

6.0 Supply and Demand

In Chapter 2, we described the derivation of a consumer's demand for any good that he might plan to buy. A consumer's demand for a particular good is shown as a demand schedule which tells us how his purchase plan would be revised if the only planning datum that altered was the price he expected to have to pay for the good – that is, a schedule that shows the quantity that the consumer would plan to buy in a given period of time at each price at which the good might be sold, *ceteris paribus*. The other things that must remain equal are the consumer's tastes and preferences (i.e. his indifference map), his income, the prices of all other goods that he might buy, and the basic aim of utility maximisation. The total or market demand for the good is obtained by adding together the demands of all the consumers in the economy who might plan to buy it.

In Chapter 4, we derived the supply curve of an existing firm on the assumption that the firm was operating in conditions of perfect competition. The firm's supply schedule shows us how its sales plan would be revised during the short-run if the only planning datum that altered was the price at which it expects to be able to sell its output; that is, it gives us the quantity that the firm would plan to offer for sale in each production period at each price, *ceteris paribus*. The other things that must remain equal are the firm's production possibilities (i.e. its isoquant map), the prices at which it expects to be able to buy its variable inputs and the objective that it is pursuing. The total or market supply schedule is obtained by adding together the supplies of all the firms in the economy that might plan to sell it.

The total demand curve summarises the role that consumers play in determining the relative price of the good as they implement their plans to buy it. The price-determining role of firms is summarised in the total supply curve of the same good. In this chapter, we shall first describe how these roles are played; second, examine some of the applications of demand and supply analysis in order to demonstrate its usefulness; and third, analyse price determination in the long-run.

6.1 Price Determination: Short-Run

In Figure 6.1.1, we measure the expected price per unit of the good on the vertical axis, and on the horizontal axis we measure the planned sales of the good by firms and the planned purchases of the good by consumers in each period of time. The market demand and supply schedules are graphed between these axes. The price will tend towards the level $\bar{p}$, for only at that price will the quantity that firms plan to sell ($\bar{x}$) be the same as the quantity that consumers plan to buy ($\bar{x}$) in each period.

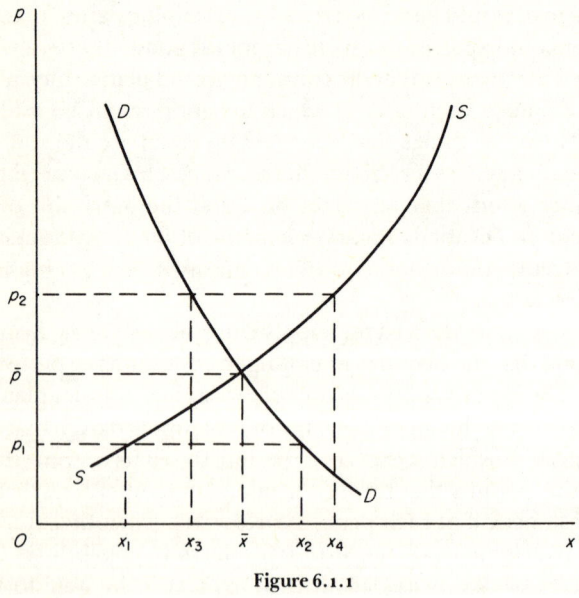

Figure 6.1.1

We can see clearly from the figure that $\bar{p}$ is the only price at which the plans of consumers and firms will be consistent with one another. Thus, if the price were p_1 firms would plan to sell x_1 during the period but consumers would plan to buy x_2. If firms actually offer for sale an amount equal to x_1, then the purchase plans of the consumers must be under-fulfilled by x_1x_2 during the period. Conversely, if the price were p_2, consumers would plan to buy only x_3, while firms would plan to produce and sell x_4. If both consumers and firms attempt to make their plans effective during this period, then the sales plans of the firms will be under-fulfilled by x_3x_4 – that is, at the end of the period, they will be left with unsold stocks equal to x_3x_4. These divergences between the planned and actual purchases of consumers, or between the planned and actual sales of firms, cannot continue, and we shall describe presently how their existence sets in motion forces that will probably lead to this commodity being bought and sold at $\bar{p}$ per unit.

The price of $\bar{p}$ per unit is called the *equilibrium* price, and the price will remain at that level, with an even flow of sales and purchases each equal to $\bar{x}$ in each period, so long as there is no change in the demand for the good or in the supply of it. We showed, in Chapter 2, that demand will alter if there is any change in consumers' tastes and preferences, their incomes, their objectives, or in the price of any other good that they might buy. If the preferences for the good become stronger, or income increases, or the prices of substitute goods rise, then consumers will plan to buy more at each price than before. This increase in demand is shown in Figure 6.1.2 by a movement of the demand curve from D_1D_1 to D_2D_2. If there is no change in supply then price will tend to rise from $\bar{p}$ to $\bar{p}_1$. The rise in price that follows any given increase in demand will be the greater the less is the price elasticity of supply, and it will be the less the greater is the price elasticity of supply.

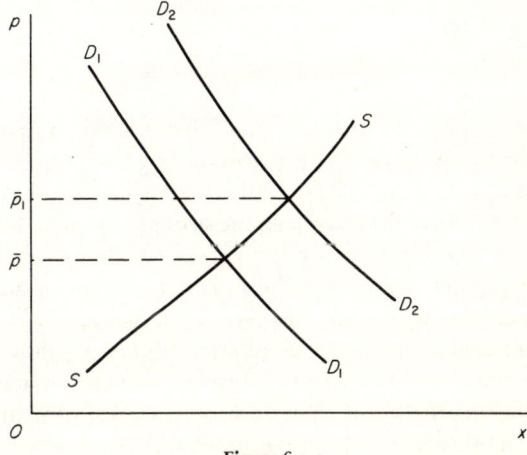

Figure 6.1.2

126   *Price Theory*

We showed in Chapter 4 that supply will alter if there is any change in the firm's production possibilities, the prices they expect to pay for the variable inputs, or in their objectives. If the prices of one or more of the variable inputs are reduced, then firms will plan to sell more at each price than before. This increase in supply is shown in Figure 6.1.3 by a shift in the supply curve from S_1S_1 to S_2S_2. If there is no change in demand, then price will tend to fall from $\bar{p}$ to $\bar{p}_2$. For any given change in supply, the ensuing change in price will be the greater the less is the price elasticity of demand, and it will be the less the greater the price elasticity of demand. The effects of simultaneous changes in demand and supply, whether in the same or opposite directions, can be illustrated simply by a similar figure.

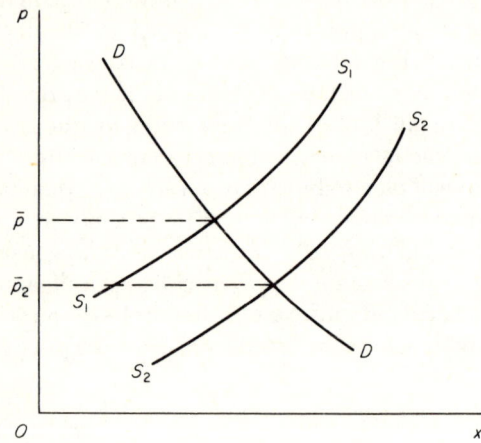

Figure 6.1.3

It must be emphasised that the preceding analysis only explains changes in the *relation* between the prices of the good in question and the prices of other things. Thus, Figure 6.1.2 shows us that if consumers' preferences for the good become stronger, its price will rise as compared with (*a*) the prices of other goods that they might buy; (*b*) their incomes, which are merely the prices at which consumers are currently selling the inputs that they own; (*c*) the prices of the variable inputs that are used to produce it. Similarly, Figure 6.1.3 shows us that if there is a reduction in the prices of the variable inputs that are used by firms producing this good, then its price will fall as compared with (*a*) the prices of other products; (*b*) consumers' incomes, which depend on the prices at which they are selling their inputs; (c) the new and lower prices of the variable inputs.

We have not yet attempted to explain how, or by whom, the price is driven up, nor have we described the precise path by which it moves from the initial to the new equilibrium position. Initially, we shall suppose that the movement to the new equilibrium price is effected by a single intermediary (or group of intermediaries acting in concert), who works without either thought or expectation of reward, so that the price at which he buys is that at which he sells. This provides a pedagogically useful model of the adjustment of price towards its equilibrium level, though it is difficult to find any actual markets in the real world to which it is a close approximation. We shall assume that the production period for firms is the same as the purchase period for consumers, each being equal to one week; that sales and purchase plans are made at the beginning of the week on the basis of the price that is expected to rule during it; and that, once made, these plans are unalterable until the beginning of the next week. Let us now suppose that there is a permanent increase in demand at the beginning of week 1: that is, that the demand curve in Figure 6.1.4 moves from $D_1 D_1$ to

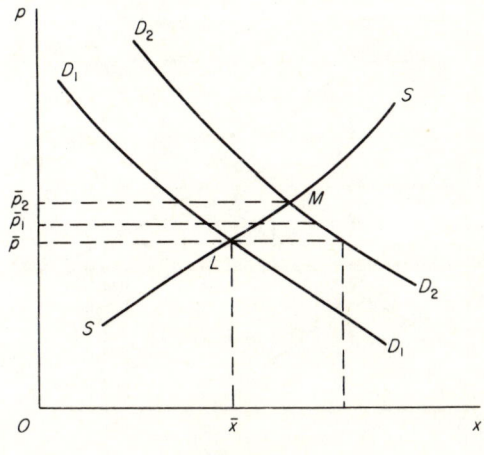

Figure 6.1.4

$D_2 D_2$. If firms and consumers have already laid their plans on the expectation that the price $\bar{p}$ will rule, then during week 1 firms will supply the intermediary with $\bar{x}$ units to sell, and he will become aware (through orders that he is unable to satisfy) that this falls short of the amount that consumers want to buy at $\bar{p}$ per unit. For week 2, therefore, the merchant will plan to buy more from firms, but to induce them to produce more, a higher price – say, $\bar{p}_1$ – must be offered. If the price is fixed at $\bar{p}_1$ for week 2, the merchant will find that his experiences of the first week are repeated, though in lesser degree. He will plan a further increase in his purchases from firms for week 3, and these adjustments will continue until the price has reached $\bar{p}_2$, for only then will the flow of the good in each week from firms to the merchant be just equal to its flow from him to consumers. The description of what would happen on these assumptions if there had been a reduction in demand is similar, and it is left to the reader. In this model, the price, in moving to the new equilibrium level, follows the path traced by the short-run supply curve between L and M.

We may alternatively assume that the product is a perishable one, so that it must all be sold within the period in which it is produced. If we again suppose that the firms producing it expect the price $\bar{p}$ to obtain in week 1, they will plan to produce $\bar{x}$ in Figure 6.1.5. If there is a spontaneous increase in demand at the beginning of week 1 from D_1D_1 to

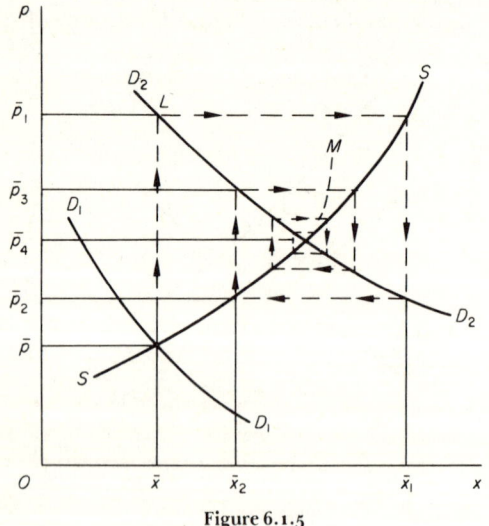

Figure 6.1.5

D_2D_2, then the price in that week will rise to $\bar{p}_1$. This increase in price may be effected by wholesalers or merchants, who are more or less aware of the enhanced demand, and who, desiring to maximise their profits, buy 'cheap' and sell 'dear' to consumers. Or it might be the result of those consumers who were first in the queue acquiring $\bar{x}$ from

The Determination of Relative Product Prices

firms at $\bar{p}$ per unit, and reselling to those behind them in the queue, these transactions continuing until the price was such that no consumer possessing the commodity was willing to resell and no consumer wanting it willing to buy – that is until the price had reached $\bar{p}_1$ per unit. We may call $\bar{p}_1$ the *market* equilibrium price, to distinguish it from the short-run equilibrium price like $\bar{p}$ or $\bar{p}_4$. What will happen to the price in the weeks that follow will depend mainly on how firms revise their production and sales plans. We shall explore briefly what would happen if each firm always expected the price in the period lying ahead to be that which ruled in the present period.

If each firm expects the price $\bar{p}_1$, to obtain in week 2, then together they will plan to produce a quantity $\tilde{x}_1$ in week 2, for in the light of their price expectations that quantity alone will promise to maximise their profits. When $\tilde{x}_1$ is actually offered for sale, the price per unit will fall to $\bar{p}_2$. If each firm expects the price to be $\bar{p}_2$ in week 3, they will plan to produce $\tilde{x}_2$. In week 3, then, the price must rise to $\bar{p}_3$. We can see from Figure 6.1.5 that, on these assumptions, the price will gradually approach the new equilibrium level, $\bar{p}_4$. The path by which the price moves from $\bar{p}$ to $\bar{p}_4$ can be seen more clearly from Figure 6.1.6, where we measure time (in weeks) on the horizontal axis, and the price that actually ruled in each week on the vertical axis. In this figure, $\bar{p}_1$ denotes price in week 1, $\bar{p}_2$ price in week 2, and so on.

The fact that price fluctuates, rather than rises monotonically, towards the new equilibrium level is a necessary consequence of our assumption about the basis of the price-expectations of firms. The fact

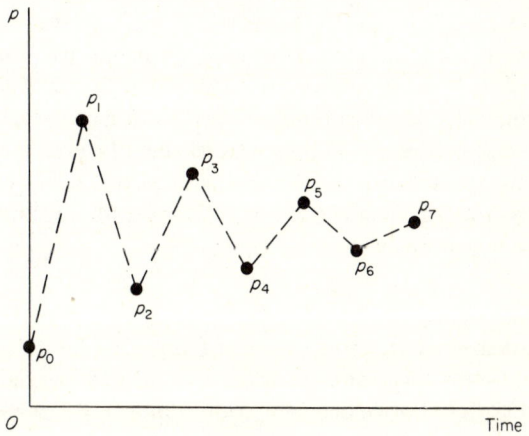

Figure 6.1.6

that we have a convergent fluctuation in Figure 6.1.5 and Figure 6.1.6 is because the new demand curve, D_2D_2, has a smaller slope at each price than the supply curve. If demand had had a greater slope than supply at each price, we would have had divergent fluctuations. If the two curves had the same slope at each price, there would have been continuous fluctuations.

These consequences of our assumption that each firm expects this period's price to rule in the next period are called the *cobweb theorem*, because of the appearance of the figure on which they are illustrated. Even if the other circumstances are favourable – a perishable commodity, no single producer of which can affect its price – it is unlikely, however, that a 'cobweb' fluctuation will develop: sooner or later, managers must observe that the assumption on which they base their price-expectations is being proved wrong by events, and that periods of high and low prices alternate with one another: there is a 'learning' process. Once this is realised, the cobweb fluctuations will be neutralised, for the more far-sighted firms will expect price to be low in the next period if it was high in this period (and vice versa), and make their production and sales plans accordingly. If the demand for the product rises, driving its price up to $\tilde{p}_1$ in Figure 6.1.5, the price will probably fall monotonically in the ensuing periods, following the path traced by the range *LM* of the new demand curve. This sharp rise in the price of a commodity, followed by a continuing decline to somewhere above its initial level, is a not infrequent consequence of actual increases in demand. In practice, it is explained in part by the manner in which firms revise their price-expectations (and it is on this that we have concentrated in our analysis above); it is in part due also to the fact that not all firms can employ more variable inputs – that is, can 'move along' their short-run supply curves – with equal ease. Those that are favourably placed can increase production quickly, but some time may elapse before others do so. Consequently, even if each firm knew what the equilibrium price was going to be, the quantity supplied would increase only gradually from period to period, causing the price to follow some path like *LM*.

6.2 Short-Run Price Determination: A Simple Algebraic Approach

Whilst diagrams frequently provide the easiest mechanism for analysing theories of price determination, simple algebra tends to do the same job more quickly. The interaction of supply and demand in

The Determination of Relative Product Prices

determining price provides a simple application of elementary algebra.

The demand curve in Figure 6.2.1 can be represented by the equation

$$x^D = a - b \cdot p. \tag{1}$$

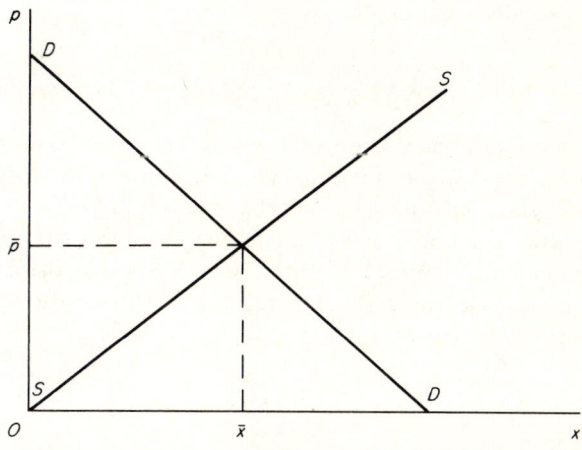

Figure 6.2.1

Notice that this is an equation for a straight line. A curvilinear demand curve would involve at least a term in $\bar{p}^2$. The supply curve (also shown as linear) could be written

$$x^S = c \cdot p. \tag{2}$$

The constants, a, b, and c, are the *parameters* of the two equations. We assume zero quantity is supplied at zero price, so that the supply curve goes through the origin. The variables p and x are referred to as *endogenous* variables. The equilibrium price $\bar{p}$ exists where demand equals supply, that is, where $x^D = x^S$. This last equivalence is the equilibrium condition – i.e. we formally write

$$x^D = x^S. \tag{3}$$

We now have a three-equation *model* of supply and demand which is easily solved by substituting equations (1) and (2) in equation (3) as follows,

$$a - b \cdot p = c \cdot p$$

which on rearrangement gives

$$\bar{p} = \frac{a}{b+c}$$

as the equilibrium price. Notice that $\bar{p}$ is expressed solely in terms of *parameters*. This is called a *reduced form* equation. The reduced form equation for $\bar{x}$ can be found by substituting the equation for $\bar{p}$ into the demand or supply equation, that is,

$$\bar{x} = c \cdot \frac{a}{b+c} = \frac{ac}{b+c}.$$

A *shift* in the demand curve would mean that one or both of the parameters of the demand curve change. If the demand curve shifts in a parallel fashion, only the value of a changes. If it shifts and its slope changes *as well*, then both a and b change. Suppose only a changes, say to $2a$. We need not repeat all the previous working: the basic result remains the same – all we have to do is substitute $2a$ for a in the reduced form equations. This gives

$$\bar{p} = \frac{2a}{b+c}, \quad x = \frac{2ac}{b+c}$$

for the system of equations

$$x^D = 2a - b \cdot p$$
$$x^S = c \cdot p$$
$$x^D = x^S.$$

The reader can experiment with changing other parameters.

6.3 Short-Run Demand and Supply Analysis: Applications to Price Control and Taxation

The demand for, and the short-run supply of, a commodity explain the level towards which its price will tend while the firm's activities are circumscribed by past commitments. While the price is, for the moment, assumed to lie beyond the control of any single buyer or seller, the ultimate effect of all buyers and all sellers revising their expectations of what the price will be, and adjusting their planned purchases and planned sales accordingly, will be a situation in which all their expectations and plans are fulfilled. This explanation of the determination of relative prices in terms of demand and supply analysis has two main uses: first, it provides a number of headings under which we may conveniently classify the causes of changes in relative prices; second, it helps us to predict the consequences of price controls, of taxes on commodities, and of other similar measures.

Let us suppose that during the past month the price of eggs has risen as compared with the prices of all other things. A knowledge of elementary demand and supply analysis enables us to organise our quest for the cause of this event. If the relative price per dozen eggs has risen, the explanation must lie in changes in demand, or in supply, or in both of these. We have called the kinds of reason why demand or supply might change the 'determinants' or 'conditions' of demand and supply: these provide us with a broad classification of the possible mediate causes of changes in relative prices. The next step is to discover which of these were operative. The system of classification that demand and supply analysis provides is, then, an aid to diagnosis: we observe the symptom, which is a rise in the relative price of eggs, and the analysis tells us on what kinds of change we should focus our attention.

We may discover that price has risen because the preferences of consumers for eggs have become more intense; this in turn might be the result of any one of an almost innumerable list of causes, ranging from climate to caprice, and to explore further we need another classificatory system. Or the cause might seem to lie in a rise in the prices of the variable inputs used by the egg producers: to probe further we can here use the classifications implicit in demand and supply analysis. The value of a classification must be judged by the help it gives in unravelling the problem at hand, and on this test all the classifications we have listed are tolerably good. They help us to localise the causes of the event in which we are interested, and if we wish to probe further, they suggest where we should look for more information.

We have so far used demand and supply analysis to work from an event to its proximate cause, and we have seen that it undoubtedly clarifies hindsight. The analysis may also be used to deduce from an event its probable consequences. If we observe, for example, that the price of poultry feed has risen, or that the government has controlled the price of eggs or imposed a tax on them, we may, assuming other things equal, predict what will happen to the price of eggs. Whether or not our predictions are proved by events to have been correct will depend on whether other things are equal. Good economic predictions can never result from the mere mechanical application of the analysis, for in a developed economy most consequences have several causes. Before hazarding a prediction in practice, we must decide whether any of the other determinants of demand and supply are likely to change. The analysis tells us what things to look at, but our judgement of how they are likely to alter, and of how we should weight the probable changes in different determinants before chancing a prediction of their net effect, is more a matter of 'feel' – that is, of that rather rare ability to measure the incommensurable and add the non-additive. Bearing this in mind, we shall explore in a more or less mechanical way the probable effects of price controls and taxes on commodities.

1. Price Controls: Let us suppose that there is an increase in demand and that the government makes it illegal for sellers to raise the price above its initial equilibrium level. At the legal maximum price ($\bar{p}$ in Figure 6.3.1), firms will plan to supply $\bar{x}$ per period and this falls short by $\bar{x}x_1$ of the quantity that consumers are planning to buy. If the

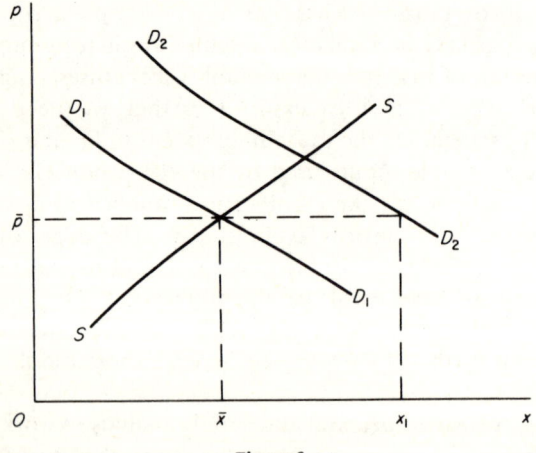

Figure 6.3.1

price control is effective, this situation can continue indefinitely, for the consumers, or the firms who serve them, dare not offer the higher prices that would eliminate this 'excess demand'. If price is thus prevented from distributing the quantity that is supplied of the commodity amongst all those who demand it, other methods must be found. Sellers may allocate the quantity $\bar{x}$ amongst those desiring x_1 on the basis of 'first come, first served', or they might hoard it 'under the counter' and distribute it on the basis of their personal feelings towards their customers or of their customers' past purchases and behaviour. When there are maximum price controls, some form of rationing is necessary, but it may be deemed socially undesirable that the choice of method should be left to sellers. In these circumstances, the government may issue to each household ration coupons, the value of each coupon being so fixed that all together they can 'buy' only the quantity of the commodity that is being supplied in each period.

It may be that the equilibrium price ($\bar{p}$ in Figure 6.3.2), the total revenue that most firms earn per period, is not sufficient to cover their total costs of production, so that sooner or later the number of firms producing the commodity will be depleted by bankruptcy. There may

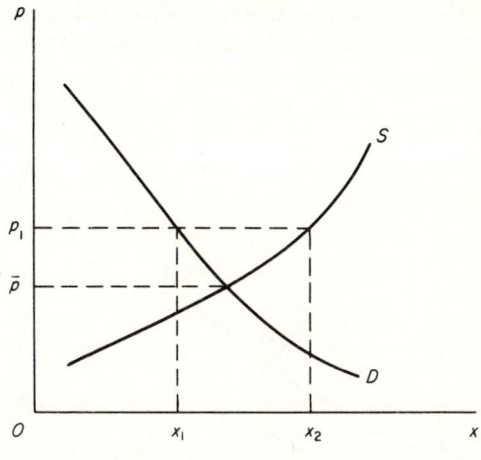

Figure 6.3.2

be political, social, strategic or humanitarian reasons why this is deemed undesirable by the government. To prevent it, the price may be fixed or 'pegged' above its equilibrium level – say at p_1. At the legal minimum price p_1, the firms will plan to produce x_2 in each period, and this will exceed the planned purchases of consumers by x_1x_2. The individual firms, whose financial straits led the government to fix the price at p_1 per unit, will not be able to accumulate stocks at a rate of x_1x_2 per period: if left to themselves, they will offer to sell at lower prices in an effort to dispose of their total output in each period and the price will fall to $\bar{p}$. To avoid this, the firms may be required to restrict their planned outputs in each period to x_1. Or the government may set up a central agency to buy $x_1 x_2$ in each period at the legal minimum price, and destroy it (as happened with Brazilian coffee in the inter-war years), or store it (as now happens in the United States with many agricultural commodities). If the latter, it may be hoped that the demand for the commodity will rise (or the supply of it will fall) in the future, so that the price p_1 will fall short of the then equilibrium level. If this should happen, the accumulated stocks could then be run down to meet the 'excess demand' for the product at the legal minimum price.

2. *Taxes:* Let us suppose that before the imposition of a tax the conditions of demand and supply are as illustrated by $D_1 D_1$ and $S_1 S_1$ curves respectively in Figure 6.3.3, and that the equilibrium price is $\bar{p}$ and sales and purchases per period are each equal to $\bar{x}$. Let us now suppose that the government decides to exact a fixed sum (say, three pence) from each seller for each unit that he sells – that is, that a *specific* tax is imposed. The immediate effect of the tax will be to shift the supply curve due northwards through a distance equal to the tax per unit.

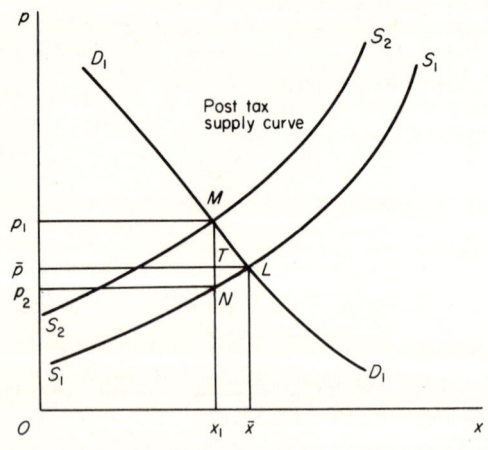

Figure 6.3.3

Each seller, given his costs of production, will only plan to produce (say) 100 units if he expects to receive, say, 10 pence per unit: if the government now exacts three pence for each unit sold, sellers will require thirteen pence per unit if they are to continue producing 100 units in each period, for only then will sellers be left with the 10 per cent per unit that they must get if their profits are to be at a maximum at this output. After the imposition of the tax, then, the equilibrium price of the commodity will rise to p_1 and the planned sales and purchases in each period will fall to x_1. By comparing the initial equilibrium (L) with the post-tax equilibrium (M) in Figure 6.3.3, we can measure the effects of the tax. Buyers now pay $p_1\bar{p}$ ($= MT$) per unit more for $\bar{x}_1\bar{x}$ ($= LT$) less of the commodity; sellers now receive TN less per unit for their lower sales of x_1 in each period. In the post-tax equilibrium, buyers spend Ox_1Mp_1 per period; of this sum sellers pass on p_2NMp_1 to the government and they are left with Ox_1Np_2. In terms of the figure, of the tax of MN per unit that has been imposed, we may say that MT is 'paid' by buyers and TN 'paid' by sellers.

When the tax is a relatively small proportion of the price of the commodity, it can be shown that the ratio of MT to TN is equal to the ratio of the elasticity of supply (e_s in the range LN of the supply curve) to the price elasticity of demand (e_d) (in the range LM of the demand curve). In Figure 6.3.3,

$$e_s = \frac{x_1\bar{x}}{O\bar{x}} \bigg/ \frac{p_2\bar{p}}{O\bar{p}}$$

and

$$e_d = \frac{x_1\bar{x}}{O\bar{x}} \bigg/ \frac{\bar{p}p_1}{O\bar{p}}$$

Therefore, $e_s/e_d = MT/TN$. If we know these relevant elasticities, we could predict the relative impact of the tax on price and output: the less elastic is demand and supply, the less will output fall and the more will price rise; the more elastic is demand and supply, the more will output fall and the less will price rise. This can be shown as follows:

Let t be the tax per unit: then $t = MT + TN$.

Now, for MT we can write $e_s/e_d \cdot TN$.

We then get:

$$t = \frac{e_s}{e_d} \cdot TN + TN = TN \frac{e_s + e_d}{e_d}.$$

Hence

$$TN = t\left(\frac{e_d}{e_s + e_d}\right).$$

Similarly: $$MT = t\left(\frac{e_s}{e_s + e_d}\right).$$

If $e_d = 0$, then $TN = 0$, and $MT = t$.
If $e_s = 0$, then $TN = t$, and $MT = 0$.
If $e_s = $ infinity, then $TN = 0$, and $MT = t$.
If $e_d = $ infinity, then $TN = t$, and $MT = 0$.

In presenting demand and supply analysis and in examining some of its more obvious applications, we have tacitly assumed that in each period planned production was identical with planned sales, and planned purchases the same as planned consumption. Consequently, in our figures the flows of production, sales, purchases and consumption were equal to one another in each period. If the commodity can be stored cheaply, this assumption is untenable, and when we drop it, other patterns of price adjustment than those we have already examined become possible. By way of example, let us suppose that there is a rise in the demand for some commodity and that its price starts to rise. We shall suppose also that this creates expectations in the minds of buyers and sellers that the price is going to continue to rise in the future. Since the commodity can be stored cheaply, these expectations will cause a change in the distribution over time of purchases and sales. Buyers may still desire an even flow of consumption in each period, but they will plan to concentrate their purchases in the present when the commodity is relatively cheap, at the expense of the future when they believe that it will be relatively dear. Purchases will exceed consumption now so that buyers accumulate stocks; planned purchases will fall short of expected consumption in the future, when these stocks are being depleted. Sellers will plan to maintain or increase production and reduce sales now; in this way, they will build up stocks that can be used to supplement current production in the future, when (or if) their expectations are fulfilled. Thus, if price is expected to rise in the future, the increase in present purchases and the curtailment of present sales will tend to raise the price more quickly now, and so justify these expectations. The reduction in purchases and the increase in sales in later periods will arrest the rate of increase in prices – indeed, it may even cause the price to begin falling and so create expectations of further price reductions.

If all this was initiated by a permanent rise in demand, it is probable that the price will ultimately settle at its new and higher equilibrium level. The path by which the price reaches this level may be similar to that shown in Figure 6.1.6. Such paths are the more likely the less aware are buyers and sellers of the nature and strength of the true cause of the initial rise in price, namely, in our example, a permanent rise in demand.

6.4 Price-Determination: Long-Run

In this chapter so far, we have confined our attention to the short-run. If the demand for a commodity rises (or falls), the firms who are producing it are limited in their responses by the possession of fixed inputs. As the past commitments that fix the quantities of certain inputs at their disposal fall due for renewal, firms will be able to make a more complete adjustment to the new demand conditions. In the remainder of this chapter we shall examine the nature of these adjustments and describe how they are likely to affect relative prices.

In the short-run, the output of the product can only be varied within the limits set by the fixed plants of existing firms. In the long-run, the output of the product can be varied by the firms who are already producing it, increasing or reducing their scale of operations by changing the nature and size of their 'fixed' inputs; it can be varied also by new firms entering the industry, or by firms that are already there, retiring. The choices facing a manager who is planning to enter or remain in an industry are summarised in his planning curve. Each manager will have a planning curve for each industry that he might enter. Given the price at which he expects to be able to sell each product, and his knowledge of the methods by which it might be produced and his expectations of the prices of the inputs these require, he can deduce the maximum profits per period he could get were he to decide to make it. He will decide to produce that product – that is, to enter that industry – that promises him the *maximum maximorum* of profits. The same choice will face a manager who has rid himself of all past commitments in an industry, for he can choose whether he will remain there or set up in another industry.

Let us now suppose that the demand for, and short-run supply of, some product are as illustrated by the D_1D_1 and S_1S_1 curves in Figure 6.4.1, and that at the price $\bar{p}$ and output $\bar{x}$ there is long-run equilibrium – that is, were the price to continue at this level, no new firm would desire to enter this industry and no existing firm would plan to leave it or vary the scale of its operations in any way. We shall presently describe how a position of long-run equilibrium may be reached. Let us suppose that there is a sudden but permanent rise in the demand for this product to D_2D_2, and that the demand is generally expected to remain indefinitely at its new level. We shall assume also that no change is expected to occur in the conditions of demand and supply in any other industry. In the short period, in which no change in either the number or size of firms is possible, the price of the product will tend towards p_1. The level towards which the price will tend in the long-run will depend on the elasticity of the long-run supply curve. The path by which the price will move towards its long-run equilibrium level will depend on the expectations that each manager has about the price of the product, and the prices of the inputs needed to produce it, when he is making his long-run decision.

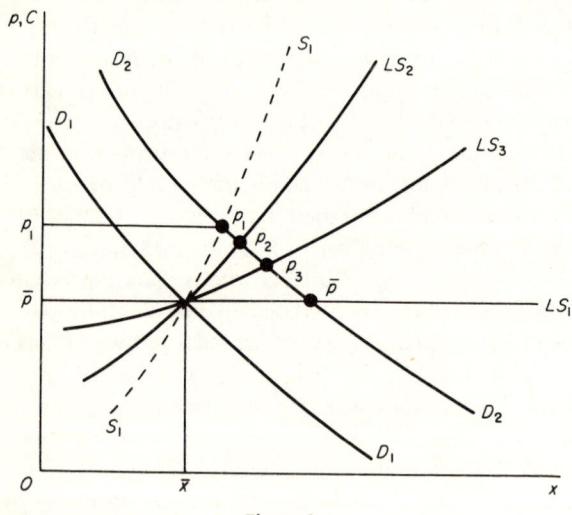

Figure 6.4.1

We have shown (p. 118) that the long-run supply curve of a firm will be perfectly elastic until the minimum point of its planning curve is reached and that it will then rise, the rising portion coinciding with its long-run marginal cost curve. Given the prices of the relevant inputs, the elasticity of the rising part of the firm's long-run supply curve will depend on (a) the physical production possibilities, and (b) the possibility of 'diseconomies' of large-scale management – that is, the possibility that as the rate of output is increased, the problem of co-ordinating the activities of the greater variety and quantity of inputs that are required will tend to raise unit costs of production. The elasticity of the long-run supply curve of the product depends not only on these but also on the relationship between the minimum points of the planning curves of the different managers who might enter the industry. If there is a very large number of managers who might remain, or start work, in this industry in the long-run; if they all have the same expectations about the prices of inputs and if the minimum expected profits required to induce each to enter this industry are the same; and if they are all equally knowledgeable about production possibilities and equally competent as co-ordinators, then their planning curves will all be identical with one another. When their long-run supply curves are added together, the resulting long-run supply curve of the product will be perfectly elastic, i.e. will appear as LS_1 in Figure 6.4.1, and the price in the long-run will return to its initial equilibrium level, $\bar{p}$.[1]

If the actual or potential managers in the industry are not equally knowledgeable about production possibilities, or if they differ from one another in the ability to make decisions and determine policy, or if the minimum expected profits needed to induce each to enter the industry are not the same for all of them, then each will have a different planning curve. The planning curves may differ in that their minimum points come at different levels or at different outputs. The minimum point of a manager's planning curve may be at a relatively high price because (a) he is unaware of some methods by which the product might be produced; or (b) he is less able than some of his fellows to co-ordinate effectively; or (c) he requires relatively large profits to attract him to this industry. The minimum point of a manager's planning curve is roughly explained, therefore, by his relative 'efficiency' in the industry to which the curve relates and by his relative 'efficiency' in the other activities in which he might indulge: the less is the former and the greater the latter, the higher will it be, and vice versa. In these circumstances, the long-run industry supply curve will be less than perfectly elastic, and the level towards which the price of the product will tend in the long-run will be between $\bar{p}$ and p_1. In general, we may say that the supply curve will be the more elastic, and the price will ultimately be nearer to $\bar{p}$, the smaller are the differences between the minimum points of the individual planning curves; and the greater are these differences, the less elastic will be the supply curve, and the

---

[1] The rising part of the firm's long-run supply curves will only begin affecting the shape of the long-run industry supply curve at an infinitely large rate of output.

nearer will be the long-run equilibrium price to p_1. These conclusions are illustrated by the curves LS_3 and LS_2 respectively in Figure 6.4.1.

The points p_2, p_3 and $\bar{p}$ on the respective LS curves represent long-run equilibria, for at each of these prices (on the appropriate assumption about the elasticity of supply) the quantity of the product that consumers plan to buy would be the same as the quantity that the firms plan to produce and sell in each period. At each of these prices, each firm's output would be at the level that promised it maximum profits, and there would be no incentive for any new firm to enter the industry or for any existing firm to leave it.

The path that price follows when moving to its long-run equilibrium level will depend primarily on each manager's expectations about the prices at which he hopes to be able to sell his product and buy his inputs during the ensuing long period. The time taken for price to traverse this path will depend mainly on how quickly long-run decisions can be made in terms of calendar or clock time. Initially, we shall suppose that each manager expects the price at which the commodity is now being sold, and the prices at which inputs can now be bought, to rule indefinitely, and that long-run decisions can be implemented quickly.[1] If the industry is in long-run equilibrium at $\bar{p}$ in Figure 6.4.2, and if there is a rise in demand for the product to D_2D_2, the price will soon rise to p_1, the short-run equilibrium. As each firm makes its long-run plan on the assumption that p_1 will rule indefinitely, the planned output per period will rise to p_1M_1 when these plans have been implemented. This exceeds purchases by consumers at p_1, so that the price will tend to fall, and as it falls, each firm will contract its output along its short-run supply curve. The price will therefore fall to p_2, where S_2S_2, the new short-run supply curve, cuts D_2D_2. If each firm again supposes that the price of the product will remain at p_2, together they will plan a long-run output of p_2M_3 per period. This will fall short of the planned purchases at the price p_2, and the price will tend to rise. As price rises, each firm will expand output along its short-run supply curve, so that the price will tend towards the level p_3, where S_3S_3, the short-run supply curve of the industry when all firms have the fixed

---

[1] A long-run decision may be implemented quickly if time is measured in days, hours or weeks; yet once implemented, the long-run decision may bind the firm for a long period of calendar time. It is probable that this assumption is reasonably true of retail trading, and of many industries that supply personal services. It may also be true in agriculture: thus, a farmer may plan in autumn to devote all his land to growing oats in the ensuing crop year, and this decision, once made, will bind him for the ensuing calendar year.

plant, etc., appropriate to the point M_3 on the long-run supply curve, cuts D_2D_2, and so on. The figure shows that there will be a convergent fluctuation towards the long-run equilibrium price p_n, and that, given the elasticities of the D_2D_2 and LS curves, the rate at which price converges on p_n will be the greater the more elastic are the short-run supply curves.[1]

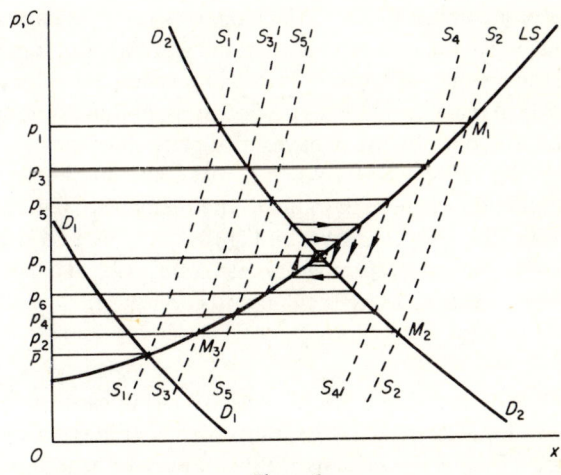

Figure 6.4.2

We would not expect to find the price of a product actually fluctuating in this way, and for three reasons. First, as many long-runs as there are 'turns' in the 'spiral' must elapse before price reaches its long-run equilibrium level, and during this time it is likely that there will be changes in demand, techniques, input prices and the alternative opportunities open to managers. Second, even if there are no changes in the conditions of demand and supply, each manager is likely to revise his belief that the price will remain at its present level. Each manager will know that, while the price of the product lies beyond his control, its level will depend on the total output of the product. In making a long-run plan, each manager may be aware that others have made, or may suspect that others may make, similar plans, and that the

---

[1] In the long-run we are unlikely to get either a divergent or a continuous fluctuation because (a) the long-run supply curve will probably be fairly elastic; (b) even if LS is less elastic at each price than D_2D_2, the short-run supply curves always have some elasticity, and their influence will probably overcome the tendency towards divergent or continuous fluctuations.

price of the product will probably fall in the future. In deciding upon what plant to build he may therefore assume that the price of the product, when the plant is in operation, will be somewhere below p_1. Third, even if neither of these reasons is operative, the price might nevertheless move more or less directly towards p_n, for long-run decisions are likely to be implemented *seriatim* rather than simultaneously. When the demand for the product rises, some existing firms whose past commitments are lapsing, or some firms new to the industry, may make long-run plans. As these plans are put into effect, the price of the product will start falling. By that time, other firms may find it possible to make their long-run decisions, and in doing so they will be influenced both by the behaviour of price since the rise in demand and by its existing level. As they make and implement their plans, there will be a further fall in price. In other words, it may take a very long time for the *LS* curve in Figure 6.4.2 to become fully operative, and while it is becoming operative, the price of the product will be falling towards p_n along the demand curve D_2D_2.

6.5 Long-Run Demand and Supply Analysis: Applications

Demand and supply analysis, in the long-run as in the short-run, has two main uses: first, it provides us with a number of headings under which we may meaningfully classify the causes of changes in relative prices; and second, it helps us (though to a very modest extent) to predict the ultimate effects on relative prices of present events, like a growing demand for the product or the discovery of a new method of producing it.

Let us suppose that during the past year or so the price of eggs has continuously fallen as compared with the prices of other things. The analysis of this chapter tells us that the explanation must lie in changes in demand and supply. The price may have declined, for example, because demand has been falling, with existing firms contracting their outputs along their short-run supply curves; or because demand rose some time ago and the producers have been adjusting along their long-run supply curves; or it may be that the explanation lies in changes in the conditions of supply, which have caused rightward shifts in either the short-run or long-run supply curves, with demand conditions remaining unaltered. Our knowledge of the economic history of the past few years may tell us whether or not demand has altered. If we feel that demand has not changed, and if, in addition, we observe that the number of firms and their size (as measured by the amount of 'fixed' inputs each employs) have remained more or less the same, we can conclude that the fall in price is largely due to rightward shifts in the short-run supply curve; and we have already shown how the analyses of Chapter 2 can help us to discover why this may have happened. If demand has not changed, but if the number and/or size of the firms producing eggs have risen, then the explanation of the fall in price is probably to be found in a rightward shift in the long-run supply curve. The analysis of Chapter 4 provides us with a classification of the reasons why this might have happened: the determinants of long-run supply are (a) the methods or techniques of production; (b) the prices of the inputs that are required; (c) the firms' objectives. The discovery of a new method of production will lower the minimum point of each firm's planning curve and probably move it to the right, for the urge to seek new methods of production springs from the desire to reduce costs. A fall in the price of inputs will have the same general effect. It may be that the input whose 'price' has fallen is management; this would happen if there were a fall in the maximum profits that managers could expect to earn in industries other than egg production. Thus, if for some reason other agricultural activities become less profitable, the 'price' that each manager would want for his services in egg production would fall.

Long-run demand and supply analysis is more useful in clarifying hindsight than in informing foresight. If the government decides to subsidise the production of some commodity, we can make a fairly firm prediction of the short-run consequences: the short-run supply curve will fall vertically through a distance equal to the subsidy per unit, as in Figure 6.5.1; the price that consumers pay will fall from $\bar{p}$ to p_1; the price that sellers receive will rise from $\bar{p}$ to p_4 (= p_1 plus the subsidy per unit of $p_1 p_4$), and sales and purchases will rise from $\bar{x}$ to x_1. Our prediction may be quite accurate, for the short-run, which we have defined in terms of operational time (that is, as time during which certain changes can or cannot take place), can usually be related to a short period of calendar time or clock time, and the shorter the calendar time the greater the likelihood that demand and supply will not alter. In forecasting the more immediate effects on price and output of a subsidy, we may then be justified in assuming that the new equilibrium is reached by firms and consumers 'moving' along their existing demand and supply curves.

If before the subsidy is introduced, the industry is in long-run equilibrium at the price $\bar{p}$ and the output $\bar{x}$, and if in the light of the existing conditions the long-run supply curve is LS, we may deduce (from a mechanical application of the analysis) that, if the subsidy continues, the price paid by consumers will ultimately fall to p_2 per unit and the output per period will rise to x_2, with firms receiving p_3 (= p_2

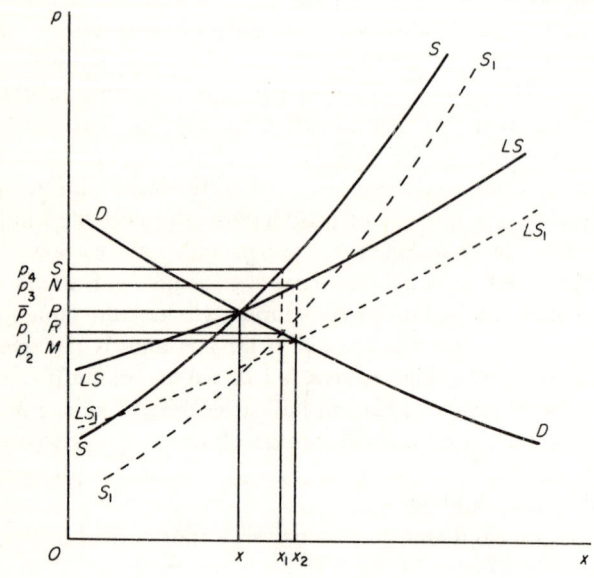

SS = Short-run supply curve before subsidy
S_1S_1 = Short-run supply curve after subsidy
LS = Long-run supply curve before subsidy
LS_1 = Long-run supply curve after subsidy
$p_1p_4 = p_2p_3$ = Subsidy per unit

Figure 6.5.1

plus the subsidy p_2p_3) per unit. Events will only confirm this prediction if all other things remain unchanged while the adjustments in supply are taking place. The long-run adjustments, however, may require months or years, and in the meantime the determinants of demand and supply will almost certainly alter: long-run changes, for example, may be occurring in other industries and the changes in the prices of their products will affect the conditions of demand and supply for the commodity in which we are interested. It would be wrong to conclude, however, that long-run demand and supply analysis is valueless as an aid to prediction. In the first place, it helps us to deduce the ultimate effects on price of any once-for-all change in the conditions of demand and supply, *ceteris paribus*. In the second place, while it seldom helps us to foresee what other changes will occur in the planning data of firms and consumers as the adjustments to some initial change are proceeding, it does provide an analytical framework within which these changes can be interpreted. We can, therefore, modify our initial prediction as events unfold.

However, not all changes in the determinants of long-run supply are equally unpredictable: there are some that we, as economists, might foresee, even though no firm in the industry may take account of them when laying its long-run plans. Economic history suggests that most industries that have expanded have at least two things in common. First, the development of new methods of production, and of new variants of the product, usually proceeds *pari passu* with the expansion of the industry; and second, that as the industry expands the prices of some of its inputs tend to rise, while the prices of other inputs tend to fall.

During the last two centuries, the rate of technological development has been increasing more or less continuously in most industries. In most developed economies, there is probably a general expectation that the flow of new techniques and of new products will continue in the future, and this is almost as strong as the general expectation that the flow of foodstuffs from the farms, or cars from the factories, will continue. This expectation would not, by itself, destroy the analytical and prognostic value of the concept of the long-run supply curve, for if all new developments were 'acts of God', or if they appeared from outside the industry, the long-run supply curve would remain as a useful summary of managers' intentions. Each manager would make his plans on the basis of present techniques, and he would revise them as best he could, as and when these random or stochastic developments occurred. In practice, however, technological research is increasingly being carried out by firms, and the 'production' of new techniques and of new knowledge is planned in the same way and on the same principles as the production of more tangible products. The planning horizon for new methods and new products may be longer than that for long-run plans of the kind we have already described. And the choice of a 'research' plan differs more in degree than in kind from the choice of a long-run production plan as described in Chapter 4: the 'outputs' are less tangible and less predictable, but their 'volume' varies roughly with the quantities and the kinds of inputs (research workers and specialised equipment) that are used. We may then think of the actual long-run plan that a manager makes (especially if he is engaged in newer industries like plastics, telecommunications, laser technology, etc.) as being the compromise, which he considers potentially the most profitable, between the exploitation of existing methods and products and the quest for new methods and products.

Enough has been said to show that in many industries managers will seldom devote all their energies to 'moving along' their long-run supply curves as we have defined them; some part of their resources will be devoted to shifting these curves. Our long-run supply curves assume that all other things remain equal, but managers will devote some effort to making some of them unequal. Conceptually, there is a choice: first, we may treat each firm as being a multi-product firm in the long-run, planning to produce both its existing products by existing methods and new methods, or new variants; or second, we may view research as being the quest for a new input, the demand for which could be described in the same way as we shall later describe the demand for a machine or a factory building; or third, maintain our definition of the long-run supply curve and assume that technological progress is continuously tending to shift it to the right. We shall choose the last of these, for the present stage of knowledge about the causes of technical progress makes it almost impossible to posit the functional relationships that either of the other two would require. The long-run supply curve, then, shows us the long-run plan that a manager would make at a point in time at each price at which he expects to be able to sell his product; technical progress means that at each successive point in time, the long-run supply curve will, *ceteris paribus*, be further to the right.

6.6 Long-Run Supply: Changing Input Prices

As an industry expands, not only may new techniques appear but the price that each firm must pay for some inputs may rise, while the price it has to pay for other inputs falls. Most industries begin with a few firms producing a relatively small output. They may each produce the specialised equipment they require, or have it made to order by firms in other industries. In either case, the relatively small demand for the machine confines the firm that makes it to the production possibilities that lie at the western end of the relevant planning curve, so that the

The Determination of Relative Product Prices

cost per machine will be relatively high, and its price will be relatively high also. As the industry grows, the demand for the specialised equipment and services that it requires will rise also: the firm (or firms) that makes the machines, for example, can then 'move along' its planning curve (assuming no change in techniques, input prices, etc.); the cost per machine will fall as the number produced rises, and hence its relative price will tend to fall also. Reductions in input prices that come about in this way are called *pecuniary external economies*; they are so called because they are external to each firm that demands these inputs. If industry A expands, and if, as a consequence, the price of one of its inputs that is produced by industry B falls, this is an external economy for each firm in industry A; but it is the result of economies that are internal to each firm in industry B, for the rise in the demand for its product makes it profitable for each firm there to 'move along' its planning curve towards its minimum point.[1]

Examples of external economies spring easily to mind. As an industry expands, it may become profitable for new firms to specialise in collecting and disseminating market information, or in marketing the industry's product, or in supplying it with consultant services. If the expanding industry is localised geographically, the external economies may be more striking: its skilled labour may be trained at local technical colleges (for at each college there may be enough students to make the employment of a full-time teacher worth while), and the public utility industries may evolve with it, being continuously adapted to its needs. In general, the external economies will be the greater the less are the differences between the products of the firms that enjoy them, and the more standardised are the inputs that are being demanded from other industries.

If the demand for industry B's product is initially large enough to enable each firm to produce at an output that lies at or beyond the minimum point of its planning curve, then when industry A expands,

---

[1] In the situation described above, we cannot assume, as we have been doing, that no single firm can affect the price at which its product is being sold. This assumption will only be valid if, *inter alia*, there is a very large number of firms producing the same product. This clearly cannot be the case initially in the machine industry in the above example before the rise in the demand for its product; for if there had been a large number of firms then, there would already have been a strong incentive for each to expand output and so reduce cost. Initially, then, the quantity of industry B's product demanded per period by industry A, must have been less than the cost-minimising output for a firm in B, with the existing techniques, etc. It may be, of course, that the expansion in A is so great that the quantity of B's output demanded per period is large enough to support a large number of firms, each enjoying its internal economies.

the price that it must pay for the input it buys from *B* will, *ceteris paribus*, remain the same if *B*'s long-run supply curve is perfectly elastic, and rise if it has any degree of inelasticity. The tendency for the price of *B*'s product to rise may, as we saw earlier, be offset by the development of new techniques of production. As industry *A* expands, the price that each firm must pay for the labour-service it uses, may rise also, and the extent of the rise in price will depend, as we shall see later, on the elasticity of supply of each kind of labour-service to industry *A*. The labour costs per unit of output in industry *A* may rise, not only because each firm must pay a higher price per unit for labour-service of the same quality, but because, while the price remains the same, the quality of the labour-service that can be hired falls. Increases in price that occur for these reasons are called *pecuniary external diseconomies*. They are so called because they are external to each firm in industry *A*: the rise in the price of the input is not caused by the expansion of any single firm in *A* but is rather the consequence of the expansion of the whole industry.

Analytically, the problems introduced by external economies and diseconomies are of the same order as those implicit in the discussion about firms planning for the long-run on the assumption that the price of the product would remain at its present level indefinitely. There, the ultimate effect of all firms implementing their plans was seen to be to reduce the price of the product. Similarly, if each firm plans on the assumption that the price of each input will remain the same over the long-run, and if there are external economies or diseconomies, the ultimate effect of all firms implementing their plans will be a change in input prices. In both these cases, when the firms have put their long-run plans into effect, the actual profit which they will be earning in each period will differ both from that which they had expected to earn before their plans were implemented, and from the maximum profit they now feel they could earn were they to plan anew on the basis of existing input and product prices. There will ensue a period of adjustment and re-adjustment culminating, after many long periods have elapsed, in a new equilibrium in which all their expectations are being fulfilled.

6.7   Short-Run and Long-Run Demand

Thus far, in analysing changes in relative prices, we have assumed sudden and permanent changes in demand, and sought to discover the

The Determination of Relative Product Prices 151

pattern of supply adjustments over time, and its consequences. We have split time into three operational periods: first, the market period in which no revision whatsoever can be made in the output plan in response to changes in the firm's expectations of the selling price of the product; second, the short-run, during which the output plan can be revised within the limits imposed by past commitments whose tangible embodiments are fixed inputs; and third, the long-run, for which virtually no inputs are fixed, so that the fullest possible adjustment can be planned to changes in the expected selling price of the product. We have seen that if demand rises, price will rise to its highest level in the market period, that it will fall somewhat in the short period, and that it will fall still further in the long period, the other things appropriate to each operational period remaining equal.

We have not so far sought patterns in the demand adjustments that occur as time passes. We shall do this now very briefly, for both the concepts and the analysis are analogous to those used for supply. We may define the market period for consumers in one of two ways. First, we may suppose that during the market period the quantity of each good that the consumer plans to buy cannot be altered: on this definition, the consumer's demand for each good that he plans to buy will be perfectly inelastic, so that if, on balance, prices are higher than the consumer expected them to be when making his plans, he will spend more than he intended during the market period, and save less, and vice versa. Second, we may assume that during the market period the planned expenditure on each good is unalterable: on this definition, the consumer's demand for each good will have unit elasticity, and if, in the market period, the actual prices are different from the prices the consumer expected to have to pay when making his plans, the consumer will enjoy lower utility than he hoped.

The consumer, like the firm, may have past commitments that limit the extent to which his purchase plan can be revised while they bind it. The consumer may have insured his life and contracted to pay the premiums in quarterly instalments, or he may be buying a television set or a motor-car on hire purchase and paying a fixed sum each month to the seller. In either case, the consumer will have certain fixed expenditures (the analogue of the firm's fixed costs) in each period. If the relative prices of one or more of the goods that he buys should change, the consumer will be limited to the combination of goods that can be bought with his planned consumption expenditure, less his fixed expenses. Some adjustment in either the planned purchases of each 'variable' good, or in the planned expenditure on it (or in both), will now be practicable, so that we would expect the consumer's demand curve for these goods to be rather more elastic in this short-run than they were in the market period. When the consumer has rid himself of all past commitments like hire-purchase agreements, he may plan a full adjustment of his purchase plan to the new pattern of relative prices. For most goods and services, we would normally expect the consumer's long-run demand curve to be more elastic than his short-run demand curve.[1]

The influence of demand on the behaviour of prices over time is illustrated in Figure 6.7.1. LD and LS are the long-run demand and supply curves respectively, and we shall suppose that initially the price is at the long-run equilibrium level $\bar{p}$. Let us now suppose that there is a sudden and permanent fall in the long-run supply to LS_1. If D_m is the 'market-period' demand curve, the immediate consequence will be a rise in price to p_1. As consumers make their short-period adjustments, the short-period demand curve D_s will become effective, and the price will fall to p_2. As their long-period demand becomes operative – i.e. as the LD curve becomes the locus of alternative purchase plans open to consumers – the price will fall further to p_3. The use of the concept of long-run demand to predict the ultimate consequences of present events is subject to the same limitations as were described on pages 144–8. We might combine Figures 6.4.1. and 6.7.1 to illustrate the effects of long-run demand and supply adjustments on price behaviour over time. If we did so, we would have to be very careful in

---

[1] The analogy between long-run demand and long-run supply decisions might be pressed further, though to do so would provide more analytical excitement than insight. We might, for example, classify the consumption possibilities that are open to the consumer when making a long-run decision into 'standards of living' or 'methods of consumption'. The goods and services that the consumer might buy (his inputs) will vary both in size (partially true of houses) and in kind (bicycle and motor-car, ice and a refrigerator, coal fires and oil-fired central heating), from one 'standard of living' or 'technique of consumption' to another. Each standard of living will have its own set of 'fixed' inputs, like a house, a car, club membership, school fees, etc., and these will probably bulk the larger, the 'higher' is the standard. The level of satisfaction that the consumer would enjoy can be varied within each standard by varying the quantities of the 'variable' inputs (current consumption goods) that are combined with the appropriate 'fixed' inputs. Given the expected prices of all inputs, we could calculate the level and behaviour of the planned total expenditure (both 'fixed' and 'variable') per period within each standard of living. Given the consumer's expectations of his planned expenditure in each period and of how he expects this to behave, he will choose that standard of living that promises the maximum satisfaction per period. If the consumer's satisfaction, like the firm's revenue, could be cardinally measured, the analogy might be pressed even further.

The Determination of Relative Product Prices 153

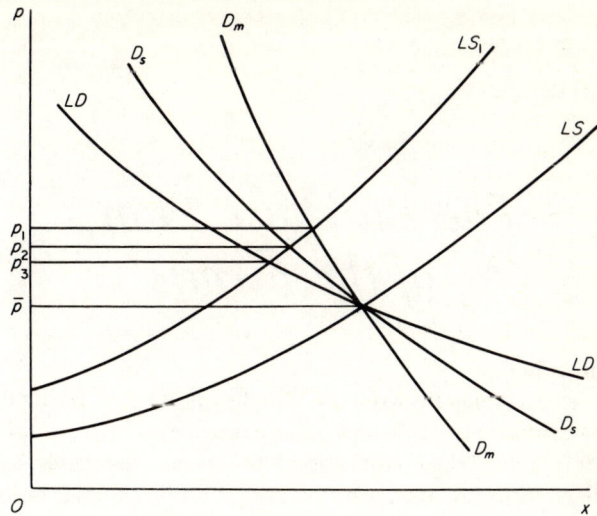

Figure 6.7.1

interpreting our results, for the calendar time required for demand adjustments to take place may differ markedly from that required for supply adjustments.

7
The Purchase Plan of the Firm

7.0 Introduction

So far, we have generally assumed that the input prices facing the firm were given, although we observed that a firm's expansion could lead to a change in input prices (see Section 6.6). Taking input prices as given, determined by mechanisms we have not yet investigated, enabled us to develop a basic theory explaining why product prices change in relation to each other, and how they respond to given changes in input prices. It is now time to reverse the assumptions and take product prices as given and analyse the determination of input prices. This chapter investigates the *demand* for inputs. Chapter 8 looks at the *supply* of those inputs provided by consumers, and Chapter 9 at the overall determination of input prices. Chapter 10 analyses the simultaneous determination of product prices and input prices.

7.1 Short-Run Demand for One Variable Input

The first case we consider assumes that only input is variable. This means that the firm is constrained to the area below $\bar{K}\bar{K}$ in Figure 7.1.1 which shows the familiar production isoquant map. We saw that such a situation defined a set of 'product curves' (see Section 3.6) repeated in Figure 7.1.2. The shape of these curves is determined by the law of non-proportional returns which operates because of the fixity of the input K. These curves relate *physical output* to the variable input L — that is, the vertical axis is measured in tonnes or yards, or numbers of cars, television sets or whatever. Accordingly, to remind us of this fact we relabel the curves *total physical product* (TPP), *average physical product* (APP) and *marginal physical product* (MPP). We can in fact translate these concepts into revenue concepts. But we must be careful to note two possible situations.

The Purchase Plan of the Firm

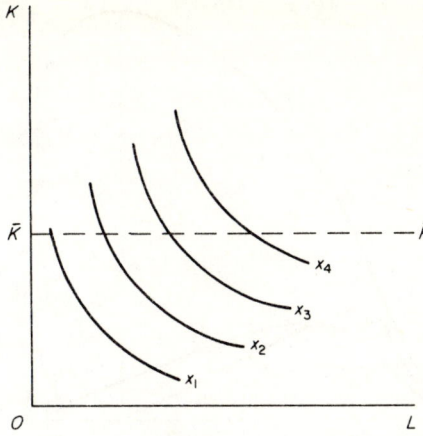

Figure 7.1.1

First, if product prices do not change as output is expanded, the extra revenue obtained by employing an extra unit of L is simply

$$MPP_L \cdot p_x = \text{Marginal Revenue Product } (MRP).$$

In this case product price is constant for the firm – that is, the firm must be a price-taker. It must be operating under conditions of perfect competition.

The second situation relates to the case where the demand curve facing the firm slopes downwards. This will be the situation when the firm is a price-maker. The equation for marginal revenue product is now

$$MPP_L \cdot MR_x = MRP.$$

Sometimes the distinction between the two is emphasised by calling the MRP, in the context where product prices are given, the *value of the marginal product*. But since price = marginal revenue in the price-taker situation, it is correct to call both of them marginal revenue product.

For the remainder of this chapter, and in keeping with the analysis so far, we work with the price-taker situation, so that the first equation for MRP is relevant. Consequently, the curves in Figure 7.1.2 can be relabelled TRP, ARP and MRP respectively. Figure 7.1.3 does this concentrating on the ARP and MRP curves only. We can now demonstrate that the part of the MRP curve below the ARP curve in Figure 7.1.3 is, in fact, the firm's demand curve for the variable input L.

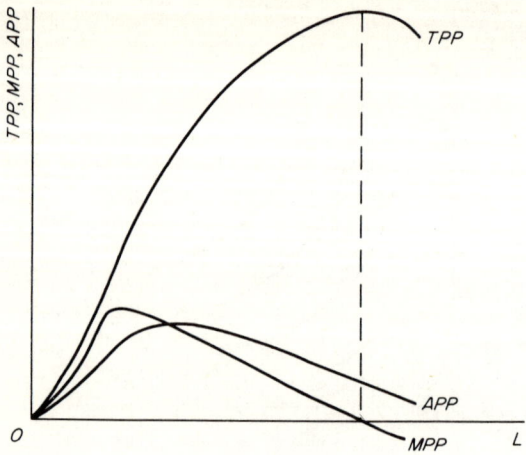

Figure 7.1.2

Suppose that the firm is faced with a price per unit of labour of W_1 – that is, the ruling wage-rate is W_1. The MRP curve shows the extra revenue the firm will obtain by employing one extra unit of labour. The extra cost of employing that labour is, of course, W_1 (assuming wages are not affected by the numbers employed). If the firm is a profit-maximiser it will not employ extra labour unless the addition to revenue from so doing is greater than the extra cost incurred – i.e. unless $MRP > W_1$. Consequently, all points on the MRP curve to the left

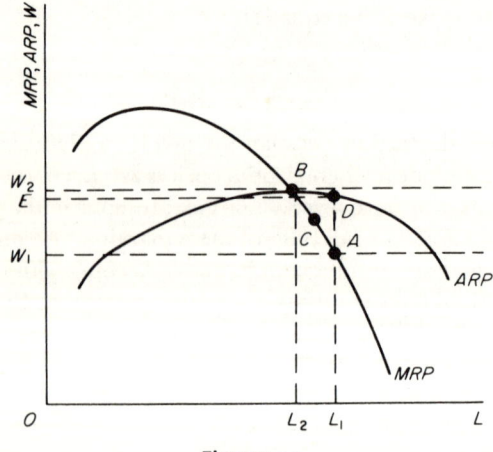

Figure 7.1.3

of point A in Figure 7.1.3 are, potentially, points at which extra labour is willingly employed. If the wage-rate is W_1, however, a point like C cannot be an equilibrium for the firm: by employing extra labour and moving from C to A the firm can increase profits (since MRP is still above W_1 between C and A). Similarly, the firm will not settle at points to the right of A if the wage-rate is W_1 since $MRP < W_1$. Point A, where $MRP = W_1$, is therefore an equilibrium for the firm.

In fact, the relationship between MRP and W is nothing more than the requirement that price = marginal cost for the price-taker profit-maximising firm. This is easily shown. We can write

$$MRP = \frac{\Delta x \cdot P_x}{\Delta L}$$

where the notation is as before: Δx is the change in output, ΔL the change in the labour input, and P_x is the product price. Similarly, if only labour can be varied, we have

$$W = \frac{\Delta C}{\Delta L}$$

where W is the wage-rate, and ΔC is the change in total cost. The condition established above for equilibrium was

$$MRP = W$$

which can now be expanded to

$$\frac{\Delta x \cdot P_x}{\Delta L} = \frac{\Delta C}{\Delta L}$$

which, on cancellation and rearrangement, is

$$P_x = \frac{\Delta C}{\Delta x}.$$

But $\Delta C/\Delta x$ is the expression for marginal cost. The requirement that $MRP = W$ is therefore another way of expressing the requirement that $P = MC$.

Obviously then, if the wage-rate changed, the new equilibrium for the firm would be where the new wage-rate cuts the MRP curve. The firm's response to a change in W is therefore to move along the MRP curve. We conclude that the MRP curve is the firm's demand curve for the variable input.

However, not *all* of the MRP curve is relevant. At a wage-rate of W_1 the firm employs L_1 of labour in Figure 7.1.3. The total variable costs of the firm in this situation are OL_1AW_1 (that is, the amount of labour employed multiplied by the wage-rate). Total revenue is OL_1DE, which is found by looking at the average revenue product curve. Consequently, the area W_1ADE measures the firm's fixed costs and any profits. For the moment, we assume that the profits earned are just sufficient to keep the firm in business, so that we can treat the entire area W_1ADE as 'fixed' costs. If we now repeat the exercise for wage-rate W_2, we see that total variable costs are OL_2BW_2. Total revenue is also OL_2BW_2 since the MRP curve cuts the ARP curve at B. Hence the revenue available to cover fixed costs is zero: the firm only just meets its variable cost charges. The firm may believe that business conditions will pick up and be prepared to tolerate just covering variable costs in the short-run. Certainly, he will not be prepared to continue production if he cannot meet even variable costs in the short-run, which would be the case at points on the MRP curve above point B. It follows that the firm's short-run demand curve for the variable input is operational only below point B. This is shown by the section of the MRP curve in Figure 7.1.3 below the ARP curve.

We have now established the firm's short-run demand curve for a variable input, given all the assumptions of the analysis.

7.2 Input Price-Elasticity

Just as it was possible to express the responsiveness of product demand to changes in price, so we can measure the responsiveness of input demand to changes in input price. As usual, the measure is 'dimensionless' and is expressed as an elasticity:

$$e_f = -\frac{\Delta L}{L} \bigg/ \frac{\Delta W}{W} = -\frac{\Delta L \cdot W}{L \cdot \Delta W},$$

so that e_f is the elasticity of demand for labour with respect to the price of labour. This expression assumes labour is the variable input. For any other variable input we simply substitute the appropriate symbol.

The price elasticity of demand for L in our example, where L is the only variable input, clearly depends on the shape of the marginal revenue productivity curve, which has the same shape as the marginal physical productivity curve, which in turn depends on the shape of the total product curve. The ultimate explanation of the elasticity of demand for L must then lie in the pattern of production possibilities open to the firm when L is the only variable input: that is, on the 'law' of diminishing returns. The more rapidly does the rate of rise in output diminish as more of L is used, the less elastic will be the demand for L, and vice versa.

7.3 The Effects of Parameter Changes

The relationship that we have called the demand for input L shows us the quantity of L that the firm would plan to buy at each price at which L might be bought, when the production possibilities that are open to it, the contractual obligations that fix the quantities of all the other inputs, its objective, and the expected selling price of the product, are all given. We shall now briefly examine what would happen to the demand for L were any one of these parameters to alter.

First, the effects of a change in the production possibilities. If the quality and kind of the fixed inputs had been different from what they are in our example, we should have a different relationship between total outputs and inputs of L. If the firm had had more of the same fixed inputs, the total, average and marginal physical productivities of each quantity of L would have been greater than in Figure 7.1.2, and the demand curve for L would have been to the right of its position in Figure 7.1.3, and vice versa. If the firm had had other kinds of fixed inputs at its disposal, we can say little more than that the total, average and marginal productivities of L, and therefore the demand for L, would have been different from what they are in our figures.

Second, the effects of the demand for L of a change in the firm's objective. The market demand for L is what it is in our example because we have assumed, *inter alia*, that the firm strives to maximise its profits per period. If the firm sought only to cover its total variable costs in each period, its demand curve for L would be the falling portion of its average revenue productivity curve. If its aim were to cover its total costs of production in each period, then the demand curve for L would be a curve lying directly below the falling part of the average revenue productivity curve and asymptotically approaching it as the input of L is increased.

Third, the effects of a change in the expected selling price of the product. If the price of the product rises, the marginal revenue productivity will be greater than it was before at each input of L, for to obtain it the marginal physical productivity (which is unchanged) is being multiplied by the higher expected selling price of the product. Each point on the demand curve for L in Figure 7.1.3 will move due northwards, so that the new demand curve for L will lie to the right of its original position. Conversely, if the expected selling price of the product falls, the demand for L will fall, and the firm will plan to employ less of L at each price than before.

Lastly, the effects of a revision in the firm's contractual arrangements with its fixed inputs. We shall deal later in this chapter with the consequences of a change in the quantity and quality of the fixed inputs that widens the range of production possibilities open to the firm. The only contractual revision that will not alter these latter is one that affects only the size of the fixed costs. If the firm has not been covering its fixed costs for some time, the fixed inputs may voluntarily accept reduction in their rewards to enable the firm to remain in business. Or the firm may have gone into voluntary liquidation and its fixed inputs may have been bought by another firm at their current valuation: the firm that bought them, therefore, will have lower fixed costs per period. Revisions of this kind, however, will have no effect whatsoever on the market demand for the single variable input: for provided the quantity and quality of the fixed inputs remain unchanged, the demand for the input is in no way dependent on the fixed costs. A change in fixed costs arising solely from a change in the rewards paid to the fixed inputs will, however, alter the length of time for which the firm's market demand for L can be maintained.

7.4 The Short-Run Demand Curve: Two Variable Inputs

The production possibilities open to a firm with two variable inputs are reshown in Figure 7.4.1. Given the prices of the two variable inputs, L and K, we can draw isocost lines each showing the different combinations of L and K that can be bought with some sum of money. When the iso-cost lines are superimposed on the isoquants, the points of tangency between them show the maximum output that can be obtained for each sum spent on the variable inputs – or, in other words, the minimum variable costs of different outputs. When these 'minimum cost' combinations are joined together, we have the expansion path, and from this we can derive the relationship between output per period and variable costs that was demonstrated in Chapter 4. Given the expected selling price of the product, and the firm's desire to maximise profits, we can discover the output that the firm will plan to produce and sell in each period. And knowing the output that promises maximum profits, say M in Figure 7.4.1, we can discover the quantities of L and K that the firm would use to produce it – that is, L_M and K_M in Figure 7.4.1. Our problem now is to discover how the quantity of either of the variable inputs that the firm uses to produce its profit maximising output will vary as its price changes – that is, to derive the demand curves for L and K.

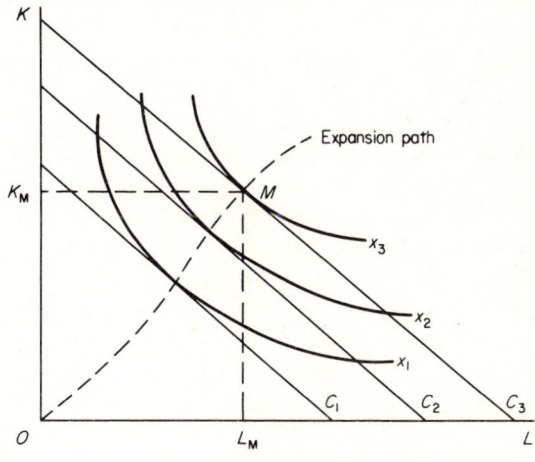

Figure 7.4.1

In Figure 7.4.2, OE_1 is the expansion path at the initial prices of L and K. Let us suppose now that the price per unit of input L falls, the price of K remaining the same. A larger quantity of L can now be bought for each sum of money, so that each isocost line in the figure will be rotated anti-clockwise about the point where it cuts the vertical axis: that is, K_1L_1 swivels to K_1N_1, K_2L_2 to K_2N_2, and so on.[1] The expansion path, now that L is relatively cheaper, will be OE_2. In Figure 7.4.3, we have drawn the relationships that are implicit in the expansion paths OE_1 and OE_2 between total variable costs and output. It can be seen that as a result of the fall in the price of L, the total variable cost curve shifts to the right, for each isocost line in Figure 7.4.2 now touches a higher isoquant – or, in other words, the variable cost of each output is now less than before. The line OR in Figure 7.4.3 shows the relationship between output and total revenue at the given expected selling price of the product. At the initial prices of the inputs L and K, the firm will plan to produce and sell x_1 of its product per

[1] To keep the figure simple, we are assuming that the fall in the price of X is such that each new isocost line touches one of the isoquants that are already drawn in the figure.

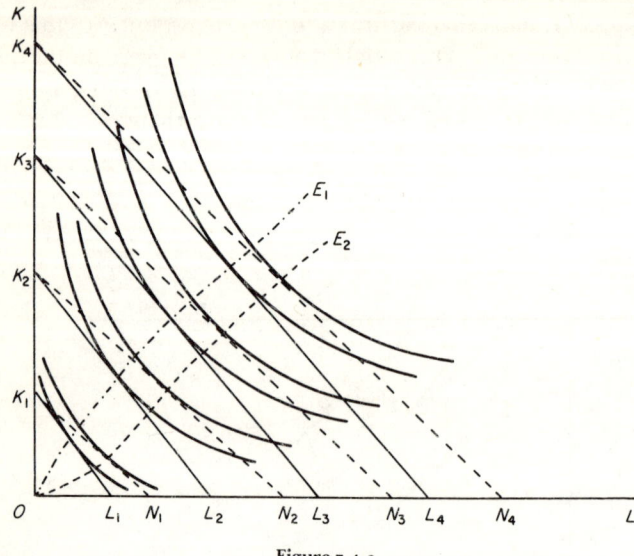

Figure 7.4.2

period, and from Figure 7.4.2 we can read off the quantities of L and K that it will plan to employ to produce this output. At the new price for L, when the total variable cost curve is TVC_2, the firm will plan to sell x_2 per period, and from Figure 7.4.2 we can discover what quantities of L

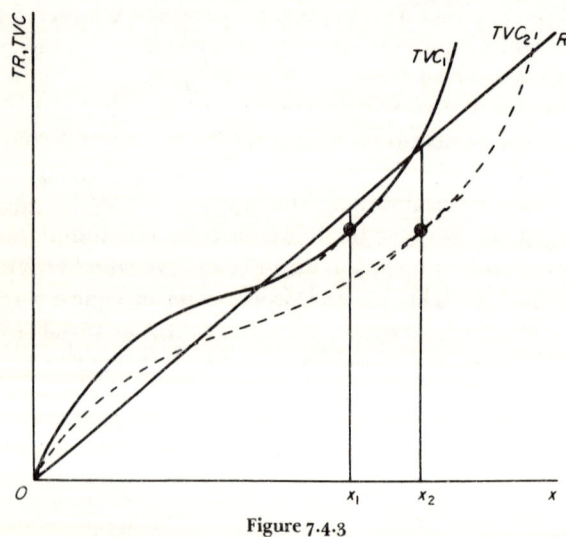

Figure 7.4.3

and K it would plan to use when doing so. It is clear that the firm will employ more of L at its new and lower price. In a precisely similar way, we can discover what quantity of L the firm would plan to buy at each other price at which L might be bought, and so obtain the demand for L. We will find that the planned purchases of L will vary inversely with its expected price.

The price elasticity of demand for L will be the greater the further is the new expansion path OE_2 to the right of OE_1. The extent of the shift in the expansion path will depend on the shape of the isoquants, and this can be confirmed by briefly revising the concepts of output and substitution effects introduced in Section 4.3.

In Figure 7.4.4, the marginal rate of technical substitution of L for K (or of K for L–$MRTS_L$) falls off rapidly – that is, the isoquants are highly convex when viewed from the origin; when the price of L falls, the isocost line shifts from C_1 to C_2, and the firm will redistribute its expenditure on the two inputs so as to buy more of both.

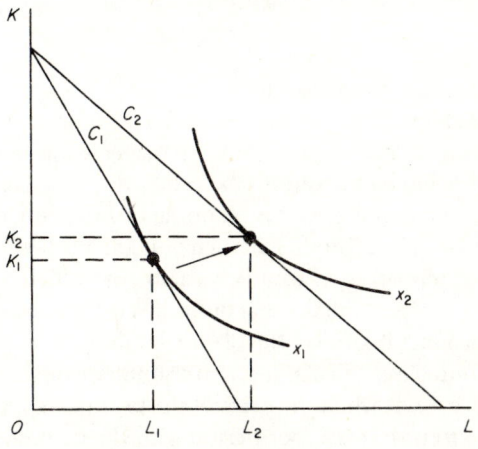

Figure 7.4.4

When a fall in the price of one of the variable inputs causes more of both to be bought, we say that the two inputs are *complementary*. In Figure 7.4.5, the isoquants are relatively flat – that is, $MRTS_{L,K}$ declines slowly; when L becomes relatively cheaper, the firm will re-allocate its expenditure between the two inputs in such a way as to buy more of L and less of K. When this occurs, we say that the two inputs are *substitutes* for one another in production. We conclude that the price elasticity of demand for L will be the greater the more easily can L be substituted for K in production, and vice versa.

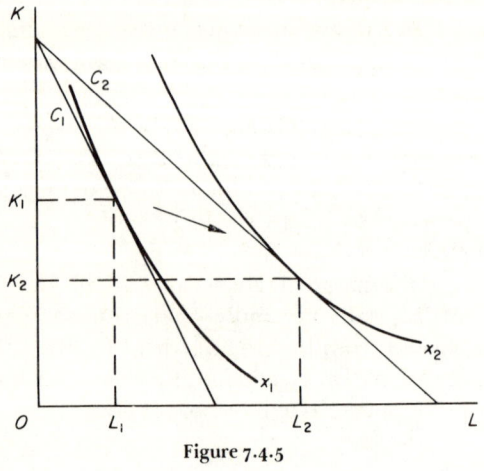

Figure 7.4.5

7.5 The Long-Run Demand Curve

The long-run demand curve may be derived in the same way as the short-run demand curve. Given the manager's knowledge of the techniques of production, and his expectations of the prices he must pay for all the relevant inputs, his planning or long-run average total cost curve can be drawn. Implicit in each point on the planning curve is a particular combination of inputs, namely that which promises the lowest average cost per unit for that output. When the expected selling price of the product is known, the planned output of the product and the planned purchases of each input are simultaneously determined. Thus, in Figure 7.5.1, when the price of the product is p_1 per unit, the firm will plan to produce x_1 per period with the quantities of inputs that give the point R on the planning curve. If the price of one input (L) should fall, then the manager will have a new planning curve lying south and east of the old one. The greater is the relative importance of L in each combination of inputs by which the product might be produced, the further south-eastwards will it lie. If the expected selling price of the product remains unchanged, the firm will plan a larger output per period, and will therefore plan to buy more of L and of those inputs that are complementary to L, and less of those inputs for which L can be substituted.

We would expect the long-run demand for L to be relatively more elastic at each price for L than the short-run demand for it, for the same reasons that the short-run demand for L will be more elastic when L is one of two variable inputs than where L alone is variable. In the previous section, we saw that when the price of L fell, L could be substituted for K: in the long-run, the possibilities of substitution are wider, for L may then be substituted not only for K but also for the other inputs that were 'fixed' in the short-run.

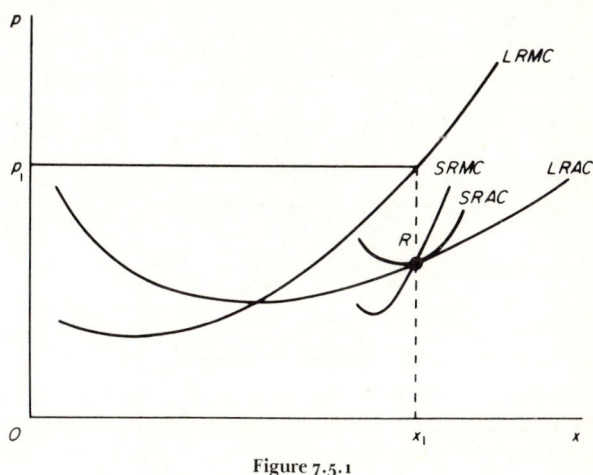

Figure 7.5.1

7.6 The Total Demand Curve for an Input

The demand of an individual firm for an input shows the quantity of it that the firm would plan to buy in each period at each price at which it might be bought, given the firm's production possibilities, its objective, the price of each other input that it uses or might use, and the price at which it expects to be able to sell its product. The role that firms play in determining the relative prices of the inputs they buy is summarised in the total demand curve for each service. If we wish the total demand curve for an input to play this role, then we cannot derive it simply by adding together the individual firm demand curves for it. We can show why this is so by exploring the implications of a total demand curve that is obtained in this way.

In Figure 7.6.1, we suppose that the short-run equilibrium price of the product is p per unit and the price of the variable input W per unit, and that the firms are buying WT of the input to help produce pR of the product per period. Let us now suppose that the price of the variable input falls to W_1: this will cause a rightward shift in the short-run supply curve of the product to S_2S_2. If all firms assume that the price of the product will remain unchanged, they will together plan to buy W_1T_1 of the input; if they simultaneously implement their purchase plans the output per period will be pU, and the price of the product

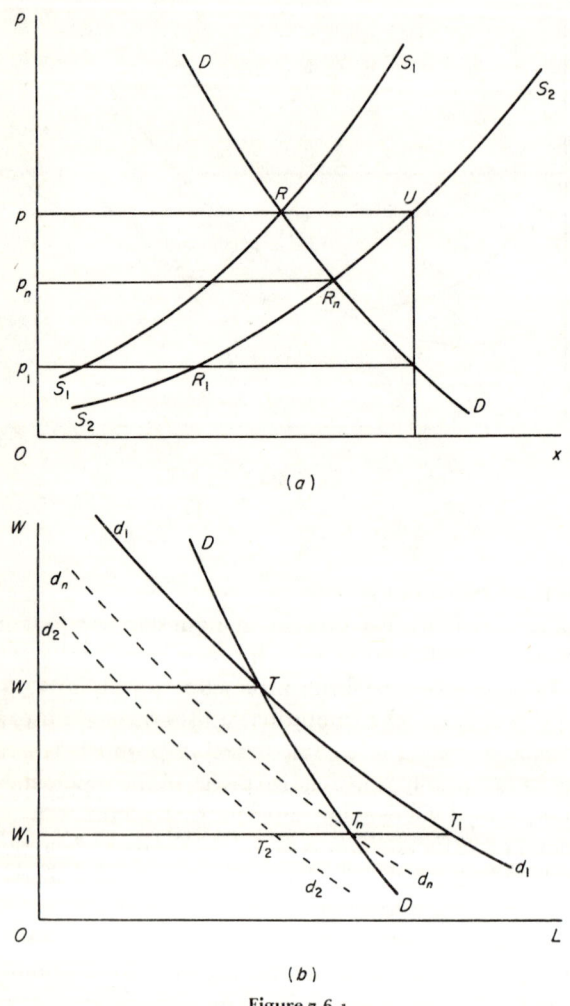

(a)

(b)

Figure 7.6.1

The Purchase Plan of the Firm

(assuming that it cannot be stored) will fall to p_1. At the price p_1 for the product and W_1 for the variable input, firms will plan to produce $p_1 R_1$ of the former with the aid of $W_1 T_2$ of the latter – i.e. the whole 'demand curve' for the input will shift leftwards to $d_2 d_2$. A cobweb-type cycle will ensue until the product price has reached p_n per unit and the final demand curve for the variable input is $d_n d_n$; firms will then be producing $p_n R_n$ per period with $W_1 T_n$ of the input. If the purchase plans are implemented *seriatim* rather than simultaneously, the supply curve of the product will move gradually to $S_2 S_2$ as the 'demand' for the input falls slowly to $d_n d_n$, so that the price of the product will fall directly to p_n and the planned purchases of the input to $W_1 T_n$. In this new position, the purchase and sales plans of the firms will again be consistent with one another. If all points such as T and T_n are joined together, we have the total demand curve for the productive service.

We are already familiar with this kind of problem: in Chapters 3, 4, 5 and 6 we saw that while each firm may make its sales plan on the assumption that the price of each input is given, one consequence of all firms implementing their plans would be to change the relative prices of some or all of their inputs. Here we see that if all firms make their purchase plans on the assumption that the price of the product is a datum, one result of all firms putting their purchase plans into effect would be to alter the relative price of the product. In both cases, that which is a datum or constant for the individual firm in an industry is a variable when all firms are taken together. In Chapter 4, we defined the short-run total supply curve in such a way that at each price, the sales and purchase plans of the firms in the industry were consistent with one another – i.e. in such a way that we could 'move along' it in predicting the probable direction of changes in relative prices. Here we shall define the total demand curve for an input in a similar way, so that at each price of the input, the purchase and sales plans of the firms in the industry are consistent with one another. This is shown by the curve DD in Figure 7.6.1.

It is clear from Figure 7.6.1 that the short-run total or industry demand curve for an input (DD) will be less elastic at each price at which the service might be bought than any of the 'total demand' curves ($d_1 d_1$, etc.) that were obtained simply by adding together the individual firm demand curves. The elasticity of the total demand curve will depend, then, not only on the degree to which each firm can substitute the input in question for others as it becomes relatively cheaper, but also on the elasticity of demand for the product. If the demand for the product is less elastic than in Figure 7.6.1, then T_n will lie further to the left of the d_1d_1-curve, and the DD-curve will be less elastic also. Conversely, if the demand for the product is more elastic at each price than in the figure, the total demand curve for the input will be more elastic also – that is, T_n will lie nearer to the d_1d_1-curve.

The long-run total demand curve for an input may be derived in a manner analogous to that illustrated in Figure 7.6.1. We shall find that the long-run total demand curve will be less elastic at each input price than the 'total demand curve' that is obtained by summing the long-run demand curves for the input of all the firms that might plan to use it over the long period. We shall find also that the price elasticity of the long-run total demand curve will vary directly with the price elasticity of demand for the product.

7.7 The Firm's Demand for a Durable Good

We have so far confined our attention to the demand for inputs supplied by men, land, machines or buildings. Firms demand these inputs because consumers (or other firms) demand the products that they help to produce, and in this chapter we have described the precise manner in which the demand curve for an input is derived from the demand curve for the product. Our analysis in this chapter would suffice if firms were always able to buy the services rendered by inputs in such quantities as they desire. Consumers frequently own land and sell only its services to firms; and firms often 'rent' or lease machines, as with computers. Generally, however, if a firm wants the services of a machine, building, or other durable good, it must buy the good itself – that is, rather than buy the *flow* of services per period, it must buy the *stock* from which it stems. We shall conclude this chapter, therefore, by describing the derivation of the firm's demand for a durable good.

Suppose that a machine can now be bought for £P, that its expected life is n periods, and that the firm borrows the money to buy the machine at a rate of interest of i per cent per period. We shall assume also that the costs of operating the machine are zero and that the firm desires to distribute the cost of the machine equally over all the periods of its life. In each period, therefore, the manager must set aside a sum of money equal to $(d + O \cdot i)$, where d is that period's contribution towards recouping the initial price of the machine, and $P \cdot i$ is the amount of interest that has to be paid in that period on the money he borrowed to buy the machine.

The Purchase Plan of the Firm

Now d, the depreciation per period, will be equal to[1]

$$\frac{P \cdot i}{(1+i)^n - 1}$$

so that the cost per period of the machine will be

$$d + P \cdot i = \frac{P \cdot i}{(1+i)^n - 1} + P \cdot i = \frac{P \cdot i (1+i)^n}{(1+i)^n - 1}.$$

Given this 'price' per period of the productive service rendered by the machine, and the price of each other input, the long-run average cost curve can be drawn. If the expected selling price of the product is p_1, in Figure 7.5.1, the firm will plan to produce x_1 units of output per period over the long-run, with the number of machines and the quantities of other services implicit in the point R on the long-run average cost curve. If the price of the machine should fall, then *ceteris paribus* the 'price' per period of its services will also fall. As a consequence, the planning curve will move south-eastwards and the manager will now plan to produce an output larger than x_1 per period, with more machines and other services. In this way, by drawing the planning curve appropriate to each price of the machine, we can derive the firm's demand curve for the machine, and it is clear that the number of machines demanded will vary inversely with their price. The elasticity of the firm's demand for the machine will depend on the ease with which its services can be substituted for other inputs.

The demand curve for a durable good may be derived in another way. The planning curve shows us the minimum unit costs of production of each output: hence, at each output on the curve, the ratio

---

[1] The sum of money that is set aside in the first period of the machine's life (d) may be lent to another firm and we shall assume that it would pay interest at i per cent per period until the lender requires repayment. The same will be true of the sum, d, set aside in each subsequent period. The value of d must be such, then, that by the end of the period n, the firm will have accumulated a sum of money equal to £P; that is,

$$d(1+i)^{n-1} + d(1+i)^{n-2} + \ldots + d = P,$$

where $d(1+i)^{n-1}$ is the value which the d lent at the end of period 1 will have reached at the end of period n, and similarly for each other term. This is a geometric progression, and when it is summed we have

$$\frac{d\{(1+i)^n - 1\}}{(1+i) - 1} = \frac{d\{(1+i)^n - 1\}}{i} = P,$$

or

$$d = \frac{P \cdot i}{(1+i)^{n-1}}.$$

between the price of each productive service and its marginal productivity will be the same for all services (see Section 4.1). At the output x_1, which promises maximum profits when the expected selling price of the product is p_1 per unit, the price of each input will be equal to its marginal revenue product, as we have already seen. When the firm is planning to produce x_1 per period with the number of machines and other inputs implicit in the point R, then the 'price' of the machine's services per period must be equal to its marginal revenue product; that is:

$$\frac{P \cdot i \cdot (1+i)^n}{(1+i)^n - 1} = MRP \qquad (1)$$

or

$$P = \frac{MRP}{i}\left(\frac{(1+i)^n - 1}{(1+i)^n}\right). \qquad (2)$$

The right-hand side of this equation (2), however, is merely the *present value* of the marginal revenue productivity of machines (when the planned output is x_1 per period) over each period of their lives, for the present value (PV) of sums of money of MRP accruing in each of the n periods for which the machine will last is

$$PV = \frac{MRP}{(1+i)} + \frac{MRP}{(1+i)^2} + \frac{MRP}{(1+i)^3} + \ldots + \frac{MRP}{(1+i)^n}.$$

The sum of this geometric progression is:

$$\frac{MRP}{1+i}\left\{1 - \frac{1}{(1+i)^n}\right\} \bigg/ 1 - \frac{1}{1+i} = \frac{MRP}{i}\left(\frac{(1+i)^n - 1}{(1+i)^n}\right).$$

Equation (2) tells us that when expected profits per period are at a maximum, the present value of the marginal revenue product per period of machines will be equal to the price at which they can now be bought. If the price per machine should fall, then the firm would plan to buy as many more machines as were necessary to reduce the marginal revenue product per period of machines to the level at which their present value was equal to the new price; for only then would the expected profit per period be at a maximum in the new conditions. The elasticity of demand for machines will depend on the rate at which their marginal revenue product per period declines as more of them are used, and this in turn depends on the degree to which the services of machines can be substituted for other inputs as machines become cheaper.

The Purchase Plan of the Firm

The choice of the number of machines that the firm will plan to buy is generally made when the manager is making his long-run plan. The firm's demand curve for a durable good, therefore, relates to the long-run, and it shows us the number of machines that it will plan to buy at each price at which they might be bought, given the manager's knowledge of the techniques of production, his objective, the price of each other durable good or input, the rate of interest, the expected life of the machine in question and the expected selling price of the product. If the rate of interest that the firm uses in making its calculations should fall, then the present value of the stream of marginal revenue products will rise, so that the firm will plan to buy more machines at each price – i.e. the whole demand curve for the machine will move to the right. If the rate of interest rises, the demand curve will move to the left. If the firm believes that the rate of technical development, and therefore of obsolescence, will be slower, and so comes to expect the life of each machine to be longer, then the present value of the machine will rise and its demand curve will shift rightwards. Conversely, if the expected life of the machine is shortened, the demand for it will fall. Changes in any one of the other determinants of the demand for a durable good will affect the demand for it in the same way as they would affect the demand for any other input.

The total demand curve for a durable good may be derived in a manner analogous to that illustrated in Figure 7.6.1. The total demand will be less elastic at each price than the 'total demand' that would be obtained simply by adding together the demand curves of all the firms that might plan to use that good in the long-run. We shall find also that, *ceteris paribus*, the elasticity of the total demand for a durable good will vary directly with the price elasticity of demand for the product that it helps to produce.

In this chapter, we have described how the total demand for a durable good or input is derived from the demands of the individual firms for it. The total demand curve for an input summarises the part that firms play in determining the relationship between the prices of the things that they buy. In the next chapter, we shall study the sales plans of consumers and try to discover how consumers, in implementing their sales plans, help to determine the relative prices of the productive services they sell.

8

The Sales Plan of the Consumer: The Supply of Effort

8.0 Consumption Time and Work Time

The members of a household or family are not just consuming units. They also own *factors of production*, or *inputs*, which they sell to production units. In the typical case, the consumer supplies some inputs to the *firm*, where the firm may be a private or public enterprise, hospital, government department, or whatever, as long as the unit is engaged in productive activity. The most important input supplied by consumers is *labour* or *effort*, and the price per unit at which this labour service is sold is the wage-rate. We can now develop the model of consumer behaviour, presented in Chapters 1–2, to explain how the level of the consumer's income is determined.

In selling his labour the worker is buying a money-income that can be used to sustain himself and his family, both now and in the future. The sustenance and satisfaction that any given money-income is expected to provide depends on the family's tastes and preferences for the goods and services of everyday consumption, and the prices that it expects to have to pay for them. When he is not working, however, the worker may play with his children, dig his garden, or watch television. Since there is a limit to the number of hours at his disposal each week, the more hours he sells for income by working the fewer hours he will have in which to indulge his other interests. How he will dispose of his time between working for money-income, and pursuing these other interests for his own pleasure, will depend on his tastes for each and on his preferences for different combinations of them. In addition, of course, the individual's supply of labour will be constrained by factory laws, safety regulations, legal contracts, union regulations, and so on. For the moment, however, we assume that the individual is free to vary his labour supply, within limits at least. His supply will be measured in units of time: hours per day or per week.

The Supply of Effort

Now, in supplying more labour the individual secures more income, but he must surrender some of his 'consumption time' – the amount of time he spends in consumption activities (including sleep). Hence, the consumer must be able to rank various alternative combinations of work time and consumption time. Since more work time means more commodities, this choice context is equivalent to choosing between consumption time (leisure) and commodities.

We now state an important proposition:

> *The individual consumer is assumed to rank alternative combinations of consumption time and commodities in accordance with the axioms of consumer preference stated in Chapter 1.*

This proposition enables us to analyse the individual's willingness to supply effort in terms of the, by now, familiar indifference map. Instead of choosing combinations of commodities, however, the individual now chooses combinations of consumption and work time, or, as it is usually described, combinations of leisure and work.

8.1 Optimal Allocation of Time

Figure 8.1.1 describes the indifference map of the individual choosing combinations of work and consumption time. Some attention needs to be paid to the units of measurement on the axes. On the horizontal axis we measure consumption time (leisure time) T_C. Clearly, however, there is a limit to T_C, set by the number of hours in a day, or in a week. To remind us of this, the vertical dashed line is included to set a 'bound' to the right-hand part of the figure. Since there is a fixed amount of time, T, it follows that time not spent in consumption activities must be spent in work time, T_E. Hence, by definition,

$$T_C + T_E = T \qquad (1)$$

and T_E is also measured on the horizontal axis: as we move along the axis T_E is reduced.

Note, too, that the region where T_C approaches zero is also unlikely to be 'occupied' by indifference curves since it implies working 20–24 hours a day. Sheer physical needs would not permit this.

On the vertical axis a 'composite commodity', X, is measured. This can be construed as some collection of all commodities to which, in turn, we can attach some composite 'price', p. The vertical axis therefore measures income, and

$$Y_C = p \cdot X \qquad (2)$$

Prices are assumed to be constant so that money-income equals real income. Assuming that the individual is not subject to the 'money illusion', the choice he exercises will be between consumption time and real income.[1]

But income is also equal to the wage-rate, W, multiplied by hours worked, T_E. Hence

$$Y_C = T_E \cdot W = p \cdot X. \qquad (3)$$

Multiplying equation (1) by W, gives

$$W \cdot T_C + W \cdot T_E = W \cdot T \qquad (4)$$

and substituting $W \cdot T_E = p \cdot X$ in equation (4) gives

$$W \cdot T_C + p \cdot X = W \cdot T,$$
or
$$p \cdot X = W \cdot T - W \cdot T_C. \qquad (5)$$

Equation (5)[2] is the equation of the relevant 'budget line', with a slope of $-W$. However, since the constraint on the individual, in this case, is not his income, the term 'budget line' appears redundant. It is *time* that is fixed in amount, so that the appropriate term might be 'time constraint line'.

The value of consumption time is given by W, and the optimal allocation of time between work and consumption time, is given by the point of tangency, A, in Figure 8.1.1. At A, an amount of time $O\bar{T}_C$ is devoted to consumption time, and $\bar{T}_C T$ to work. The corresponding income level is $\bar{Y}_C$. Thus, *given* the wage-rate W, the consumer's income is determined by his preferences for work and leisure.

Just as commodity prices were assumed to be exogenously determined in the previous model, so the current model assumes the wage-rate is determined in the market for labour.

At the point of tangency, the rate of substitution of income for consumption time (the slope of the indifference curve) therefore equals the wage-rate, that is,
$$\frac{\Delta Y_C}{\Delta T_C} = W.$$

---

[1] We are all familiar with the idea that money-income can rise without us being any better off in 'real' terms. This will happen if the rise in money-income is counterbalanced by a change in prices such that we can only buy the same amount of goods as before. If a consumer reacts to an increase in money-income by purchasing more goods, even though his real income is constant, he is said to be subject to a 'money illusion' (see Section 2.0).

[2] The equation could of course have been derived immediately since $p_x = W \cdot T_E = W(T - T_C) = W \cdot T - W \cdot T_C$.

The Supply of Effort 175

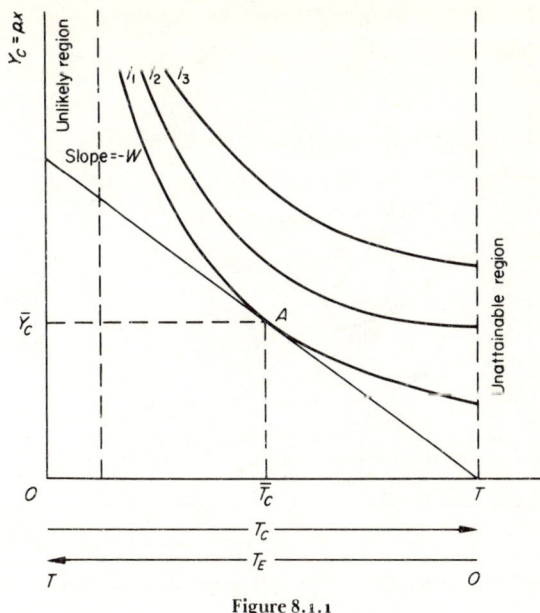

Figure 8.1.1

8.2 The Supply Curve of Labour

Equation (5) shows that a change in (a) the worker's tastes and preferences for leisure and income; or (b) commodity prices; or (c) the wage rate; will alter the amount of labour supplied.

If the prices of the goods and services that the individual plans to buy should rise, then each sum of money-income will buy less of these things than before. From the individual's point of view, then, it is as if the prices of the things he buys remain unchanged while the hourly wage-rate falls. The consequences of changes in product prices therefore will be similar to changes in opposite directions in the wage-rate.

The possible reactions to changes in the wage-rate are illustrated in Figures 8.2.1 and 8.2.2. The figures are drawn so as to exclude the 'unlikely' and 'unattainable' regions noted in Figure 8.1.1. Since income rises, the individual is able to secure the same amount of consumption time as before, and more income. Hence the time constraint line shifts outwards to the right, pivoting about the point A in each figure. Each new line corresponds to a higher wage-rate. The steeper

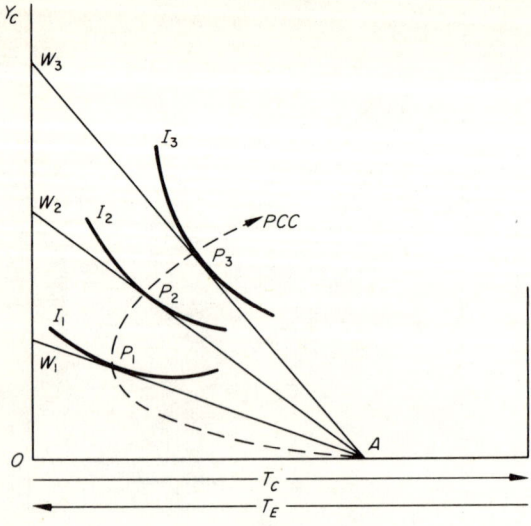

Figure 8.2.1

the line, the higher is the wage-rate (we showed that the gradient equalled the wage-rate in Section 8.1).

In Figure 8.2.1 the effect is to *increase* the amount of time devoted to consumption, a result which seems intuitively acceptable. As wage-rates rise, then, the individual *reduces* his supply of effort, as is shown in Figure 8.2.3. In Figure 8.2.2, however, increased wages lead to *reduced*

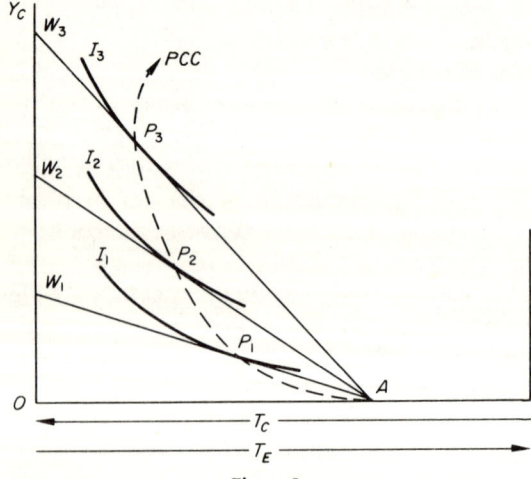

Figure 8.2.2

The Supply of Effort

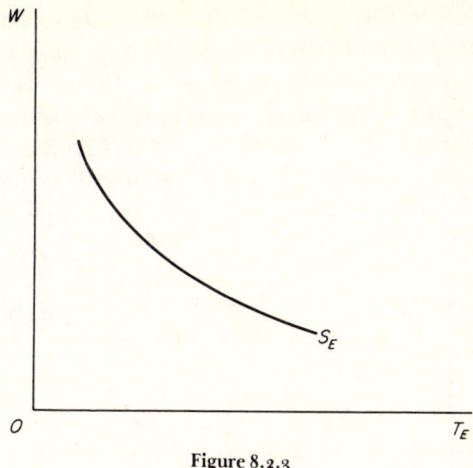

Figure 8.2.3

consumption time, and hence increased work time. This corresponds to the situation shown in Figure 8.2.4. Notice that neither curve is defined for very low wage-rates since individual needs will be such as to *force* people to work at subsistence level incomes: no notion of *ranking* work and leisure time is applicable at these points.

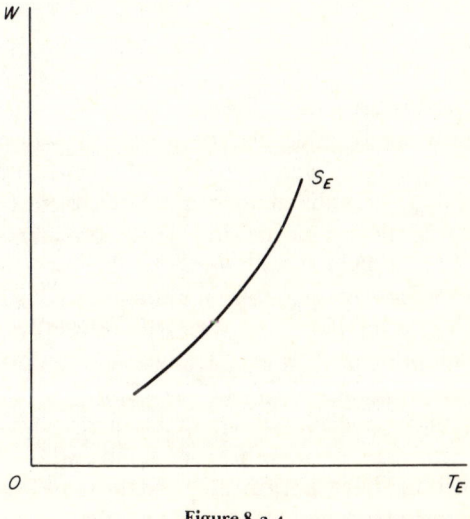

Figure 8.2.4

Figure 8.2.2 contains a hint that the supply curve of labour might comprise both aspects of Figures 8.2.3 and 8.2.4. Thus, at W_3 the PCC curve – analogous to the PCC curves of Chapter 2 – is beginning to slope to the right, as in Figure 8.2.1. It is reasonable to suppose, therefore, that the supply curve will appear as in Figure 8.2.5: sloping upwards at first, and then bending backwards as the individual becomes more affluent and places higher and higher values on his leisure time.

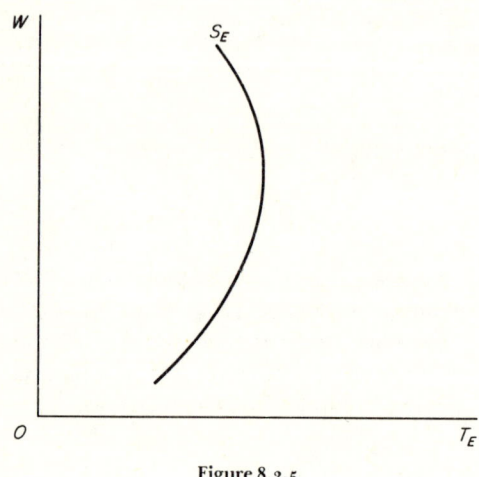

Figure 8.2.5

8.3 Income and Substitution Effects

Thus far we have merely shown that the direction in which the number of hours that the worker is willing to work will alter when the wage-rate changes depends on his indifference map. The characteristics of the indifference map that determine the kind of reaction can be described in another way. In both Figures 8.2.1 and 8.2.2 the worker is 'better off' the higher is the hourly wage-rate, for the points P_1, P_2, P_3, lie on progressively higher indifference curves. We may think of the rejection of P_1 and the adoption of P_2, when the wage-rate rises from W_1 to W_2, as a 'movement' along the curve $P_1P_2P_3$. The 'force' (namely, the rise in the wage-rate) that pushed the worker in this direction can be thought of as being the resultant of two other forces. First, when the wage-rate rises, the worker may have more income and the same leisure, or more leisure and the same income. Either way he is better off. It is as if the wage-rate had remained unchanged and the worker had been given a sum of money equal to AB in Figures 8.3.1 and 8.3.2. A time constraint line is drawn through B, parallel to the initial one through A. The move from P_1 to P_3 in each figure is an 'income effect', because the increase in consumer satisfaction that follows a rise in the wage-rate is as if the consumer had received an income of AB from some source other than his labour.

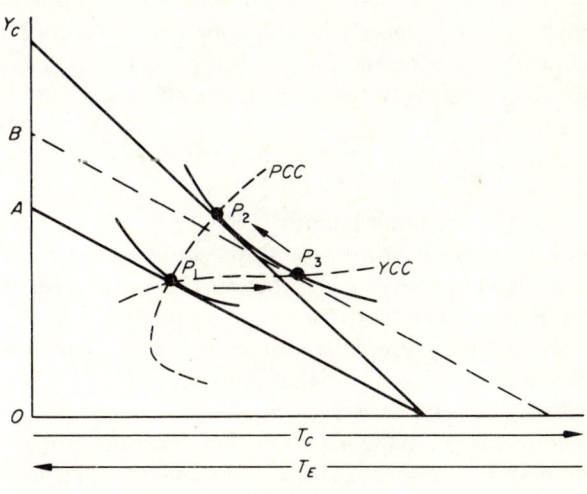

Figure 8.3.1

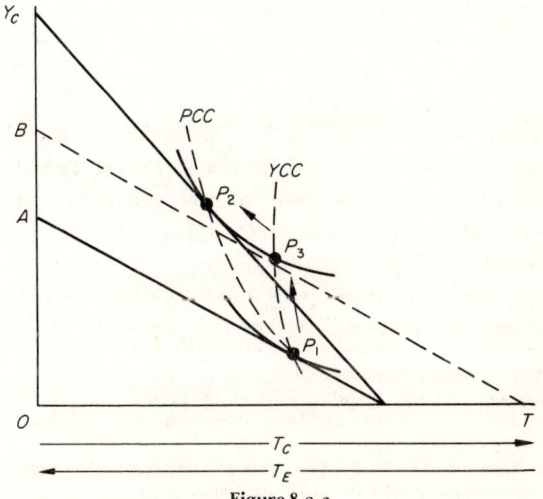

Figure 8.3.2

If the income effect alone operated, the effect in Figure 8.3.1 is to lead to *more* consumption time being chosen, and in Figure 8.3.2 to a smaller reduction in consumption time. The movement from P_3 to P_2 is, in each case, the substitution effect: as the wage-rate rises, leisure becomes relatively more expensive since the sacrifice of work time for leisure time involves the surrender of increased purchasing power over commodities. Hence, the substitution effect is always positive with respect to an increase in the wage-rate: income will tend to be substituted for leisure, and more labour is supplied. In Figure 8.3.1 the combined result of the income and substitution effects is to *reduce* the supply of effort, whereas in Figure 8.3.2 the effect is to increase the supply of effort.

8.4 The Effort-Demand for Labour[1]

It is possible to describe the previous results in an alternative fashion. Table 8.4.1 shows the relationship between the wage rate and the number of hours worked. The schedule corresponds to Figure 8.2.5 – the backward-sloping supply curve. In selling his effort, the worker is buying income. The 'effort-price' that he must pay for £1 of income is the number of hours he must work in order to earn £1 at the ruling hourly wage-rate. Thus, if the wage-rate is 30 pence per hour, he must work for $100/30 = 3.3$ hours to earn £1. The amount of income which he demands is equal to the hourly wage-rate multiplied by the number of hours for which he would plan to work: thus, when the wage-rate is 30 pence per hour, he is willing to work for 36 hours – that is, he is demanding an income of 30 × 36, or 1,080 pence per week. The effort-price of a unit of income is calculated for each hourly wage-rate in column (4), and the total income that the worker demands at each wage-rate is set out in column (3) of Table 8.4.1. In Figure 8.4.1 we plot the income that would be demanded at each effort-price of income; when the points are joined together, we have the individual's demand curve for income in terms of effort.

The effort-price elasticity of this demand curve may be measured by the total expenditure method described in Section 2.5. Thus, when the

---

[1] The 'effort-price' approach is not fashionable in current writing. It derives, perhaps, from a desire to produce analyses which look comparable to the Marshallian price-quantity demand curve. This section may be omitted without any loss of continuity. For a discussion of the effort-price approach, see L. Robbins, 'On the Elasticity of Demand for Income in Terms of Effort', *Economica*, 1930, reprinted in American Economic Association, *Readings in the Theory of Income Distribution* (Allen and Unwin, London, 1950).

The Supply of Effort

Table 8.4.1

Wage-rate (pence per hour)	Hours worked per week	Total income demanded (pence per week)	Effort-price per unit of income (hours per £1)
(1)	(2)	(3)	(4)
30	36	1080	8·0
31	40	1240	7·7
32	44	1408	7·5
33	48	1584	7·3
34	47	1598	7·1
35	46	1610	6·85
36	45	1620	6·67
37	44	1629	6·5

effort-price is 8 hours per £1 (i.e. when the hourly wage-rate is 30 pence), a weekly income of 1,080 pence is demanded, and the worker's total expenditure of effort in buying this income is 36 hours; when the effort-price falls to 7·7 hours per £1 (i.e. when the hourly wage-rate is 31 pence), a weekly income of 1,240 pence is demanded, and the

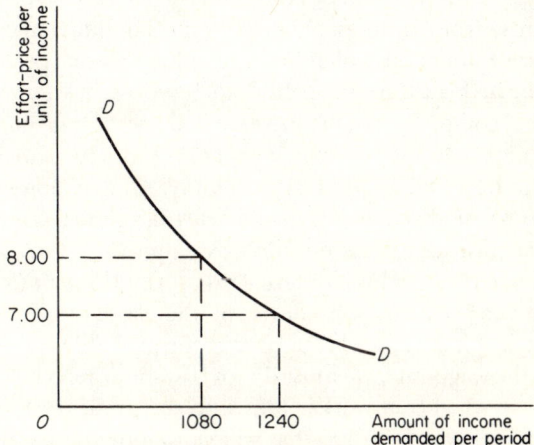

Figure 8.4.1

worker's total effort-expenditure is 40 hours. In this range of the demand curve, the total effort-expenditure rises as the effort-price falls – that is, the worker's demand for income in terms of effort is relatively elastic. It is clear that the effort-expenditure is merely the number of hours that the worker is willing to work at a particular wage-rate – and these are given in column (2). By comparing columns (4) and (2) of Table 8.4.1, then, we can see immediately whether the worker's demand for income in terms of effort is relatively elastic or relatively inelastic: as the effort-price falls from 8·0 to 7·3 hours per £1 (i.e. as the wage-rate rises from 30 to 33 pence per hour), the demand for income in terms of effort is relatively elastic; at effort-prices lower than 7·3 hours per £1 (i.e. at wage-rates higher than 33 pence per hour), the demand for income in terms of effort is relatively inelastic.

We may sum up thus far as follows: It has been observed that when the hourly wage-rate rises, some workers offer more hours of their labour for sale and some offer less. From these facts we inferred the shape of the leisure-income indifference curves. The fruit of our indifference analysis was not an explanation of why a worker reacts to higher hourly wage-rates in the way that he does, but rather a classification (under the headings: tastes and preferences for income and leisure, prices of products, etc.) of the different influences that affect his decision. The segregation of the substitution and income-effects of a rise in hourly wage-rate, and the concept of the elasticity of the demand for income in terms of effort, merely offer alternative ways in which these same facts can be communicated to others: if, when the wage-rate rose from 30 to 33 pence per hour, an individual reduced the number of hours for which he was willing to work per week, we may describe his behaviour in precisely these words, or we may say that for him the income-effect of the increase in the wage-rate outweighed the substitution-effect, or we may say that his elasticity of demand for income in terms of effort was less than unity. All this, however, does not help us to predict how he would react if another wage change should occur, for we cannot establish by empirical investigation the precise characteristics of his indifference map, or the relations between his income- and substitution-effects, or the elasticity of his effort-demand for income. If we wish to predict the probable consequences of a rise in the wage-rate, we must discover some criteria by which we can recognise whether a worker falls into the group that will work fewer hours, or into the group that will work more hours, per week. We look at this issue briefly.

Where the wage-rate has been at a certain level for some time, so that the worker has become accustomed (or reconciled) to the standard of living that it can command, we commonly find that the number of hours worked falls as the wage-rate rises. This tendency will be the stronger the more exhausting the work that he is doing, and the more numerous the opportunities for passing leisure-time inexpensively. Where the prevailing wage-rate does not enable the worker to achieve the standard of living to which he aspires, or to maintain the standard to which he has become accustomed in the past, the number of hours that he is willing to work will usually vary directly with the wage-rate per hour. The prospect (or fact) of marriage and children, for example, and the expenses that attend them, may induce this kind of behaviour. Indeed, it is conceivable that more hours may be worked, not merely because the worker aspires to a higher standard of living, but because he aspires to more expensive hobbies.

We have now derived the supply curve of labour-service of an individual worker. The total or market supply curve of labour-services in a particular industry is obtained by summing together these curves – that is, by adding the number of hours that each worker is willing to work at each hourly wage-rate. The shape of the total supply curve of labour-service from those possessing a particular skill will depend on the degree of their preferences for leisure as opposed to income. If the preferences for leisure are strong, we would expect the total supply curve to have the same shape as that drawn in Figure 8.2.3; if the individual indifference maps are, on balance, like that illustrated in Figure 8.2.2, we would expect the total supply curve to be like that drawn in Figure 8.2.4.

8.5 Long-Run Supply

In this chapter so far we have assumed that the worker's current behaviour is circumscribed by past decisions. Some time in the past he acquired a certain skill. While this decision binds him, he is limited in revising his sales plan to the various ways in which the total time at his disposal can be allocated between leisure and work; and we have illustrated his choice of that allocation of his time that promises him the maximum utility, given his expectations about the hourly wage-rate and the prices of the products he may want to buy. We shall call an analysis that is so confined a *short-run* analysis, and contrast it with a *long-run* analysis which explores the choice of a sales plan when the worker may *choose* what skill to acquire. We shall now describe the choice of a long-run sales plan by consumers, and show how the long-run supply curve of a particular kind of labour-service may be derived from the manner in which consumers revise their sales plans as relative wage-rates alter.

When a worker makes a long-run sales plan, he is deciding what kind of labour-service to sell – that is, what skill to acquire. Our problem is to describe the range of choice that faces the worker and the considerations that influence his final decision. We shall seek its solution by taking the simplest example, namely, that of someone who has reached the legal minimum age at which he may undertake full-time employment. The range from which he must choose is merely a catalogue of all the skills or 'occupations' of which he is aware. Some of these may be eliminated by his assessment of his own abilities and potentialities. From the occupations that he feels competent to enter, he will make his choice in the light of (a) his attitude towards the type of work – whether manual or mental, monotonous, or exciting, hazardous or safe – that each occupation requires, and the conditions in which it must be performed – whether outdoor or indoor, sitting or standing, and so on; (b) his estimate of the time and cost of preparing himself for each occupation; and (c) his expectations of the income per period that he might earn were he to enter each occupation. For many workers, the second of these may drastically narrow the range of choice, for they may neither possess nor be able to acquire the money that is needed to meet the costs of being trained for certain occupations: for them, it is as if the costs of becoming a doctor or lawyer or school-teacher were infinitely large. As economists, we can say little more than that the worker will choose that occupation that he prefers, and we presume that in making his choice he in some way adds together the relative income he would hope to earn were he to pursue each occupation, the relative attractiveness to him of the kind of work it requires, and the relative social esteem in which it is held. A worker who already possesses a skill will be influenced by similar considerations in deciding whether or not to acquire a new skill.

The long-run decision of a worker will be revised if there is any significant change in his estimate of his own capacities, in his attitudes towards the type and condition of work in different occupations, in the relative costs of preparing himself for different occupations, or in the relative money-incomes he expects to earn were he to enter them. We cannot derive a long-run supply curve for the individual worker from the way in which his sales plan would be revised when the relative prices of different kinds of labour alter, for in the long-run the worker is choosing between different full-time occupations. Given all the other influences that affect his choice, at one set of relative prices he might decide to become a school-teacher; at another a carpenter; and at yet another he might plan to become an agricultural labourer. From the manner in which each individual worker will revise his long-run sales plan as relative wage-rates (or relative salaries) alter we can, however, derive the long-run supply curve of carpenters, or of school-teachers, or of workers to any other occupation. We can do this in the following way.

Let us suppose that all the influences that we have listed remain the same, but that the hourly wage-rate of, say, carpenters rises. As a consequence, we would expect more new entrants to the labour market to plan to become carpenters, and some of those who had previously chosen other occupations to revise their decisions and train as carpenters. Initially, the 'new' carpenters would probably be drawn from occupations that required similar abilities and offered similar conditions to the trade of carpentry. As the wage-rate that carpenters might earn rose further, however, the 'new' carpenters might be drawn from semi-professional or professional occupations – for there is some wage-rate that might induce even professors and surgeons to ply this trade. The higher is the wage-rate that firms are willing to pay for carpenters' services, therefore, the larger the number of workers who will plan to become carpenters, and vice versa, so that the long-run supply curve of carpenters will slope north-eastwards as in Figure 8.5.1.

The elasticity of the supply of carpenters is the responsiveness of the number of carpenters to changes in the relative wage-rate, and it is measured by dividing the proportionate change in the number of workers who are planning to work as carpenters by the small proportionate change in the expected wage-rate. In the absence of special measures by trade unions or professional associations to exclude new entrants, we would expect the long-run supply curve of labour-service to any particular occupation to be relatively elastic, for as the wage-rate that can be earned in it rises, workers will be drawn from other occupations that are held in comparable social esteem and that require similar abilities and training expenses. The elasticity of the long-run supply of labour-service to an occupation will generally be positive, and it will always be greater at each wage-rate than that of the short-run supply curve, for in the long-run the entry or exit of new workers will generally outweigh variations in the number of hours for which each man that is in the trade is willing to work. It is possible that the long-run supply curve of labour to an occupation that lies at the bottom of the 'occupational ladder' may have a negative elasticity over a part of its range: for this to happen, it must be so unremunerative that workers are not drawn into it from occupations that lie immediately above it in the occupational scale, even when its wage-rate rises over this range.

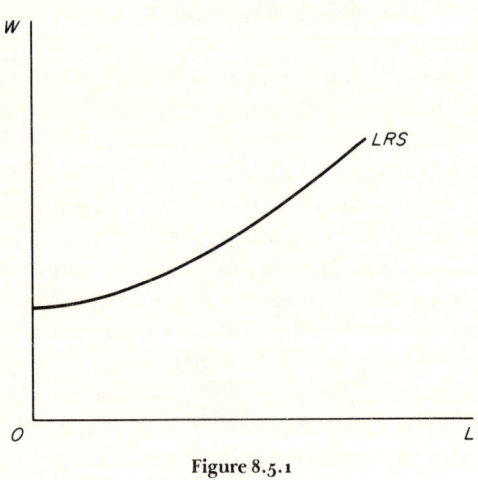

Figure 8.5.1

8.6 The Sales Plan for the Services of Land

Some consumers are likely to be landowners and can therefore sell land or the services of land. Just as the consumer could decide to use part of the fixed time available to him for supplying a labour-service and the remainder for 'leisure', so the landowner can supply part or all of his land for productive purposes – housing, agriculture, and so on – and retain part or all of it for his own consumption purposes – as a garden or amenity area for his personal use. The decision about how best to use the land is therefore analogous to the decision about how best to use available time. The basic difference is that the consumer cannot supply productive services for the entire period of time available to him – he needs *some* leisure – but he can supply all of his land if he so chooses.

In supplying land, therefore, the consumer's problem is to select the best current *use* of that land. We can define the short-run as a period within which the current use cannot be changed. Obviously, the short-run will vary according to the type of land and its current use: agricultural land may be quickly converted into building land, but not vice versa. In the short-run then, the supply of land by individual consumers will be fixed and hence the market supply curve will be fixed (perfectly inelastic) as well. In the longer run, of course, the use can be changed. If the consumer behaves in the same manner as suggested in Chapters 1 and 2, he will switch the use of his land as soon as the expected flow of services from that land, when changed to another use, exceeds the value in its current use. More strictly, the use will change when the present value of the net yields from the alternative use exceeds the present value in the current use. Of course, the consumer may be comparing a land use that has an income flow – renting the land for agricultural use, say – with one that has no cash flow, e.g. preserving the land for amenity purposes. Nonetheless, the principle remains the same. All that we need to say is that he compares the respective present values of the *utility* from each use.

Where markets function properly, these alternative use values can be compared by looking directly at the current price of land. Land values are, in effect, market expressions of the present value of the services that the land can provide.

9

The Sales Plan of the Consumer: Saving and Savings

9.0 The Saving Plan

By *saving* we mean that part of a consumer's income that he decides not to spend. To date, we have assumed all income was spent – i.e. that the consumer operated at a point *on* the budget line. This analysis remains correct provided we modify the budget line to refer to income available for consumer-good expenditure – i.e. that income left over after the saving decision has been made. For any period t then, we have

$$S_t = Y_t - C_t$$

where S_t is saving, Y_t is income, and C_t is consumption expenditure. What we are now interested in is not the way in which C_t is distributed over alternative goods, but the prior decision to distribute income between saving and consumption-expenditure.

Saving is distinguished from *savings*: the latter refers to the consumer's wealth at any point in time. The consumer's problem as far as *savings* is concerned is how to distribute his wealth over the various assets – i.e. in what form to hold his savings. This decision is investigated in Sections 9.1 and 9.2.

In making a saving plan, the consumer is deciding how much of the income he expects to receive in the period lying ahead he will plan to spend on buying consumption goods during that period, and how much of it to reserve for buying consumption goods in future. The manner in which he will dispose of any given income between consumption and saving will depend on the relative intensity of his desires for consumption now and consumption in the future, and on his estimate of its relative capacity to satisfy these desires. We shall illustrate the influence exercised by each of these by a simple example. Let us suppose that the consumer is making his plan at the beginning of period t, and that his planning horizon encompasses two consecutive periods – period t (the present) and period $t + 1$ (the future). In Figure 9.0.1, we measure quantities of present goods on the vertical axis (C_0), and quantities of future goods on the horizontal axis (C_1). Each point that lies between these axes will represent a combination of some quantity of present goods with some quantity of future goods, and each combination will promise some level of unity to the consumer. The consumer's preferences as between different combinations of present and future goods can be illustrated on the figure by indifference curves. We have assumed that each indifference curve is convex to the origin.

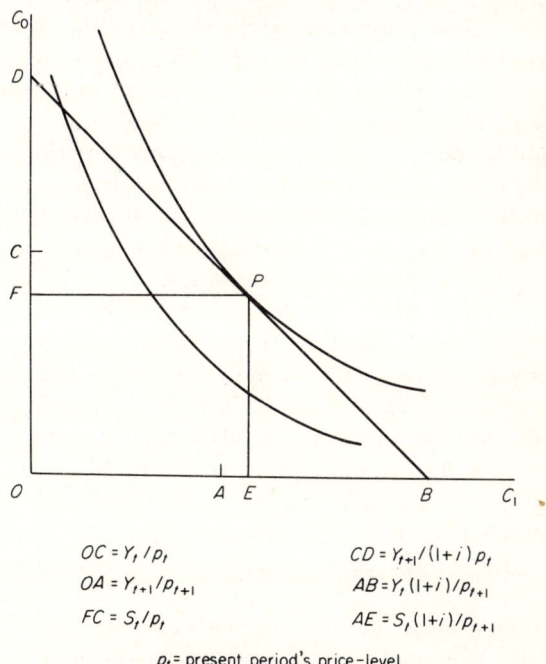

$OC = Y_t/p_t$ $CD = Y_{t+1}/(1+i)p_t$
$OA = Y_{t+1}/p_{t+1}$ $AB = Y_t(1+i)/p_{t+1}$
$FC = S_t/p_t$ $AE = S_t(1+i)/p_{t+1}$

p_t = present period's price-level
p_{t+1} = next period's expected price-level

Figure 9.0.1

Our assumption that each indifference curve is convex to the origin can be stated in another way. We shall define the marginal rate of substitution of future for present goods as the quantity of future goods the loss of which in the estimation of the consumer would just be compensated by an additional unit of present goods. The assumption that the curves are convex is, then, an assumption that the marginal rate of substitution of future for present goods decreases. An alternative name for this marginal rate of substitution is the *marginal rate of time preference*. The indifference map in Figure 9.0.1, then, shows us the consumer's tastes (as at the beginning of period t) for present and future goods and his preferences as between different combinations of them.

The ability of the consumer to obtain present and future goods will depend on the incomes he expects to receive and the prices he expects to have to pay for consumption goods and services in periods t and $t+1$ respectively, the rate of interest, and the stock of savings he possesses at the beginning of period t. The way in which these limit his ability to satisfy his present and future desires can be shown in Figure 9.0.1. We shall suppose that the expected incomes are Y_t and Y_{t+1} respectively, that the rate of interest is i per cent per period and that savings are initially zero. If the consumer were to eschew all present expenditures, the total monies at his disposal in period $t+1$ would consist of the income he expects to receive in that period plus the value of his current income and the interest he could earn on it by lending it, rather than spending it, during period t – i.e. in period $t+1$ he would have $Y_{t+1} + Y_t(1+i)$ available for spending on consumption goods and services. Given the prices that the consumer expects to rule in period $t+1$ – p_{t+1} – we can calculate the quantity of goods that this money would buy: in Figure 9.0.1, we assume that Y_{t+1} would buy OA goods ($= Y_{t+1}/p_{t+1}$), and $Y_t(1+i)$ would buy AB goods ($= Y_t(1+i)/p_{t+1}$), so that the consumer's total command over $t+1$ goods if all his spending were done then would be represented by OB. If the consumer were to concentrate all his spending in period t, the sum of money at his disposal would consist of the income of period t – i.e. Y_t – and the 'present value' of the income he expects to receive at the beginning of period $t+1$. If the consumer wants to spend next period's income now, he must borrow now from other consumers or firms, and pay interest on the loan until it can be repaid when the income of Y_{t+1} accrues at the beginning of period $t+1$. The sum which he borrows must be such that the principal and the interest on it will be equal to Y_{t+1} at that time – i.e. it must be $Y_{t+1}/(1+i)$.[1] Given the expected prices of consumption goods and services during period t, Y_t will buy OC (= Y divided by p_t, which is an index of the prices of consumption goods in

---

[1] If $Y_{t+1}/(1+i)$ is borrowed at the beginning of period t, the sum that the consumer will owe at the beginning of period $t+1$ will be $Y_{t+1}/(1+i)$ plus $i \cdot Y_{t+1}/(1+i)$, which is $Y_{t+1}/(1+i)$ all multiplied by $(1+i)$ or Y_{t+1} – i.e. the sum of money available at the beginning of $t+1$ to repay the principal of the loan and pay the interest on it.

period t), and the present value of Y_{t+1} will buy CD ($= Y_{t+1}/p_t(1+i)$), so that if all the consumers spending were done during period t, he could buy OD present goods.

The straight line joining D and B passes through all the combinations of present and future goods that the consumer could enjoy given expectations about his income, the relative prices of present and future goods and the rate of interest. Of these, he will prefer that denoted by P, where the line DB is tangential to one of the indifference curves: that is, he will plan to consume OF present goods during period t, and OE goods during period $t+1$. During period t, he will save a sum of money (S_t) that would command FC present goods; in period $t+1$, he will spend Y_{t+1} plus the then value of S_t, which will be $S_t(1+i)$ and which will command AE goods in that period. He is planning to save in period t and to dis-save in the subsequent period. In Chapter 1, we assumed that the consumer had already decided upon his planned consumption expenditure per period; we have now shown how that choice is made.

The consumption-saving plan represented by the point P in Figure 9.0.1 will be revised if there is any change in the consumer's tastes and preferences, expectations about present and future incomes and prices, the rate of interest, or in the stock of savings. We shall illustrate the consequences of a change in any one of these.

First, the effects on the consumption-saving plan of a change in tastes and preferences. Let us suppose that a consumer plans to save more and spend less on consumption, while savings, incomes, prices and the interest rate remain unchanged. The cause of this revision in his plan must lie in some change in his tastes and preferences – he may have experienced some sudden psychological conversion that leads him to value future goods more highly than before. The new pattern of tastes and preferences is illustrated in Figure 9.0.2: there, each indifference curve is relatively steeper near the vertical axis and relatively flatter as it approaches the horizontal axis, so that P_1 in Figure 9.0.2 lies south and east of P in Figure 9.0.1. Alternatively, we may say that the quantity of future goods that the consumer would surrender for each unit of present goods is now less than before. Conversely, if the consumer plans to save less, *ceteris paribus*, it must be because he has become less thrifty, and the implications of this change in his tastes and preferences can be seen by assuming that Figure 9.0.2 illustrates the initial position and by comparing this with Figure 9.0.1.

Second, the effects of a change in the rate of interest. In Figure 9.0.3

all the combinations of present and future goods that the consumer could buy at the given expected prices and incomes and rate of interest of i per cent per period lie on the line BD. If the rate of interest should fall to i_1 per cent per period, *ceteris paribus*, this 'budget' line will move to B_1D_1, for now that the interest rate is lower, the command of the consumer over present goods will be greater and his command over future goods will be less. The power to acquire present goods rises

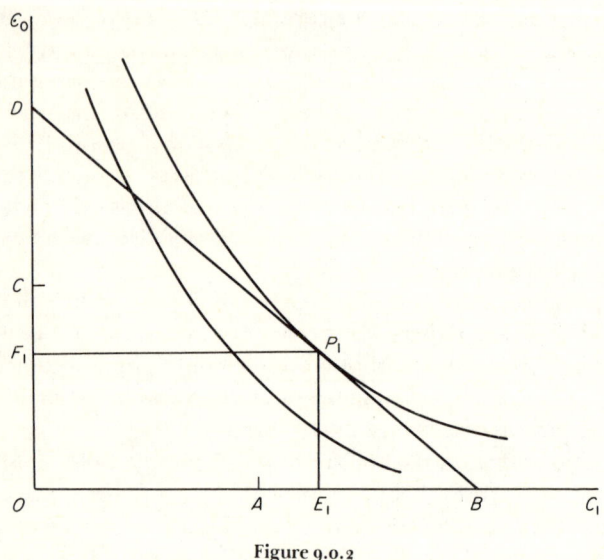

Figure 9.0.2

because the present value of next period's income (CD in Figure 9.0.1) rises when the interest rate falls; command over future goods falls because the value in the next period of this period's income (AB in Figure 9.0.1) falls when the interest rate falls. Of the combinations lying on B_1D_1, the consumer will choose P_1 where B_1D_1 touches an indifference curve. We know from experience that planned saving may fall or rise as a result of a relatively small fall in the interest rate. By introspection, we can easily adduce reasons why either reaction may occur. If the lower rate of interest is expected to rule indefinitely, and if the consumer is intent on enjoying a given income from his savings over some span of future periods or on accumulating a given stock of savings at some future date, he may plan to save more now than before; and his tastes and preferences as between present and future

Saving and Savings

goods would be illustrated in Figure 9.0.3(a). Typically, however, we would expect planned saving to fall when the rate of interest falls, for if all other things remain the same, each sum of money that is set aside now will command a smaller quantity of goods in the next (or any

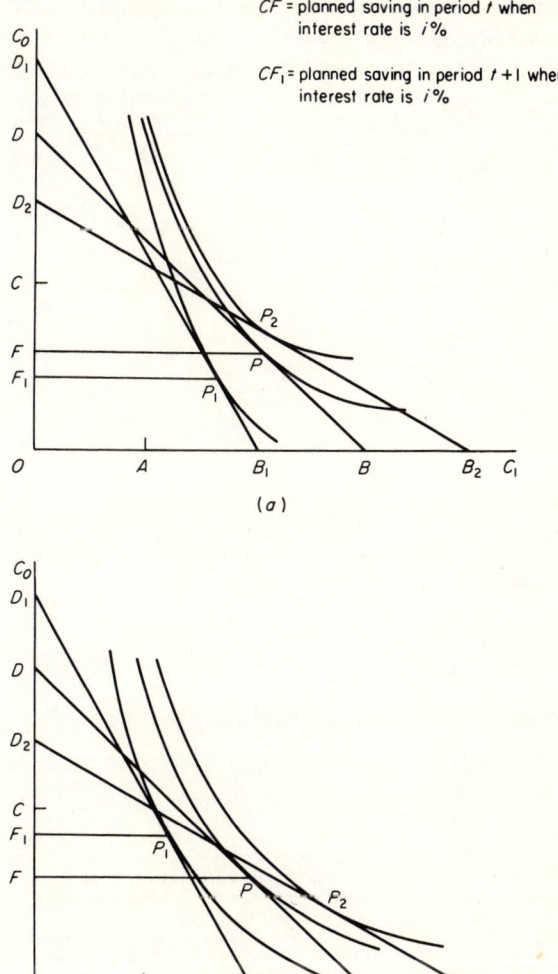

Figure 9.0.3

future) period the lower is the rate of interest: this more usual reaction is shown in Figure 9.0.3(b). Conversely, if the rate of interest were to rise to i_2 per cent per period, the 'budget line' would move to B_2D_2, and the new consumption-saving plan would be denoted by P_2. At P_2, planned saving will generally be greater than at P, though it might be less. The relationships between planned saving and the rate of interest that are implicit in Figures 9.0.3(a) and (b) are shown explicitly in Figures 9.0.4(a) and (b). Irrespective of the direction of the change in planned saving, there is evidence to suggest that its magnitude is

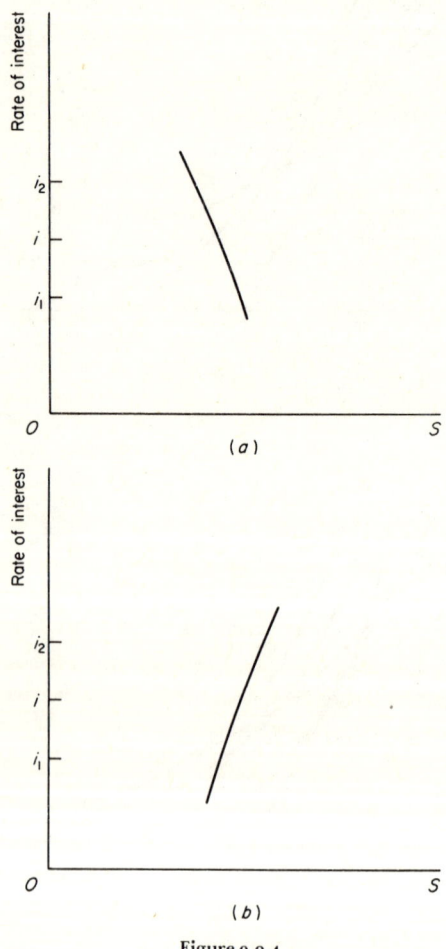

Figure 9.0.4

small: that is, in our jargon, the interest-elasticity of saving, while it may be positive or negative, will usually be 'low' – that is, near to zero.

Third, the effect on the consumer's consumption-saving plan of a change in present and future incomes. Let us suppose that income in period t rises, tastes, the rate of interest, and expectations about future income and present and future prices remaining the same. The consequences are illustrated in Figure 9.0.5 by a movement of the 'budget line' from BD to B_1D_1,[1] and a change in the consumption-saving plan from that denoted by P to that denoted by P_1. The consequences of any

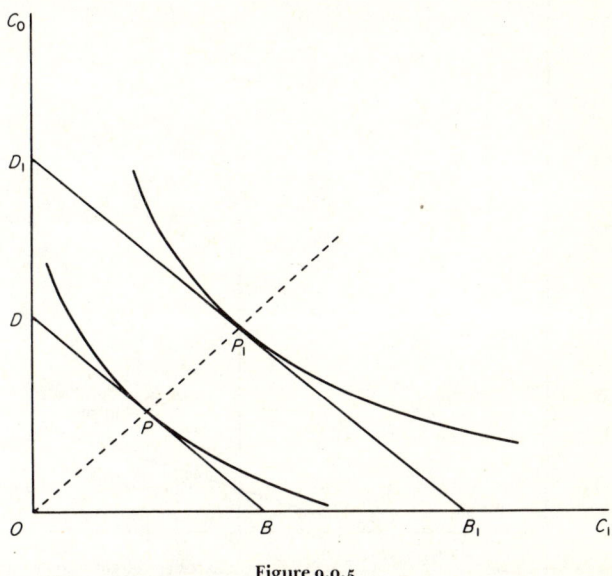

Figure 9.0.5

other possible change in present income, all other things remaining the same, can be illustrated in a similar way. The relationship between present income and planned saving that is implicit in the points P, P_1, etc., in Figure 9.0.5 as shown in Figure 9.0.6. Most empirical studies have concluded that planned saving varies in the same direction, though not, of course, in the same proportion, as income, and the shape we have given to the indifference curves in Figure 9.0.5 is such as

---

[1] It can easily be shown that B_1D_1 will be parallel to BD. The slope of BD is equal to $Y_t + Y_{t+1}/(1+i)/p_t$ divided by $(Y_{t+1} + Y_t (1+i))p_{t+1}$ – that is, to $p_{t+1}(1+i)/p_t$. The slope of B_1D_1, which is the 'budget line' when the present income has risen to Y_t is $(Y_t + Y_{t+1}/(1+i)/p_t$ divided by $(Y_{t+1} + Y_t(1+i)/p_{t+1}$, – that is, $p_{t+1}(1_t+i)/p_t$.

to give this kind of behaviour. At very low incomes, savings may be negative – that is, there may be *dis-saving* – for the consumer might then be forced to realise his past savings, or, lacking these, to borrow money to supplement his income; as his present income rises, saving soon becomes positive as it rises also. The relationship between the consumer's planned saving and his present income that is portrayed in Figure 9.0.6 is called his *propensity to save*. Implicit in this is a

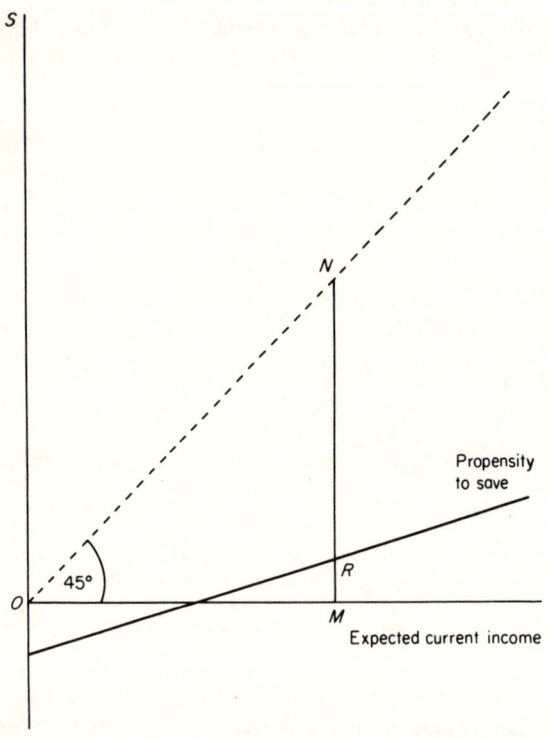

Figure 9.0.6

relationship between planned consumption-expenditure and present income. This latter can be shown on the figure by drawing a line with a slope of 45° through the origin: since the consumer plans to spend that part of income that he does not plan to save, the planned consumption-expenditure at each income will be equal to the vertical distance between the propensity-to-save line and the 45° line at that income. Thus, if the present income were *OM* (= *MN*), planned saving would be *MR* and planned consumption-expenditure *RN*. The relationship between consumption and present income is shown explicitly in Figure 9.0.7, this relationship is called the *propensity to consume*.

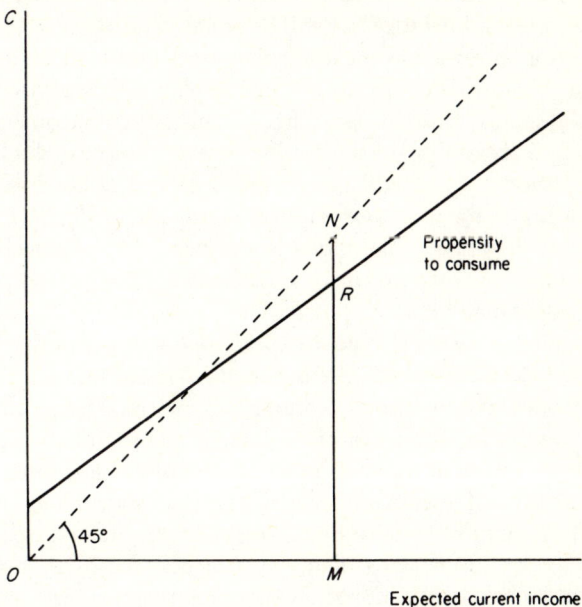

Figure 9.0.7

The propensity to save (consume) schedule that is graphed in Figure 9.0.6 (Figure 9.0.7) shows us the amount that the consumer would plan to save (consume) at each level of present income, if his tastes and preferences, the rate of interest, his expectations about his future income and about present and future prices, all remained unchanged. The proportion of each income that the consumer would plan to save (consume), *ceteris paribus*, is called the *average propensity to save (consume)*: in Figure 9.0.6, the average propensity to save when present income is *OM* is equal to *MR/OM*, and the average propensity to consume at the same level of income is equal to *RN/OM*. As we have drawn the schedule, the former rises continuously and the latter falls continuously as income rises. The rate of change in planned saving (consumption) as present income changes is called the *marginal propensity to save (consume)* and it is measured by the slope of the propensity-to-save (consume) line over the appropriate range of income. In our figures, the propensities to save and consume are drawn as straight lines, so that the marginal propensities to save and consume are the same at each income. From the manner in which we have measured them, it is clear that the marginal propensities to save and consume, at each level of income, when added together will be equal to unity.

In the same way, we may illustrate diagrammatically the manner in which the consumer's consumption-saving plan will be revised if his expectations about future income changes, his present income and all the other data remaining the same. If he expects to receive a higher income in period $t + 1$, B will move eastwards and D northwards in Figure 9.0.1, and the new consumption-saving plan will generally be such that planned saving in period t is less than before. Conversely, if the expected future income falls, the consumer will generally plan to save more now than before.

Fourth, the effects of a change in expected present and future prices. If present prices rise, then, *ceteris paribus*, the consumer's present money income, and the present value of his expected future income, will command a smaller quantity of present goods and services; the purchasing power of next period's income and of the then value of the present income will remain unchanged. The new 'budget line' will rise less steeply than the old one, and, it is shown by BD_1 in Figure 9.0.8. In the new consumption-saving plan, which is denoted by P_1, the consumer is planning to save more now that present goods have become dearer relative to future goods – his flow of consumption-spending is being redistributed over time in favour of those periods in which goods and services now appear to be relatively cheaper. Conversely, if present prices fall, the consumer will now plan to save less and to spend more now than before.

Lastly, the influence of savings on the consumption-saving plan of the consumer. We have assumed so far that the consumer has no savings when planning at the beginning of period t, and the indifference curves that we have drawn reflect his tastes and preferences for present and future goods in his knowledge that savings are zero. In our examples, the consumer will have accumulated savings by the beginning of period $t + 1$. In describing his consumption-savings plans for period $t + 1$ and $t + 2$, however, we cannot assume that his indifference map is unchanged, for the possession of savings will affect his relative valuations of present and future goods. His present savings give him command over future goods, so that we would expect his desire to add to savings – that is, to save during period $t + 1$ – to be less intense. If we were to draw an indifference map that reflected the existence of savings, we would expect each curve in it to have the shape illustrated in Figure 9.0.1 rather than the shape shown in Figure 9.0.2. We shall not attempt to portray the influence of savings on tastes and preferences for present and future goods. Intuition, introspection and observation all suggest, however, that if savings increase, the typical

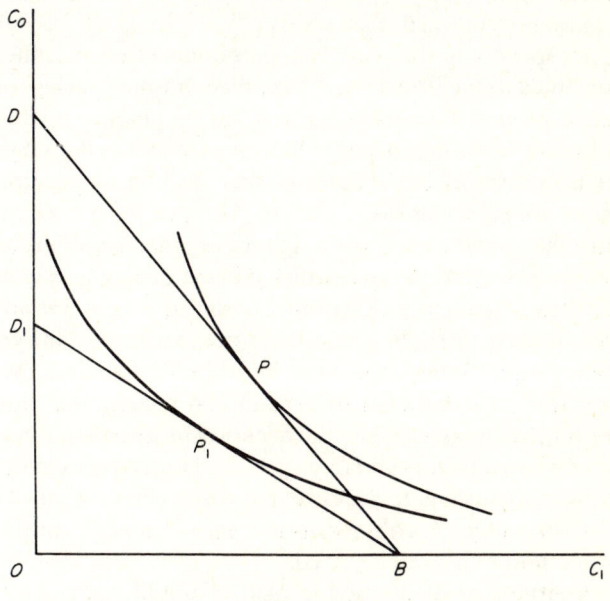

Figure 9.0.8

consumer will plan to save less and consume more of his present income, with given expectations about its future incomes, present and future prices and the interest-rate; and if the value of his savings declines, we would expect him, *ceteris paribus*, to plan to save more and spend less out of each level of present income. The influence of the value of savings on planned saving and consumption expenditure is called the '*Pigou Effect*'.[1] We shall return, though in no great detail, to the role of savings, for presently we shall be describing the forms in which a consumer may hold his savings and one 'form' in which

[1] See A. C. Pigou, 'The Classical Stationary State', *Economic Journal*, 1943. The 'Pigou effect' plays a central role in some macroeconomic models. See, in particular, D. Patinkin, *Money, Interest and Prices* (Harper Row, London, 1967).

savings may be held is consumption goods and services – that is, at any point in time the consumer may decide to spend all or a part of his savings.

We have assumed, so far, that only consumers save or have savings; in practice, however, firms do both. The income of a firm is its profits – that is, the sum of money that it expects to be left with after the fixed and variable costs of production have been paid out of the expected total revenue. A firm may either spend its income – that is, distribute it to the consumers in which the owners of the firm reside – or save it – that is, not spend it in this way. That part of the firm's income that is not distributed to the firm's owners is called 'business saving' or 'undistributed profits'. Our problem is to list the things on which the planned saving of the firm depends. If we regard the whole of the profit that the firm earns as accruing in the first instance to its consumer-owners, who then decide how much of it to spend and how much to save, then the preceding analysis might suffice: that part of the income that a consumer-owner receives which it does not plan to spend is left with the firm as undistributed profits. It may be tolerably realistic to view some firms in this light – especially firms that are owned by one or by a few people. Where the firm is a limited liability company, however, the nexus between ownership and control that this view assumes is much weaker. While the firm may be owned by many, it is controlled by its directors and managers, and the interests of these do not necessarily coincide. It is these latter who decide how much of the firm's profits will be distributed to its owners (to augment their incomes) and how much will be saved.

The determinants of the saving plan of the firm are similar to, though not the same as, those of the consumer's plan. We shall rest content with merely listing them. The analogue of the consumer's tastes and preferences as between present and future goods is the range of opportunities for earning profit that the firm expects to be open to it both now and in the future; we would expect the return per pound spent on buying inputs to decline, in future, as the firm planned to spend more and more pounds in the future and fewer and fewer pounds now, and vice versa. Second, the firm's saving will depend on its expected present and future profits: if profit is expected to decline in future as compared with its present level, we would expect the firm to plan to save more now than it otherwise would. Third, the firm's plan will be influenced by the present relationship between input and output prices and how this is expected to behave in future: if input prices are expected to fall, *ceteris paribus*, we would expect the firm to save more now so that it will be in a better position to exploit the relatively cheaper inputs in the future. Fourth, the rate of interest: it is probable that business saving, like individual saving, is relatively unresponsive to changes in the interest rate. Lastly, there are a number of influences that affect the firm's decision but which have no close counterpart with the individual. A firm may desire to grow, and current saving is one method by which this objective may be achieved. Furthermore, firms may plan to borrow to meet future commitments or grasp future opportunities, and the strength of their desire to save now will tend to vary inversely with the ease and cheapness with which they expect to be able to procure money in the future when they need it. Given all these, we would expect business saving, like individual saving, to vary in the same direction, though not necessarily in the same proportion, as current business income.

We have now described how the consumption-saving plan of the individual consumer (or the analogous plan of the individual firm) will be reviewed if there is any change in expectations about present or future incomes, the expected prices of present and future goods, or in the rate of interest. From these revisions, two relationships are commonly derived, namely, the relationship between planned saving and the rate of interest, and that between planned saving and current income. We shall call the former the individual's *supply of saving*, and we have called the latter his *propensity to save*. And our discussion in the previous pages has shown the direction in which each of these schedules will shift if any other planning datum should alter. The total supply curve of saving in each period may be obtained by adding together the planned saving of each individual at each rate of interest: while some of the individual supply curves may have negative slopes and elasticities, it is unlikely that these will be reflected in the shape of the total supply curve, for the majority of individuals will plan to save somewhat more as the interest rate rises. The total curve, like its components, will be interest-inelastic. It might be thought that the role that individuals play in determining the relationship between the rate of interest and other prices is summarised in the total supply curve of saving, in the same way as their role in determining the relative prices of other inputs is played by the total supply curves of them. This, however, is not so, and for two reasons. First, interest is the price received by those who lend money and paid by those who borrow it. This price is formally determined by the supply of, and the demand for, loans. The supply of loans – that is, of money for lending – is not, however, the same as the supply of saving, saving is merely not spending on the purchase of current consumption goods and services: the money that is not so spent may be used in many ways, only one of which is to lend it. Second, as we shall see later (Chapter 11), the relative prices of labour and of the services rendered by land are determined by the disposition of the total stock of labour and of land among their different uses. Saving, however, is not a stock: rather, it is a flow per period that augments the stock of savings. The flow of saving in any period is small as compared with the existing stock of savings; being small, we can neglect it as we did implicitly with the additions to the labour force (through, for example, a net excess of births over deaths) or to the stock of land (through reclamation, for example). We shall see in the next chapter how consumers and firms, in deciding upon the forms in which to hold their savings, help to determine the rate of interest.

The propensity to save of all individuals and firms in an economy is a relationship between the economy's income (that is, the income of all firms and individuals) and planned saving. This cannot be obtained by simply 'adding together' the propensities to save of all the individual firms and consumers, and we can see why not by taking a simple example. We shall suppose that there are but two consumers in the economy and that their propensities to save are as drawn in Figure 9.0.9. Before we can calculate the total planned saving out of each level of the economy's income, we must know how the total income is distributed between the constituent individuals. Thus, if the total income is 1,000 per period, and if it is distributed equally between the two individuals, the total planned saving will be R_1S_1 plus R_2S_2 or RS in Figure 9.0.9(c). If the same income had been distributed in the proportions 1 : 3, with individual A (who has the 'higher' propensity to save) receiving 250, and B (who would plan to save less out of each income than A) receiving 750 per period, the total planned saving would be less at RT. If the income had been distributed in the proportions 3 : 1, planned saving for the economy as a whole would have been greater at RV. This may be confirmed by supposing that A's propensity to save is given by the equation $S_a = -50 + \frac{1}{2} \cdot Y_a$, and B's by the equation $S_b = -100 + \frac{1}{3} \cdot Y_b$, where S and Y denote saving and income respectively, and the suffixes a and b particular consumers. If total income is 1,000, and if A and B each receive 500 per period, A will plan to save 200 and B 67, so that RS will be equal to 267. When A receives one-quarter and B three-quarters of this income, A will save 75 and B 150, so that RT is 225. When A gets three-quarters and B one-quarter, A saves 325 and B saves minus 17, so that RV is 308.

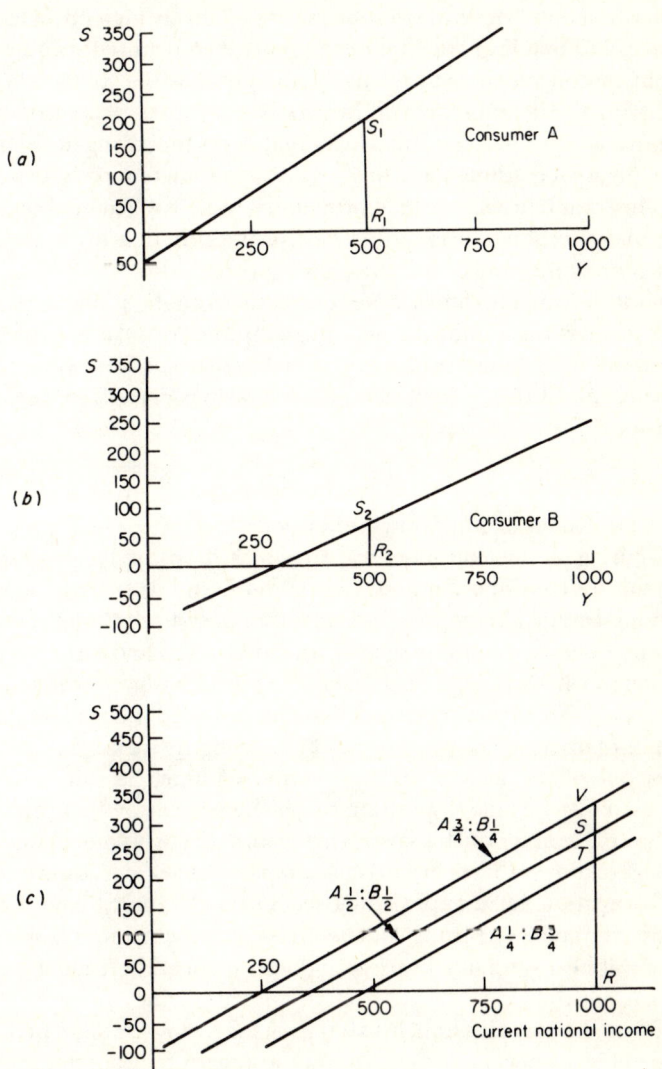

Figure 9.0.9

We could show in precisely the same way that the planned saving by both consumers at each level of total income will depend on how that income is distributed between them. It is clear, then, that the propensity to save of the economy as a whole will rise, *ceteris paribus*, if income is redistributed in favour of consumers with relatively high propensities to save, and that it will fall if the economy's income is redistributed in favour of consumers with relatively low propensities to save. When specifying the determinants of the propensity to save of an economy, we must add to the list of influences that affect the saving decision of the individual consumer and firm, the distribution of income between consumers and firms. The total propensity-to-save schedule shows the role that consumers play, and a part of the role that firms play, in determining the level of the economy's income.

In this section thus far we have concentrated on the saving decision; once this has been implemented, the consumer or firm must decide how it will hold the sum of money that it has saved until it requires it at some future time. We shall examine this savings decision in the next section.

9.1 The Savings Plan: Money and Bonds

In Figure 9.0.1 the consumer was shown as choosing to spend some amount on consumption goods in period t, and to save some other amount. Implicit in the analysis is that the consumer's choice is a simple one – between consuming now, and saving now and earning a rate of interest on his savings. Such a simple approach obscures an important aspect of the saving decision: that the consumer will have available to him many ways in which to hold his saving. If we assume that he saves out of his income in each period of time, he will have accumulated *savings* the disposition of which presents another problem of choice. He may hold his savings in the form of government bonds or bills, as ordinary shares in a private company, as Local Authority loan stock, or in the form of physical assets such as property, land, works of art, antiques. The list is endless, particularly when we realise that there will be a substantial variety of government and private industry stock in which he can 'invest' – that is, hold his savings. In any period, of course, he may also hold his savings in the form of money, perhaps to spend in the next period or as precaution against unexpected events, but also as an asset. The decision to distribute savings over various assets, including money, is called a *portfolio decision*. If accumulated savings are, say, £1000, a possible *portfolio* might be £100 cash + £400 on deposit with the bank + £500 ordinary shares. Obviously, however, there are many other combinations. For the moment, we imagine that only one asset exists other than money, called 'bonds'. The consumer's decision concerns the allocation of savings between money and bonds. Bonds may be held because they yield an income annually, or because their purchase and sale (or vice versa) yields a capital gain – a difference between the buying and selling value. We shall assume that individuals are interested in capital gains.

It is as well to understand the relationship between the price of a bond and its rate of interest. Suppose the only bonds in question are issued by central government. They are issued 'at par' at a price of £100 each. This price is the *nominal value* of the stock. It will have been issued at a particular rate of interest, say $3\frac{1}{2}$ per cent: this means that the central government promises to pay £3.50 each year to the holders of each £100 nominal value of stock. This initially declared rate of interest is called the *coupon yield*. The stock is likely to have a redemption date, say 1980, at which the full £100 will be repaid to the holders of the stock. Until then, its *market price* will vary with supply and demand. Suppose, for example, that the market price is now £50 and that there is *no* redemption date. Each holder of stock still receives £3.50 each year, even though purchase of the stock in the market would cost only £50. If we express £3.50 as a yield on £50, it is 7 per cent and this is the *market rate of interest*. The following table shows how the price and rate of interest are related.

Market price	Nominal yield %	Market yield = Rate of interest %
£100	£3.50	£3.50
£80	£3.50	£4.37
£50	£3.50	£7.00
£20	£3.50	£17.50

The table shows clearly that as the market price falls, the rate of interest rises. This relationship is general: price and yield vary inversely.

In fact we could have calculated the rate of interest from the following formula:

$$\text{Market Price} = \frac{\text{Coupon Yield in year 1}}{(1+i)} + \frac{\text{Coupon Yield in Year 2}}{(1+i)^2} + \text{etc.}$$

or

$$P = \frac{C_1}{(1+i)} + \frac{C_2}{(1+i)^2} + \frac{C_3}{(1+i)^3} + \ldots + \frac{C_n}{(1+i)^n}$$

where n is the number of years to maturity. Where the bond is a perpetuity, as we have so far assumed, we have $n = \infty$, and the series is a geometric progression with sum C/i. Where the bond has a redemption date of, say, 10 years, $n = 10$ and the final yield will be £3.50 *plus* the nominal value of £100. By substituting values for P and C in the equation, we can solve for i, the market rate of interest, hereafter called simply the *yield*.

The problem from the consumer's point of view is that the future yield on bonds is not known. Supply and demand vary over time and bond prices will therefore fluctuate. If the consumer held such a large holding of bonds that he could influence the market price by buying and selling, he would of course have some idea of future price trends. We assume he cannot influence price in this way and that the future is therefore characterised by a state of *uncertainty* about bond prices. What matters then is the consumer's *expectations* about future prices. At the simplest level, if he expects bond prices to rise (the yield to fall), he may buy bonds now, when their price is low, and sell them later when the price has risen (assuming his expectations are fulfilled). In this way he makes a *capital gain*. We might therefore formulate a fairly simple proposition about the consumer's behaviour. If bond prices are low already, the consumer will expect them to rise: he will buy bonds and part with money to do so. If, on the other hand, bond prices are already high, he will have much lower expectations of a price rise. Perhaps he buys just a few bonds only. In other words

the higher the existing price, the lower the expectations about a rising future price, and hence the lower will the demand for bonds be.

The behaviour of the consumer who obeys this proposition is depicted in Figure 9.1.1. The current bond price is measured on the vertical axis OL. Equally, we could show this axis in terms of yields. To avoid confusing the figure, we show the current yields corresponding to each market price on the right-hand side vertical axis L_1N. Notice that this axis goes from top to bottom, with low yields at the top: this is because the yield bears an inverse relation to the bond price. Along the horizontal axis is measured the total amount of savings available to the consumer, OM, and which he has to distribute between money and bonds.

Saving and Savings

At a bond price of 80 and a yield of 4.37 per cent (the coupon rate being $3\frac{1}{2}$ per cent in keeping with our original example), the consumer feels there is no possibility of prices rising any further. Consequently, he chooses to hold all his savings in the form of money. His portfolio is then OM of money and zero bonds. When the price is 70, and the yield is 5 per cent, the consumer expects a price rise, but considerable uncertainty attaches to such a change. Hence he 'invests' only part of his money, the amount OA. This leaves AM held in money, so the portfolio is now OA bonds and AM money. The curve O_1M traces out the consumer's demand curve for bonds given current bond prices.

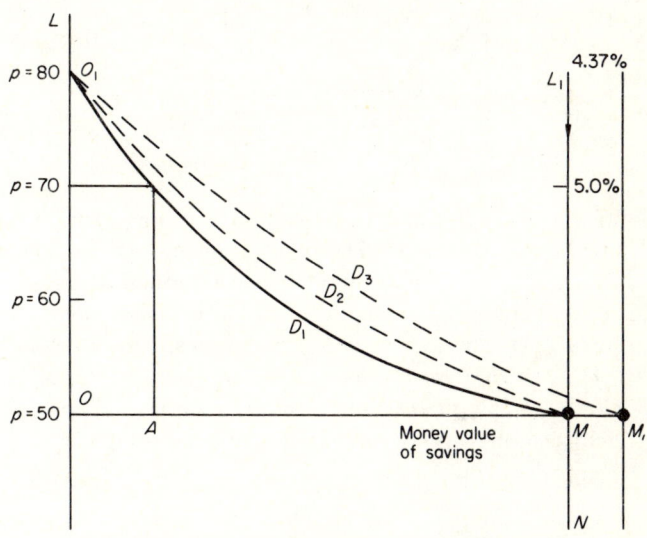

Figure 9.1.1

From Figure 9.1.1 we can derive various curves along the consumer's demand for bonds and for money. Thus, Figure 9.1.2 shows a demand curve for bonds. It is in fact identical to curve O_1M in Figure 9.1.1, but at prices below 50, at which point the consumer puts all his savings into bonds, the curve has unitary elasticity – that is, if savings are increased by 10 per cent, bond holdings are increased by 10 per cent. We can also construct a supply curve of the consumer's willingness to hold bonds. Such a curve is shown in Figure 9.1.3, but note that it shows bond holdings measured against the yield on bonds. This curve will have unit elasticity about the yield of 7 per cent. (The reader should recall that unit elasticity in a supply curve appears as a positively sloped straight line).

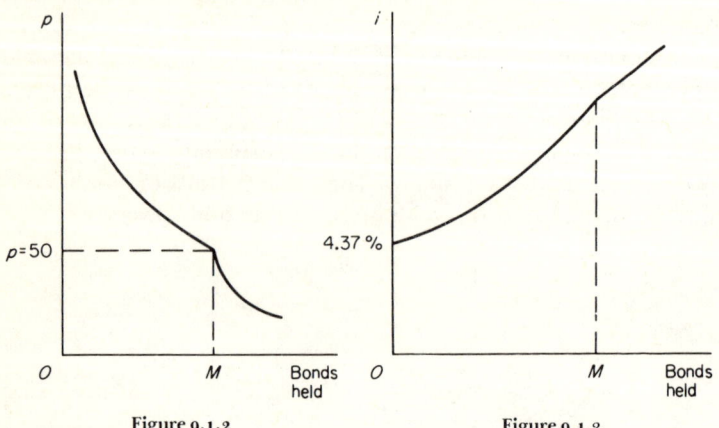

Figure 9.1.2   Figure 9.1.3

Equally, the curve in Figure 9.1.1 can be shown as a supply curve and demand curve for money. Figure 9.1.4 shows the demand curve. At a yield of 4.37 per cent all savings are held as money. At rates below 4.37 per cent, therefore, the quantity of money held does not increase. At the rate of 7 per cent savings are held as bonds and the 'demand' for money is zero. In Figure 9.1.5 this same relationship is expressed as a supply curve: at low prices the consumer's supply of money (i.e. savings held as money) is low, and at high prices it is high.

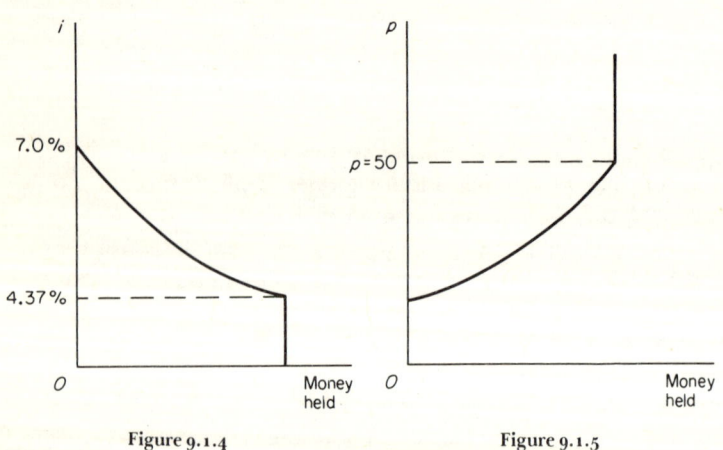

Figure 9.1.4   Figure 9.1.5

If the consumer's expectations about future bond prices change, the curves in the previous figures will shift. Suppose that prices are expected to be higher in the future than was previously imagined. The expectation of capital gain is therefore increased and the consumer will wish to hold more bonds than before. The curve in Figure 9.1.1 will shift to the right to D_2. Notice that the 'end points' of the new demand curve are the same as the old end points. This is because we assume that the consumer retains his belief about the very low rate of interest of 4.37 per cent – that is, he doesn't believe yields can go lower than this. And he still has the same total savings, so the new curve must also end at M.

If the consumer's savings are higher, at OM_1 instead of OM in Figure 9.1.1, the demand curve becomes D_3. Again it is assumed that the upper and lower interest rates remain the same. The reader can experiment on Figures 9.1.1 to 9.1.5 to show the effects of these two changes on those figures.

Notice that the analysis presented so far will not differ materially if the consumer's savings at the beginning of the period are held entirely in money (as we have so far implicitly assumed) or in an existing portfolio of some bonds and some money.

To obtain an overall demand curve for bonds, or money, we simply add the individual demand curves. If the majority of bond holders (firms and consumers) revise their expectations in the same direction, the total demand curve will shift, just as it did for the individual consumer. If, on the other hand, part of the market revises its expectations upwards and the remainder revises them downwards, the total demand curve will remain fairly stable.

The aim of this section has been to show the relevance of the consumer's portfolio decision to the determination of the interest rate. We now turn, briefly, to the more complex situation in which the portfolio choice is wider than that between money and bonds.

9.2 The Savings Plan: Wider Portfolio Choice

In the previous section, the consumer was shown to exercise a choice between money and bonds. If the consumer knew exactly what would happen to the price of bonds – that is, if there was complete certainty about the future – there would be little point in holding money at all. Bonds could be converted at any time as the need for cash arises, and holding cash on its own would be an unprofitable venture since it yields no rate of interest. Indeed, holding cash is itself risky in a world where the general goods price level is rising since the real value of cash holdings is eroded over time. The reason that individuals, companies and institutions do not hold all their assets in the form of cash is therefore obvious. Equally, since the future is not certain it is easy to see why not all assets are held as bonds. Uncertainty is therefore the basic reason for the existence of *mixed portfolios*. We could add to this the fact that switching in and out of different types of asset is not costless: there are *transactions costs* (brokerage fees, bank charges, and so on). Hence, even in a certain world, we would not expect all assets to be held as bonds because it would be costly to switch out of bonds and into cash when it was needed. These are the basic reasons for holding mixed portfolios. In practice, of course, the competition of a portfolio can be varied over an almost infinite range because of the wide variety of assets available to any 'investor'. In this section we look briefly at the portfolio decision when more than two assets are available.[1]

We shall concentrate on portfolios of assets which have a positive yield. We have already observed that each asset has a risk attached to it: we do not know what the future yield will be. We may, however, know the range of values the yield is likely to take and the probability that each yield will occur. For example, we may know that there is a 60 : 40 chance the yield will be either 9 per cent or 14 per cent. We may then take a weighted average of these two possible outcomes: this average is called the *expected value*. In our example it will be

$$(0.6 \times 9) + (0.4 \times 14) = 5.4 + 5.6 = 11.0 \text{ per cent.}$$

More probably, the range of variations will be wider, perhaps from 8 to 15 per cent and there will be probabilities that 8, 9, 10, 11, 12, 13, 14 and 15 per cent will occur. The computation of the expected value follows the same rule given above, however. If we knew that the corresponding probabilities were 5, 10, 15, 20, 20, 15, 10 and 5 per cent respectively, the expected value would be

$$(0.05 \times 8) + (0.10 \times 9) + (0.15 \times 10) + (0.20 \times 11) + (0.20 \times 12)$$
$$+ (0.15 \times 13) + (0.10 \times 14) + (0.05 \times 15) = 11.50 \text{ per cent.}$$

But the decision to hold this asset cannot be made on the basis of expected value alone. Figure 9.2.1 shows why. The vertical axis

---

[1] Strictly, we have already considered the three-asset case since our analysis embraces goods, money and bonds. The holding of goods is analysed under the demand for goods.

Saving and Savings

measures the probability that each value will occur, the horizontal axis measures the values the yield may take. Curve A shows the asset we have just considered. Curve B shows a different asset which has the same expected value but clearly shows a wider 'spread' of values.

The problem is that the asset holder can expect to be more certain that the expected value of A will occur than that the expected value of B will occur, even though the two expected values are the same. If he dislikes riskiness (that is, if he is a *risk-averter*) he will prefer asset A to asset B. A measure of the 'spread' taken on by the values in each case is the *variance* or *standard deviation*.[1] These are symbolised by σ^2 and σ respectively. If we call the expected value E, the suggestion is that the consumer looks at assets in terms of their corresponding values of E and σ.[2]

If the consumer does look at assets in terms of expected value and variance, we would expect his indifference map to look as in Figure 9.2.2. Notice that this map is drawn for a risk-averter. *Risk-lovers* could have convex indifference curves and preferred positions would lie to the right of the asset-yield space.

If we consider points B and C we see that C has a higher E and a higher σ. The consumer may therefore be indifferent between B and C because although C has a higher risk it also has a higher expected value, and the latter compensates the former. Point A lies on a more

---

[1] The underlying idea of a measure of variance is to observe the deviations of actual values of the yield from the expected value. But inspection shows that some of the values will be greater than E and some lower. Simply adding up the deviations would not produce a sensible result because the plusses would cancel out the minuses. Consequently, the squares of the deviations are taken since this is one way of eliminating the + and − signs. Thus, if the expected value is $\bar{X}$ and any actual value is given by X, then the variance is measured by

$$\frac{1}{n}\left[(X_1-\bar{X})^2 + (X_2-\bar{X})^2 + \ldots\right]$$

where n is the number of observations of the value of X. Introducing the summation sign this becomes

$$\sigma^2 = \frac{1}{n}\sum_i (X_i - \bar{X})^2$$

or

$$\sigma = \sqrt{\frac{1}{n}\sum_i (X_i - \bar{X})^2}$$

[2] In fact this is only correct if the distribution of values appears as in Figure 9.2.1 – i.e. if values are normally distributed. In practice they may well not be and further measures of the distribution are required. Unfortunately this tends to complicate the entire analysis rather severely.

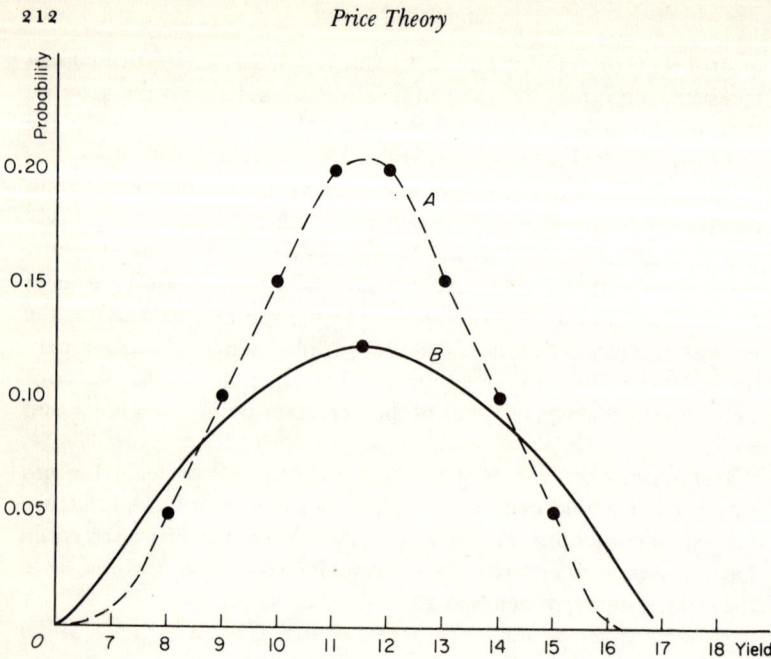

Figure 9.2.1

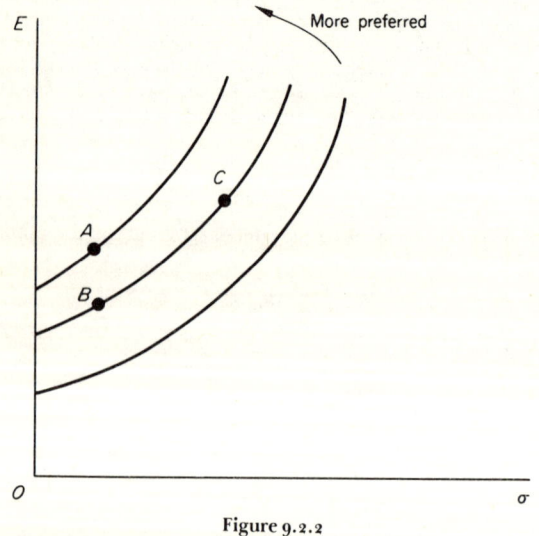

Figure 9.2.2

preferred curve because it has a higher E than asset B, without any increased risk. Now points A, B and C can just as easily refer to entire portfolios – that is, collections of assets. To calculate the expected value of a portfolio we simply calculate the individual expected values of each of the assets it combines. Calculating the variance of an entire portfolio is less straightforward, but suffice it to say that it can be done.[1]

Just as the consumer, faced with product indifference curves selected the optimum, so we assume the asset holder does the same thing. But in this case the construction of the relevant constraint contour – analogous to the budget line – is more difficult.

Suppose that the consumer knows the expected values, variances and covariances for the various combinations of assets open to him. Figure 9.2.3 shows some examples of the resulting values for E and σ

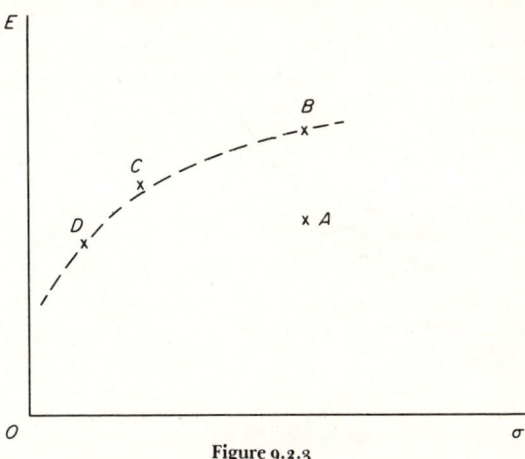

Figure 9.2.3

for the various portfolios that are possible. It should be obvious that a portfolio like A is not worth considering since portfolio B lies directly above it – i.e. B has a greater E for the same level of risk. We can dub portfolio A 'inefficient'. None of the portfolios we have depicted lies

---

[1] The main point about the variance of a combined-asset holding is that the variation in one asset may offset another if yields vary inversely. A measure of the extent to which yields may move together or inversely is the *covariance*. For an asset with values X and another with values Y, the covariance is defined as

$$COV_{XY} = \frac{1}{n} \sum (X_i - \bar{X})(Y_i - \bar{Y}).$$

above B, so B is an 'efficient' portfolio – it represents a possible portfolio from which we might choose.

Portfolio C, on the other hand, has a lower risk and a lower expected value than B. But no portfolio lies above it so it, too, is 'efficient'. In general, we might expect a cautious investor to prefer C to B but the exact nature of the consumer's preferences are shown by his indifference map. Portfolio D is also efficient. Notice that all the portfolios lying below an imaginary line through D, C and B are inefficient. They can therefore be precluded from consideration.[1]

Figure 9.2.4 shows the composite picture with the 'efficiency locus' and the individual's indifference map superimposed. For the risk-averting individual the equilibrium will exist at A on the highest attainable indifference curve. Thus the individual selects the portfolio

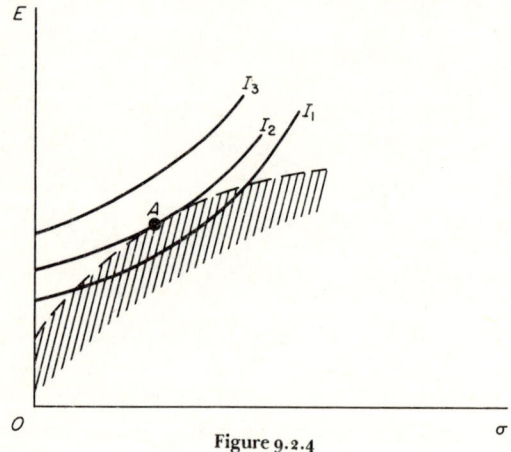

Figure 9.2.4

corresponding to point A and in so doing his demand for each of the assets it contains is determined. In turn, this constitutes one element in the total demand for each of the assets – the total demand being the sum total of the individual demands. This demand is then one side of the picture in determining the market price of the asset, and hence its

---

[1] Which is just as well. If we have to select two assets from three, they can be combined in three ways. If we select two from four, the possible combinations are six; two from five gives ten. The formula is nCr, where C denotes a combination. nCr reduces to $n!/(n-r)!\,r!$ So, if the choice is 5 from 50 the combinations are $50!/45!\,5! = 2,118,760$ ways. Of these the vast majority will be 'inefficient'. If they were not, it would be virtually impossible to behave according to the rules suggested above because of the informational difficulty. As it is, the empirical applications of the method suggested are not in the least easy.

yield. Notice that, just as it was in the money–bonds choice situation, it is expectations about yields that determine demand and hence the actual yields. This relationship between a price and what people expect the price to be turns up repeatedly in economics.

10

The Determination of Relative Input Prices

In Chapter 7, we described the derivation of a firm's demand for any input that it might plan to buy; in Chapters 8 and 9, we derived the individual's supply of any productive service that he might plan to sell. By aggregating these, we obtained the total or market demand and supply schedules respectively. The total demand for an input summarises the role that the firms that buy (or might buy) it play in determining its relative price as they implement their purchase plans. The price-determining role of the sellers of inputs is summarised in the total supply curve of each input. In this chapter, we shall describe how these roles are played, both in the short-run and in the long-run.

10.0 Relative Wage-Rates

The short-run supply curve of the services of carpenters, for example, is a schedule that shows us how the sales plans of carpenters would be revised if the only planning datum that altered was the expected hourly wage-rate – that is, it shows the number of hours of carpenters' services that all carpenters together would plan to sell in a given period of time at each price at which these services might be sold, *ceteris paribus*. The other things that must remain equal are the number of carpenters, the tastes and preferences of each for real income and leisure, the prices of the goods and services that they might plan to buy, and their objective. The short-run demand for the services of carpenters is a schedule that shows us the number of hours of carpenters' services that firms would plan to buy in a given period of time at each hourly wage-rate, *ceteris paribus*. The other things that must remain equal are the number of firms, the range of production possibilities open to each of them, the demand for the products that the firms are planning to produce, the price of each other variable productive service that the firms are

The Determination of the Relative Input Prices

buying or which they might plan to buy, and the firms' objectives. The total demand and supply curves are graphed in Figure 10.0.1: on the vertical axis we measure the hourly wage-rate of carpenters (W), and on the horizontal axis we measure the number of hours of carpenters' services that firms would plan to buy, or consumers plan to sell, in each period of time. The hourly wage-rate will tend towards the level $\overline{W}$, for only at that level will the purchase plans of firms, shown by the demand schedule D, and the sales plans of consumers for carpenters' services, shown by the supply schedule, S, be consistent with one another.

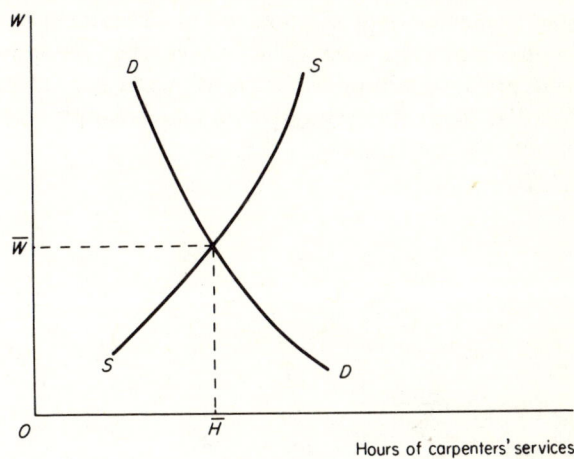

Figure 10.0.1

The wage-rate will remain at $\overline{W}$ per hour, with an even flow of sales and purchases each equal to $\overline{H}$ in each period for so long as there is no change in the demand for carpenters' services or in the supply of them. The demand curve will shift to a new position, causing a change in the wage-rate in the same direction, if any one of the determinants of demand that are listed in the previous paragraph should alter; and we described in Chapter 7 how the demand would alter in response to a change in any one of these. The supply curve will shift if there is any alteration in any one of these determinants of supply, and we have already shown in Chapter 8 how supply will change when any one of these is altered.

It must be emphasised that the preceding analysis explains changes in the relationship between the hourly wage-rate of carpenters and the prices of products and of other inputs. Thus, if the preferences for leisure of carpenters become stronger, the supply curve in Figure 10.0.1 will shift to the left, and the hourly wage-rate will rise as compared with (a) the prices of the goods and services of everyday consumption, and (b) the prices of other inputs.

In the long-run, an individual may change the kind of labour-service that he is selling: thus, in the long-run, a carpenter may renounce his skill and train as a bricklayer or bus-driver, or an agricultural labourer may become a carpenter. In the long-run, a firm may change its method of production and so substitute carpenters for other inputs, and vice versa. The influence of these long-run adjustments on the relative price of carpenters' services is illustrated in Figure 10.0.2. The short-run demand and supply curves are

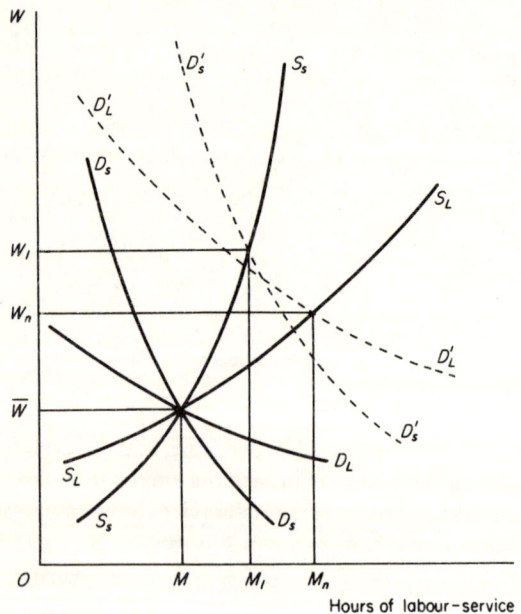

Figure 10.0.2

represented by $D_s D_s$ and $S_s S_s$ respectively, and the long-run demand and supply curves by $D_L D_L$ and $S_L S_L$ respectively. As these curves are drawn, they portray a position of both long- and short-run equilibrium, for they all intersect at the hourly wage-rate $\bar{W}$. Let us now suppose that there is a permanent change in the preferences of consumers for the products that carpenters help to produce. This will cause an increase in the demand for carpenters' services, that is illustrated by rightward shifts in the short- and long-run demand curves from D_sD_s and D_LD_L to $D'_sD'_s$ and $D'_LD'_L$ respectively. In the ensuing short period, the hourly wage-rate will rise to W_1, and the planned purchases and sales of carpenters' services will rise from M to M_1. In the long-run, as consumers and firms revise their plans, the hourly wage-rate will decline towards W_n, and the number of hours of work that are bought and sold will rise towards M_n.

It is clear from Figure 10.0.2 that the level towards which the hourly wage-rate will tend in the long-run will depend on the elasticity of the long-run demand and supply curves. For any given shift in the former, W_n will be the nearer to $\bar{W}$ the more elastic is S_LS_L, and vice versa. For any given shift in the long-run supply curve, W_n will be the nearer to $\bar{W}$ the more elastic is D_LD_L. The path by which the hourly wage-rate moves from $\bar{W}$ to W_n will depend on the expectations that each firm has about the price of its product and the hourly wage rate which it expects to have to pay for carpenters, and on the expectations of each consumer about the future level of the carpenters' wage-rate when contemplating a change in the nature of his labour-service. By making alternative assumptions about these expectations of firms and consumers, we may deduce a variety of paths by which the long-run equilibrium might be reached. These exercises are left to the reader, for they can be simply performed in the manner described in Chapter 6.

This explanation in terms of demand and supply analysis of the relationship between the hourly wage-rate of carpenters and the prices of products and other inputs has two main uses. First, it offers us a number of headings under which we may usefully and conveniently classify the causes of changes in the relationship between carpenters' wage-rates and other prices. The headings are what we have called the 'determinants' of the demand for, and of the supply of, carpenters' services. Second, it helps us to predict the probable consequences of economic events on relative input prices. It would be tedious to dwell upon the usefulness of the above analysis in diagnosing causes and exploring consequences, for there is little to add to what has already been said in Chapter 6. Rather, we shall rest content here with describing how demand and supply analysis may help us to interpret in a rather rough fashion the process of collective bargaining.[1]

Let us suppose that all existing carpenters are members of a trade union, and that all new entrants to the trade are eligible for membership. We shall suppose that the union's objective is to raise the hourly wage-rate. It may pursue this aim by restricting the supply (i.e. by shifting $S_L S_L$ to the left in Figure 10.0.2),[2] by raising the demand (that is, by shifting $D_L D_L$ to the right),[3] or simply by submitting a claim for a higher wage rate to employers. If employers grant this claim, perhaps to avoid a strike, the implications for the union may be illustrated in Figure 10.0.3, in which the curves have the same meaning

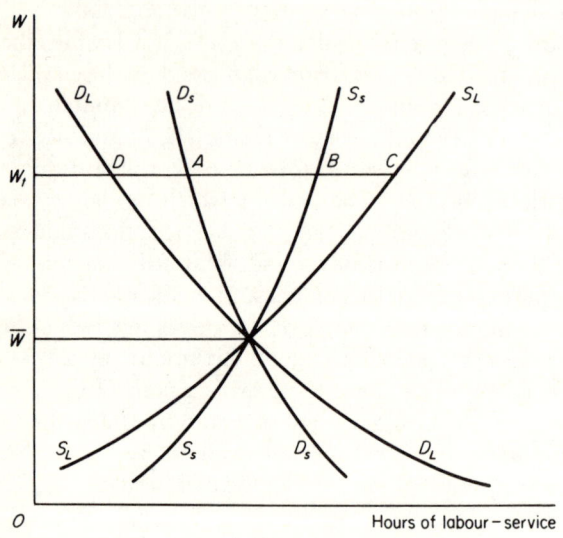

Figure 10.0.3

as in Figure 10.0.2. If the trade union threatens to strike unless the wage-rate is raised to W_t, then the short-run supply curve of carpenters' services becomes $W_t B S_s$, and in each period there will be an 'excess supply' represented by AB – that is, there will be unemploy-

---

[1] It must be emphasised that demand and supply curves are very crude tools for the interpretation of the process of collective bargaining. An alternative approach for elucidating this problem is described later in Chapter 17 under the heading 'Bilateral Monopoly'.

[2] This may be effected, for example, by limiting the number of hours for which each of its members might work per week.

[3] For example, by co-operating with employers in introducing new techniques of production.

The Determination of the Relative Input Prices

ment or underemployment of carpenters. The long-run supply curve will be W_tCS_L, and when long-run adjustments have been completed by employers, there will be an 'excess supply' of carpenters' services shown by DC. But perhaps the employers refuse to capitulate so easily. Following the submission of the claim, negotiations may ensue, and the arguments by which the claim is supported and countered as these proceed can be roughly interpreted in terms of our demand and supply analysis.

Let us suppose that the existing wage-settlement was effected some time ago at t_0, and that the hourly wage rate of OW, that was fixed at that time, was the then long-run equilibrium rate. This is a convenient simplifying assumption; whether or not it is true makes no difference to the substance of our argument. The short-run and long-run demand and supply curves at time t_0 are shown by D_sD_s, D_LD_L, S_sS_s and S_LS_L respectively, in Figure 10.0.4. Let us suppose that the trade union submits a claim for a wage rate of W_n at the beginning of period t_n. In supporting its claim, the union may argue that the prices of the goods and services of everyday consumption (that is, the 'cost of living') have risen since time t_0. If this were the only change that had taken place since the last settlement, then the S_sS_s and the S_LS_L curves would now lie in positions that are different from those they assumed at time t_0. The union may argue that the tastes and preferences of its members for leisure and real income are on balance such that the new curves lie to

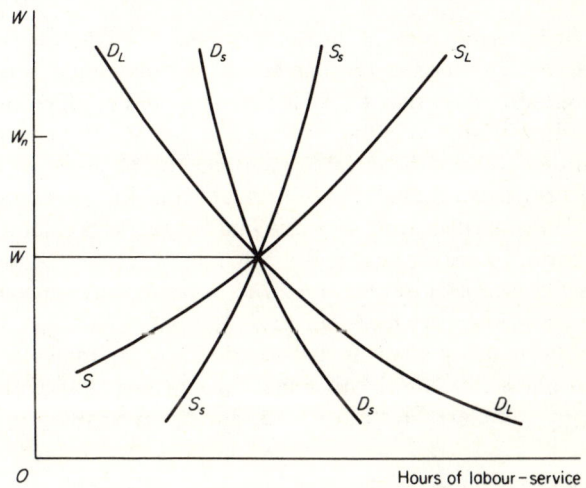

Figure 10.0.4

the left of the old ones. Secondly, the union may argue that the wage-rates in similar or comparable occupations have risen: if this alone had happened, then the long-run supply curve of carpenters' services would now lie to the left of its position at t_0. Third, the union may argue that the profits of the firms that employ its members have increased. The increase in profits may be attributed to a rise in demand for the products that carpenters help to produce and/or to an increase in their physical productivities. In either case, the implication of this argument is that the short-run and long-run demand curves for carpenters now lie to the right of $D_s D_s$ and $D_L D_L$ respectively. The total effect of all such arguments is to suggest that the demand and supply curves at time t_n intersect at the wage-rate W_n. The employers may deny the force of the union's contentions or question its estimate of the extent of the changes in prices, in wage-rates in alternative occupations, or in profits. In these ways, the employers may support their view that the long-run equilibrium wage-rate, appropriate to the conditions at time t_n, lies below OW_n. We are not here concerned, however, with the determination of the final outcome of the negotiations, for that requires a more refined analysis, some approaches to which will be described later in Chapter 17. At this stage, we wish merely to show how the arguments and counter-arguments may be interpreted in a rather crude way within the framework of demand and supply analysis.

10.1 The Determination of the Relative Price of a Durable Good

We have already derived the demand of an individual firm for a durable good (see Section 7.7). This demand will be operative only when the firm is implementing its long-run plan. During any period, the total demand for the durable good may be obtained by adding together the demands of all the individual firms that are planning to buy it as they put their long-run plans into effect. This total demand for the good, let us suppose it is a machine of some description, is shown in Figure 10.1.1 by the curve DD. The position and shape of this demand curve may vary from one period of time to another, depending on the number of firms that are deciding to implement their long-run plans. The short-run supply of machines and their long-run supply curve are illustrated by S_s and S_L respectively in Figure 10.1.1.

We shall suppose that the demand for these machines has remained stable at DD for long enough to enable the firms that produce and sell them to make complete adjustments to it, so that the price per machine is initially $\bar{P}$. Let us now suppose that there is a permanent rise in demand to $D_1 D_1$. In the ensuing short-run, the firms will expand their rate of output 'along' S_s, and the price will rise to P_1. Over the long-run, as the number and size of the firms that produce machines increases, the price will tend to fall to P_2, and the number of machines that are being demanded and supplied in each period will tend to rise to Q_2.

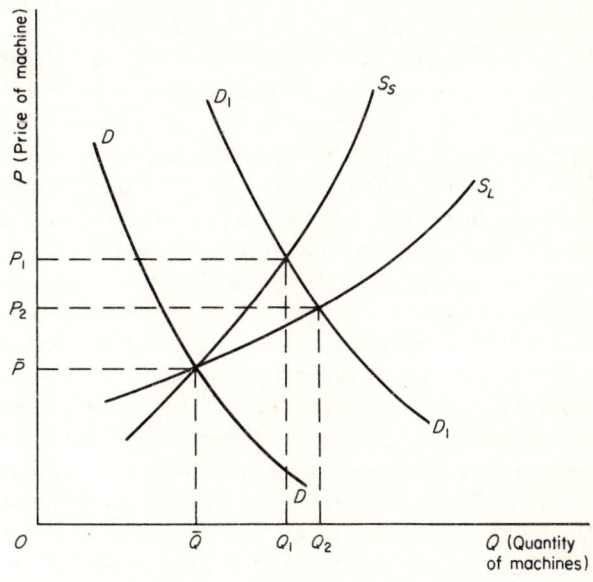

Figure 10.1.1

We know from Chapter 7 that the relationship that we have called 'the demand for a durable good' depends, *inter alia*, on the conditions of demand for the product(s) that it helps to produce, the price of each other durable good and input in conjunction with which it may be used, and on the rate of interest, and that the relationship that we have called 'supply' depends, *inter alia*, on the price of the inputs that are needed to produce it. If the rise in the demand for the machine in Figure 10.1.1 is the consequence of a change in consumers' tastes and preferences for the product(s) it assists in producing, then the rise in the price of the machine from $\bar{P}$ to P_1, and its fall in the long-run to P_2, represents changes in the relation between the price of the machine and the prices of products, other durable goods and inputs, and the rate of interest.

10.2 The Pricing of the Services of Durable Goods

The price that is paid for the services rendered by a durable good in each period is called 'rent' in everyday usage. The durable good may be a house, a factory building, a plot of land or a machine. The explanation of the relative price of the services rendered by these is formally the same as our explanation of the wage-rate of carpenters in the first section of this chapter; we shall, therefore, deal with it briefly. If the shelter that houses provide is bought by consumers, then the demand curve for it may be derived in the way described in Chapter 2, and we may, if we like, distinguish between the short-run and long-run demands for the services of houses. If the services of the durable goods are being bought by firms to assist in the production of other goods and services, we may obtain the short-run and long-run demands for them in the manner described in Chapter 7. In the short-run, the number of units of each durable good will be more or less fixed; there will, for example, be a given number of houses available for renting, and of plots of land suitable in site and quality for the particular use we have in mind. The short-run supply curve of the services rendered by these will, therefore, be perfectly inelastic. In the long-run, the number of houses may be depleted by dilapidation and by the use of houses for other purposes, and it may be augmented by the building of new houses and the conversion of buildings that are now being used in other ways. The long-run supply curve of house-room will be more elastic than the short-run supply curve, and its elasticity will be the greater the greater is the elasticity of the long-run supply curve of buildings, and the lower is the cost of converting houses to other uses and of making buildings now used in other ways suitable for habitation. The same will be true of the long-run supply curve of land to a particular use: in the long-run, land that is being put to other uses may be made suitable for the use in question, and land now being used in this way may be made suitable for other purposes.

The determination of the relative price of house-room, and its behaviour over the long-run, *ceteris paribus*, are illustrated in Figure 10.2.1. We have supposed that at the rent period $\bar{R}$, there is initially both short-run and long-run equilibrium, and that this is upset by a permanent increase in the preferences for house-room. As a consequence, the short-run and long-run demand curves move to $D'_sD'_s$ and $D'_LD'_L$ respectively. The rent per period will rise to R_1 and tend over the ensuing long-run towards R_2. In Figure 10.2.2, we have illustrated the determination of the relative price of the house itself. In the initial

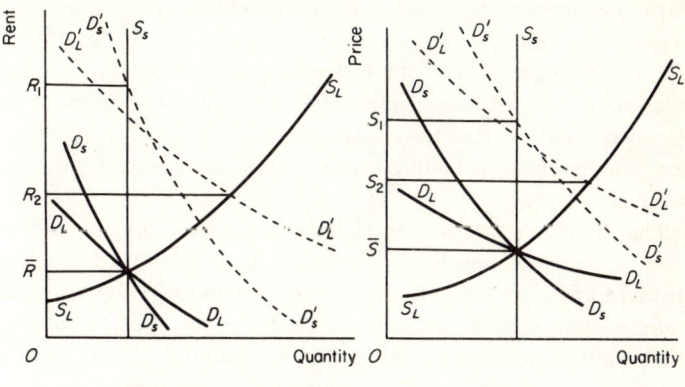

Figure 10.2.1 Figure 10.2.2

equilibrium, the price is $\bar{S}$. If we ignore operating and maintenance costs, and if we are given the expected life of the house and the rate of interest (i), we know (see Section 7.7) that

$$\bar{R} = \frac{\bar{S} \cdot i \cdot (1+i)^n}{(1+i)^n - 1}.$$

When the demand for house-room rises, the derived demand for the houses that provide this service will rise also: the price of each house will rise to S_1 in the short-run, and tend towards S_2 in the long-run. The price of existing houses in the short-run (S_1) and the rent per period of existing houses (R_1) will be such that

$$R_1 = \frac{S_1 \cdot i \cdot (1+i)^n}{(1+i)^n - 1}.$$

The price S_1 exceeds the costs of building new houses; as these are provided, both the rent per period and the price per house will fall towards R_2 and S_2 respectively, and these must be such that

$$R_2 = \frac{S_2 \cdot i \cdot (1+i)^n}{(1+i)^n - 1}.$$

10.3 Classifying Inputs: A Note on Human Capital

At one time it was customary in economics to classify inputs into three groups – land, labour[1] and capital, and to call the price paid for the use of the inputs that fall into each class rent, wages and interest respectively. This classification may be workable when an economy is in the initial stages of economic development, for individual inputs may then fall easily into one or other of these groups. Further, it may then be useful, for each member of the economy may then own only inputs that fall into a single group, so that this classification of inputs and of the rewards paid to them may correspond fairly closely to the social classes landowners, proletariat and capitalists respectively. In a modern economy, however, what we ordinarily call 'land' is land to which has been added capital and labour, and what is ordinarily called 'labour' is human beings whose skills have been developed by education and training. In these circumstances, if we maintain the customary classification of inputs, we must discard the classification of their rewards that accompanied it: for the price paid for the use of a plot of land whose quality has been improved by drainage and artificial fertilisers will then consist partly of rent (that is, the price paid for the use of land *per se*) and partly of interest; and the price paid for a doctor's services will be partly wages and partly interest also. Further, in modern social democracies, we do not find the same simple correlation between input groups and social classes, for fewer and fewer individuals now derive their incomes wholly from interest, and with the diffusion of the ownership of capital goods, more and more individuals derive at least a part of their incomes from interest and dividends. Lastly, if a man decides to hold his money-savings in the form of land, the price he receives by selling the use of the land will appear to him mainly as interest. In this chapter, our prime concern is to explain the determination of the relative prices of the things that firms buy. We have classified these things roughly into inputs, which make the whole of their contribution to production in the period in which they are bought, and durable goods, which yield their services over a succession of production periods. In calling the prices of some of these 'rents' and 'wages', we follow ordinary usage. In explaining relative price behaviour, there is no need to try to break down the price

---

[1] Labour is sometimes divided into entrepreneurial and other labour, and the distinction between these is based on function. Entrepreneurship or enterprise may be defined as the labour which plans or co-ordinates the use of all other factors. It is sometimes defined as the factor which bears uncertainty – i.e. whose reward reflects the existence of uncertainty. (See below, Chapter 12.)

of any particular service or durable good into the notional components appropriate to the three-fold classification of inputs – that is, into 'rent', 'wages' and 'interest'.

One important development which centres on the inadequacy of defining labour as if it were 'free' of capital, relates to the theory of *human capital*. Only the basic ideas underlying this theory can be treated here. Instead of thinking of labour as an input which yields its services in the period in which it is employed, the theory of human capital treats labour in the same way as we have treated durable goods – as an input whose services accrue over several periods of time. 'Investing' in human capital essentially takes the form of enabling individuals to acquire productively useful knowledge, skills and techniques. Education, therefore, becomes a particular form of investment activity not significantly different, *prima facie*, from investment in machines and buildings. The cost is incurred in the immediate future in the form of university, technical college and schooling costs, or in the form of on-the-job training, and the returns accrue later when the acquired skills and knowledge are put into practice.

Looked at in this way, it is possible to conceptualise the consumer's demand for a product like education. Education is tantamount to a durable good. In deciding whether to 'buy' more education or not, the consumer will weigh up the advantages accruing in the future. The costs incurred may be personal expenditure in the form of fees, or, in state-aided systems, they will consist largely of earnings forgone by spending time at college instead of earning an income. Note that as far as the consumer's *private* decision is concerned, he will ignore the fact that society at large will be subsidising his education. The costs borne by society would be relevant, however, if we were deciding on how much education *society* should sponsor. For the private individual only the private costs matter. His returns will be less easy to measure. It is a fairly obvious fact that skilled labour generally earns a higher wage or salary than unskilled labour, and empirical studies tend to show that the differential is systematic and permanent. This suggests that the difference in earnings reflects (at least partly) the return to the investment in skill and training. The future returns to be set against the costs could therefore consist of the sum of these future differentials.

Thus, if a consumer 'spends' (in actual expenditure or in forgone income) £3,000 on a university education, and secures a job at the end which yields £1,600 per annum compared to, say, £1,200 he would otherwise have earned, the investment decision will appear as follows:

Cost = £3,000
Returns = £400 for 30 years.

The life of the investment will be determined by the life of the owner of the capital (note that the two cannot be separated!) and his retention of knowledge. What should the interest rate be? Strictly it should be equal to the rate the consumer could have obtained had he invested £3,000 in capital equipment, shares or whatever. Suppose this is 10 per cent. The net present value of the interest is then[1]

$$£400 (9.43) - £3,000 = £3,772 - £3,000 = £772.$$

The investment is worthwhile.

Of course, the idea of treating education as investment in human capital has many pitfalls. Many people do not decide to 'buy' education on an investment basis. They derive some satisfaction from the education process, particularly where the form of education is not geared to productive needs. Such people are buying education as a consumption good, just like any other good. Similarly, the earnings differential may have nothing to do with education: it may reflect a 'natural flair' for the job, innate intelligence or purely social factors. Nonetheless, the idea that labour cannot be distinguished from capital in the classical sense is an important one.[2]

10.4 A Note on Differences in Efficiency between Units of the 'Same' Input

In explaining the relative price of carpenters' services per hour in the first section of this chapter, we assumed that each carpenter *qua* carpenter was identical with each other. This meant that for employers an hour's work from any one carpenter was a perfect substitute for an hour's work from any other. In practice, however, carpenters may differ widely from one another in efficiency – that is, all other things (such as the lay-out and organisation of the other inputs) being constant, an hour's work from carpenter. *A* may yield a different output from that by *B*. In these circumstances, our explanation of the relative wage rate must be modified.

Little modification is needed (*a*) if carpenters can be divided into sub-classes each containing carpenters that are of the same efficiency;

---

[1] £9.43 is the value of £1 held for 30 years at 10 per cent.
[2] For a detailed advocacy of the human–capital concept, see T. W. Schultz, *Investment in Human Capital* (The Free Press, New York, 1971).

or (b) if the labour-service that is being supplied by each carpenter can be reduced to a common denominator. If carpenters can be graded according to efficiency, and if within each grade there is a relatively large number of homogeneous carpenters, then the determination of the relative hourly wage-rate of each grade may be illustrated by a diagram similar to Figure 10.0.2. The demand curves for the services of carpenters in each grade will be much more elastic than those shown there, for the services of grade I carpenters can now be substituted for those of the men in grades II and III, etc. If each carpenter differs from each other, so that sub-classification is impossible, it may be possible to reduce hours of work by heterogeneous carpenters to some common unit of efficiency. Thus, suppose that the services of carpenter A are taken as the standard: if eight hours' work per week from carpenter B is substituted for eight hours' work per week from A, the relationship between the total outputs before and after the substitution will give a relationship between the efficiency of A and B, so that B's services can be measured in the same units as A's. If a controlled experiment of this kind were performed for all carpenters, their services might be reduced to the common efficiency unit, and this being done the relative price per efficiency unit might be explained in the way illustrated by Figure 10.0.2.[1]

If the contribution of each worker to output is identifiable and measurable, it may be possible to relate the wage to the output rather than to the time that is worked – that is, to have piece-rates rather than time-rates. When the price of labour-service is expressed as a simple piece-rate, the implied unit, in terms of which the work is being measured, is 'labour-service per unit of (homogeneous) output', and this provides a fair approximation to the efficiency units that were described in the previous paragraph. Where there are simple piece-rates, the hourly wage-rate will vary between one carpenter and another roughly in proportion to their relative contributions to output – that is, to their marginal product. The less efficient worker, however, will tend to receive rather more than his marginal net product and the more efficient rather less: thus, if in one hour A's output is four times that of B, B's hourly wage will be one-quarter that of A, but since the quantities of the services of machines, plant and management required for each unit of B's output are four times the

---

[1] This unit is called a 'corrected natural unit' by J. Robinson. See her *Economics of Imperfect Competition* (London, Macmillan, 1933) App. Sec. 4, p. 332. In fn. 2, p. 332, some defects of this measure are described.

quantities required for each unit of A's output, A's marginal net product will be more than four times greater than that of B.

If our purpose were to explain the precise wage that is being received by each carpenter, we would be forced to explore in much greater detail the implications of the fact that carpenters differ widely from one another in efficiency. We are primarily interested in this volume, however, in explaining changes in the relationship between the wages of carpenters and the prices of products and other inputs. If the spread of efficiency among carpenters and the system of wage-payment are given, then our demand and supply analysis provides a useful framework within which to explain and interpret variations in the relative wages of carpenters. Thus, if the demand for the products that carpenters help to produce increases, then, *ceteris paribus*, we would expect the wage received by each carpenter to rise; if the wage-rate in other comparable occupations should fall, then, *ceteris paribus*, we would expect the average wage of carpenters to tend to fall.

10.5 A Note on 'Economic Rent'

Economic rent is the difference between the actual earnings of a unit of an input and its supply price.[1] The actual earnings of a unit of an input is the price that it receives for selling its services for a given period of time. Its supply price is the minimum sum of money that is required to retain it in its existing use. If the costs of transfer from one use to another are zero, then this will be equal to the maximum sum it could earn per period in any other use; if these costs are positive, its supply price will be equal to its highest earnings per period in an alternative use less one period's share of the transfer costs. Thus, if a carpenter can earn £15 per week by working as a carpenter, and if the minimum sum that would induce him to do so is £13 per week, his economic rent is £2 per week.

If each carpenter is identical with each other carpenter, each will receive the same weekly wage, which will be determined by the demand for and the supply of carpenters' services. If all carpenters are identical not only *qua* carpenters but in all other respects also, then each will have the same supply price to carpentry, for the maximum earnings in alternative uses and the costs of transfer will be the same for each. In these circumstances, the long-run supply curve of carpenters' services will be perfectly elastic as in Figure 10.5.1, and the weekly wage will be

---

[1] 'Opportunity cost' and 'transfer earnings' are synonyms for supply price.

the same as the supply price of a week's work from each carpenter, so that no part of the earnings of any carpenter will be economic rent. If actual or potential carpenters are not equal in all other respects, then the long-run supply curve of carpenters' services will be less than perfectly elastic, as in Figure 10.5.2. They may differ from one another in that they are not equally versatile, so that the range of alternative occupations open to them varies from one to another: the most remunerative alternative use for one might be driving a bus, for another acting as a waiter. They may have different attitudes towards the nature and conditions of the work in the various occupations open to them, and this by itself will mean that the wage that would induce A to become a carpenter might differ from that which B would demand.

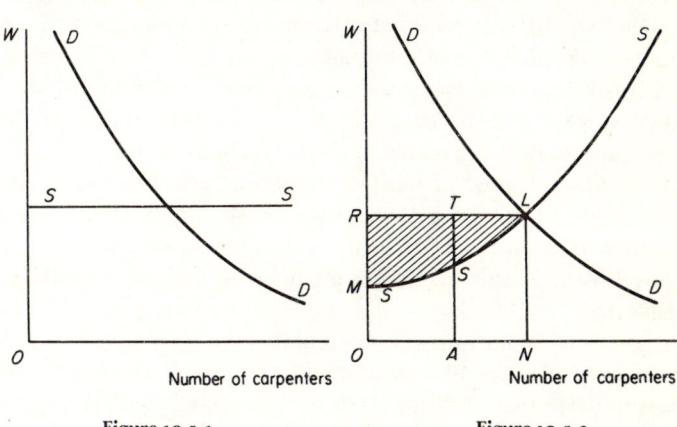

Figure 10.5.1   Figure 10.5.2

Lastly, the costs of transferring from other occupations to carpentry and vice versa might vary widely from one man to another: thus, to take the simplest example, A might live beside the firms which are demanding carpenters' services and B might live five miles away near a textile factory; other things being equal, A's supply price to carpentry will be less than B's. It is clear that economic rent will be a component of the earnings of most carpenters and the size of the component for any particular carpenter is illustrated in Figure 10.5.2. Thus, the economic rent received by the Ath carpenter will be equal to ST, the difference between his actual earnings OR and his supply price AS; that of the Nth carpenter will be zero, for the weekly earnings of OR are just sufficient to induce him to acquire or retain this skill. The shaded area

RML shows that part of the total earnings of all carpenters who are at work (*ONLR*) that is economic rent.

It is clear from Figure 10.5.2 that economic rent will be a more important constituent of the actual earnings of an input the less elastic is its supply curve. The elasticity of its supply curve will depend, *ceteris paribus*, (*a*) on the manner in which we define an input and the uses to which it might be put, and (*b*) on time. If we adopt broad definitions of input and use, economic rent will be the greater, and vice versa. Thus, if we group all the natural, non-human agents of production together and call them 'land', and if we define agriculture as the sole use of land, then the supply curve of land to agriculture will be perfectly inelastic, for on these definitions land is quite specific to agriculture so that its supply price is zero: the whole of the actual earnings of landowners will, therefore, be economic rent. Given the definition of an input, economic rent will be the less, the narrower are our definitions of use: thus, if we distinguish between the use of land for growing corn, wheat, potatoes, apples, and so on, the supply price of land to each of these uses will be positive, so that only a part of its actual earnings in any particular use may be called 'economic rent'. If we go further and define as a separate use the growing of potatoes for Mr Smith, who is one of many growers of potatoes in a locality, then the supply of land to him will be perfectly elastic, for the supply price of land to him will be its market price.

On any set of definitions of input and use, the supply price of a unit of an input to any use will depend on the range of alternative uses that is open to its owner, and this tends to vary directly with time. If we define the short-run as a period within which a unit of an input cannot move from one use to another, then its supply price to its present use will be zero, and the whole of its current earnings will be economic rent. In the long-run, units of an input may move from one use to another: thus, carpenters may become bricklayers, and a firm whose past savings are embodied in a machine may realise these from depreciation allowances and use them to buy another machine. In the long-run, therefore, the supply price of each unit of an input to its existing use will be what it could earn in its next most remunerative use (if we ignore transfer costs), and not the whole of its actual earnings will be economic rent. Economic rents that appear in the short-run have been called *quasi-rents* to draw attention to the fact that in whole or in part they are likely to be temporary. It would seem, then, that wide definitions of inputs and use have the same effect on the size of the economic rent as a narrow planning horizon, and that narrow definitions have similar consequences to a lengthening of the planning horizon.

As we have defined economic rent, it is a surplus: if, when the price of each product and input were at its long-run equilibrium level, all economic rents were appropriated by the state, no unit of any input would have any incentive to change its use, for post-tax earnings of each would be equal to its supply price to its existing occupation. For this reason, the notion of economic rent has been of some importance in the history of public finance theory: with its aid, it was possible to conceive of a system of taxation that would not directly affect the pattern of resource-use within an economy. For example, land rents in urban areas consist of a return to capital invested and an element reflecting locational advantage. The latter is called 'site rent' and advocates of land taxation have long suggested taxing site rents because such taxes would not affect the patterns of land use. Even if such a tax system were practicable, however, it would alter the distribution of income between the owners of inputs. Since tastes and preferences differ from one person to another, there would be a change in the pattern of demand, and hence in the pattern of relative product and factor prices, and this in turn would cause a change in the pattern of resource-use in the economy.

10.6 The Rate of Interest

By a rate of interest we mean the price per unit that is paid for a loan of money for a period of time. Conventionally, the unit of money is £100, and the period of time is one year, so that the price is usually expressed as a rate *per cent* per annum. In this section, we shall attempt to explain how this price is determined. In doing so, we shall simplify heroically by assuming that all loans are riskless,[1] that all are made for an infinitely long period of time, and that borrowers borrow by selling irredeemable bonds and lenders lend by buying them. We shall suppose also that the number of bonds that is currently issued in any period of time is insignificantly small as compared with the quantity of bonds that have already been issued. On these assumptions, all bonds will be homogeneous, the market price of bonds will be determined primarily by the demand for the existing stock of bonds, and the

---

[1] That is, no-one defaults on the payment of interest. Distinguish this from uncertainty about the future price of the bond.

relationship between the market price of bonds and the coupon rate on them will give us the current or market rate of interest.[1] Later, we shall modify our explanation by assuming that bonds are not homogeneous, either because they are issued for different periods of time, or because there is uncertainty about whether borrowers will meet their promises to pay the nominal rate of interest on their bonds and repay the principals.

We have already seen that the manner in which a consumer will plan to distribute his savings between money and bonds during the period that lies ahead depends on the current bond price (rate of interest), expectations about the future level of the bond price and his objective. In Chapter 9, we have shown what the planned disposition of savings would be at each current bond price, assuming that the consumer's expectations and objective remained unchanged. From this relationship, we derived the consumer's supply of the willingness to hold money, his demand for money as a store of wealth, his demand for bonds and his supply curve of the willingness to hold bonds. By adding together the demand curves for bonds of all consumers and firms in the economy, we obtain the total demand for bonds. This shows us the number of bonds that the firms and consumers would plan to buy at each current bond price, given their objectives, their expectations about the future level of the bond price (market rate of interest), the initial distribution of the savings of each consumer and firm between money and bonds, and the initial distribution of the existing stocks of money and bonds between consumers and firms. These last two determinants of the demand for bonds mean, in effect, that both the number of bonds and the quantity of money in the form of which savings might be held, must be assumed constant. At each point in time, there will be a given stock of bonds – that is, their supply curve will be totally inelastic (SS). These demand and supply curves are graphed in Figure 10.6.1, where we measure the current price of bonds on the vertical axis and the number of bonds demanded and supplied on the horizontal axis. The market price of bonds will tend towards the level R, for only at that price will the number of bonds that firms and consumers plan to purchase be equal to the number of bonds that are available for purchase – that is, only at the price R will the public be willing to hold the existing stock of bonds. If the bond price is R, and if the nominal rate of interest is $3\frac{1}{2}$ per cent, then the market rate of interest will be $3\frac{1}{2} \cdot R$.

[1] See above, Chapter 9.

The Determination of the Relative Input Prices

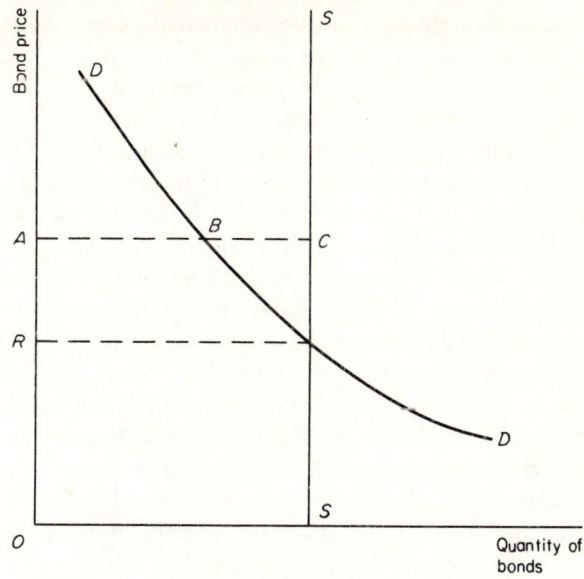

Figure 10.6.1

It can be seen from the figure that consumers and firms will only be willing to hold the existing stock of bonds when the current bond price is R. Thus, if the bond price were now A, the members of the economy as a whole would be holding BC more bonds than they wished to hold at that price: those holding more bonds than they desire would attempt to sell them, and the pressure to sell bonds would lower their price. As the bond price fell, the pressure to sell bonds would diminish, and the inducement to buy them would rise. And conversely, if the current bond price were less than R: the 'excess demand' for bonds will, *ceteris paribus*, raise their price to R. If all firms that borrow money do so by selling bonds that are identical with those already in existence, and if the flow of new bonds in any period of time is insignificantly small when compared with the stock of bonds already issued, then the sales of new bonds will not affect the bond price – that is, the market rate of interest of $3\frac{1}{2}$. R will be that at which new loans can be obtained.

The bond price will move to a new level if the demand for bonds alters. If, on balance, firms and consumers expect that the future bond price will be higher than they had previously supposed, then the demand for bonds will increase and the current bond price will tend to rise; and conversely. If there is an increase in the quantity of money that is available for holding as an asset, then, *ceteris paribus*, the demand for bonds will rise; for the demand for bonds of each individual firm and consumer that receives a part of the increase in the quantity of money will swivel rightwards so that the total demand will rise also. The increase in the quantity of money available for use as a store of value might be a consequence of a redistribution of an existing stock of money between this and other uses, or of an increase in the total stock of money. In many modern economies, the increase in the total stock of money is effected by the purchase of bonds by the monetary authorities, and the stock of money is depleted by the sale of bonds. The purchases and sales of bonds by the monetary authorities with the aim of changing the quantity of money are called 'open-market' operations. If the demand curve in Figure 10.6.1 is defined as the total of the demands for bonds by the public and by the monetary authorities, and if the quantity of money is increased by bond purchases by the latter, then to the increased demand for bonds by the public as a consequence of the increased quantity of money we must add the demand for bonds by the monetary authorities. In these circumstances, the bond price will rise by more than it would have risen if the quantity of money had been increased by other means. Alternatively, if the demand curve in Figure 10.6.1 is defined as the total demand by the public for bonds, then the effect of bond purchases by the monetary authorities will be illustrated by a leftward shift in the supply curve of bonds, for now that more bonds are held by the authorities fewer will be available to the public.

The explanation of the determination of the current bond price (rate of interest) may be presented in terms of the demand for and supply of money. From the manner in which the individual would plan to revise the disposition of his savings between money and bonds in response to changes in the current bond price, we can derive his demand curve for money as an asset. When the individual demand curves of consumers and firms are summed together, we obtain the total demand for money as a store of wealth. This shows us the number of units of money that the firms and consumers in the economy would plan to hold at each current rate of interest, given their objectives, their expectations about the future level of the bond price (rate of interest), and the economy's stocks of money and bonds.

At any point in time, there will be a given quantity of money in an economy. The whole of this, however, will not be available to function as a store of value, for some part of it must act as a medium of exchange. We have already described the purchase and sales plans of consumers: when the sales plan is implemented, goods and services are exchanged for the money that constitutes the consumer's income; when the purchase plan is implemented, the sum of money that we called the planned consumption expenditure is exchanged for goods and services. Since the consumption expenditure is mainly financed from income, money is here acting as a medium through which the inputs that the consumer owns are exchanged for the goods and services that he wants. If each consumer received payment for what he sells at the same moment as he pays for what he buys, he would require no stock of money to finance this exchange. Typically, however, incomes are received at discrete intervals, while consumption spending takes place more or less continuously, so that at each instant of time, a consumer will have some sum of money designed for spending which is as yet unspent. Given the pattern of spending, this sum will be the greater the larger is the consumer's income and the less frequently it is paid. Thus, if a consumer receives £20 on Friday evening in payment for the services sold during the previous seven days, and he sets aside £14 for consumption spending at an even rate of £2 per day during the seven days that follow, his average daily stock of money-for-spending will be £6.[1] If the weekly income had been £40, planned spending £28 and daily expenditure £4, then, *ceteris paribus*, the average daily holding of money would have been £12. The amount of money that a consumer holds to bridge the gap between receipt of income and its expenditure is called his *transactions balance*.

For each firm in an economy, money acts as a medium through which its flow of products is exchanged for the flow of inputs needed to make them. Since the inputs are used to make the firm's products, payment for the former may (and generally does) precede the receipts of money from the sale of the latter. Given the customary intervals at which the firm pays for the things it buys and receives payment for the things it sells, it will require some sum of money to bridge the gap between its payments and receipts. This sum is called its 'working capital' or transactions balance. Given the relationship between the frequency of receipts from sales and the frequency of its expenditures on the purchases of inputs, the size of a firm's transactions balance will

---

[1] Assuming that the spending is done first thing each morning, his stock of money on Saturday will be £12, on Sunday £10, and £8, £6, £4, £2 and £0 on Monday, Tuesday, Wednesday, Thursday and Friday respectively. The average daily stock will be the sum of these divided by 7 – that is, 42/7 or 6.

be the greater, the greater are its receipts. The receipts of all the firms in an economy will depend largely on the level of spending by all the consumers, and that, in turn, will depend on the aggregate income of the consumers. That part of the total quantity of money that is required to facilitate the current transactions of consumers and firms will, therefore, depend mainly on the level of the economy's income.

If we are given M, the number of units of money available for all uses in an economy, and if we are given the quantity (M_1) that is required for the transactions balances, then $M - M_1$ or M_2 will be the number of units available to satisfy the demand for money as a store of value. If M is assumed given, and if we suppose that the transactions balances will not vary with any likely change in the rate of interest, we may conclude that M_2 will be inelastic with respect to the rate of interest over the range in which it is likely to cut the demand curve for money. In Figure 10.6.2 we measure the market rate of interest on the vertical axis, and the quantity of money demanded and supplied for use as a store of value on the horizontal axis; DD is the demand for money and SS the supply curve of it, and for simplicity's sake the latter is drawn as being perfectly inelastic. The market rate of interest will be $\bar{i}$, for only at that level will that part of their savings that the public wish to hold in the form of money be equal to the quantity of money that is available for

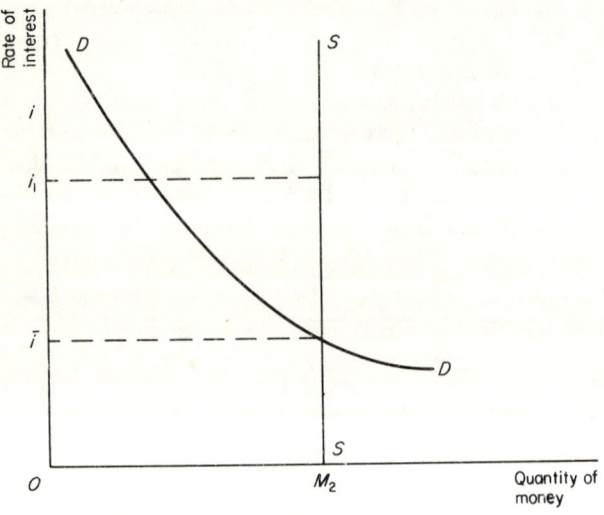

Figure 10.6.2

acting as a store of wealth. If the market rate of interest were at i, then firms and consumers taken together would find themselves holding a larger part of their savings in money than they desire. This would impel them to reduce their holdings of money by buying bonds, so that the bond price would tend to rise and the market rate of interest to fall. The desire to reduce their money holdings would persist until the rate of interest had fallen to i. The market rate of interest i corresponds to the bond price of R in Figure 10.6.1.

The rate of interest will move to a new level if there is any change in the demand for money as a store of wealth – for brevity's sake, we shall follow common usage and call this the *speculative* demand for money – or in the quantity of money available for meeting this demand. Thus, if the public on balance expect the rate of interest to be higher in the future than they had previously supposed, the speculative demand for money will increase, and the market rate of interest will rise. If the level of income should rise, then M_1 will rise, and if M remains the same, M_2 must fall, and, *ceteris paribus*, the rate of interest will rise. If, while the economy's income remains unchanged, M is reduced by the sale of bonds by the monetary authorities – that is, by open-market operations, then, *ceteris paribus*, the rate of interest will rise. If the DD-curve in Figure 10.6.3 shows the demand of consumers, firms and the monetary authorities for money, then these open-market operations will shift the demand curve for money to the right through a horizontal

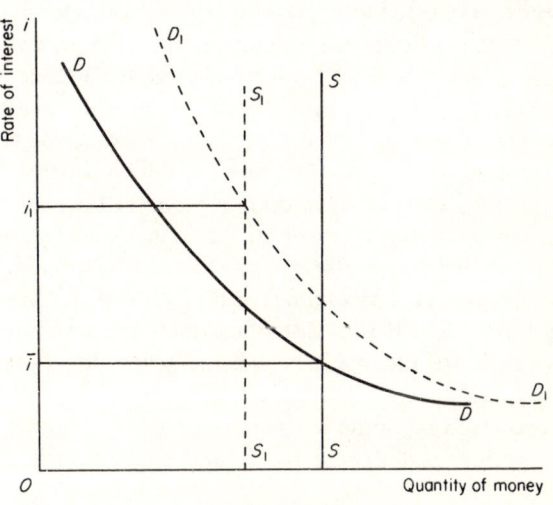

Figure 10.6.3

distance equal to the value of the bond sales; if SS represents the initial supply of money for speculative uses, it will shift leftwards to $S_1 S_1$ as a consequence of the open-market operations. In these circumstances, it can be seen that the market rate of interest will rise to i_1 – that is, when M_2 is reduced by bond sales by the monetary authorities, the rate of interest will rise by more than it would have risen had the same reduction in M_2 been effected without open-market operations.

In this section thus far, we have concentrated on explaining the determination of the market rate of interest. Let us now suppose that at the beginning of some period t, there is a permanent rise in the speculative demand for money. As we have already seen, the interest rate will rise: but will the interest rate remain stable thereafter at its new and higher level, or will the new interest rate cause changes that will in their turn tend to move it towards some long-run equilibrium level? It will be recalled that similar questions were asked in Chapter 6 and in the earlier sections of this chapter: we have seen that if there were a permanent rise in the demand for, say, butter, its price will rise in the short-run; this will lead firms to revise their long-run sales and purchase plans and as these are implemented the price of butter will tend to fall to some long-run equilibrium. The long-run behaviour of the interest rate lies rather outside the limits of this volume. We shall, nevertheless, offer a brief sketch of one way in which we may seek to explain it; for a fuller description of the relationships that we shall use, the reader is referred to any text on macro-economics.[1]

We shall define the long-run equilibrium rate of interest as that rate at which the economy's income will remain stable from one period to another: thus, if we denote total income by Y, and successive time periods by the subscripts $t, t+1, t+2, \ldots t+n$, when the rate of interest is at its long-run equilibrium level, Y_t will be equal to Y_{t+1}, and Y_{t+1} to Y_{t+2}, and so on. By the economy's total income we mean the value at current market prices of all the inputs sold by consumers within a period plus the profits earned by firms in that period. We shall define a period as the length of time required for expenditures by consumers and firms on the purchase of currently produced goods and services to generate income. The income-generating expenditures within each period may be roughly classified into expenditures on currently produced consumption goods and services, which we shall call consumption and denote by C, and expenditures on newly

---

[1] E.g., D. C. Rowan, *Output, Inflation and Growth* 2nd edn (Macmillan, London, 1974).

produced investment goods, which we shall call investment and denote by I. Within any period t, then, on these definitions: $Y_t = C_t + I_t$. We have already seen that the level of consumption spending and of saving depend, *inter alia*, on income, and for our present purposes we shall suppose that planned consumption and saving for any period depend upon, and together exhaust, the previous period's income: that is, $C_t + S_t = Y_{t-1}$. If $Y_{t-1} = Y_t$, then $S_t = I_t$. When the interest rate is at its long-run equilibrium level, on our definitions, then in each period planned saving must be equal to planned investment expenditure.

In Chapter 9, we derived a saving supply schedule for an economy: this was a relationship between the rate of interest and planned saving, given the tastes and preferences for present and future goods, current and expected future incomes and prices, and the distribution of income. In Chapter 7, we described the purchase plan of a firm for an investment good: the number of units of any investment good (such as a machine) that the firm will plan to buy will depend on its price, the firm's knowledge of productive techniques, the price of each other investment good and input, and the rate of interest. And we saw that the number of machines that the firm would plan to buy in any period would vary inversely, *ceteris paribus*, with the rate of interest. If we suppose that the prices of all goods and services are constant (as they would be if the total supply curve of each of them was perfectly elastic), we may obtain for each firm a relationship between the value of the investment goods that it would plan to buy and the interest rate, and by adding these together we will get a relationship between planned investment expenditure in each period by all firms and the rate of interest. Our definition of the long-run equilibrium rate of interest requires that this relationship between planned investment expenditure and the rate of interest and the economy's saving supply schedule must remain stable from period to period.

The diagrams in Figure 10.6.4 portray an initial position in which the market rate of interest is at its long-run equilibrium level: diagram (a) shows the speculative demand for money and the part of the total quantity of money that is available to meet it; diagram (b) shows the saving and investment schedules. At the rate of interest $\bar{\imath}$, the part of their savings that the public wish to hold in the form of money is equal to the quantity of money that is available for acting as a store of value, and planned saving is equal to planned investment expenditure. Let us now suppose that at the beginning of period 1, this equilibrium is upset by a permanent rise in the speculative demand for money to D_1D_1, so that the market rate of interest rises to i_1. We shall suppose also that during the ensuing periods there is no change in (a) the tastes and preferences for present and future goods; (b) the prices of consumption goods and services; (c) the distribution of income; (d) the prices of inputs and durable goods; (e) the techniques of production and firms' awareness of them; (f) the quantity of money, and that the planned investment expenditures are independent of the level of the economy's income. At the new market rate of interest i_1 that rules at the beginning of period 1, planned saving for that period will exceed planned investment spending by ab. On our definition of a period, the income of the economy will fall by ab during period 1. This fall in income will mean

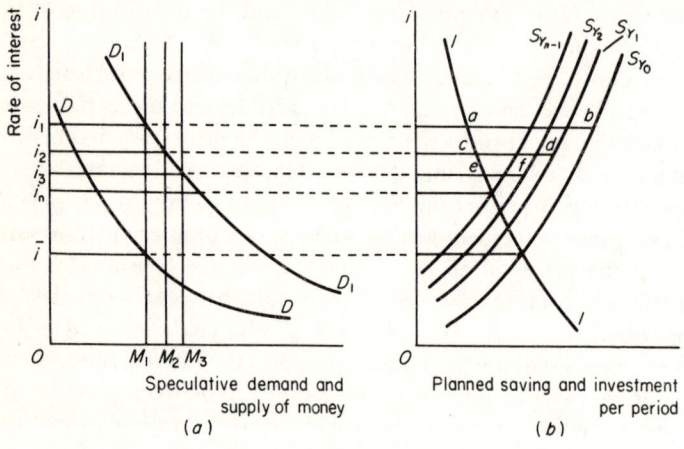

Figure 10.6.4

that fewer units of money are required for transactions purposes, so that by the end of period 1 the number of units available to meet the speculative demand will have risen – from M_1 to M_2. If we assume that changes in the supply of money that is available for speculative purposes during any period affect only the market rate of interest at the beginning of the next period, then at the beginning of period 2 the rate of interest will be i_2.

As a consequence of the fall in the economy's income during period 1, the saving supply schedule for period 2 will be to the left of its initial position at S_{Y_1}, for we assumed that saving is related to the previous period's income. At the market rate of interest of i_2, planned saving will exceed planned investment expenditure by cd, and during period 2 the economy's income will fall by this amount; this fall in income will reduce the demand for money as a medium of exchange, so that by the end of period 2 the quantity of money that can act as a store of value will have risen to M_3. For period 3, the market rate of will be i_3, and the saving supply schedule S_{Y_2}. During period 3, planned saving will exceed planned investment-spending by ef; this will cause a further rise in the amount of money available to meet the speculative demand, and so a further fall in the market rate of interest. It can be seen from Figure 10.6.4 that the reductions in income become smaller and smaller with each ensuing period, so that the reductions in the market rate of interest become smaller and smaller also. Eventually, the rate of interest will reach some new long-run equilibrium level at i_n, at which planned saving (with the saving supply schedule $S_{Y_{n-1}}$) will be equal to the planned investment expenditure.

In this analysis of the long-run behaviour of the interest rate in response to some initial change, we have assumed that variation in the economy's real income is the sole equilibrator. Our analysis can be easily modified to allow for changes in some of the other things that we have assumed to remain equal. Thus, if we assume that the investment schedule is not independent of income and posit some functional relationship between it and real income, we may trace another path of adjustment of the rate of interest to a different long-run equilibrium level. We may make the investment schedule simply dependent on the previous period's income as we did with the saving schedule; if we do so, the long-run equilibrium level of the rate of interest will be lower than in our example. We may assume that the investment schedule depends on the rate of change of income in the recent past – that is, that investment expenditure in period t is a function not only of the interest rate but also of $Y_{t-1} - Y_{t-2}$; if we do so, we shall find that the interest rate will fluctuate over time, either converging towards, or diverging from, some long-run equilibrium level.[1] In Figure 10.6.4, we have assumed that all prices are constant (because all supply curves are perfectly elastic) so that changes in money incomes represent changes of the same proportion in real income; an alternative analysis of the long-run behaviour of the interest rate might be based on the

---

[1] See P. A. Samuelson, 'Interaction between the Multiplier Analysis and the Principle of Acceleration', *Review of Economics and Statistics*, 1939. Reprinted in J. Lindauer, *Maroeconomic Readings* (The Free Press, 1968).

assumption that the real income of the economy is stable, so that changes in money income represent changes only in prices. To do this, we must posit functional relationships (at the least) between money income and planned saving and investment and the demand for money as a medium of exchange. There will, therefore, be as many long-run equilibrium rates of interest as there are long-run equilibrators;[1] our aim is neither to catalogue them nor to choose between them, but merely to indicate one way in which the long-run adjustments, with any given equilibrator(s), may be analysed.

With the aid of an analysis of the same kind as that illustrated in Figure 10.6.4, we may offer a first approximation to an interpretation of the role that the productivity of investment goods and the tastes and preferences of savers play in determining the interest rate. A change in the former will shift the investment schedule, *ceteris paribus*; a change in the latter will shift the saving supply schedule at each level of real income, *ceteris paribus*. Such changes will affect the rate of interest in the model portrayed in Figure 10.6.4 through changes in the economy's real income. The detailed argument is left to the reader, for its form is similar to that described earlier.

Thus far in this section, we have assumed a world in which there are only two assets, namely money and homogeneous, perpetual bonds. We shall briefly indicate how our analysis may be formally extended to a world in which there are n assets, $A_1, A_2, A_3, \ldots, A_n$. The relationships between the prices of these will be determined by the demand for, and the supply of, each of them. We shall suppose that at any point in time the quantity of each asset is given, and that over rather short periods of time the amount by which the stock of any one of these assets can be augmented or depleted is negligible: the supply of each asset will then be perfectly inelastic. Given the stock of each asset, the demand for any asset, A_n, will depend on the public's tastes and preferences for it as compared with each of the others, and on the current market price of $A_1, A_2, \ldots, A_{n-1}$. The way in which relative demands are formulated was indicated in the section on portfolio analysis (Section 9.2). The demand curve for each asset will generally be relatively elastic, for it may be substituted for other assets, and others may be substituted for it, in response to changes in relative asset prices. In an equilibrium position, the relationship between the prices of the different assets will be such

---

[1] In Figure 10.6.4, the main equilibrator is real income. An alternative equilibrator might be money incomes and prices. The equilibrating process may be assisted by changes in real or money investment.

that the public, taken as a whole, will just be willing to hold the existing stock of each asset. If the equilibrium is upset, through a change in the public's preferences for some assets as compared with others, the demand curve for each asset will move to a new position as a consequence, and there will ensue a process of adjustment during which there will be further shifts in the demand curves in response to changes in relative asset prices, until a new equilibrium position is reached. Thus, if assets $A_1, A_2, \ldots, A_{12}$ are riskless bonds of progressively longer currencies, ranging from a three months' bill to an irredeemable bond, and if the public as a whole expects the general level of bond prices to be higher in future than they had previously thought, then the demand curve for each of these will rise, with that for A_{12} rising most and that for A_1 rising least, and the demand curves for money and other assets will tend to fall. These initial changes in the demands will alter relative asset prices and so lead to further shifts in the demands, and these will continue until, in the light of these new expectations about the future bond prices, the public are just willing to hold the given stock of each asset. In such a world, there will be no such thing as *the* rate of interest: rather there will be as many rates of return as there are assets. The rate of interest that any individual firm, X, must pay for a loan of money will depend, *inter alia*, on how potential lenders feel about X's capacity to pay the interest and repay the principal, and on the period for which the loan is required. These will be reflected in the tastes and preferences of the public for the bond (asset) that X, the borrower, is selling. The price that X will get for his bond gives us the rate of interest that he must pay, and the price he can get will be the market price of those existing bonds that are in all respects identical with that which he is offering for sale.

In this way, we may explain the price that any firm X must pay for a loan of money for a given period of time. If we define interest as the price that is paid solely for the use of money, then the price that X pays will consist of more than interest, for those who sell the use of money to X are selling also their willingness to bear the risks of X's default. We will get a rough notion of the part of the price that X pays that may be called 'pure' interest from the price that a riskless borrower (like a central government) pays for a loan of the same size for the same period of time. Our prime purpose in this chapter, however, is to explain the determination of the relative prices of the things that firms buy. In this pursuit, there is no need to break down the price of any input into such notional components as 'pure interest', 'rent' and 'wages'.

11

The Determination of Relative Prices: General Equilibrium

11.0 General and Partial Analysis
The preceding chapters have described the roles of consumer preferences and firms' behaviour in the determination of the prices of commodities and inputs. All the analysis so far has been conducted in terms of particular assumptions about the state of economic markets. In particular, it has been assumed that firms are price-takers such that no individual firm can influence the price of the product he sells by varying the quantities he produces. We retain this assumption of *perfect competition* for this chapter. Although each individual firm and each individual consumer has no control over commodity and input prices under perfect competition, it is none the less true that the total supply and total demand for each commodity and input determine their respective prices. That is, prices are constants for each individual producer and consumer, but variables for all of them.

But all the analysis so far has been *partial*. We mean by this that the analysis has been confined to analysing only *some* of the effects of the behaviour of economic agents. A change in the tastes and preferences for a good, for example, was shown to affect the price of that good. Further consequences of this event were not enumerated. However, we know that the ramifications of a change in tastes will not end there. If demand for good X changes, and its price alters, this will affect the demand for substitute and complementary goods. Changes in the prices of all of these will in turn alter the demand for inputs used in producing each of these goods, thus altering input prices, and so on. We investigate these effects in more detail below. For the moment we can observe the important fact of *interdependence* between the prices and quantities of commodities and inputs. It is this fact of interdependence that leads many economists to feel that purely partial analyses convey only limited, and possibly misleading, information about the consequences of economic events. Because of this they argue that the proper mode of analysis should be *general*. General analysis attempts to take into account the existence of interdependencies between prices.

The previous chapters showed that supply and demand combined to determine equilibrium prices for commodities and inputs. These prices are equilibrium prices – that is, there is no tendency for them to change unless one or other of the parameters changes – only in the sense that other things have been held equal. In other words, interdependence is ignored in the analysis of partial equilibrium. However, it seems reasonable to suppose that it must be possible for a complete set of prices to exist such that all the plans of purchasers and sellers are consistent with each other. Such a situation, if it existed, would be one of *general equilibrium*. Thus the price of good X would depend not only on the prices of the inputs used to produce it, and on the demand for it, but on all other prices as well.

It remains true that most economic analysis is still taught in partial equilibrium terms. In part this reflects different historical traditions. Schools of thought trained in the Marshallian tradition tend to be preoccupied with partial analysis. Those that owe their origins to continental writers, especially Walras, stress the general approach.[1] But there is also a positive debate over the relevance of partial equilibrium analysis. Partial analysis has several advantages. First, it concentrates our attention on the causes of a change in individual behaviour or price. If it is possible to argue that the next order of effects, for example the effect of a change in the price of a good on the price of substitute goods, is small, then we may be satisfied that partial analysis picks up the most important consequences of an economic event. Second, partial analysis considerably simplifies the investigation of economic problems. This simplicity is lost if we have to trace out all the conceivable effects of, say, a price change. Not only would the latter exercise be immensely complex to handle in any verbal exercise, but even a mathematical approach would be difficult if many interdependencies are involved. Third, any empirical analysis in a general equilibrium context would run foul of the immense problems of finding data to fit the model.

---

[1] Leon Walras (1834–1910) was a French economist and his most influential work was *Elements of Pure Economics*, published in French in 1874. The necessity of taking the general approach was stressed earlier by Alfred Cournot in his *Investigations of the Mathematical Foundations of the Theory of Wealth* in 1838.

Whilst the simplicity and low informational content of partial models are powerful incentives to stay in the partial world, these advantages can only be bought at the expense of a possible loss of realism. And this loss of realism can only be discovered by carrying out a general equilibrium analysis. In other words, the adequacy of the partial approach can only be tested by carrying out a general analysis! None the less, although the conceptual basis of general equilibrium analysis is well developed, progress in the field of empirical general analysis – that is, actually building up a model of an economy using observed data – has been slight, despite the immense efforts that have gone into it. The partial–general debate therefore continues.

11.1 The General Consequences of an Economic Event

In order to illustrate verbally the type of effect incorporated into general equilibrium analysis, consider the results of a change in consumer preferences such that the demand for a good, X, increases. The following will happen.

(*a*) Since the demand for X increases – that is, the demand curve for X shifts to the right – the price of X will rise, the extent of the rise depending on the elasticities of supply and demand.

(*b*) The rise in the price of X causes the marginal revenue product curve for the inputs used to manufacture X to shift to the right. Given the supply curve for these inputs, their price will therefore rise.

(*c*) If consumers' incomes are fixed, the effects under (*a*) above will involve an increased expenditure on X and hence there will be less income available to spend on other commodities. Accordingly, the demand for at least some of these commodities will fall, the extent of the fall depending on how large these products loom in the consumers' general pattern of expenditure. Quite possibly, then, the demand for substitute products Y and Z, say, will fall, altering their prices in a downward direction. Prices of other products may not be affected, while the prices of complementary goods will rise as demand for them increases.

(*d*) The shifts in demand for the substitute and complementary goods in (*c*) above will cause shifts in the marginal revenue productivity curves for the inputs used to produce those goods. Their prices too will change.

(e) The changes in prices for substitute and complementary goods will feed back to the initial demand for good X. Now that substitute goods are cheaper this will ameliorate the increased demand for X, but only partly. The change in input prices will lead firms to substitute the now cheaper inputs for the now more expensive inputs, thus altering their prices again. Again, these effects will not offset the initial changes in the prices of inputs, but they will reduce the magnitude of the initial effect.

(f) In the long-run yet more changes may occur. Firms may now switch production away from the goods with relatively low demand and towards goods with relatively high demand. The changes in relative prices may lead to a switch in inputs such that labour trained in one use seeks retraining to enter another industry.

(g) The changes in the relative prices of inputs will lead to a change in the distribution of income between the owners of the inputs, again altering the pattern of demand if preferences are different among the different input-owning groups. Saving plans may alter, perhaps sufficiently to affect the determination of the overall national income and structure of interest rates.

Enough has been said to illustrate the almost boundless effects of one simple shift in demand for one product. The process of tracing through the consequences of such an event would be complex enough, but, in practice, many events giving rise to such effects will be taking place at the same time. This will complicate the analysis even further to the extent that it will make it more difficult to disentangle cause and effect.

11.2 The Uses of General Analysis

We have already seen that, if it can be executed, a general analysis will be more realistic than a partial analysis. This will be so because, in theory at least, general analysis enables us to trace out all the effects of an independent economic event such as a change in the demand for a product caused by a change in preferences. Against this we must recall again the argument that the important affects of an individual event may well be detected by partial analysis.

A major aspect of general analysis is that it reminds us forcefully of the interdependence of economic events. The fact of interdependence, however, is the major explanation of why economists cannot predict with a great degree of accuracy the detailed effects of an individual action such as the raising of a particular tax rate or tariff. Such a reminder is necessary if only because economists are frequently criticised for their failure to achieve exactly this.

General analysis also demonstrates the role of prices in an economy typified by the market structure we have so far discussed. Prices are seen to be the 'signals', the feedback mechanisms, by which firms learn of changing demand patterns. Firms change their plans accordingly until, ultimately, planned sales are made consistent with planned purchases. Similarly, planned sales and purchases of inputs are made consistent through changes in input prices. The final pattern of commodity and input prices then produces results for the three major decisions to be made in any economy.

First, what commodities shall be produced? The pattern of commodity prices will reflect the pattern of consumers' preferences and will thus act as signals to firms to inform them of what consumers want. In a purely private enterprise system, with all goods being provided in private markets, all goods will be supplied in response to those preferences with prices acting as the intermediary between the two aspects of commodity provision.

Second, how will commodities be produced – that is, with what combination of inputs? Again, the answer is that input combinations will be determined by relative input prices which in turn reflect the demand for the products they produce. Again, it will be consumers' preferences that determine this pattern of input use.

Third, who is to receive the commodities? Obviously, some consumers will consume more than others. How is this pattern determined? Obviously, the higher the individual's income the greater is his command over goods. Hence the pattern of incomes will determine the pattern of consumption. In turn, it is traditionally argued that this income pattern will depend on what inputs the individual supplies, his return for providing a single unit of it, and the amount he chooses to supply. The pattern of consumption will therefore depend on the role played by the individual in providing the resources necessary to produce commodities to meet consumer demands. It is perhaps as well to point out here that no prescriptive statement can be derived from this outcome: even if the existing income distribution reflects marginal productivities, this can be no *justification* for the particular income distribution that results. It is a significant feature of the mainstream of modern economics that many economists make exactly this mistake: they speak of 'optimal' allocations of resources without considering income distribution. To do this is to assume that the existing income distribution is itself optimal: if it is not, we would have to consider what society as a whole prefers by way of an income distribution. But since we have no justification for supposing that it is optimal, we are logically involved in finding out what income distribution is preferred. Such an exercise is fraught with even more difficulties than those associated with looking at the purely allocative aspects of economic behaviour. Our concern is simply to point to the arbitrariness of looking at the allocation aspects alone.

11.3 A Formal Approach to General Equilibrium

The preceding analysis has been entirely verbal. It is useful to look at general equilibrium in a more formal way since it illustrates some further theoretical problems associated with the concept of general equilibrium.

Suppose we have the following knowledge about our economic system.

1. *Demand Equations:* The demand (x) for any commodity i will depend on its own price, p_i, on the prices of other goods p_1, p_2, etc., and on incomes. Incomes in turn depend on the prices at which inputs are supplied – i.e. on f_1, f_2, etc. We take preferences, tastes and objectives as given. Thus we have

$$x_i = F_i(p_1, p_2, p_3, \ldots, p_n; f_1, f_2, f_3, \ldots, f_m) \tag{1}$$

where F_i merely denotes a functional relationship between x_i and the variables inside the brackets. Note that we have n commodities and m inputs.

2. *Cost of Production:* Commodity prices will also depend on the firm's cost functions, which will in turn be determined by the quantities of inputs $(n_1, n_2,$ etc.) used to produce goods, and their prices $(f_1, f_2,$ etc.). We denote the *rate* at which inputs are transformed into outputs by t, so that t_{12} will refer to the quantity of input 2 used to produce commodity 1. Then,

$$p_i = G_i(t_{i1} \cdot f_1, t_{i2} \cdot f_2, t_{i3} \cdot f_3, \ldots, t_{im} \cdot f_m) \tag{2}$$

so that $t_{i1} \cdot f_1$ is total expenditure on input 1 in the production of one unit of good i.

Under perfect competition, in long-run equilibrium, price equals average total cost. In this case we can drop the functional relationship in equation (2) and make the relationship additive such that

$$p_i = t_{i1} \cdot f_1 + t_{i2} \cdot f_2 + t_{i3} \cdot f_3 + \ldots + t_{im} \cdot f_m. \qquad (2a)$$

3. *Supply of Inputs:* The supply of each input (n_j) will depend on input prices (f_j) and commodity prices (p_i). Hence

$$n_j = F_j (f_1, f_2, f_3, \ldots, f_m; p_1, p_2, p_3, \ldots, p_n). \qquad (3)$$

4. *Demand for Inputs:* The demand for an input to use for the production of one unit of output (t_{ij}) will depend on input prices. Hence

$$t_{ij} = H_j (f_1, f_2, f_3, \ldots, f_m). \qquad (4)$$

5. *Full Employment:* We shall assume the total supply of any input is equal to the total demand for that input. Hence

$$n_j = t_{1j} \cdot x_1 + t_{2j} \cdot x_2 + t_{3j} \cdot x_3 + \ldots + t_{nj} \cdot x_n \qquad (5)$$

since $t_{ij} \cdot x_1$ is the total amount of j used in producing x_1 of commodity 1.

We now have five equations in n commodities and m inputs. We designate commodity 1 the *numeraire*. That is we set its price equal to unity. In doing this we are effectively modifying the analysis so to explain the prices of the other $n-1$ commodities in terms of the price of commodity 1. We shall therefore be explaining only the price of *relative* prices and not *absolute* prices. Note, too, that we could have selected *any* commodity as numeraire. By setting $p_1 = 1$ we must now modify the equations. If consumers spend all their incomes we shall have

$$p_1 \cdot x_1 = x_1 = (f_1 \cdot n_1 + f_2 \cdot n_2 + \ldots + f_m \cdot n_m)$$
$$- (p_2 \cdot x_2 + p_3 \cdot x_3 + \ldots + p_n \cdot x_n). \qquad (6a)$$

This equation tells us that the demand for good 1 is equal to the total incomes of consumers minus the amount they spend on commodities 2 to n.

For the remaining commodities the equations are as in equation (1), but without the price of the numeraire, that is,

$$x_2 = F_2 (p_2, p_3, \ldots, p_n; f_1, f_2, \ldots, f_m) \qquad (6b)$$

up to $\qquad x_n = F_n (p_2, p_3, \ldots, p_n; f_1, f_2, \ldots, f_m). \qquad (6c)$

The Determination of Relative Prices

Equation (2a) presupposed a perfectly competitive state such that commodity prices equal average total costs of production. This situation produces the following equations:

$$p_1 = 1 = t_{11} \cdot f_1 + t_{12} \cdot f_2 + \ldots + t_{1m} \cdot f_m \qquad (7a)$$
$$p_2 = t_{21} \cdot f_1 + t_{22} \cdot f_2 + \ldots + t_{2m} \cdot f_m \qquad (7b)$$

up to
$$p_n = t_{n_1} \cdot f_1 + t_{n2} \cdot f_2 + \ldots + t_{nm} \cdot f_m. \qquad (7c)$$

The equations for the supply of inputs (see equation 3) can be similarly modified. We do not repeat the exercise here, but merely call these modified equations group 8. Similarly, the input demand equations (see equation 4) can be presented as group 9. The final group of equations, group 10, shows the full-employment conditions, so that

$$n_1 = t_{11} \cdot x_1 + t_{21} \cdot x_2 + \ldots + t_{n1} \cdot x_n \qquad (10a)$$
$$n_2 = t_{12} \cdot x_1 + t_{22} \cdot x_2 + \ldots + t_{n2} \cdot x_n \qquad (10b)$$

down to
$$n_m = t_{1m} \cdot x_1 + t_{2m} \cdot x_2 + \ldots t_{nm} \cdot x_n. \qquad (10c)$$

We can now proceed to add up the number of equations in our system. There are n demand equations (group 6) and n equations relating price to cost (group 7). Group 8, the input supply equations, will number m since there are m inputs. The group 9 equations for input demand will number nm since the expansion t_{ij} relates each of the n commodities to each of the m inputs. Finally, there are m equations in group 10, so that we appear to have in all $n + n + m + mn + m = 2n + 2m + mn$ equations. But the unknowns can be listed as

$n-1$ commodity prices (not n, since $p_1 = 1$)
n quantities of commodities
m input prices
m input quantities
mn technical coefficients (the t_{ij}).

This gives $2n-1 + 2m + mn$ unknowns – that is, one less unknown than the number of equations. For there to be a *prima facie* case for supposing that a set of prices exist which would ensure the complete consistency of purchase and sale plans we require the number of equations to *equal* the number of unknowns.

Inspection of the sets of equations (6) to (10) shows that equation (6a) is not in fact independent of the others. We can demonstrate this as follows. Take the equations in group (7), and multiply each successive one by $x_1, x_2, x_3, \ldots, x_n$ respectively. Then take the equations in group (10) and multiply successive equations by $f_1, f_2, \ldots, f_m$ respectively. Now add the resulting equations together. It will be found that the sum of the right-hand sides of each set of equations is the same. Hence their left-hand sides must be equal, that is

$$x_1 + p_2 \cdot x_2 + p_3 \cdot x_3 + \ldots + p_n \cdot x_n = f_1 \cdot n_1 + f_2 \cdot n_2 + f_3 \cdot n_3 + \ldots + f_m \cdot n_m.$$

Hence

$$x_1 = (f_1 \cdot x_1 + f_2 \cdot x_3 + \ldots + f_m \cdot x_m) - (p_2 \cdot x_2 + p_3 \cdot x_3 + \ldots + p_n x_n)$$

which is, of course, the first equation in group (6).

Thus, instead of $2n + 2m + mn$ independent equations, we have $2n-1 + 2m + mn$, which is now the same as the number of unknowns. We have at least a *prima facie* case for supposing that there exists a set of unique prices which secure overall general equilibrium, by which we mean that each input and commodity has only one price respectively and this price 'clears' the market for each input and commodity.

11.4 The Existence of General Equilibrium Prices

Unfortunately, the equivalence of the number of unknowns and the number of equations in the system described in Section 11.3 is not sufficient to *guarantee* that a set of general equilibrium prices exists. This problem arises because we have not specified the actual equations involved: they were shown only as general functions relating dependent variables to independent variables. Figure 11.4.1 illustrates the problem. In the figure there are two unknowns, X and Y, and two equations relating the variables. In diagram (a) the curves intersect to produce a unique equilibrium; in (b) the curves do not touch at all so that no equilibrium exists; in (c) the curves intersect several times, and one of the intersections produces a negative equilibrium value of X. Each of the situations in the diagrams is consistent with the requirement that the number of unknowns equals the number of equations, however.

Figure 11.4.1 illustrates a number of problems that occur with the analysis of general equilibrium systems. In diagram (a) the equilibrium exists such that the equilibrium values of X and Y (x^* and Y^*) are unique. Obviously, unique solutions are desirable features, so

The Determination of Relative Prices

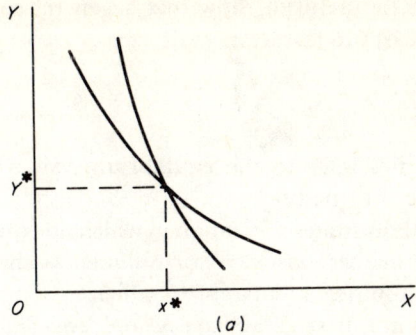

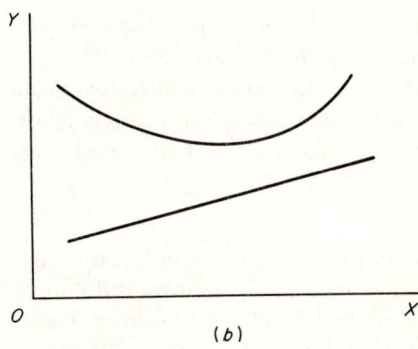

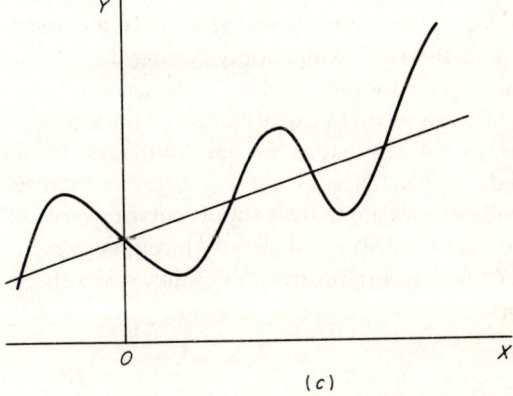

Figure 11.4.1

that it would be useful to show that a general equilibrium system possesses at least two features:

(i) *Existence*;
(ii) *Uniqueness*.

These properties refer to the equilibrium values which solve the equation system in question.

Diagram (*b*) illustrates a situation in which no equilibrium solution exists: hence neither existence nor uniqueness characterises such a system; (*c*) illustrates a situation in which existence is proved, but uniqueness is not. Indeed, we have *multiple equilibria* in this situation. Further, one of the equilibria gives a negative quantity of X. Translated into our previous model, this could mean that some products would have negative prices, or some inputs negative rates of reward.

Theorems which state that existence and uniqueness exist have been developed in the recent economic literature. Walras's own approach was limited to counting equations and unknowns. We can go no further in this text than indicating that this further literature exists.[1]

11.5 The Stability of General Equilibrium Prices

As it happens, existence and uniqueness do not exhaust the desirable features of a general equilibrium system. We also require that the system should be *stable*. The idea of stability can again be illustrated by concentrating on just two variables and two equations. Figure 11.5.1 shows two situations. We can in fact see the two curves as supply and demand curves and they are labelled as such. In the first diagram the curves are 'well-behaved' with supply cutting demand from below, giving a unique price for the product. In the second, however, supply cuts demand from above. If we concentrate on the second situation for the moment, we can see that to the right of the equilibrium at A demand exceeds supply. There is, therefore, no mechanism to induce suppliers to move back along their supply curve towards A. To the left of A supply exceeds demand providing no incentive to expand production to move towards A. The direction of the arrows shows the actual forces at work.

---

[1] Proofs of existence rely on 'fixed-point theorems'. An introductory treatment to such theorems is given in Professor W. J. Baumol's excellent text '*Economic Theory and Operations Analysis*', 3rd ed. (Prentice-Hall, New Jersey 1972). ch. 21.

The Determination of Relative Prices

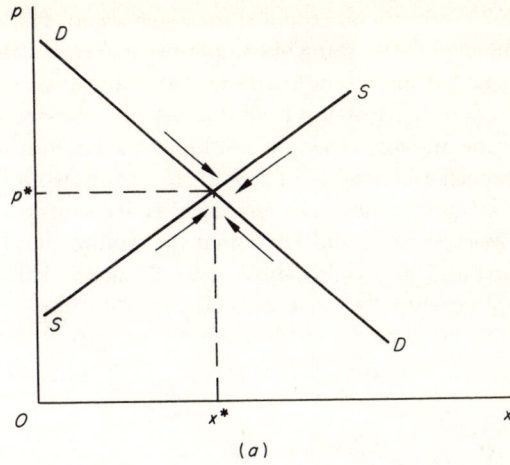

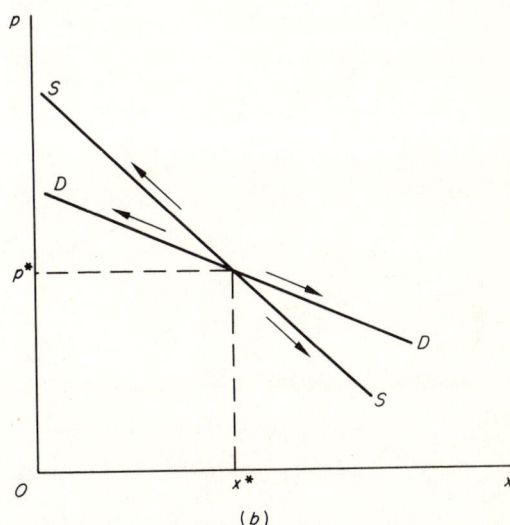

Figure 11.5.1

The arrows move away from A showing that a small disturbance which moves the situation away from A will not set up forces causing a return to A. In diagram (a), however, the forces do operate so as to generate a return to A. The situation in (a) is a *stable* one; in (b) it is *unstable*. Note that in both (a) and (b), p^* and x^* indicate unique solutions which exist.

Walras believed general equilibrium systems were stable. His basic argument likened the working of competitive markets to an auction. If demand exceeded supply the auctioneer would raise price, lower it if supply exceeded demand and hold it constant if the two were equal. Obviously, the auctioneer would not know the equilibrium price to which he expects to converge. Thus, his first move would be to raise price by an arbitrary amount if demand exceeded supply. If excess demand still existed, he would know that the equilibrium had not yet been reached and he would adjust upwards again. This *tatonnement* process would eventually converge on the equilibrium.

12

Market Behaviour and Market Morphology

12.0 The Methodology of Market Models

The analysis of the previous eleven chapters has been conducted almost entirely in terms of a 'perfectly competitive' model in which consumers and firms have been assumed to be price-takers and quantity-adjusters. That is, each firm and consumer is assumed to face a market price for inputs and outputs, that market price having been determined by the behaviour of supply and demand in the total market. Firms' and consumers' behaviour has then been analysed in terms of adjustments to the given prices, and the adjustments have consisted mainly of changing the quantities of inputs or goods purchased or offered for sale when prices change.

While the model used has been internally consistent and logical, it is clearly 'unrealistic' in that many firms, for example, are price-makers and quantity-adjusters. Equally, consumers are not always individually unable to exert influence over price. The question is whether the 'unreality' of the model used matters. There are several schools of thought on this issue, and a substantial debate has developed in which two polar views can be discerned. At one extreme are those who argue that the ability of a theory to yield useful hypotheses about economic events depends critically on the empirical validity of the assumptions of the model. In this respect, a theory would be held to be not useful if its assumptions failed to reflect the facts. At the other extreme are those who argue that the realism of a model's assumptions is irrelevant. On this argument, the only test of whether or not the assumptions have succeeded in isolating the most important elements is whether or not the hypotheses they yield are confirmed by events.[1]

---

[1] See M. Friedman, 'The Methodology of Positive Economics', in his *Essays in Positive Economics* (University of Chicago Press, Chicago, 1953).

Not surprisingly, then, those who argue for securing the empirical validity of assumptions tend to reject the use of perfect competition models. The 'positivists', who select assumptions on the grounds of their predictive power, would tend to argue in favour of the retention of unrealistic assumptions if they yield hypotheses which fit the facts. Accordingly, the former school tends to concern itself with the development of theories of market behaviour based on more realistic assumptions. In large part this explains the emergence of the substantial body of theory that now exists on 'imperfectly competitive' markets, and which forms the subject matter of Chapters 13 to 16.

There are difficulties with both views of economic methodology and it would be wrong to suggest that the polar extremes described above exhaust the possibilities of methodological standpoint. One danger with the 'realism of assumptions' argument is that we shall forever refine our assumptions to allow for a more and more complete description of human behaviour. In the limit, a statement of assumptions would simply become a statement of how the world is, making generalisation, which is after all the object of any investigation, impossible. But the positivist view is not free of difficulties either. Suppose we have several sets of assumptions, all equally unrealistic, from which we can choose. How do we select the 'right' set of assumptions? Presumably, the positivist approach would be to try them all and test their 'predictive power' against the facts. This in turn implies that there is some measuring rod of predictive accuracy. This requires some list of implications which must be explained by the theory for it to be judged a sound theory. The danger is that there are no clear rules for deciding on the evidence. Further, if the theory does succeed in predicting accurately, it might be taken to imply that the assumptions are themselves accurate descriptions of reality, even though observation might suggest otherwise.

On the purely practical level, there is much to be gained by adopting the positivist standpoint. The assumptions of perfect competition, say, are simple and greatly facilitate subsequent deductions because of the identity of so many variables (e.g. demand and marginal revenue). Thus Marshall's original classification of markets was simpler than those that now tend to be used in economics, and it is arguable that other market models have done little to discredit the general predictive power of Marshallian analysis. But we leave the reader to judge. What follows is a classification of markets. The next four chapters, then, look at each classification in turn.

12.1 Pure Competition

A state of pure competition exists when the price of any commodity X is a datum for each consumer and for each firm. For this to be the case the following conditions must be simultaneously fulfilled:

(i) The number of sellers (firms) of X must be so large that the amount that each seller offers for sale in each period constitutes so small a proportion of the total quantity being supplied by all sellers that he, acting alone, is powerless to affect the price by varying the amount that he offers for sale. This number is incapable of being expressed cardinally. We can only define it operationally: the number of sellers must be so large that any practicable variation in the planned sales of any seller will not shift the market supply curve by enough to cause a change in the price, in the given conditions of demand.

(ii) The number of buyers of X must be so large that the planned purchases of any buyer at any price constitutes an insignificantly small proportion of the total planned purchases at that price. This assumption is necessary for the same reason as (i) above, namely, to eliminate any appreciable or significant interdependence between the decisions of different buyers.

(iii) The product X that is being bought and sold must be homogeneous. The product will be homogeneous if each buyer (seller) is indifferent as to which unit(s) of a seller's production (buyer's purchases) he buys (sells), and if each buyer (seller) is indifferent as between sellers (buyers). If buyers are to regard each unit of X as being a perfect substitute for each other unit of X, then it is not only necessary that the different units of X must be physically identical; in addition, the spatial distribution of buyers and sellers within a geographical area must be such that no preference can arise for reasons of distance for the product of any seller, and the circumstances that surround the buying and selling of X must be identical for all transactions – for example, all sellers must be equally polite or equally rude.

(iv) Each buyer, acting independently, aims to maximise utility subject to the limits set by his income and wealth, and each seller of X, acting independently of other sellers, attempts to earn the maximum profit per period by producing and selling it. This assumption is probably necessary to ensure that, when conditions (i), (ii) and (iii) are fulfilled, each buyer and each seller in fact behaves as a price-taker: the desire to maximise utility or profit impels those who operate in the market to acquire enough knowledge about its main characteristics to realise that the price of X lies beyond the control of each of them. This assumption is certainly necessary if we are concerned with the efficiency with which a market in which conditions (i) to (iii) are fulfilled transforms inputs into products and distributes the products amongst consumers – that is, if our interest lies in welfare economics rather than in positive economics, if we are trying to answer the question: how well does the price system work? and not simply the question: how does it work?

(v) The existence of a market in which there are large numbers of buyers and sellers of a homogeneous commodity does not by itself guarantee that each and every purchase and sale of the commodity will be transacted at the same price. Assumptions (i) and (iii) are necessary conditions for the sameness of price, but they are not sufficient conditions. In addition, we must make some assumption about the amount of knowledge that each buyer and seller must possess to ensure that all units of the commodity are sold at the same price. And given this assumption and assumption (iv) above, we know that this price must also be an equilibrium price.

It is customary to assume that all buyers and sellers must have complete knowledge of all prices and all price offers if all transactions are to take place at the same price. If we accord this 'perfect' knowledge to each buyer and to each seller, however, we make it impossible for the market in which they operate *not* to be in equilibrium, and we remain in ignorance about the way in which the equilibrium comes to be established. What is wanted, rather, is an assumption that answers the question: how much knowledge about what things must each buyer and seller possess if their joint actions are to be successful in establishing an equilibrium? We shall attempt to answer this question by examining the short-run equilibrium described in Chapter 6. The objective facts that underlie an equilibrium in the market for a particular product X are the tastes of each buyer, the production possibilities open to each seller (which depend on the physical productivities of the inputs that he uses), the price of each variable input, and the price of each product other than X. These define the environment of the market for X, and any equilibrium in that market must be relative to that environment. The equilibrium that actually emerges will depend on the knowledge that each buyer and seller possesses of these facts, and there will be as many equilibria as there are degrees of knowledge. If the equilibrium is to reflect fully all these facts, then each buyer must be aware of (*a*) his own tastes; (*b*) product prices; and (*c*) the relative capacity of different products to meet his preferences, and each seller must be aware of (a) the quantity of X that he will actually obtain from any possible combination of the relevant productive services, and (b) the price of each input. The equilibrium that we described in Chapter 6 was of this kind: it was an 'ideal type' chosen to simplify our analysis by giving us a unique and determinate equilibrium. If we wish this equilibrium to be established in our model, then we must assume that each buyer and each seller possesses full knowledge of each of the things listed above.

In any actual market where conditions (i) to (iv) above are fulfilled, however, consumers and firms may possess less than complete knowledge of the relevant data, and the degree of incompleteness of their knowledge will vary from one market to another. If we want some assumption to guide us when dealing with such markets, other than the assumption of 'complete' or 'perfect' knowledge, we may assume that each buyer and each seller possesses that knowledge of the relevant data that he is bound to acquire as he implements and revises his plans. Thus, a consumer may make his initial purchase plan on the basis of certain expectations about the capacity of certain products to satisfy his wants; as he actually buys and consumes these products he will gain some clearer notions about the satisfactions they provide, and his purchase plan for subsequent period will be laid on the basis of these. Similarly, a firm will acquire a fuller knowledge of the actual physical productivities of the inputs it uses as it compares, and seeks to account for, the difference between the profit it expected to earn and that which it actually succeeded in earning. The knowledge that is acquired in this way will be the fuller, the more stable are the elements of the market environment. Even if the environment is absolutely stable, however, the knowledge that is so acquired need never be complete, for there may be certain relevant data that a consumer or firm never becomes aware of through putting his (its) plans into effect. Thus, if a consumer is initially unaware of the existence of commodity Y, which would satisfy the same want as X, Y will not appear in his purchase plan and the implementation of that plan will not necessarily call Y to the consumer's attention. For the present, however, we shall assume that each buyer and seller has complete knowledge of his 'segment' of the market environment: this simplifies our analysis in that it gives us a unique equilibrium price for market X when conditions (i) to (iv) obtain.[1]

---

[1] On assumption (v), see F. A. Hayek, 'Economics and Knowledge', *Economica*, IV, New Series, 1937, pp. 33–54.

When the structure of the market for a commodity is accurately described by the five assumptions that we have listed above, we shall say that those who buy and sell in it are operating under conditions of *pure competition*, or that in that market there exists a state of pure competition. When a state of pure competition exists in the market for X, each purchase and sale of X takes place at the equilibrium price and each consumer is buying in each period a quantity of X such that his utility is maximised, and each firm is selling the quantity of X that promises it the maximum profits per period. Alternatively, we may say that each consumer's purchases of X are such that the marginal rate of substitution between X and each other product is equal to the ratio of their prices, and each firm's sales of X in each period are such that (*a*) the marginal cost of production is equal to the equilibrium price, and (*b*) the marginal rate of technical substitution between any two of the productive services used to produce this quantity of X is equal to the reciprocal of the ratio of their prices.

In delineating the morphology of a purely competitive market, we have confined our attention to a market for a product. Pure competition may also exist in the market for an input. The assumptions that must be fulfilled to give us a purely competitive input market are very similar to those listed above, and a statement of their precise contents is left to the reader. It should now be clear that in our explanation of the determination of product and factor prices in Chapters 6 and 10, we assumed that a state of pure competition existed in the product and input markets respectively.

12.2 Perfect Competition

If pure competition exists in the market for some commodity X, then we know that at each moment of time each buyer and seller of X will be a price-taker, and the price of X will be such that the planned purchases of all buyers will be the same as the planned sales of all sellers. If the market environment alters, however – as a result, for example, of a general change in the intensity of the desires for X – the existence of pure competition tells us nothing about the relationship between the prices of X at successive moments of time: it tells us merely that at each instant the price is such that the market is cleared; it does not tell us anything about the path that will be traced by the price of X as time passes. We saw in Chapter 6 that the time-path of prices following some initial event depends primarily on the adjustments that are effected in the firm's sales plans. We classified all the adjustments that might occur into two groups, namely, short-run and long-run adjustments. In the short-run, the only revisions of sales plans that are possible are those that can be made by the firms already producing the product, within the limits set by the quantities of plant, equipment, managerial and executive labour, etc., at each firm's disposal; in the long-run, the total supply of the product may be augmented or depleted by changes in both the number and size of firms. We have already seen that the ease with which these long-run adjustments can be effected is reflected in the price elasticity of the long-run supply curve of the product: if no long-run adjustment was possible, then the long-run and short-run supply curves would coincide with one another; if all long-run changes could be accomplished with perfect ease and without cost the long-run supply curve would be perfectly elastic, and following any initial rise in demand the price of the product would ultimately subside to its initial level. We shall now list the things on which the elasticity of the long-run supply curve of a product depend, and it is convenient to do so by stating the conditions that must be fulfilled if the long-run supply curve is to be perfectly elastic.

If the long-run supply curve of a product is perfectly elastic, we shall say that the industry is in a state of *perfect competition*, or that the firms in it are operating under conditions of perfect competition. Alternatively, we may say that *free* competition obtains, where 'free' means both the total absence of any restrictions of any kind on the entry of new firms or the exit of old firms, and, a consequence of this, that an increase in the output of the industry may be obtained in the long-run without any increase in the average total cost of production per unit of the product, and therefore without any rise in the price.

An economist would predict that the price of a commodity X would ultimately return to its initial level, after an initial long-run equilibrium has been upset by a rise in demand, if (a) there are no legal and institutional barriers in the way of new entrants to the industry, and (b) if the managers that enter the industry are identical in quality with existing managers and if they can buy inputs of the same quality and at the same price as those that are already there. For these conditions to obtain, the following assumptions must be descriptively accurate:

(a) There must be no legal or institutional restrictions on the entry of new firms into the industry that produces X. New entry may be restricted by government or by the firms already in the industry. In the United Kingdom, for example, there is only one firm in the coal, electricity and rail transport industries, and the entry of new firms is prohibited by statute. The firms already in an industry may discourage new entrants by threatening to undercut their prices, by boycotting buyers who patronise them, by collectively acquiring the source of some of the processes by which alone it can be produced: until the patent expires, new firms can only enter by paying licence fees to the substantial advertising campaigns designed to reduce the initial profits of the new entrant. Existing firms may have patented the product, or some of the processes by which alone it can be produced: until the patent expires, new firms can only enter by paying licence fees to the patent-owners and these may put them in a disadvantageous position. It is only when all such obstacles are absent that new firms will be able to enter the industry and operate in it on terms that are no less favourable than those which obtain for the firms that are already there.

(b) If the prices of inputs are to remain unchanged as the industry expands, then each must be in perfectly elastic supply to the industry. If the input in question is the product of other firms, it will be in perfectly elastic long-run supply to the industry producing X only if the firms that produce it are themselves operating under conditions of perfect competition, so that the pre-conditions of perfect competition (that we are at present enumerating for industry X) must be fulfilled also in the industries producing the services that X buys. An input (like a particular kind of labour-service) will be in perfectly elastic supply to industry X if the following conditions are fulfilled:

(i) Each unit of it must be perfectly mobile, both geographically and occupationally. Let us suppose that the service is carpentry, and that the demand for X (in whose production carpenters assist) rises. As new managers are attracted to the production of X, the demand for carpenters' services will rise. If the actual (or potential) carpenters who might meet this new demand are not living in the same places as the firms that want their services, then a higher wage-rate might have to be offered to them – a wage sufficiently higher to amortise the initial, and cover the recurrent, costs of moving. By perfect geographical mobility of a resource, we mean the absence of any money cost in transferring it from one place to another. For as many more carpenters to be forthcoming at the existing wage-rate as are required, that rate must be sufficient to cover the costs that workers with other skills would incur in changing their occupation. A high degree of occupational mobility implies the absence of any legal or institutional barriers in the way of new entrants to any trade; in addition, it requires either that the precise skills in different occupations are closely similar, or that enough workers are highly versatile and flexible in intellectual ability and manual dexterity. If there is occupational immobility, then a progressively higher wage-rate must be offered to carpenters to induce new workers to acquire that skill. What we have said of carpenters applies equally to managers: they, too, must be perfectly willing to move, into the industry that produces X and at the rewards that can be initially earned there, from the industries and places in which they are at present engaged.

(ii) Each unit of each input must have full knowledge of the alternative opportunities that are open to it. Each worker, for example, must know the different jobs for which he is by natural endowment suited, and the wage-rate that might be earned in each of them. If potential carpenters were ignorant of these things, then a rise in the carpenters' wage-rate might pass unnoticed and so cause no increase in the number of carpenters. When the demand for product X rises, causing an increase in the profits of the firms that make it, managers in all other industries must be aware of this fact; at least some of them must have enough knowledge of the methods and costs of production of X to realise that the higher net revenues that firms now making X are earning might be earned by them also. If managers in other industries are ignorant of these things, then no new firms may be set up following the increase in the demand for X.

(iii) Each unit of each input must not only have full knowledge of present opportunities: it must also have unique expectations about how the range of opportunities, and the reward that each promises, will vary in the future. Let us suppose that the wage-rate of carpenters rises in the short-run, as a result of a rise in the demand for their services. This need not evoke an increase in the number of carpenters, even if all the conditions that we have already listed are fulfilled, for potential carpenters may not respond because they are uncertain about the future behaviour of the carpenters' wage-rate, and because, being uncertain, they may be loath to acquire a new skill that would force them to live in the presence of uncertainty as they practised it. Thus, the range of values within which potential carpenter A believes the wage-rate will lie at some date in the future, or fluctuate over the future, may be wider or narrower than that which carpenter B has in mind, or the two ranges may overlap one another. In these circumstances, even though A and B are in all other respects identical, the wage-rate that will induce A to become a carpenter need not induce B to do so or to remain so. Different expectations about the future behaviour of the carpenters' wage-rate may, therefore, by themselves explain a less than perfectly elastic supply curve of carpenters in the long-run. Even if A's expectations are identical with those of B – even if they both feel that the wage-rate in future will not be more than 25 per cent greater or 25 per cent less than its present level – they may differ in their attitudes towards uncertainty.[1] If A is venturous, and B timorous and happy only if his future earnings seem stable and secure, then A may move into carpentry while B remains where he is. What we have said of carpenters applies equally to the owners of machines and equipment and to those who are venturing their savings. Uncertainty, and the attitudes towards uncertainty, may therefore explain why the long-run equilibrium price of an input may rise if there is a permanent increase in the demand for it. We may think of this higher price as being a reward to those who earn it for 'bearing' uncertainty or for 'living with' it; or we may view it as being caused by the unwillingness of others to bear the uncertainty.

Uncertainty may exert its strongest influence in shaping the decision of the manager. It is the manager whose initial decision creates the firm: it is he who hires or buys inputs and organises their transformation into saleable products, and who obtains a reward for himself and for the shareholders in each period from the difference between the revenue and the total expenditure on all imputs. In calculating the profit he might earn were he to enter some industry X, he must estimate the present level and probable future behaviour of the price of the product, and of the prices and physical productivities of the inputs. Uncertainty bears more heavily on him, therefore, largely because there are more variables about whose values he may be uncertain. He may eliminate some of the uncertainty by making long-term contracts with the owners of inputs, though his inclination to do so will reflect his own attitude towards uncertainty. Even though the existing firms in industry X are currently earning high profits, therefore, other managers may not enter it: they may doubt that similar profits would accrue to them were they to begin producing X or they may be uncertain about the behaviour of profits in that industry in the future. The

---

[1] We are here assuming that the range of expected values of the wage-rate is independent of the attitude towards uncertainty. While this seems reasonable, it may not be realistic.

relatively higher profits that the firms now producing X are earning may therefore be explained by the fact that the existence of uncertainty makes the supply of units of an otherwise homogeneous managerial factor less than perfectly elastic; alternatively, we may view these profits as being, in part, the reward that accrues to managers already in the X-industry for 'bearing' the uncertainty.

It is clear, then, that if each input is to be in perfectly elastic supply to industry X, each owner of each input must have perfect foresight about the future behaviour of the price of the service that he sells. Alternatively, we may assume that the owners of an input are equally uncertain about the future and what it holds for them, and that they all have the same attitude towards uncertainty. The former assumption is merely the limiting case of the latter when the 'value' of the uncertainty is zero.

(iv) Lastly, we must assume that each input is perfectly divisible. Let us suppose, by way of example to show the necessity for this assumption, that carpenters are an indivisible input. In Figure 12.2.1, we measure the hourly wage-rate on the vertical axis; on the horizontal axis, we measure both the number of carpenters and hours of work, assuming that carpenters and those who employ them regard a working week of 40 hours as 'normal' when the wage-rate is at its long-run equilibrium level of $\overline{W}$. The curve S_1S_1 shows the short-run supply of hours of work when one carpenter only is employed, and similarly the curves S_2S_2 and S_3S_3. We suppose that the demand for carpenters' services is initially DD and that the wage-rate is $\overline{W}$: at this wage-rate, two carpenters are just willing to offer the 'normal' hours of work in each week and no actual (or potential) carpenter elsewhere feels attracted to this industry. Let us now suppose that the demand for carpenters' services rises to D_1D_1. In the ensuing short-run, the hourly wage-rate will rise to W_1; this rate will appear attractive to workers in other occupations, but when a third carpenter enters, the wage-rate will fall to W_2. In these circumstances, if a wage-rate of $\overline{W}$ is sufficient to retain a third carpenter in that industry in the long-run, and if he possessed perfect foresight, he would not decide to enter the industry until the short-run rate had reached W_3; for a present rate of W_3 is needed to ensure for him the long-run rate of $\overline{W}$ after he has actually begun work in the industry. When the demand for carpenters rises continuously, therefore, the number of hours of work that are being supplied per week will rise discontinuously along the path $\overline{W}ABCDE$ ... The existence of indivisibility – or, more accurately, the fact that the quantity of an input cannot be increased by the same proportion (with no change in its price) as the change in the demand for it – means that the long-run supply curve of it may be less than perfectly elastic over at least a part of its range. When this occurs, we shall only observe a perfectly elastic long-run supply curve for the input if the demand for it rises discontinuously also by the same steps as the discontinuities caused by the indivisibility.

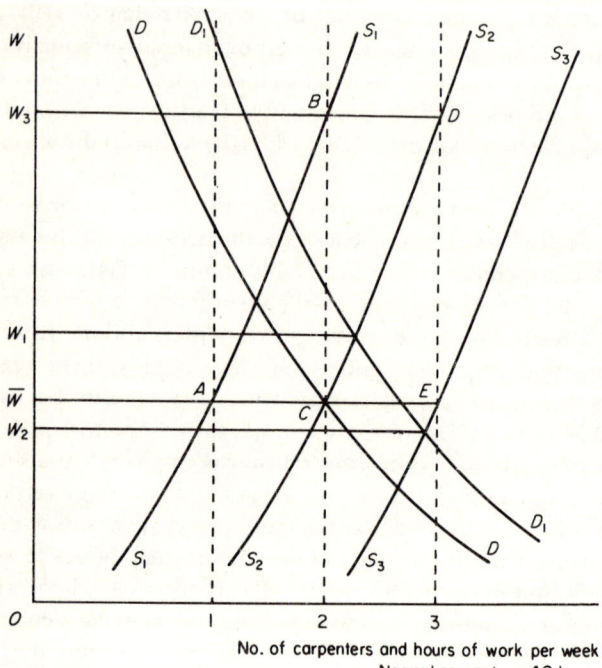

Figure 12.2.1

Indivisibilities may explain why there is a permanent rise in the profits of firms producing some product X following a rise in the demand for it, in the same way as they explain why the hourly wage-rate of carpenters may remain higher than its initial level following a rise in the demand for their services. The indivisible factor may be the manager: it may happen, for example, that the quantities of all inputs that he must employ to give him the lowest average cost per unit of output would so enhance the output of the product that its price would fall to a level that would give the new manager (and those already in the industry) a negative profit. Alternatively, the dominant indivisibility may lie in the machines, equipment or processes that are required in industry X: in these circumstances, the advent of a new firm using the indivisible machine or process would so enhance the industry's output that no firm earned a positive profit.

When there are no legal or institutional obstacles in the way of new firms entering industry X, and when all the inputs required to produce X are perfectly mobile and perfectly divisible, and their owners perfectly knowledgeable and possessed of perfect foresight, then conditions of perfect competition obtain in that industry. When these conditions prevail, then each firm producing X will be of the same size – that is, each firm will be enjoying the same advantages as each other: each firm will be employing the same quantity of each input as each other firm and all will be producing and selling the same output in each period; and the total revenue being earned by each firm will just suffice to cover its total costs of production – that is, to pay for the imputs that it uses at their current market prices.

The pre-conditions of pure competition that we listed earlier define the shape of the demand curve for the product that each firm sells and for the services that each consumer sells: the demand curve that faces each seller of a product or input will be perfectly elastic at the ruling market price. The pre-conditions of perfect competition, in their turn, define the relationship between the demand and cost curves of the individual firm: the demand curve for its product and the average total cost curve will be tangential to one another, so that the firm's total revenue just covers its total costs of production, as shown in Figure 12.2.2.

It should be noted that conditions of pure and perfect competition need not necessarily co-exist. It is conceivable, for example, that there might be pure competition in an industry, but that the entry of new firms is prohibited by government; this is unlikely, however, for government intervention is usually the consequence of organised lobbying by the firms already in the industry, and once they have enjoyed the fruits that co-operation bears they are unlikely to return to a situation in which they must act independently of one another. If perfect competition exists, however, then it is probable that pure competition exists also: for example, if all inputs are perfectly divisible – one of the pre-conditions of perfect competition – then this by itself suggests that there will be a large number of firms already in the industry. The concepts of pure and perfect competition are, therefore, logically

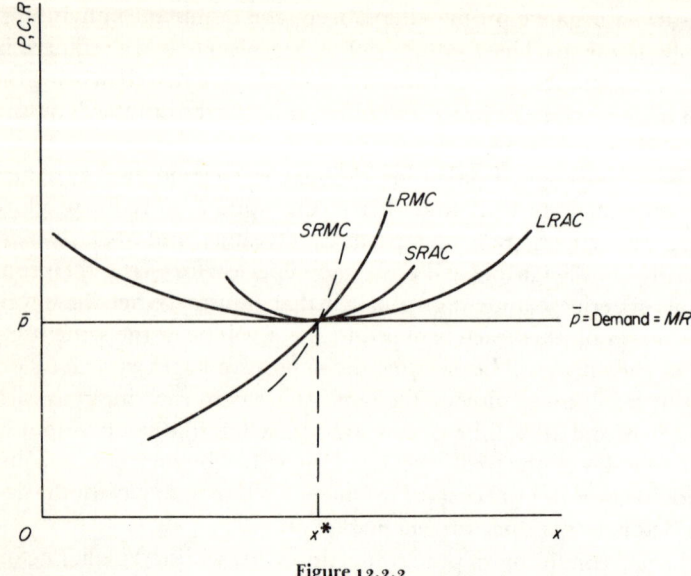

Figure 12.2.2

separate: the former defines the equilibrium of each firm in an industry; the latter defines a particular equilibrium position for the whole group of firms that constitute the industry.

12.3 A Classification of Markets

If all the assumptions that we have stated in the previous two sections were simultaneously true of any actual market, then those operating in that market would be doing so under conditions of pure and perfect competition. The most cursory knowledge of actual markets suffices, however, to convince us that these assumptions are generally, if not always, descriptively inaccurate. While generally lacking in empirical validity, these assumptions nevertheless provide us with the criteria on which a rough and workable classification of actual markets can be based. The manner in which they help us in this respect becomes clear if we interpret each assumption as being compounded of a statement that a certain variable exercises a determining influence on the behaviour of firms, and of a statement that this variable is assumed to have a particular value. Viewed in this light, each of our assumptions becomes the 'product' of a 'multiplicand' which is simply a statement that something is relevant if we are concerned with a firm's behaviour,

Market Behaviour and Market Morphology

and of a 'multiplier' which is the precise value that is attached to this relevant variable. Thus, the assumption that to have pure competition, we must, *inter alia*, have a large number of firms in the industry means that the behaviour of each firm (whether it will be a 'price-taker' or a 'price-maker') will depend on the number of other firms producing the product, and that to the relevant variable 'number of firms' we have attached the value of infinity. Again, the assumption that the product that is being produced by the many firms must be homogeneous means that the 'degree of homogeneity' is a relevant variable, and that we have given it a value of infinity. Lastly, we have asserted that the behaviour of the price of a product following an increase in the demand for it will depend on the mobility and divisibility of inputs and on the knowledge and foresight possessed by their owners and we have given each of these the value of 'perfect'.

Our judgement that the assumptions underlying pure and perfect competition are 'unrealistic' can now be expressed more precisely: each of our assumptions isolates a relevant variable, and it is the value that we have attached to each of these that is 'unrealistic'. A classificatory system into which actual markets can be fitted may therefore be developed by giving realistic and typical values to the relevant variables. The completeness of the classification that emerges will depend on whether or not all the relevant market characteristics have in fact been included in our model. The test of its completeness is partly logical and partly empirical. In our models of pure and perfect competition we obtained determinate equilibria and this suggests that nothing that was relevant was excluded. Most actual markets at the present time can be brought within the classification by varying the values that we attach to the characteristics that we have isolated. Lastly, the success with which we can explain economic events and predict their main consequences with the help of hypotheses derived from these assumptions could be argued to suggest that all the major influences that affect the behaviour of relative prices have been included.

The variables whose value helps to determine the actual course of particular prices are (i) the number of sellers; (ii) the number of buyers; (iii) the amount of knowledge that each possesses; (iv) their objectives; (v) the degree of homogeneity of the product they buy and sell; (vi) the unimportance of legal and institutional barriers to the entry of new buyers and sellers; (vii) the mobility and (viii) the divisibility of inputs; (ix) the degree of knowledge and (x) of foresight possessed by their owners. Each of these may assume any value from zero to infinity, and since we believe that this list includes all the relevant variables, there must exist a set of precise values for each of them that will accurately describe the morphology of any particular market in the economy. The infinite number of possible market morphologies that may emerge in that way has customarily been fitted into a primary classification that arises in the following manner: a value of zero is given to variables (vi) to (x) inclusive, and variables (iii) to (v) inclusive are given the same values as under pure competition, and alternative values are given to the numbers of buyers and sellers of the product.

Economists have long been aware that a high degree of correlation exists between the number of sellers (or of buyers) of a commodity and the market behaviour of each of them, so that the values that were accorded to these variables were the critical values necessary to isolate the different kinds of market behaviour. On this basis, the following classification emerged:

1. *Monopoly*: This is the name given to the market form in which there is one seller, an infinitely large number of buyers, and in which the values assumed by variables (iii) to (v) are the same as when conditions of pure competition exist, and the value of each of the variables (vi) to (x) inclusive is zero. Where this kind of market exists, we would expect the single seller to be an 'independent price-maker' – that is, to possess some power to determine the price of his product – and we generally find that these expectations are confirmed. The complementary market form is *monopsony*, where there is one buyer, and an infinitely large number of sellers, and where all the other variables have the same values as for monopoly.

2. *Oligopoly*: This is a market in which there are a few sellers, and in which the values assumed by all the other variables are the same as when there is monopoly. When oligopoly exists, we would expect each of the small number of sellers to have some power to choose the price at which he will sell his product, but this power is limited by the existence of a few other firms selling the same product. For brevity's sake, we shall say that each oligopolist is an 'interdependent price-maker' – that is, his power to set a price for his product is circumscribed by the decisions of his rivals. The complementary type of market is *oligopsony*, where we have a few buyers and an infinitely large number of sellers, and where all the other variables have the same values as for oligopoly.

3. *Bilateral Monopoly*: Here, there is one buyer and one seller, and each of the other relevant variables has the same value as for monopoly or oligopoly. When bilateral monopoly exists, the single buyer and the single seller of the commodity or productive service each possesses some power to fix the price at which the transactions between them shall be finally effected.

4. *Monopolistic Competition*: This form of market was first explicitly isolated by E. H. Chamberlin in his *The Theory of Monopolistic Competition* (Harvard University Press, 1933). A state of monopolistic competition exists when all the variables (save (v) and (vi)) are given the same values as under conditions of pure and perfect competition. It is assumed that each unit of the product which is being produced by many firms and bought by many households is a close, but not a perfect, substitute for each other unit, and that there is some legal obstacle (such as the laws relating to patents and trade-marks) that prevents any firm from producing and selling a product that is in *all* respects identical with that being currently offered by any other firm.

If we wish to make this list of market prototypes exhaustive, we must add the market forms with which we are already familiar:

5. *Pure Competition*: In its simplest form, this type of market requires the values for variables (i) to (v) that we have listed above, and zero values for the variables (vi) to (x).

6. *Perfect Competition*: This type of market logically requires that pure competition exists also, so that for it to occur we must give the pure competition values to (i) to (v) and the values of infinity to variables (vi) to (x).

In the chapters which follow, we shall concentrate mainly on the kinds of competition that are to be found in the markets in which products are bought and sold.

13

Monopoly

13.0 The Nature of Monopoly

A monopoly market will be said to exist when there is one seller and many buyers of a homogeneous commodity. Because of this dominance of the market by one seller, we shall discover that a monopolist has power to fix the price for the product he sells.

We shall take the simplest case of monopoly for our 'ideal type'. Let us suppose that there is one seller of commodity X, that pure competition exists in the markets in which he buys his inputs so that the price of each of them is a datum for him, and that there is a very large number of knowledgeable buyers who buy his product in each period of time. We shall further suppose that the monopolist believes that there is no possibility, either now or in the forseeable future, of any new firm(s) being set up to produce X, and that, in pursuing his objective of earning maximum profits per period, he believes that his actions do not affect in any way the prices of any other products or the behaviour of the firms that make and sell them. By these assumptions, we, *inter alia*, exclude monopsony in the markets in which the monopolist buys his inputs and we eliminate all elements of oligopoly in the market in which he sells his product. Starting with this simple model of monopoly, we shall attempt to do three things: first, to describe the typical market behaviour of a monopolist; second, to indicate the wide variety that may exist amongst the individual markets that are classified together as monopolies, and this we shall do by modifying some of the assumptions on which the simple model of monopoly rests and examining the consequent modifications in the monopolist's plans; and third, to catalogue the methods by which monopoly might be created and the measures by which it might be perpetuated.

13.1 The Equilibrium of the Monopolist

Since the monopolist can, *ex hypothesi*, influence the price of the product he sells, the demand curve he faces will be downward-sloping. In turn this means that his total revenue curve (*TR*) must appear as in Figure 13.1.1. If we superimpose a total cost curve (*TC*) the equilibrium of the monopolist will be determined by his objective, which is likely to relate to some connection between *TR* and *TC*. Thus,

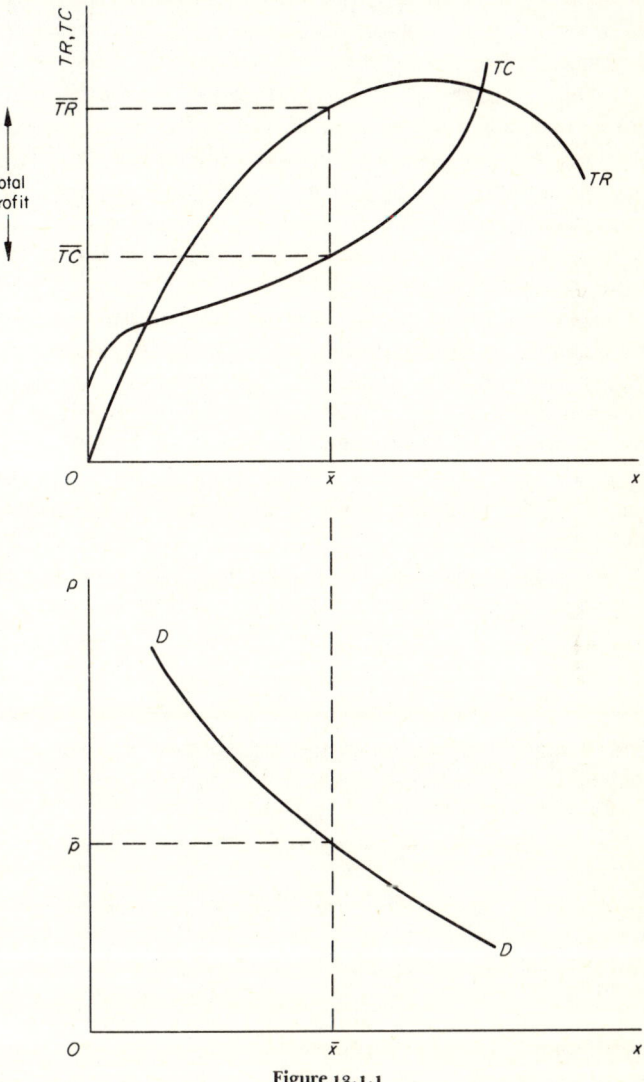

Figure 13.1.1

if the monopolist is a profit-maximiser he will seek the point where the distance between TR and TC is greatest. This is shown on the figure and corresponds to total revenue of $\overline{TR}$, total costs of $\overline{TC}$ and output $\overline{X}$. This output level can be translated to the monopolist's demand curve as is shown in Figure 13.1.1. The profit-maximising price is $\bar{p}$.

We observed in Section 4.4 that the equilibrium of the price-taker could be expressed in terms of *marginal revenue* and *marginal cost*. This equivalence is also true for the profit-maximising behaviour of the monopolist. In Figure 13.1.2 we repeat Figure 13.1.1 but we show, in addition, marginal revenue and, marginal cost, and average cost curves. Since marginal revenue is the extra revenue obtained from the sale of an extra unit of output, it can be seen that it corresponds to the *slope* of the TR curve ($\Delta TR/\Delta x$) in Figure 13.1.2. Equally, marginal cost is the slope of the TC curve ($\Delta TC/\Delta x$). It can be seen that the profit-maximising equilibrium coincides with the equivalence of MR and MC. The reason for this equivalence is identical to that given in Section 4.4 for the price-taker firm. If $MR < MC$ the firm will add more to costs than to revenue and hence will reduce profits by expanding output. Only when $MR = MC$ are profits at a maximum. In Figure 13.1.2 maximum profits are shown either by the distance $\overline{TR} - \overline{TC}$ on the top diagram, or by the shaded area in the lower diagram. The 'profit-margin' on each unit sold is $\bar{p} - \overline{AC}$ in Figure 13.1.2, so that total profits are $\bar{x}\,(\bar{p} - \overline{AC})$.

We can express the monopolist's equilibrium in one other way. Returning to the definition of marginal revenue, we can write

$$MR = \frac{TR_1 \text{ (after price fall)} - TR_0 \text{ (before price fall)}}{\text{Change in quantity}}.$$

Let the change in quantity be Δx and the change in price be Δp, then

$$\Delta x \cdot MR = (x_0 + \Delta x)(p_0 - \Delta p) - x_0 \cdot p_0$$
$$= x_0 \cdot p_0 - x_0 \cdot \Delta p + \Delta x \cdot p_0 - \Delta x \cdot \Delta p - x_0 \cdot p_0.$$

Cancelling out, and ignoring $\Delta x \cdot \Delta p$ as being of negligible magnitude, we have

$$\Delta x \cdot MR = \Delta x \cdot p_0 - x_0 \cdot \Delta p$$

$$= p_0 \cdot \Delta x \left[1 - \frac{x_0 \cdot \Delta p}{p_0 \cdot \Delta x}\right]$$

but $x_0 \cdot \Delta p/p_0 \cdot \Delta x$ is the expression for the *reciprocal* of the price elasticity of demand, $1/e_p$. Hence we can write

$$\Delta x \cdot MR = p_0 \cdot \Delta x \left(1 - \frac{1}{e_p}\right).$$

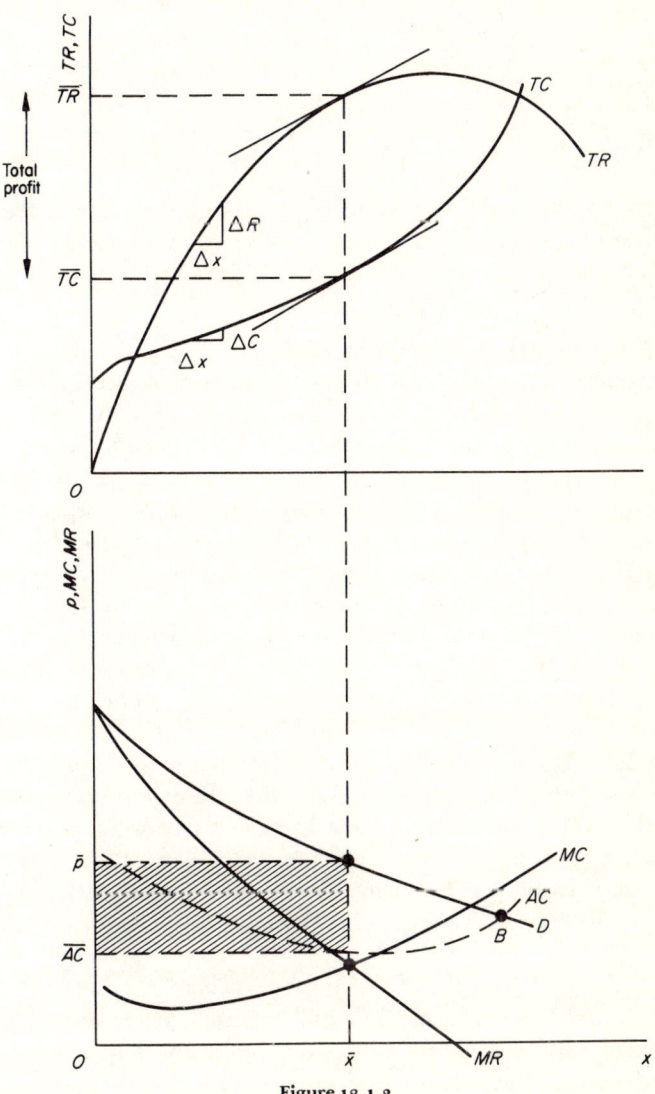

Figure 13.1.2

So that

$$MR = p_0 \cdot (1 - \frac{1}{e_p}).$$

Since in equilibrium $MR = MC$ we can write

$$MC = p_0 (1 - \frac{1}{e_p})$$

so that, in general, we can write

$$p = \frac{MC}{(1 - \frac{1}{e_p})}.$$

The monopolist's profit-maximising price can therefore be expressed in terms of marginal cost and the price elasticity of demand.

13.2 The Objectives of the Monopolist

The equilibrium of the monopolist has been described in terms of profit maximisation.

This objective is the same as that of a firm operating under conditions of perfect competition. For a firm in those conditions, however, that objective is obligatory: it is not so much a separate element in the market morphology as a necessary consequence of all the other elements, for if a firm is to survive in a perfectly competitive market it can only hope to succeed in doing so by seeking the maximum profit from its current operations. A firm that is operating under conditions of otherwise pure competition might regard this objective as permissive in the short-run, but if competition is also perfect it must pursue it to avoid bankruptcy in the long-run. Our monopolist is not compelled, however, to choose this objective, for there is no other firm, either now or in the future, to so compel him. The assumptions by which we have defined the environment in which he operates will not help us, then, to say what particular aim he will have, for that will depend largely on the individual idiosyncracies of the person who plays the role of monopolist in our model. While in these circumstances our model will not help us to predict the precise price and output that will be fixed in any particular case, it nevertheless helps us to delimit the range of highly probable prices and outputs. The monopolist will not fix a price that lies below that at which the average cost and demand curves intersect one another in Figure 13.1.2

– i.e. at B. For at prices below that his total revenue would not cover his total costs. Equally, he is unlikely to fix his price above the price at which the profit per period would be at a maximum.

It is possible that the monopolist will aim to maximise *revenue* instead of profits. If this is the case, he will operate at output x_1 in Figure 13.2.1 instead of at the profit-maximising output $\bar{x}$, his revenue and cost curves being TR and TC. Since TR is at a maximum, MR must be zero, so that the price-output rule becomes one of setting price such that $MR = 0$. Note that profits at x_1 output are only cd in Figure 13.2.1 compared to ab if the firm maximised profits.

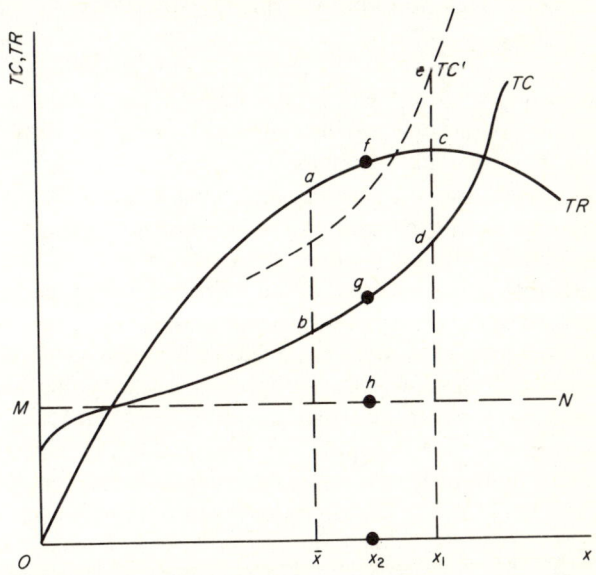

Figure 13.2.1

Of course, revenue maximisation as a single objective will be self-defeating if the cost curve in Figure 13.2.1 was further north, as indicated by the dashed curve TC'. In this case revenue maximisation would lead to net losses of ce per period, and even a monopolist is unlikely to sustain this for any period of time. It is more reasonable to suppose therefore that the monopolist will aim to maximise net revenue subject to some constraint about minimum necessary profits.[1] Suppose the minimum necessary profits are shown by MN in Figure

[1] See W. J. Baumol, *Business Behavior, Value and Growth* (Macmillan, New York, 1959).

13.2.1. Then the monopolist cannot produce at x_1 if TC and TR are his cost and revenue curves since profits are only cd and this is less than the minimum necessary profits. Instead, he will operate at output x_2 where profits are $fg = x_2h$, the minimum necessary profits. The firm has gone as far along the TR curve as is possible, given the constraint.

13.3 Monopolistic Price Discrimination

In our analysis of monopoly so far, we have assumed, *inter alia*, that the consumers who bought this product were as knowledgeable as they would have been had conditions of pure and perfect competition obtained. A necessary consequence of this assumption was that each unit of the monopolist's output would be sold at the same price: if he fixed a higher price for group A of buyers than for group B, the former would buy from the latter and the latter alone would buy from him; in these circumstances, since all units of the product must be sold at the same price, the monopolist will earn the maximum profit by fixing the price of each unit at $\bar{p}$ in Figure 13.1.2. We shall now suppose that the potential buyers of the product do not constitute a single and knowledgeable group, but that they are divided into several groups, and that each buyer is aware of the prices at which any other buyer in the same group is buying, but quite unaware of (or unable or unwilling to profit by) the price at which any buyer in any other group is buying. Each such group of buyers will then constitute a separate and independent market for the monopolist's product. The markets may be separated by ignorance, or by laws that prohibit the movement of the commodity from one market to another, or by accepted social conventions and customs that frown upon transactions between members of different groups. Our analysis may easily be extended to encompass several markets. The monopolist remains the sole producer and seller of X to all markets, and there will be a separate demand for his product in each market, depending on the tastes and planned expenditures of the buyers who buy within it and on the prices of all the other goods that they might buy. The monopolist's problem is to fix a price for his commodity in each market, and its formal solution is illustrated in Figure 13.3.1, where we assume that there are two markets (A and B), that the monopolist knows the demand for his product in each of them and the relationship between his total costs of production and his rate of output, that his objective is to earn maximum profits and that the cost of transporting his product to either market is zero.

Monopoly

The demand curve for the product in A is shown by $D_a D_a$ in Figure 13.3.1(a), and that in B by $D_b D_b$ in Figure 13.3.1(b). The monopolist's marginal costs of production are shown by MC in Figure 13.3.1(c).

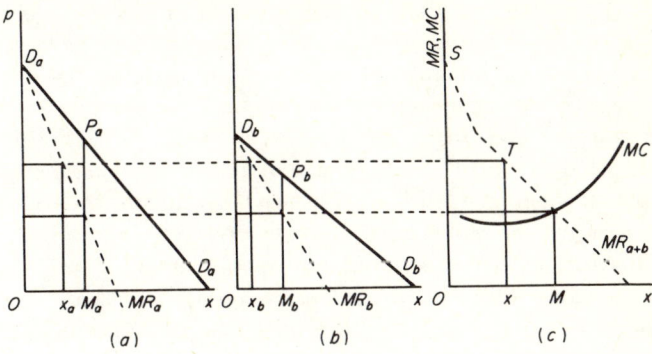

Figure 13.3.1

When the monopolist is earning maximum profit from the production of his product and its sale in markets A and B, he will be producing the output at which marginal cost and marginal revenue are equal to one another, for that is merely another way of saying that profits are maximised, and he will be distributing his output between the two markets in such a way that the last unit sold in each market adds the same sum to his total revenue, for if that is not so then a higher total revenue can be obtained from the sale of the same output by transferring sales from A to B, or vice versa. We can discover the output and price for each market at which both these conditions will be fulfilled with the help of Figure 13.3.1. The marginal revenue curves of markets A and B are added together to give us the curve MR_{a+b} in Figure 13.3.1(c). This curve shows the maximum total revenue that can be obtained by selling any output: thus, $OxTS$ is the greatest sum of money that can be earned by selling an output of x, and this is earned when a quantity x_a is sold in A and x_b in B.[1] The MR_{a+b} curve thus illustrates the second condition mentioned above. The first condition is fulfilled when the monopolist is producing an output of M per period, for at that output marginal cost and the addition to revenue from selling the M-th unit are the same. The monopolist will therefore plan

[1] Since the MR_{a+b} curve was derived by adding together the sales in each market at each level of marginal revenue, x_a plus x_b must be equal to x.

to produce M per period and to sell M_a in market A at a price of p_a per unit and M_b in B at a price of p_b per unit.

We know (see *supra*, page 280) that at any level of sales in any market marginal revenue $= p(1 - 1/e)$, or $p = MR(e/e - 1)$. If the demands in markets A and B are such that at each price the price elasticity of demand is less in A than in B, then the marginal revenue yielded by selling an additional unit in A will be less than the marginal revenue in B. Conversely, if the marginal revenues are the same in A and B, then the price must be greater in A than in B. If at each price the price elasticity of demand in A is the same as that in B then when the marginal revenues in the two markets are the same, the monopolist will be charging the same price in both markets. We conclude, then, that if the demand curves in the separate markets A and B are equally elastic, the monopolist will earn the maximum profit by charging the same price in each market – i.e. there will be no price discrimination between them, for if different prices were charged the profit would not be maximised; if the demand curves are not equally elastic, then when profit is greatest the price will be higher in the market where the price elasticity of demand (at each price) is lower.

We shall not explore the mechanics of price discrimination further.[1] Where there exist several independent markets for a monopolist's product, he may earn a larger profit by charging a different price in each of them than by lumping them together and treating them as a single market. As a corollary, if the practice of price discrimination promises a higher rate of profit, a monopolist who faces a single market for his product will have an incentive to divide it into separate markets, and we would expect him to attempt to do so provided the expected costs of dividing the market did not outweigh the expected gains from exploiting the divided market: that is, a monopolist may behave not only as a 'price-maker' but also as a 'market-divider'. Generally, the total revenue that he can earn from the sale of any given output can always be increased if the market is divided into sectors, in each of which the price elasticity of demand is different at each price from that in each other, and if he can effectively prevent the movement of his commodity from one sector to another. The division of the market may be effected in various ways. The monopolist, for example, may persuade the political authority in the part of the market where

---

[1] The classic treatment, not only of the mechanics, but also of all aspects of price discrimination is to be found in J. Robinson, *Economics of Imperfect Competition*, v (London, Macmillan, 1933).

the demand is relatively inelastic to impose duties on the importation of his product from the part(s) of the market in which he plans to sell it at a lower price because the demand is there relatively elastic. Again, it may be that the elasticity of demand varies according to the use to which the product is put, and that a unit of it that is bought for one use cannot be resold to a buyer that wants it for another: thus, to take an approximate example, a railway company might vary its charges per ton-mile according to the value of the commodity that it is asked to transport. Lastly, a monopolist might effectively divide the market if he successfully convinces the buyers whose demand is relatively inelastic (and who pay a relatively high price) that the product they are buying is not the same as that which is being bought by buyers whose demands are relatively elastic (and who are therefore paying a lower price).

13.4 Advertising

The monopolist may know or suspect that all potential buyers are not aware of his product or of its relative ability to satisfy their desires. In these circumstances, the monopolist can increase the demand for his product by calling its existence and properties to the attention of all potential buyers by advertisement. He may, indeed, go further and attempt not only to increase the knowledge of buyers so that their existing tastes and preferences may be more fully satisfied, but also to intensify their preferences for his product. For a monopolist in this position, the demand curve for his product is not a datum (as it was for the monopolist in our simple example) but a variable whose value is at least partly dependent on his own actions. We shall not attempt to represent diagrammatically the choice of a sales plan by a monopolist who advertises, but shall rest content with delineating the range of choice that faces him. Each sum of money that he contemplates spending on advertisement may be spent in an infinite number of different ways, and the effect of its expenditure on the position and shape of the demand curve will depend on the way in which it is spent. Thus, a sum of £1,000 per period may be used to buy space in weekly journals or in daily newspapers, or it might be spent on handbills or posters, neon signs, television commercials, or it might be used to pay the wages of salesmen who hawk the product from door to door. If spent on newspaper advertising, there may be a whole-page advertisement in one issue of a national daily, or a smaller advertisement in a number of successive issues. There will be a different change in demand for each way in which this sum is spent. There may be an increase in the planned purchases at each price as with D_1D_1, DD_2 and $D'D_3$ in Figure 13.4.1, or an increase in planned purchases at some prices as with DAD_1 and $D'BD_2$ in Figure 13.4.2. D_1D_1 and $D'D_3$ are less elastic than the old demand curve at each price in Figure 13.4.1. DAD_1 is more elastic at lower prices, and $D'BD_2$ less elastic at higher prices, in Figure 13.4.2. For each new demand curve that he might have by spending £1,000 per period on advertising, the monopolist can calculate the price and output that promises him the maximum excess of total revenue over total *production* costs,[1] and from this he must deduct the £1,000 he spends on advertisement to get his profits. A similar calculation can be made for each other level of advertising expenditure. For each sum of money that he spends on advertising, there will be a particular way of spending it that promises the greatest profit. From all these maximum profits he will choose the *maximum maximorum*, and in doing so he will be simultaneously fixing the price of his product, the output that he will produce in each period, the level of advertising expenditure and the manner in which to spend it.

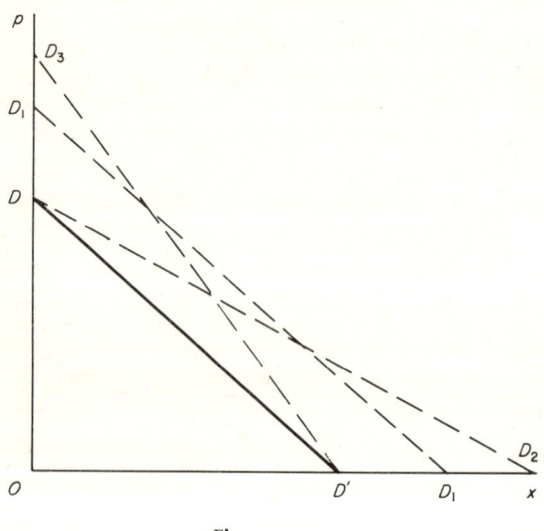

Figure 13.4.1

[1] We shall assume, for simplicity's sake, that there is no change in the physical characteristics of the product so that the costs of production remain unaltered.

Monopoly

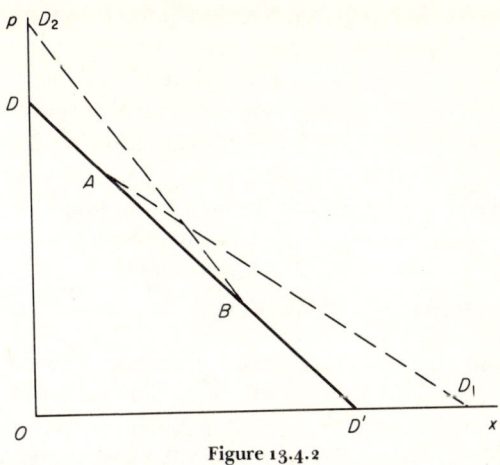

Figure 13.4.2

In the previous paragraph we have assumed that the product remains the same for the monopolist, and that he attempts to earn a higher profit through expanding his sales of the given product by advertisement. It may be possible, however, to increase his profits by altering the design, colour, packaging, or any other attribute of the product. The mechanics of this decision may be indicated briefly. The costs of production and the demand will vary from one variant of the product to another. For each possible variant of the product, he can calculate the maximum profit that he would earn per period by producing and selling it, and in choosing the *maximum maximorum* profit he will be simultaneously choosing the product-variant, the price at which to sell it and the quantity to produce of it in each period.

13.5 Potential New Entrants

We shall now examine how the monopolist's aims and behaviour might be modified if he believes both that new firms might be formed to produce the same or a closely similar product and that whether or not they will actually be set up depends on his present actions. Assuming that there are no legal or institutional barriers that effectively prevent new entry, new firms will be attracted into this field by the prospect of earning a higher profit. They may base their belief that they could enhance their profits by competing with the monopolist on

(a) the present price of the commodity;

(b) the size of the profit that the monopolist is now earning;

(c) a feeling that the monopolist is not effectively catering for the market for his product, either because many potential buyers remain ignorant of its existence or because some or all buyers would prefer a variant of the product that the monopolist appears unwilling to offer them; and

(d) a belief that they could produce the monopolist's product more cheaply either by using newer techniques of production or by more efficient organisation and management within the technique that the monopolist is now using.

If the monopolist is aware that these are the criteria on which potential competitors will base their decisions, and if he wishes to retain the whole market for himself over the long-run, then he will attempt to fix values for the price of his product, his profit, his advertising expenditure and technique of production that effectively discourage new entry. We may call his objective in these circumstances the maximisation of the 'present value' of the stream of profits per period over the long-run – i.e. of the sum of the expected profit in each future period discounted to a present value at what is for him the relevant rate of interest. It is not possible to indicate with any degree of precision the value that the monopolist must give to his price, profit, advertising expenditure and costs of production if potential competitors are to be permanently discouraged. All that we can say is that a monopolist who seeks to remain a monopolist will pay more attention to the magnitude and method of his advertising and will experience a stronger urge to improve the techniques by which his product might be produced and so lower its costs of production. Having done all this, if he feels that new entry still threatens, he will reduce his price below the level that promises the maximum profit in the current conditions of demand for the product, and so lower his present profit.

In Figure 13.5.1 we know that this 'entry-forestalling' price will be below $\bar{p}$ and above p_1. Exactly where the price will be established will depend on the monopolist's estimates of what the average cost curves of potential firms are, and what profit he judges they would need to attract them to enter the market. Suppose the monopolist has sufficient information to establish that potential new entrants have cost curves like $LRAC'$ in Figure 13.5.1. Then the (expected) $LRMC$ for new entrants is $LRMC'$ and their 'entry price' becomes p_2. To forestall entry, our monopolist must charge just below this price. If he does so he still makes profits, but not such high profits as he would have made in the absence of the threat of new entry. For the monopolist, the demand curve that faces him effectively becomes 'kinked' at a in Figure 13.5.1, as shown by $p_2 a D$.

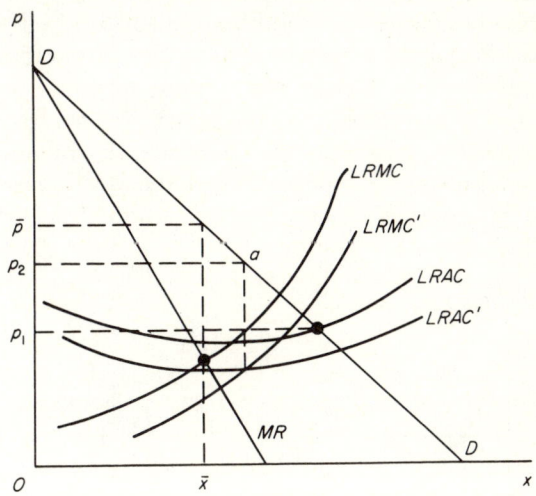

Figure 13.5.1

A monopolist who is not harassed by the threat of competition may nonetheless fear that his customers, or some consumer protection body, or some institutional agency, will judge his profits to be too high and that they will seek to curtail them through legislative action. If so, the monopolist is likely to respond to this threat in the same way as he responds to the threat of potential new entrants. If, on the other hand, he feels that he is unable to prevent the threat of competition or government control he will continue to maximise profits as long as he can in order not to jeopardise future profits.

13.6 Long-Run Decreasing Costs

We know that the long-run average cost curve, or 'planning curve', facing a firm would slope downwards if increasing returns to scale prevail. It is interesting to contrast the firm's equilibrium under monopoly and under perfect competition when increasing returns prevail. In Figure 13.6.1 we show a perfectly competitive firm with a declining *LRAC*. *LRMC* lies below *LRAC* since *LRAC* is declining. It is tempting to think that the profit-taking firm's equilibrium is at A where $\bar{p} = LRMC$, the normal profit-maximising condition. But it is obvious that this cannot be an equilibrium since increases in output to the right of A reduce losses and eventually produce increasing profits. In fact, $\bar{p} = LRMC$ is not sufficient to establish a profit-maximising condition. We also require that the demand curve cuts *LRMC* from above. But no equilibrium exists in Figure 13.6.1 since *LRMC* is continually declining. In short, the price-taker context entails that no equilibrium exists when decreasing costs prevail. The firm will continue to produce ever-increasing quantities of output, a situation which appears to contradict the very assumptions of perfect competition.[1]

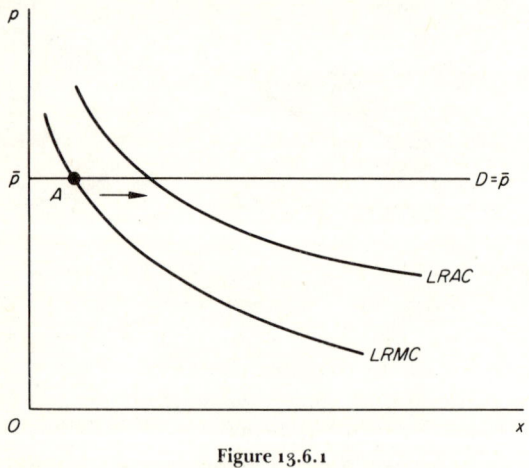

Figure 13.6.1

We may contrast this with the monopolist facing a declining *LRAC* curve. Figure 13.6.2 shows that an equilibrium will exist, with a profit-maximising output of $\bar{x}$ and profit-maximising price of $\bar{p}$. Profits are shown by the shaded area.

13.7 Genesis of Monopoly and Maintenance of Monopoly

Monopoly may be a natural consequence of the fact that (for some commodities and services) the unit costs of production are lower for

---

[1] For the *locus classicus* on this see P. Sraffa, 'The Laws of Returns under Competitive Conditions', *Economic Journal*, 1926.

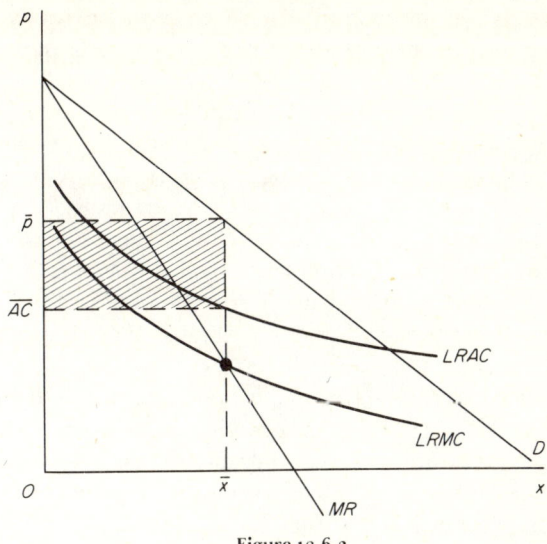

Figure 13.6.2

large than for small outputs, or it may be the result of conscious efforts directed towards establishing it. The output in each period from the plant that gives the lowest average total costs per unit of the product may be large enough to meet the planned purchases of buyers at all prices at which it is likely to be sold. If more than one such plant existed, some or all of them would earn negative profits and thus be driven into bankruptcy. Monopolies that arise for this reason are called 'natural' monopolies, and the industries supplying water, gas, electricity and rail transport are typical examples. In most countries, these natural monopolies are nationalised, municipalised or subjected to rather strict control by the government.

While some firms may have monopoly thrust upon them by the current pattern of relative prices and state of the technical arts, it is probable that most monopolies are the result of deliberate and purposive effort. The independent firms producing a commodity may merge together to form a single firm that thereafter is the sole producer and seller; or one firm may either acquire control of all the others or drive them out of business; or the firms, while preserving their separate identities as producers, may agree to act in concert as sellers. In the recent past, such efforts to establish monopoly have frequently enjoyed the blessing, if not the active support, of governments. While the methods by which monopoly may be established are legion, their objective is generally the acquisition of power. When there are many independent sellers of a commodity, the power of any one of them to fix a selling price for his output is effectively circumscribed by the existence of all the others; when there is a single seller (or group of sellers acting in concert) the power to fix the price is limited only by the conditions of demand for his product. The power that monopoly confers may be sought, then, because of the higher rate of profit that can be earned by its possessors. It may be sought also to enhance the bargaining strength of those possessing it *vis-à-vis* the government or another monopolist (for example, a trade union) and thus to maintain or to increase their profits.

The gains that currently accrue to the monopolist wholly depend on his position as the sole seller of the product; if they are to be his permanently then his position as sole seller must be assured by the effective prevention of new entry. The market for the product of a natural monopolist is protected in the long-run by 'indivisibilities' of inputs; even here, however, the protection is not absolute, for the invention of new substitutes for his product or the development of new techniques by which relatively small outputs may be produced at a unit cost as low (or lower) than that which he is now incurring may expose him to competition from new firms. A monopoly that is formed by merger, combination or agreement may enjoy no such 'natural' protection, and if it is to remain as the sole seller of the product the entry of new firms to compete with it must be prevented either by law or by its own actions. A government may protect the national market of a monopolist by imposing tariffs on the same or similar products imported from other countries. The monopolist may have patented his product or some of the processes by which it is produced so that any firm desiring to compete with him must pay him royalties or licence fees and thus suffer higher costs of production. A monopolist may deprive new entrants of markets for their output or of sources of supply of basic raw materials. He may do the former by making long-term contracts with his customers, by offering them substantial rebates that depend either on their buying solely from him or on the quantities of his product that they buy, or he may attempt to bind his customers wholly to his product by substantial and sustained expenditure on advertising. He may do the latter by making long-term contracts with the firms that supply him or by buying these firms and so assuring their output permanently to himself. To the extent that a monopolist indulges in these practices, the costs that a new firm must incur if it is to compete effectively with him are increased, and they may be made so large that new entry is prevented in practice. Lastly, new firms may be deterred from setting up to compete with the monopolist by the fear that he will drive them into bankruptcy before they are established: he might do this by depriving them of customers by deliberate price-cutting or by bribing and coercing their employees and suppliers.

14

Monopolistic Competition

14.0 The Nature of Monopolistic Competition

As our 'ideal type', we shall take the simplest case of monopolistic competition. We shall suppose (a) that there is a very large number of independent sellers of some class of commodity (like tea, motor-cars or toothpaste); (b) that the product of any seller is an equally close substitute for that of any other seller and that the products of all sellers are sufficiently alike to be called by the same class-name, such as motor-cars or toothpaste; (c) that all inputs (including the services of managers) are in perfectly elastic supply to the production of this class of commodity; and (d) that there is a large number of knowledgeable buyers of the class of product that the firms are selling. We shall further suppose (e) that in the long-run, competition is perfect except in that no firm (new or old) may decide to produce and sell a product that is a perfect substitute for a product that is being currently offered by any other seller. Given these assumptions, there will be a separate demand curve for the product of each seller, showing the quantity of his product that buyers would plan to buy at each price in each period, given their tastes and preferences, planned consumption expenditures, and the price (*inter alia*) that is being charged by each other seller for his product. The demand curve for each firm's product will be highly elastic at each price, because there exist many close substitutes for it. Furthermore, the demand curve for the product of any seller will be independent of his own behaviour: since he is only one of a very large number of sellers and since his product is an equally close substitute for that of any other seller, if he lowers his price his gain in sales will be distributed more or less equally over all the other firms so that the extent to which any other firm suffers will be negligible, and, being negligible, will evoke no change in the price at which it is currently selling its product.

14.1 Short-Run Equilibrium under Monopolistic Competition

Given the circumstances described in Section 14.0, each seller will have some choice in fixing the price of his product. It was pointed out that the demand curve facing each firm will be highly elastic. This is the essential difference between monopolistic competition and monopoly as far as a diagrammatic illustration of the firm's equilibrium is concerned. Thus, in Figure 14.1.1 the short-run equilibrium for a profit-maximising firm is seen at output M and price $\bar{p}$. The figure is essentially similar to that for a monopolist, but demand is seen to be very elastic. Profits are shown by the shaded area.

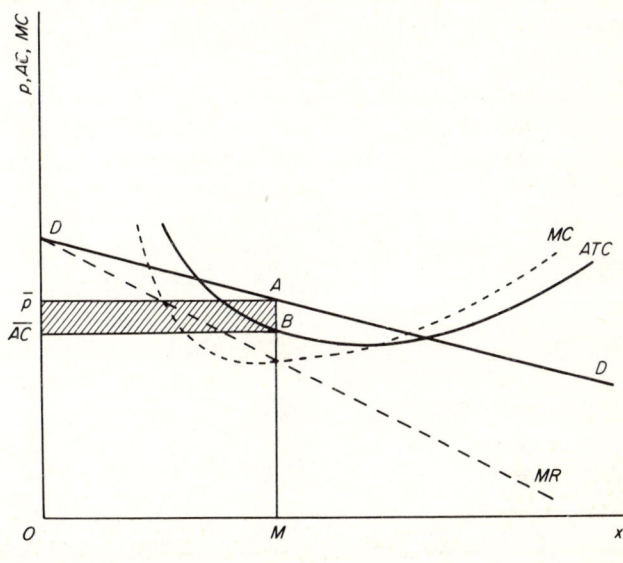

Figure 14.1.1

If existing firms are earning positive profits in the short-run, then in the long-run they may vary the quantities of plant, equipment, etc., that they use, and new firms will plan to produce similar products. Each existing firm will be planning to earn the *maximum maximorum* rate of profit that can be extracted from the expected demand per period for its product in the long-run. It is not unreasonable to assume that the long-run demand for any firm's product will be more elastic at each price than the short-run demand for it. If we ignore advertising expenditures, each firm will believe that the position of the long-run demand for its product is not affected by its present behaviour: since each firm acts independently of each other firm, and since the products that are currently being produced and those that may ultimately be produced by new firms are all equally substitutable for one another, no firm will have any incentive to behave like a monopolist who seeks to discourage potential competition, for by doing so it will forgo profits in the present and it will enjoy no compensating gain in profits in the future. The sales plan that each existing firm will hope to be implementing in each period in the long-run is illustrated in Figure 14.1.2 *LD* and *LRMR* are the long-run demand and marginal revenue curves respectively and *LRAC* and *LRMC* are the long-run average cost and marginal cost curves. The firm will be planning to produce $\bar{x}$ per period at a price of $\bar{p}$ per unit.

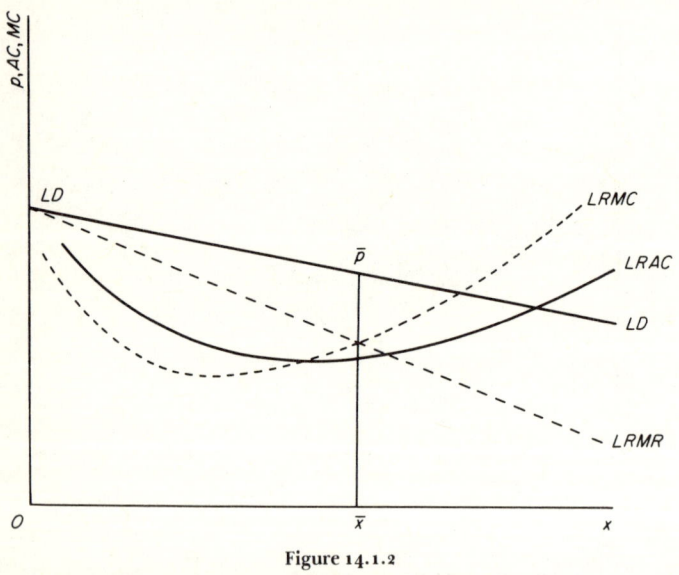

Figure 14.1.2

14.2 Long-Run Equilibrium Under Monopolistic Competition

As each new firm is set up in the long-run to produce a product that is similar to those being offered by existing firms, the demand curve for each existing product will shift negligibly to the left as some of its clients forsake it in favour of the new substitutes. The effect of continuous new entry will be continuous, and appreciable falls in the demand for each existing product and new entry will continue so long as the demand for existing products promise those who produce and sell them positive profits. It will only cease when each firm is implementing the sales plan illustrated in Figure 14.2.1 – i.e., when each firm is producing a rate of output of $\bar{x}$ and selling it at a price of $\bar{p}$ per unit, and in doing so, is just earning a revenue that covers its total costs of production in each period.

This simple model of monopolistic competition deviates from pure and perfect competition in two respects only: first, the product of any seller is not a perfect substitute for that of each other seller, and second, in explanation of product differentiation, no seller may produce a product that is a perfect substitute for that of any other seller. Thus far, then, differentiation of the products has been based 'upon certain characteristics of the product itself, such as exclusive patented features; trade-marks; trade-names; peculiarities of the package or container, if any; or singularity in quality, design, colour, or style'.[1]

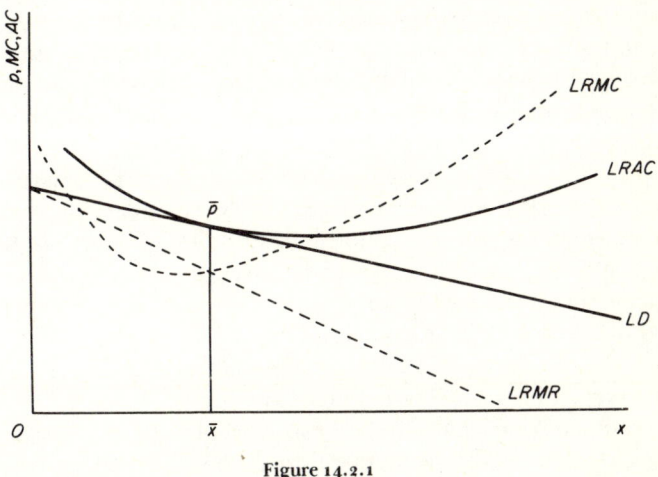

Figure 14.2.1

Differentiation of the products may also arise because the inputs that any firm uses are not perfect substitutes for those being used by any other firm: thus, in retail trade, there may be differences between one firm and another in 'the convenience of the seller's location, the general tone or character of his establishment, his way of doing business, his reputation for fair dealing, courtesy, efficiency, and all

[1] E. H. Chamberlain, *Theory of Monopolistic Competition*, 5th ed. (Harvard University Press, 1947) p. 56.

the personal links which attach his customers either to himself or to those employed by him. In so far as these and other intangible factors vary from seller to seller, the "product" in each case is different, for buyers take them into account, more or less, and may be regarded as purchasing them along with the commodity itself.'[1] If the differentiation arises for these reasons, our analysis requires little modification: if the heterogeneous inputs are perfectly mobile between firms, then in the long-run each firm will be earning zero profits as in Figure 14.2.1; if it is the managerial factor that is heterogeneous, then in the long-run only the manager that is least 'efficient' will be in this position, and all the others will be earning positive profits which are commensurate with their relative efficiencies in the production and sale of this class of commodity.

14.3 Full-Cost or Average-Cost Pricing[2]

The full-cost or average-cost theory of price purports to be a description of how the typical businessman actually fixes the selling price of his product. This theory usually rests on statements by businessmen or on questionnaires which they have completed. It may be summarised as follows:[3]

(i) 'The price which a business will normally quote for a particular product will equal the estimated average direct costs of production plus a costing margin.' It is assumed that the average direct cost function is equivalent to what we have called average variable costs, and it will tend to be a horizontal straight line over a part of its length if the prices of the direct cost factors are given.

(ii) 'The costing-margin will normally tend to cover the costs of the indirect factors of production (inputs) and provide a normal level of net profit, looking at the industry as a whole.' Once chosen, the costing-margin will remain constant, 'given the organisation of the individual business, whatever the level of its output'. It will tend to vary, however, with 'any general permanent changes in the prices of the indirect factors of production'. Indirect costs are taken to be what we have called fixed costs.

---

[1] Chamberlain, *op. cit.*, p. 56.

[2] On this subject see P. W. S. Andrews, *Manufacturing Business* (Macmillan, London, 1949).

[3] All the quotations in this description of the full-cost theory are taken from Andrews, *op. cit.*, p. 184.

(iii) 'Given the prices of the direct factors of production, price will tend to remain unchanged, whatever the level of output.'

(iv) 'At that price, the business will have a more or less clearly defined market and will sell the amount which its customers demand from it.'

This method of fixing prices, which is said to be followed by all or most price-makers, is illustrated in Figure 14.3.1. In accordance with the assumption in (i) above, the average direct cost curve (and therefore the marginal cost curve) is a horizontal straight line over a part of its length. If we equate the indirect costs with what we have called fixed costs, then they, together with the profit which the firm expects, hopes or plans to earn, will give a fixed sum of money which will be a datum for any existing firm making a short-run plan. The absolute amount of the costing-margin is derived from this sum of

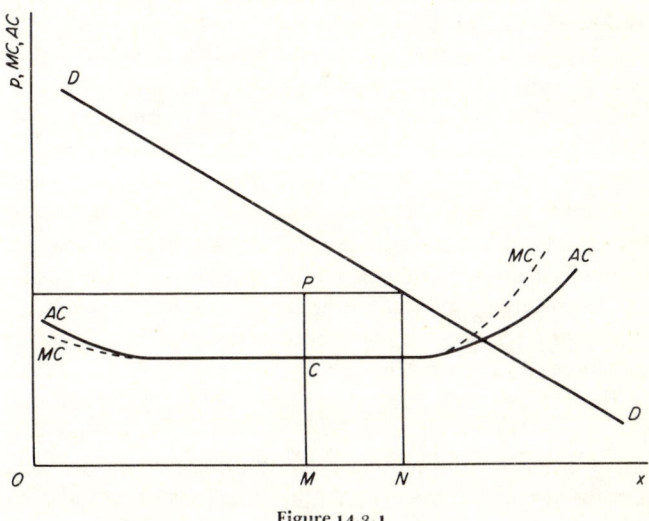

Figure 14.3.1

money by dividing it by some output. This output might be determined either (a) as a percentage of capacity output, where capacity is interpreted as an engineering fact; (b) as the output which was sold in the preceding production period, or the average of realised sales over a number of past production periods; or (c) as the minimum, mean, median or modal output that the businessman expects to be able to sell in a future period. If the firm is a new one, or if it is an existing firm introducing a new product, then only the first and third of these interpretations will be relevant; in these circumstances, indeed, it is likely that the first will coincide roughly with the third, for the capacity of the plant will depend on expected future sales. We shall assume that the firm chooses the output OM as the basis for its choice. Its selling price will therefore be equal to MC plus the costing-margin PC — that is, to MP. If DD is the demand curve for the firm's product, then at the price MP per unit the firm will succeed in selling ON per period. This price will not be altered in response to changes in demand, but only in response to changes in the prices of the direct and indirect factors.

One difference between the average-cost theory and that in the preceding chapters lies in the shape of the average direct (or variable) cost curve. The shape given to the average-cost curve in Figure 14.3.1 is in general accord with the results of empirical investigations into cost behaviour.[1] The shape which we have generally given to the average variable cost curve was explained by the law of variable proportions and by our assumption that the businessman when making a long-run plan had in mind some precise output which he will decide to produce with the bundle of 'fixed' and other inputs that promises him maximum profits. If a manager expects his sales per period to vary widely, however, it may be profitable for him to choose inputs which limit the rate at which physical returns diminish and thus promise virtually constant average variable costs over a wide range of outputs. This difference, however, is not crucial, for our previous analysis and conclusions would need no substantial revision were all the average variable cost curves given flat bottoms.

In Figure 14.3.2, we compare the average-cost theory with profit maximisation. If the firm is in any degree a profit maximising price-maker, it will plan to sell OM per period at a price of MP per unit. We may say that the firm chooses this price by taking its average variable costs of production and adding a costing-margin. In the marginal analysis, the size of the costing-margin, PC, depends *inter alia* on our assumptions that the firm knows (or thinks it knows) the costs and demand for its product and that it seeks to earn the maximum profits from its operations. In the average-cost analysis, the costing-margin may be PC, or it may be adjusted to approximate towards PC. If the costing-margin suggested by the average-cost theory differs from PC, the explanation might lie in the fact that the businessman (*a*) is quite unaware of his costs and demand, or (*b*) pursues some maximand other than money profit. A firm is unlikely to be completely ignorant

---

[1] See J. Johnston, *Statistical Cost Analysis* (McGraw-Hill, New York, 1960).

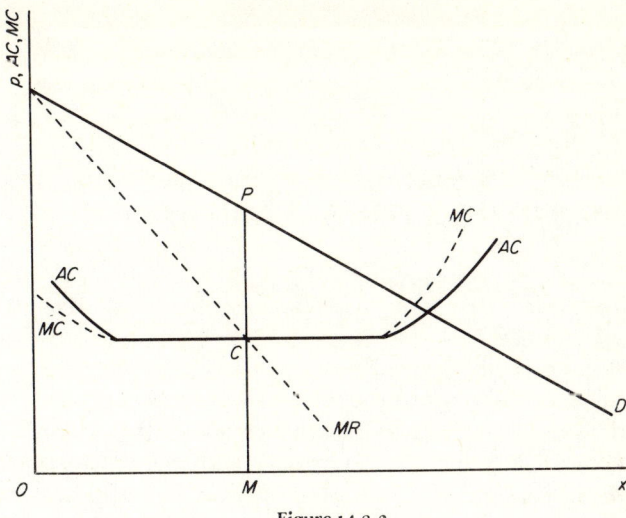

Figure 14.3.2

of the demand for its product, for at worst it can ascertain something about the current demand for products that are close substitutes. A multi-product firm may find it too costly both in terms of time and of money to proceed in the manner described for the profit-maximiser; it may, therefore, take that part of the costs of production which can be unambiguously attributed to any product X, and determine the price of X by adding a margin. If the firm is trying to maximise its profit, however, we would expect that the addition of this margin would give a price which would approximate towards that suggested by our analysis of the multi-product firm. It would appear, therefore, that if the two theories suggest different prices, the cause must lie in firms which follow the average-cost theory pursuing some objective other than maximum money profits.

15
Monopsony and Monopsonistic Competition

15.0 Monopsonistic Markets

This chapter deals briefly with monopsonistic market structures, for they add little to the substance (though they add much to the variety of illustrative geometry) of our treatment of monopoly and monopolistic competition. For our 'ideal type' of monopsony, we shall suppose (a) that there is one buyer of input X; (b) that X is the only variable input that he buys; (c) that X is supplied to him by a purely competitive industry; (d) that he is only one of a large number of knowledgeable sellers of the product that X helps to produce, and (e) that the monopsonist believes that there is no possibility, either now or in the foreseeable future, of other firms deciding to buy X. The relationship between the planned sales of X to the monopsonist and the price that he offers for it is the market supply curve of X. Since the monopsonist is the sole buyer of X, the supply curve of X describes the whole range of purchase plans that is open to him in each period: if he plans to buy relatively much of X he must offer a relatively high price per unit, and vice versa. The quantity that he decides to buy, and therefore the unit price that he must pay for it, will depend on his objective. This choice is illustrated in Figure 15.0.1, where we assume that the monopsonist seeks the maximum profit per period from his operations, that he knows the market supply curve of X, and the relationship between inputs of X and outputs of his product. The MM-curve shows the relationship between inputs of X and the marginal revenue product of X, and it is calculated in the manner described in Chapter 8. There, however, what we now call the MM-curve was the firm's demand curve for X, for we assumed that the price of X lay beyond the firm's control; here, the MM-curve shows simply the additions to the firm's total revenue that would result from the use of successive units of X. The SS-curve is the market supply curve of X. The MSP-curve shows the

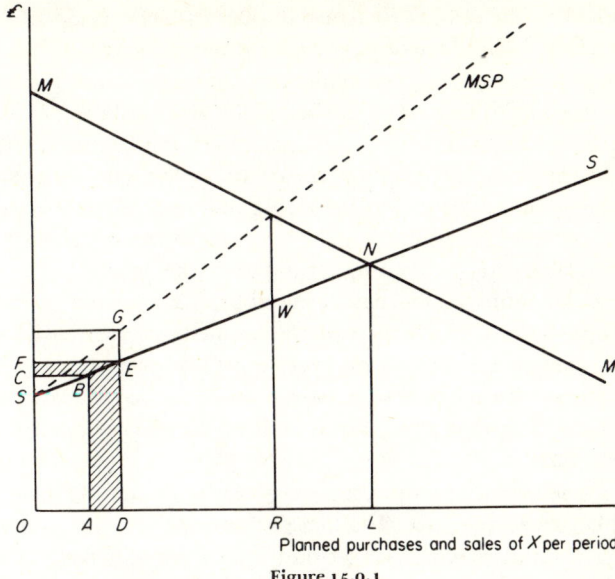

Figure 15.0.1

amounts by which the firm's total expenditure on X would rise as successive units of X are purchased: thus, to buy OA units of X would cost the firm $OABC$, and to buy OD (= OA plus one unit) would cost it $ODEF$; the difference between $ODEF$ and $OABC$ (= the shaded area $ADEFCB$) is the amount by which the firm's total costs will rise as a result of its buying the OD-th unit of X, and this is represented by the distance DG.[1] The monopsonist will earn the maximum profit per period by purchasing OR units of X at a price of RW per unit: if he were to purchase one unit more than OR his expenditure on X would rise by more than the additional revenue that he would earn by selling the products it helped to produce: to purchase one unit less of X would take more from his revenue than it would from his costs.

15.1 Equilibrium under Monopsony

The simple model of monopsony may be modified in the same way as we modified the simple model of monopoly. Thus, the monopsonist is

[1] The MSP-curve bears the same relationship to the SS-curve as does the marginal revenue curve to the demand curve. The MSP-curve must not be confused with the firm's marginal cost curve. The behaviour of the latter depends not only on the former, but also (in our simple model) on the relationship between inputs of X and outputs of the product.

not obliged by the market structure to pursue maximum profits per period: irrespective of the objective he chooses, however, his planned purchases of X per period are unlikely to fall below OR or rise above OL, and its price is unlikely to fall below RW or rise above LN. If X is being produced in several, independent, purely competitive markets, and if the elasticities of supply of X vary between them, the monopsonist may enhance his profits by paying different prices in different markets, and the price he pays will be lower in the market where X is in relatively elastic supply, and higher in the market where X is in relatively inelastic supply. It will pay the monopsonist to divide the market in which he buys X into sectors between which no transfers of X are possible, provided the costs are less than the additional revenue he expects to earn from doing so. Lastly, it may pay the monopsonist to advertise for new sources of X and so shift the market supply curve of X to the right.

We have seen that monopolistic competition may exist if buyers are not indifferent as to which seller they patronise; if, *inter alia*, sellers are not indifferent as to which buyer they sell to, we may have monopsonistic competition. For our ideal type of monopsonistic competition, we shall suppose (*a*) that there is a very large number of sellers of an input, S, which may be a particular kind of labour-service; (*b*) that each unit of S is a perfect technological substitute for each other unit; (*c*) that there is a large number of firms buying this input and that it is the only variable input that they buy; (*d*) that each firm is a price-taker for the product it sells and for each input that it buys; (*e*) that sellers are not indifferent as to which buyer they offer their services; and (*f*) that the only limitation on the entry of new buyers is that there may appear no buyer who is identical in the estimation of sellers with any existing buyer. Given these assumptions, the supply curve of S to each buyer will be highly, but not perfectly, elastic: if he offers a higher price, more (but not all) sellers will patronise him; if he offers a lower price, only some of those who now supply him will forsake him. The choice of a purchase plan by an individual buyer is illustrated in Figure 15.1.1 where we assume that he knows his demand for S and the supply of S to him. The sales plan for its product is shown in Figure 15.1.2. The firm will be buying OR of S at a price of RW per unit in each period and producing with this (in conjunction with the fixed quantities of other inputs at its disposal) an output of $\bar{x}$ per period; when doing so, it will be earning maximum profits. The excess of total revenue over total variable costs is shown by the areas ALM and $BWLC$ in Figure 15.1.1

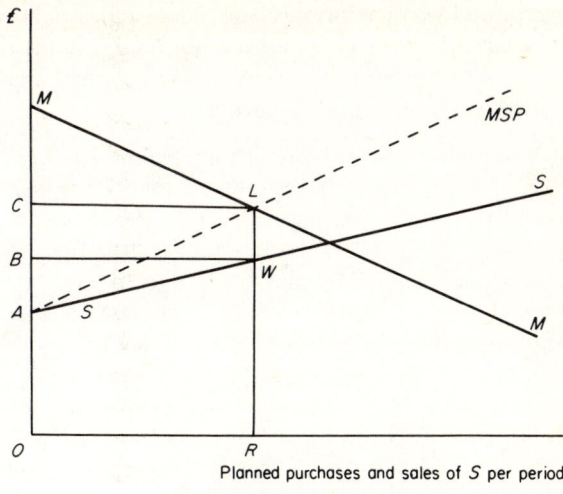

Figure 15.1.1

and $EFGH$ in Figure 15.1.2. If this excess is more than enough to cover the fixed costs of existing firms, and if any new firm can enjoy all the advantages that are being enjoyed by existing firms (save that of being equally esteemed by the sellers of S), then new sellers of the product (buyers of S) will appear in the long-run. As new entry proceeds, the price of the product will fall, and as this occurs, each firm's demand for S will shift to the left; furthermore, the supply of S to each firm may

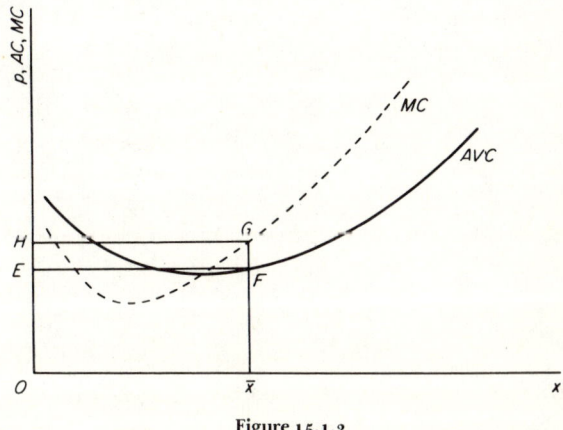

Figure 15.1.2

shift leftwards and become more elastic. These adjustments will continue until each firm is earning an excess of total revenue over total variable costs in each period that just suffices to cover its fixed costs – i.e. until each firm is earning a zero profit.

16

Oligopoly

16.0 The Nature of Oligopoly

All markets in which there are a small number of sellers are classified under the heading 'oligopoly'. The adjective 'small' must be interpreted operationally: the number of sellers of a homogeneous or differentiated product must be such that each believes that any change in his selling price and sales, or in the quality of his product, or in his advertising expenditure, or in any other variable whose value is under his control, is likely to evoke retaliation from most or all of the other sellers. When the number of sellers is small in this operational sense, we generally find that there is a small cardinal number of sellers – that is, not less than two and perhaps not more than twenty. It is for this reason that economists decide whether or not to classify any particular market as an oligopoly by counting the number of firms: this provides a recognisable, objective and measurable criterion for classification, whereas the awareness of mutual interdependence of sales, purchase, production and advertising plans is less easily established, for it is always a matter of degree and frequently a matter of opinion.

In this chapter, we shall study a number of models of oligopolistic markets. Each model explores the probable consequences of a particular assumption that is made by each oligopolist about his rivals' reactions. The models are not listed in any simple logical order. The order in which they appear below is roughly one of increasing knowledge by each oligopolist about his rivals' reactions. Since each oligopolist is the more likely to make a correct assumption about rivals' behaviour – that is, an assumption that accurately describes their reactions as he acts on the basis of it – the greater is the degree of tacit or overt agreement between them, the order is also roughly one of increasing degrees of agreement or collusion. The greater the degree of collusion, however, the nearer might oligopoly approximate towards simple monopoly, so that the order in which we list the models is very roughly one of increasing profits for some or all of the firms.

16.1 The Cournot Model[1]

In this first model, we shall suppose that (a) there are only two non-collusive firms – that is, there exists the simplest example of oligopoly, namely, *duopoly*; (b) each produces and sells a product that is a perfect substitute for that of the other; (c) the product is perishable and cannot be stored, so that in each period the total output of it must all be sold; (d) there are many knowledgeable buyers of the product; (e) each duopolist knows the market demand curve for the product; (f) the two firms have identical cost curves, and to simplify the geometry we shall assume that for each duopolist the cost of production for each output is zero; (g) each duopolist makes an output plan at the beginning of each period setting out the quantity of the product which he plans to produce during it, and, once made, an output plan cannot be revised; (h) neither sets a price for his output, but each accepts the price at which the total planned output can be sold, and (i) each duopolist seeks the maximum profit in each period. Lastly, we shall suppose that (j) while the duopolists are aware of the mutual interdependence of their output plans, each is quite ignorant of the direction and magnitude of the revision in his rival's plan that would be induced by any given change in his own; each, however, in making his own plan must make some assumption about his rival's reactions and we shall suppose that each duopolist assumes that irrespective of the output plan that he implements in any period $t + 1$, his rival will maintain his output at the same level as in period t.

Given assumptions (a) to (h) inclusive, we can illustrate the range of profit possibilities that is open to each firm. In Figure 16.1.2 the *DD*-curve shows the total quantity of the product that consumers would plan to buy in each period at each price at which it might be sold. In Figure 16.1.2, we measure the alternative outputs that duopolist A might produce in each period on the horizontal axis, and, on the vertical axis, we measure the output of his rival B. Any point that lies between these axes represents a particular combination of the output

---

[1] See Augustin Cournot, *Recherches sur les principes mathematiques de la theorie des richesses* (Paris, 1838). There is an English translation by N. T. Bacon, entitled *Researches into the Mathematical Principles of the Theory of Wealth* (Macmillan, New York, 1897).

of A and of B. Beside each point we can write the profits that each duopolist would be earning when they are producing the outputs which that point denotes. Thus, the point L denotes an output of OV per period by A and of OW per period by B. By transferring these outputs to the horizontal axis in Figure 16.1.1, we can discover the selling price per unit: thus, OR is equal to OV and RS to OW, and the total output (OV plus OW, or OS) can be sold at a price of $\bar{p}$ per unit. Since

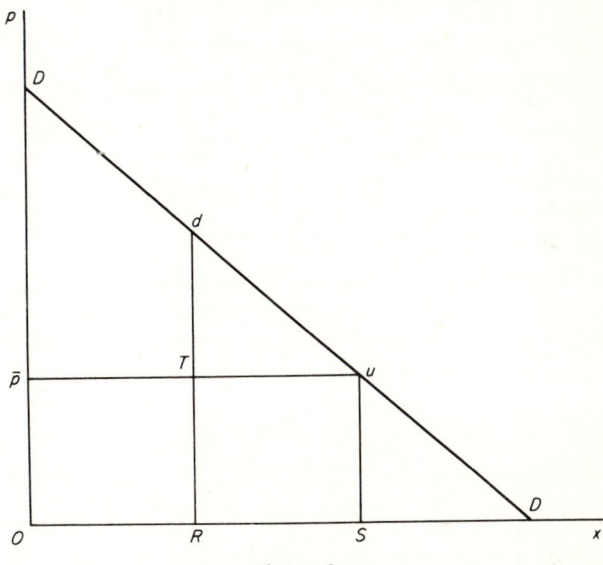

Figure 16.1.1

we have assumed that each duopolist has zero costs of production, A's profits are represented by the area $ORT\bar{p}$, and B's profits by the area $RSuT$. In precisely the same way, we may obtain the profits that each of the duopolists would be earning were they producing the outputs denoted by any other point lying between the axes in Figure 16.1.2. When this has been done for each point, we obtain a visual representation of the profit possibilities open to A and to B. We can order the profit possibilities that are open to either duopolist by drawing profit-indifference or *iso-profit* curves, each of which passes through all combinations of A's and B's output which promise A (or B) the same sum of profits per period. In Figure 16.1.3, the profit-indifference curves of A and B are drawn and we may easily explain the shape that we have given them.

310   Price Theory

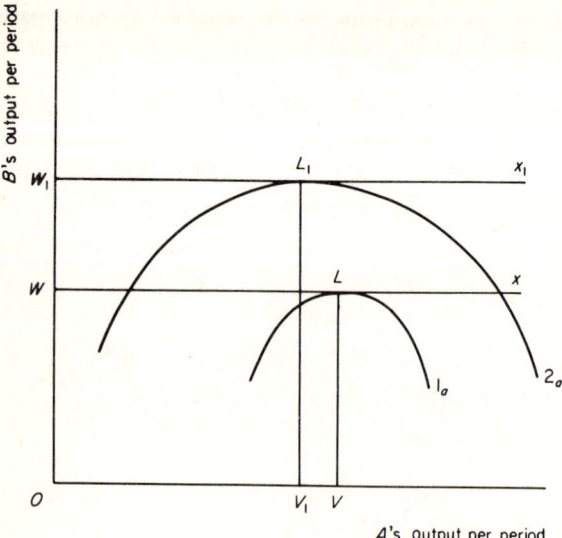

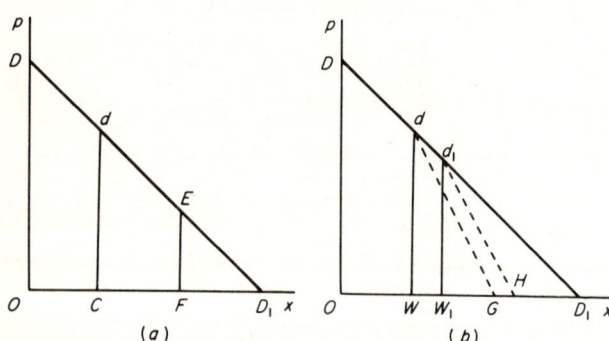

Figure 16.1.2

Let us take any value for B's output, and, keeping this constant, examine what happens to A's profits as A's output increases. In Figure 16.1.2(a), DD_1 is the market demand curve for the product, and OC is B's output. The relationship between A's output and the selling price of the product is shown by the range dD_1 of the demand curve: since this curve is relatively elastic between d and E, A's total receipts (which are also his profits since his costs of production are zero) will rise as his output per period increases from zero to CF; at prices lower than FE, the dD_1-curve is relatively inelastic, so that as A increases his output per period from CF, his profits will continuously decline, reaching zero when his output is CD_1. Next, let us take any value for A's output, and examine what happens to A's profits as the value of B's output rises. In Figure 16.1.2(a), if we suppose that OC represents A's output, it is clear that A's profits will continuously decline as B increases his output from zero to CD_1, for A's profits are represented by the area bounded by OD, OC, Cd and a horizontal line drawn at the selling price of the product, and as B's output rises the price of the product continuously falls so that this area becomes progressively smaller. These two conditions – namely, that at any value for B's output, A's profits will rise, reach a maximum and then decline as A's output is increased, and that at any value for A's output, A's profits will continuously fall as B's output is increased – are both fulfilled by profit-indifference curves that are concave when viewed from the axis on which we measure A's output. Lastly, we must explain why the maximum points of successive iso-profit curves of duopolist A lie progressively nearer to the axis on which we measure B's output. If B is producing the output OW in Figure 16.1.2, the alternative profits that A might earn by varying his output will lie on the line Wx; if A seeks the maximum profits per period, he will plan to produce the output at which this line is tangential to one of his iso-profit curves. Let us suppose that when B is producing OW per period, A's profit-maximising output is OV – the output where the line Wx just touches the maximum point L of the profit-indifference curve 1_a. If B's output were higher at OW_1 per period, then the output at which A's profits would be greatest would be OV_1 – the output at which the line W_1x_1 touches the maximum point L_1 of the iso-profit curve 2_a.

The output OV_1 is less than OV, and we can quite easily confirm why this must be so from Figure 16.1.2(b). When B is producing OW, A's profits will be at a maximum when A's output is $WG (= OV)$, the output where the marginal revenue curve corresponding to the range dD_1 of the market demand curve cuts A's marginal cost curve; when B's output is OW_1, A's profit-maximising output will be $W_1H (= OV_1)$, the output where the marginal revenue curve corresponding to the range d_1D_1 of the demand curve cuts the horizontal axis which is A's marginal cost curve. Since in our example the market demand curve is a straight line, $WG = \frac{1}{2}WD_1$, and $W_1H = \frac{1}{2}W_1D_1$; W_1D_1 is less than WD_1 so that $W_1H (= OV_1)$ must be less than $WG (= OV)$. The profit-maximising output of A will be lower, therefore, the higher is B's output per period:

that is, the apices of A's iso-profit curves must lie progressively nearer the axis on which B's output is measured. The general properties of B's iso-profit curves may be established in a precisely similar fashion.

The assumption that A (or B) makes about B's (or A's) reactions when deciding what output to produce in the ensuing period can be illustrated in Figure 16.1.3, wherein are drawn the profit-indifference maps of A and B. If A assumes (see assumption (j), *supra*, page 308) that B will always maintain his output at its level of the previous period irrespective of the output which he (A) produces, then the profit-maximising output of A for each level of B's output will lie on the line MN which passes through the maximum points[1] of A's iso-profit curves. The line MN is called A's *reaction curve*, for it shows us how A will

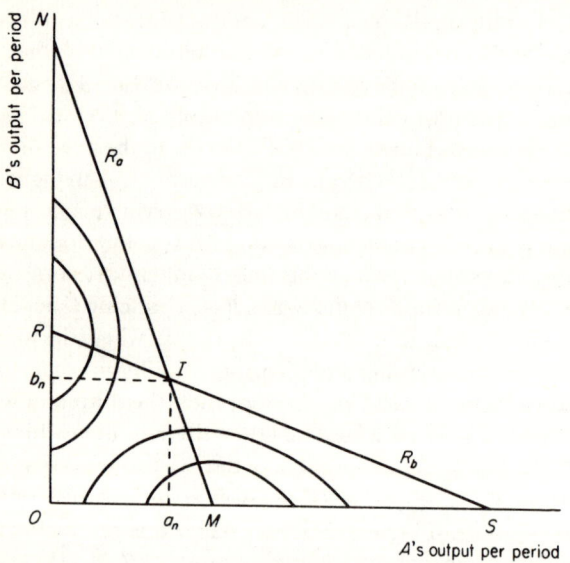

Figure 16.1.3

react to any change in B's output. In Figure 16.1.3, A's reaction curve is a straight line because we have assumed that the market demand curve is a straight line and that A's marginal costs of production are constant (at zero). The output OM is the 'monopoly' output, for it is that which A would plan to produce if B's output were zero – that is, if A were the

---

[1] By the 'maximum point' of any one of A's iso-profit curves, we mean the point furthest from the horizontal axis on which A's output is measured.

sole producer and seller of the product. The output ON is that which B would have to produce to induce A to choose a zero output. We can see from Figure 16.1.3 that ON must be the output at which price and marginal cost are equal, and since this is the output that would be offered for sale in each period had the product been produced under conditions of pure competition – i.e. by many firms each of which had zero costs of production – we shall call it the 'competitive' output. Since A and B are in all respects identical, OM will be equal to OR and ON will be equal to OS.

If each duopolist seeks the maximum profit per period and if each assumes that his rival's output will be maintained at its level of the previous period irrespective of the output which he now produces, then they will ultimately be producing the outputs denoted by the point I at which the two reaction curves intersect one another – i.e. A and B will be producing Oa_n and Ob_n respectively. This necessarily follows from our assumptions (a) to (j) above. We can trace the path by which the equilibrium denoted by I is reached by supposing that A is initially a monopolist and that a competitor B suddenly and unexpectedly appears at the beginning of period 1. In period 1 A's output is OM in Figure 16.1.4, where the reaction curves appear uncluttered by the profit-indifference maps. The new firm, B, assuming that A will continue to produce OM in period 1, plans to produce Ob_1; A, assuming that he will have no rival, plans to produce OM. The combination of outputs that will actually be produced in period 1 is denoted by the point 1 on B's reaction curve. In period 2, B will plan to produce Ob_1, for that is the output that promises him the maximum profits if A produces OM, and he assumes that A *will* produce OM; A will plan to produce Oa_2 since he assumes that B will maintain his output at Ob_1. In period 2, the total output of the product will be Oa_2 plus Ob_1 – that is, that denoted by the point 2 on A's reaction curve. In period 3, if each duopolist continues to take the output of his rival in the previous period as a datum, A and B will produce Oa_2 and Ob_3 respectively. It is clear from the figure that these adjustments will continue until A and B are producing Oa_n and Ob_n respectively.

The Cournot model is analytically attractive because it yields a unique and stable equilibrium for each duopolist. This equilibrium is denoted by the point I in Figure 16.1.4 where the two reaction curves intersect one another. The nature of this equilibrium is largely determined by assumption (j) and its precise content is mainly explained by assumptions (a) to (i). If we maintain the former assumption and if we vary the latter assumptions within the general framework of an oligopolistic market, we still get a single equilibrium, provided that the output which each oligopolist would produce if each of his rivals was producing nothing is less than the outputs which they would have to be producing to induce him to produce nothing – that is, provided that the output OM (or OR) in Figure 16.1.4 is less than OS (or ON).

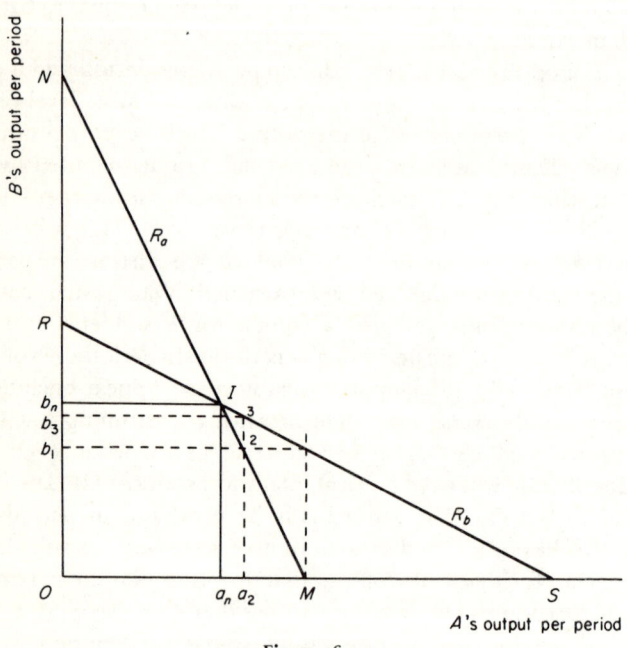

Figure 16.1.4

Assumption (j) stated that each duopolist supposes that irrespective of the output plan which he may decide to implement in the current period, his rival will maintain his output at the same level as in the previous period. In other words, each duopolist behaves as if a change in his own output will not cause a change in the output of his rival: thus, in Figure 16.1.4, A assumes that if he reduces his output from OM (its level in period 1) to Oa_2 (its level for period 2) B will continue to produce Ob_1. When an oligopolist acts on this kind of assumption about rivals' behaviour, we shall say that he behaves *autonomously*. We have shown that an equilibrium will be reached if each oligopolist con-

Oligopoly

tinues to act autonomously; we shall now examine the likelihood of their continuing to do so.

It is clear from Figure 16.1.4 that the assumption which each duopolist makes about his rival's reaction is not being confirmed by events. Thus, in period 1, A expects B to produce zero, but B actually produces Ob_1; in period 2, B expects A to produce OM, but A actually produces Oa_2; in period 3, A expects B to produce Ob_1, but B actually produces Ob_3, and so on. We would therefore expect each duopolist to observe that changes in his own output are followed by changes in the opposite direction in the output of his rival. Whether or not he attributes a causal role to changes in his own output will depend on the length (in terms of calendar time) of each production period, and on the general stability of the market environment. If the production period is relatively long, he may not relate a current change in his rival's output to a change in his own output that occurred some considerable time ago; if demand and cost conditions vary appreciably from one period to another, he may ignore, because he cannot isolate or measure, the effect on his rival's output of changes in his own. If the production period is relatively short and the market environment relatively stable, each duopolist is likely to cease behaving autonomously and to seek some alternative and more 'correct' hypothesis about his rival's behaviour. Each duopolist might assume, for example, that changes in his rival's output are functionally related to changes in his own: thus, to take the simplest example, A might suppose that if he reduces his output from any level by 10 per cent, B will raise his output by 5 per cent. When A or B acts on this kind of assumption, he is said to act *conjecturally*. If each duopolist acts conjecturally, then reaction curves can be drawn, and their point of intersection (or one of their points of intersection) may denote a position of stable equilibrium. This equilibrium, however, is no more likely to be attained in practice than that denoted by I in Figure 16.1.4: if the reaction curves do not coincide with one another, then each duopolist will observe that his conjectures are not being fulfilled by his rival's actual behaviour, and each is therefore likely to seek some more 'correct' hypothesis about his rival's reactions. We shall explore further the nature and consequences of conjectural behaviour in the model which follows.

It is unlikely, therefore, that we shall ever find an actual oligopolistic market that is accurately described by the simple Cournot model wherein each oligopolist acts autonomously and output is the sole 'parameter of action'.[1] In this sense, the model is not useful. It is useful, however, in the sense that it illustrates the distinguishing feature of an oligopolistic market, namely, the fact of mutual interdependence. During the progress towards the equilibrium denoted by I in Figure 16.1.4, it is clear that a change in B's output causes A to change his output, and that A's reaction causes a further change in B's output, and so on. We make this mutual interdependence clearer to us by making our duopolists unaware of it or so bemused by it that each of them ignores it when choosing his plans. The main justification for the assumption of autonomous behaviour is, then, the pedagogic usefulness of the model that is based on it. The Cournot model with output as the parameter of action suffices for this purpose. We shall not, therefore, examine the Bertrand model,[2] in which each oligopolist acts autonomously and price is the action parameter, nor shall we consider models of autonomous behaviour in which the oligopolists produce differentiated products and in which product quality or advertising expenditure is the parameter of action.

16.2 Leadership Models

We shall consider three leadership models, and a definition of leadership will emerge from the first of them. In our first model, we shall maintain the assumptions (a) to (i) inclusive, which we listed for the Cournot model above, and alter only assumption (j). In its place, we shall suppose (i) that A conjectures that B will accept A's output as a datum when he (B) is making an output plan, and (ii) that B actually behaves in this way – that is, acts autonomously. Given assumptions (a) to (i) inclusive, we can, as before, draw the profit-indifference curves of each duopolist. Some of these are drawn in Figure 16.2.1. Our assumption that A knows that B will act autonomously means that A knows B's Cournot reaction function, which is shown by the line RS. This line shows us (and A) the output which B would plan to produce (and actually does produce) in each period at each level of A's output. The points at which this line cuts A's profit-indifference curves show the alternative profits per period that are open to A while B behaves in

---

[1] An action parameter means any variable whose value lies within a firm's control. Thus, the sole parameter of action for a firm that operates under conditions of pure competition is the quantity of its output; the parameter of action for a monopolistic competitor is price or output, or product quality, or advertising expenditure.

[2] For a fuller consideration of the Cournot and Bertrand models, see W. Fellner, *Competition Among the Few* (Alfred A. Knopf, New York, 1949) pp. 55–97.

Oligopoly

this way. Of these, A will choose that denoted by the point L_a where B's reaction curve just touches one of his (A's) profit-indifference curves: L_a will promise A the maximum profits per period, for any point either to the right or to the left of it on RS lies on a lower[1] iso-profit curve. A will therefore plan to produce an output of Oa_r per period, and B will produce Ob_r per period. In this model, A is the 'output-leader' and B the 'output-follower': A leads in that he chooses the output which he will produce in the light of his (correct) conjectures about B's reactions; B follows in that he accepts any output that A might produce as a datum. In the leadership model, the leader has no reaction curve, for he chooses that point on the follower's reaction curve which promises him the greatest profits. There is, therefore, no 'path' by which the leadership equilibrium will be reached, for the point L_a will be established immediately by A. When A acts (and is allowed by B to act) as the output-leader, his profits will be higher and B's lower than they would have been had both A and B acted autonomously. In Figure 16.2.1, the dotted line MN shows A's reaction curve when he acts

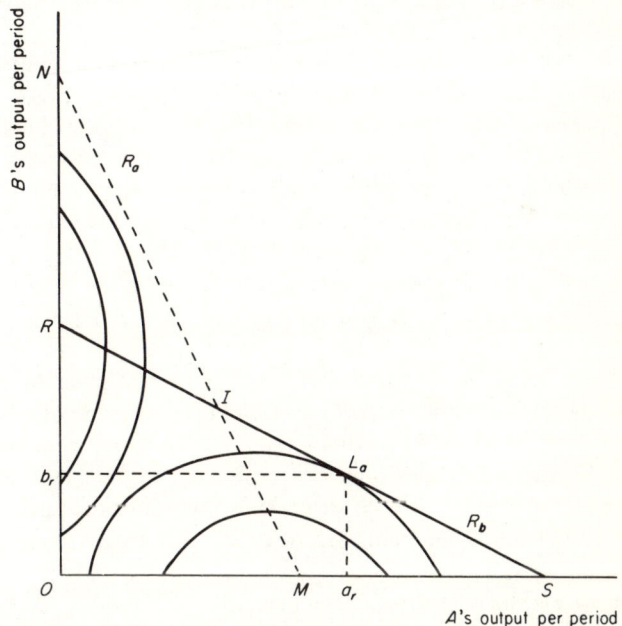

Figure 16.2.1

[1] Lower in terms of profit, but 'higher' in terms of position on the diagram.

autonomously. The point I, at which the two reaction curves intersect one another, lies above L_a in A's profit-indifference map and below L_a in B's indifference map – that is, A will prefer L_a to I, and B will prefer I to L_a.

If the leadership equilibrium is to be maintained over a succession of periods, then A must be willing to accept B's present pattern of reaction as shown by the curve RS, and B must remain ignorant of the fact that A knows his (B's) reaction curve. It is clear from Figure 16.2.1 that A would earn larger profits per period if he could force B on to a reaction curve that lay below RS and so touched a higher[1] iso-profit curve of A; and A, by threat and rumour, might try to persuade B to react along such a curve. If B suspects that A is aware that he (B) is acting autonomously, B may attempt to convince A that he will react along a curve that lies above RS and in such a position that the point L_a which A will choose on it lies on a lower indifference curve for A and on a higher profit-indifference curve for B. It is likely, therefore, that even in this simple leadership model, each duopolist will seek to alter to his own advantage the assumption which he thinks his rival is making about his reactions.

In our second model, we shall suppose that each duopolist is striving after leadership. We shall continue to make assumptions (a) to (i) listed in Section 16.1 above. In addition, we shall suppose that each duopolist assumes that his rival will act autonomously. The probable consequences of these assumptions are illustrated in Figure 16.2.2. We shall suppose that A has been a monopolist and that B suddenly and unexpectedly appears to compete with him. No *modus vivendi* has yet been reached, and each is laying his plans for period 1, the first period of their co-existence. On our assumptions, A believes that B will react along RS, so that he (A) will plan to produce Oa_r in period 1, expecting B to produce Ob_1; B assumes that A will react along MN, so he (B) plans to produce Ob_r, expecting A to produce Oa_1. In period 1, therefore, the total output of the commodity will be Oa_r plus Ob_r, or that denoted by the point G. Since G lies on a lower iso-profit curve in A's map than L_a, and in B's map than L_b, the profits which each duopolist earns in period 1 will be much less than what he expected to earn. In this way, each duopolist will discover that his rival is not behaving as he expected him to behave. During the periods which follow, each will

---

[1] The adjectives 'higher' and 'lower' when applied in this and later paragraphs to an indifference curve refer to the value of the profits which it represents and not to its position in the figure.

Oligopoly

seek some more 'correct' conjecture about his rival's reactions: he may do this by observing how his rival's output responds to experimental variations in his own; or he may try to force his rival to react along some reaction function that he prefers.

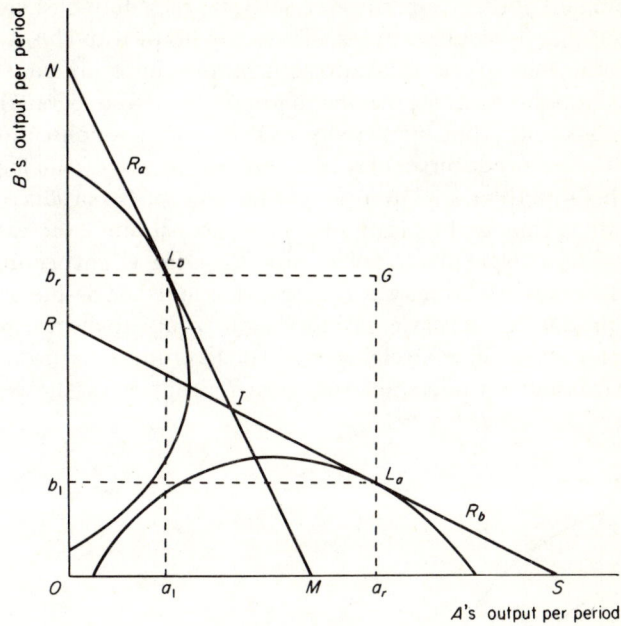

Figure 16.2.2

We see, then, that when each duopolist aspires to leadership, the hypothesis that each makes about his rival's behaviour will be proved wrong as soon as it is tested, and the assumptions by which the model was defined do not help us to identify what new hypothesis each duopolist will choose.

This kind of model nevertheless helps us, for it can be used to illustrate the prelude to bargaining or collusion. Let us, for the sake of variety, take another member of the same family of models.[1] Let us suppose that (a) there are only two independent firms; (b) each produces and sells a product that is a close, but not a perfect, substitute

---

[1] The model we have chosen, and which we define below, is almost the same as that described in Hans Brems, *Product Equilibrium under Monopolistic Competition* (Harvard University Press, 1951) pp. 196–204.

for that of the other; (c) the product of each duopolist is perishable, so that in each period all that is produced must be sold; (d) there are many knowledgeable buyers of each firm's product; (e) the parameter of action is product quality, and this is measured by the weight (in milligrammes) of their respective products; (f) each duopolist knows the profits that he would earn for all values of his own and his rival's action parameter; (g) prices and advertising expenditures are data; and (h) each duopolist seeks the maximum profits per period. Given these assumptions, the profit-indifference map of each duopolist can be drawn. The iso-profit curves of A (and of B) will be as shown in Figure 16.2.3, because (i) at any given weight per unit of A's product, A's profits will decline as the weight of B's product per unit is increased; (ii) at any given weight per unit of B's product, as the weight per unit of A's product rises, A's profits will rise for a while and then decline as the costs of producing the heavier product begin to outstrip the rise in the demand for it; and (iii) the weight per unit of A's product that promises him the maximum profits will be the greater, the greater is the weight per unit of B's product.

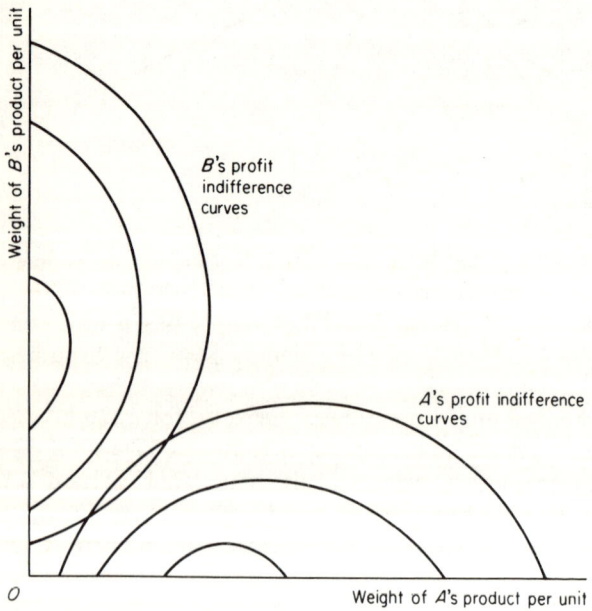

Figure 16.2.3

Oligopoly

Let us now suppose that A and B have agreed to meet to fix the weights of their respective products. For brevity's sake, we shall call the weight of A's product per unit, x, and the weight per unit of B's product, y. Neither duopolist will accept any combination of values for x and y that promises him profits which are less than those that he believes he could earn by acting independently of his rival. The maximum profits that A (or B) might expect to earn if no agreement is reached may be determined as follows. The profit-indifference map of A is drawn in Figure 16.2.4(a). When there is no agreement, we shall suppose (taking the simplest case) that A believes that B will act autonomously – that is, that A assumes that B will react to changes in his (A's) parameter along RS, which is B's Cournot reaction curve when product-quality is the action parameter. A will therefore plan to fix the weight of his product at Ox_r, believing that B will choose Oy_r, and A will expect to earn the profits denoted by the iso-profit curve on which L_a lies if no agreement is reached. Similarly, we shall suppose that B acts conjecturally – that he believes that A will react along MN in Figure 16.2.4(b): if no agreement is concluded, B will expect to earn the profits denoted by that one of his iso-profit curves on which lies L_b. The diagrams in Figure 16.2.4 are superimposed on one another in Figure 16.2.5. Any combination of values for x and y that is likely to emerge from the negotiations must lie within the shaded area, which is enclosed by the iso-profit curves of A and B on which lie L_a and L_b respectively, for any point within this area lies on a higher iso-profit curve for each duopolist. A will not accept any combination of values for x and y such as that denoted by F, for since F lies on a lower one of his profit-indifference curves than L_a, it promises him profits which are less than those which he feels he can command by independent action. Similarly, B would not accept any combination of values for x and y such as that denoted by G. Of the values for x and y that lie within the shaded area, some are more likely to be agreed upon than others: thus, if the negotiators begin by considering the values denoted by J, they are likely to discover that each duopolist could earn higher profits by accepting higher values for x and y, for by moving north-eastwards from J they will reach a higher iso-profit curve for each of them; similarly, if they are initially contemplating the values denoted by K, they are likely to discover that each duopolist could reach a higher iso-profit curve by moving south-westwards from K. It would seem, then, that if the two firms are roughly similar in size, resources and in the personalities of those who control them, the values of x and y that they will agree upon will lie near the centre of the area of negotiation.[1]

A model in which each duopolist acts conjecturally may, therefore, help us to illustrate the limits within which bargaining may take place.

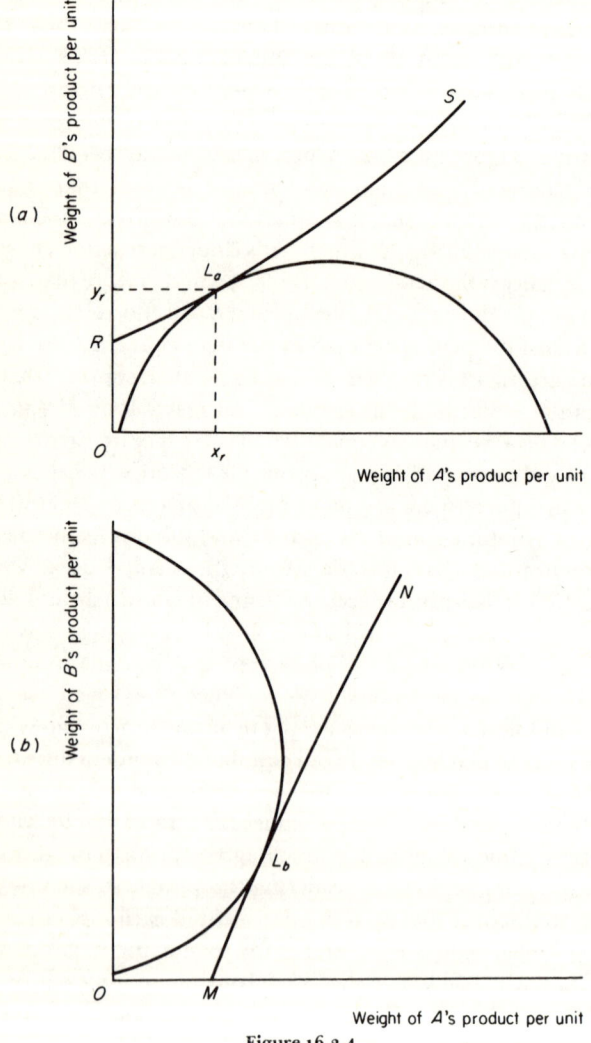

Figure 16.2.4

[1] If the profit-indifference curves on which lie L_a and L_b do not overlap when superimposed on one another, then neither duopolist will be willing to negotiate, for each will believe that he can earn higher profits by independent action.

Oligopoly

If the duopolists accept the area of negotiation, then the hypothesis which each makes about his rival's behaviour may not be tested. The negotiations may break down if either duopolist questions the bargaining range (as shown by the shaded area in Figure 16.2.5); if they do, then each must seek a new hypothesis about his rival's behaviour and reactions, for the old one will have been proved untenable by events. If either duopolist suspects the kind of conjecture that his rival is making about his reactions, he may attempt to alter it, for each will gain if he succeeds in lowering the bargaining limit of the other. It can be seen from Figure 16.2.5 that when the iso-profit maps are given, the size of the area of negotiation (and therefore the extent of the increase in profits that agreement might promise to either participant) depends on the position of RS and MN. If A suspects that B expects him to react along MN, it will clearly be to A's advantage to persuade B that he (A) will react along a curve that lies to the right of MN; similarly, it will be to B's advantage to convince A that his (B's) reaction curve lies above RS. In that way, A (or B) might hope to convince B (or A) that he would earn lower profits if no agreement is reached.

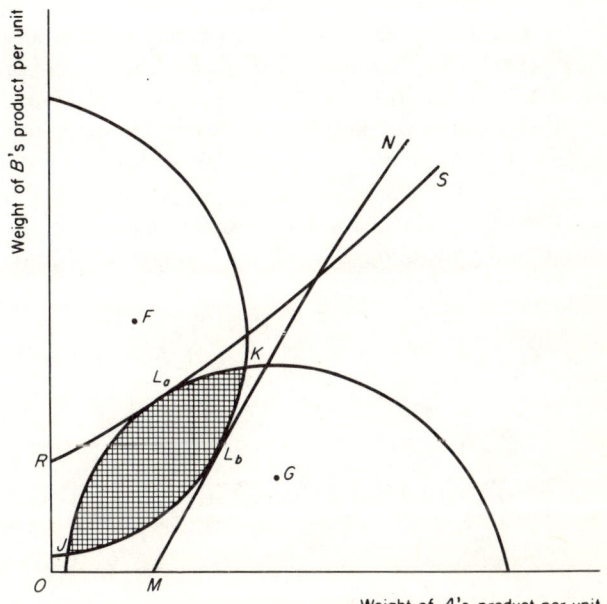

Figure 16.2.5

324   Price Theory

Our third and last leadership model is one in which there is price-leadership. There is price-leadership when firms in an industry sell their products at a price commenced by one 'dominant' firm. In this model, we shall take the simplest example: we shall suppose that (a) there are two independent firms; (b) each produces a product that is a perfect substitute for that of the other; (c) the product is perishable so that in each period the output of each duopolist must all be sold; (d) there are many knowledgeable buyers of the product; (e) each duopolist knows the market demand curve for the product; (f) each seeks the maximum profits in each period; and (g) A assumes that B will always charge the same price as that which he (A) fixes, and B actually behaves in this way. Given these assumptions, we can illustrate the choice of a price by A, the price-leader. In Figure 16.2.6(b) DD is the total demand curve for the product, and MC_b and AVC_b are the marginal and average variable cost curves respectively of B, the price-follower; in Figure 16.2.6(a), MC_a and AVC_a are the marginal and average variable cost curves respectively of A, the price-leader. At each price which A fixes, B will offer for sale the quantity that promises him the greatest profits, and the amount by which the total quantity of the product that is demanded at that price exceeds B's sales will be available for A. If A fixes the price at OC per unit, B will produce and sell CH per period – the output at which his marginal cost of production is equal to OC; at this price, B will be supplying all that buyers wish to buy, so that A's sales will be zero. The point C in diagram (a) will therefore be one point on A's 'conjectural demand or sales curve'. If A fixes the price at OD, B will offer DM per period, and MJ (= DQ_1 in diagram (a)) will be available for A; if A were to fix a price of OE per unit, B would offer EN, and NK (= EQ_2 in diagram (a)) would be left

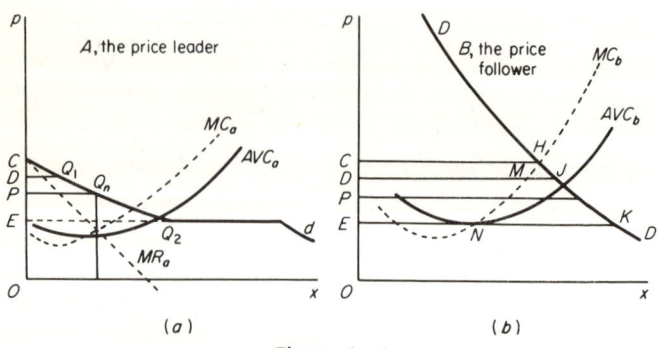

Figure 16.2.6

to A. At prices below OE, the whole of the market demand will be open to A. The curve CQ'_2d in (a), then, shows the quantity that the leader expects to be able to sell at each price. The leader will fix the price at the level which promises him the greatest profits – that is, at OP, where MR_a (the marginal revenue curve corresponding to CQ_2) cuts MC_a. By charging OP per unit, and satisfying the residual demand of PQ_n per period, the price-leader is maximising his profits within the limits set by the follower's behaviour.

We may develop variants of this model of price-leadership by increasing the number of oligopolists, by introducing differentiated products, and by positing other relationships between the leader's and the followers' cost curves than that shown in Figure 16.2.6. These variants, however, add less to the economics of leadership than they do to its geometry. Price-leadership in some form is common in actual oligopolistic markets. It is probable that when it occurs it is based on some kind of agreement. It may be a result of tacit or implicit agreement: if there is one large firm, and several small firms, in an oligopolistic industry, the latter will be malleable to the wishes of the former, for they have little ability to inflict losses on the dominant firm and less capacity to bear the losses which it might inflict on them. The dominant firm need not consult with the smaller firms in order to establish its leadership: it need merely punish them if they do not accept it. If it forces its rivals to act as price-followers, we must presume that this is the kind of reaction that is most profitable for the leader. If the oligopolists are more or less the same size, then the agreement on which leadership is based is likely to rest on firmer foundations than tacit acceptance.

16.3 The Kinked Oligopoly Demand Curve

In this model, we shall suppose that (a) there are several firms in an oligopolistic industry; (b) each produces a product that is a close substitute for that of each other firm; (c) product qualities are constant, advertising expenditures are zero, and some relationship between the prices of the differentiated products has already been established and is now obtaining; (d) each oligopolist believes that if he lowers the price of his product, his rivals will lower the prices of their products *pari passu*, and that if he raises his price, they will maintain their prices at their existing levels. Given these assumptions, each oligopolist will believe that the relationship between his price and his sales will be similar to that shown by the curve *dPD* in Figure 16.3.1.;[1] if he were to raise his price above $\bar{p}$, he would expect his sales to fall off markedly, for his product would become relatively dearer; if he were to lower his price below $\bar{p}$, he would expect no appreciable increase in his sales, for his product would be prevented from becoming relatively cheaper by the price reductions of his rivals. We shall call *dPD* the oligopolist's 'conjectural demand or sales curve', for it shows the relationship between his price and his sales given his conjecture about the reactions of his rivals. The position of this curve is defined by the location of *p*

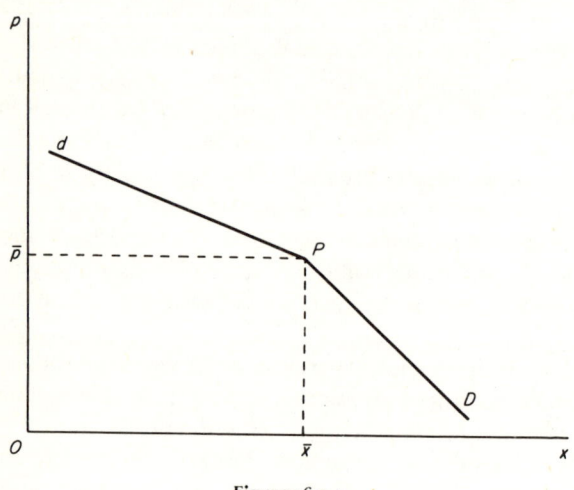

Figure 16.3.1

and the co-ordinates of *p* are $\bar{p}$, the price at which the oligopolist now happens to be selling his product, and $\bar{x}$, the quantity of it that he is currently selling in each period. The price $\bar{p}$ is a datum, and not something determined by this model. An oligopolist is more likely to make assumption (*d*) above, if the price $\bar{p}$ has been fixed by some informal agreement or by a rival who is accepted as the price-leader; in these circumstances, the assumption will reflect each oligopolist's assessment of the penalties that his rivals will inflict on him if he tries to act independently. If the price $\bar{p}$ is a result of an explicit agreement, we

[1] This is the kinked or kinky oligopoly demand curve. Its co-inventors (or discoverers?) were R. L. Hall and C. J. Hitch, *Price Theory and Business Behaviour*, Oxford Economic Papers, No. 2, May 1939, and P. M. Sweezy, 'Demand under Conditions of Oligopoly', *Journal of Political Economy*, 1939.

are unlikely to find a kinked demand curve for the individual oligopolist, for there will probably be specified and known penalties for deviating from it.

The price $\bar{p}$, however fixed, is not necessarily inconsistent with the maximisation of profits. In Figure 16.3.2, MC is the oligopolist's marginal cost curve, and MR is the marginal revenue curve corresponding to dPD; since the former cuts the latter vertically below P, the price MP is that which promises the greatest profits per period. With given marginal costs of production, MP is the more likely to be the profit-maximising price, the longer is the vertical portion of the marginal revenue curve. The length of the 'discontinuity' depends on the relative elasticities of demand at P of the curves dP and PD. This

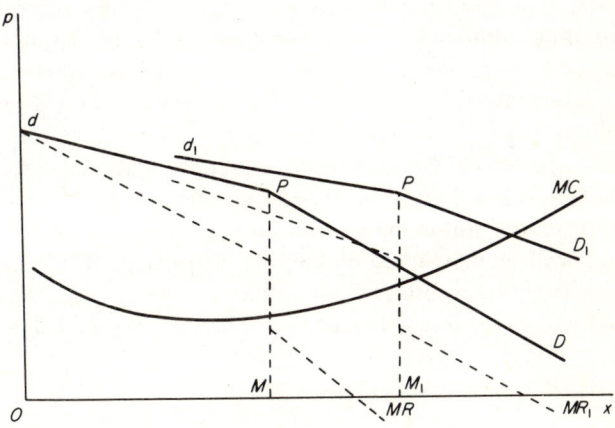

Figure 16.3.2

can be easily confirmed: we know that marginal revenue at MP is equal to $MP(1 - 1/e)$; it follows that the greater is the elasticity at P on dP, and the less is the elasticity at P on PD, the greater will be the differences between the two marginal revenues, and the greater therefore will be the length of the discontinuity. The elasticity of dP will reflect the degree to which the oligopolist's product can be substituted for that of his rivals; in the extreme case, if the oligopolists' products are homogeneous it will be perfectly elastic. The elasticity of PD will reflect the elasticity at each price of the 'demand' for the class of product that the oligopolists are producing.

While the hypothesis about rivals' reactions that gives us the kinked demand curve does not explain why the price is at its present level, it does explain why the price might remain stable at that level as time passes. If the demand for the product of oligopolist A (who makes this hypothesis) rises, he will become aware of it by an increase in his sales. Since the assumption that he makes about the probable reactions of his rivals is in no way dependent on the level of his sales, an increase in demand will not, *per se*, induce him to seek an alternative hypothesis: that is, A will interpret a rise in the demand for his product as a rightward shift of the dPD-curve to d_1PD_1 in Figure 16.3.2. This maintenance of the price at MP in the face of a rise in demand is not necessarily inconsistent with the maximisation of profits. In Figure 16.3.2, we have assumed that the dPD and d_1PD_1 curves are iso-elastic, and the marginal cost curve MC cuts the marginal revenue curve (MR_1) corresponding to the new demand curve within the discontinuity, so that M_1P $(=MP)$ continues to be the price at which the oligopolist's profits will be maximised. Similarly, it can be shown that the profits of oligopolist A may still be greatest at the price MP, even after his costs of production have risen. Thus, in Figure 16.3.3, the marginal cost curve rises from MC to MC_1; since MC_1 cuts the marginal revenue curve corresponding to dPD within the discontinuity, his profits in the new cost conditions will be maximised by keeping his price at MP. If the increases in demand and costs are not confined to a single oligopolist but affect all firms producing that class of product, then it is likely that a

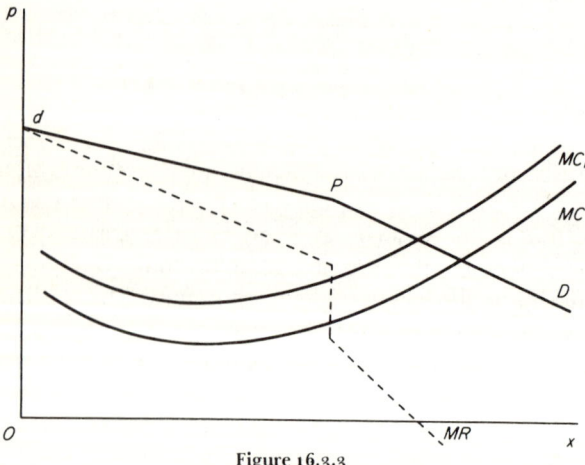

Figure 16.3.3

new informal agreement will be made or that the price-leader will adjust his price; if all the oligopolists are affected by the increases in demand and costs, we would expect the price of their products to rise.

16.4 Collusive Oligopoly[1]

In the simple Cournot model, and in the models in which each firm aspired to leadership, there was no agreement whatsoever between the oligopolists. In the models in which one firm was accepted as the price- or output-leader, there was agreement between the oligopolists on the method by which the value(s) of the action parameter(s) should be fixed. In the kinked demand curve model, we supposed that the firms had already agreed upon a set of values for the prices of their products, and we explored one way in which these values might be maintained. In this, the last section on oligopoly, we shall discuss the economics of agreements between the firms in an oligopolistic industry. We shall first suppose that the oligopolists have agreed to extract the *maximum maximorum* of profits per period from the market(s) for their product(s), and we shall illustrate the choice of values for the variables under their control which promises to achieve this aim. We shall then examine how and why they may be prevented from achieving this objective or deterred from pursuing it.

Initially, we shall suppose that (a) there are only two firms in the oligopolistic industry; (b) each produces and sells a product that is a perfect substitute for that of the other; (c) the product is perishable; (d) there are many knowledgeable buyers of the product; (e) each knows the market demand for the product; (f) the two firms have different cost curves; (g) each firm has the same expectations about the prices and productivities of the productive services which they use; (h) the price of the product is the sole parameter of action of each firm; and (i) they are contemplating whether or not to agree upon a value for the price that will promise the *maximum maximorum* of profits per period to both of them jointly. The choice of this price, and its implications, are illustrated in Figure 16.4.1. The average and marginal costs of production of duopolist A are shown by AC_a and MC_a respectively in diagram (a); AC_b and MC_b in (b) show the average and marginal costs respectively of B; the DD-curve in (c) is the market-demand curve for the product. When A and B are jointly earning the *maximum maximorum* of

[1] For a fuller treatment of collusive oligopoly, see Fellner, *Competition Among the Few*, Alfred A. Knopf, New York, 1949) pp. 3–54 and 120–239.

profits per period from the production of the product in their respective plants and its sale in their common market, they will together be producing the output at which marginal cost and marginal revenue are equal to one another (for that is merely another way of saying that profits are being maximised), and this total output will be distributed between their respective factories in such a way that the last unit produced by each adds the same sum to the costs of production of each, for if that is not so then the sum of their total costs can be lowered by transferring output from A to B, or vice versa.

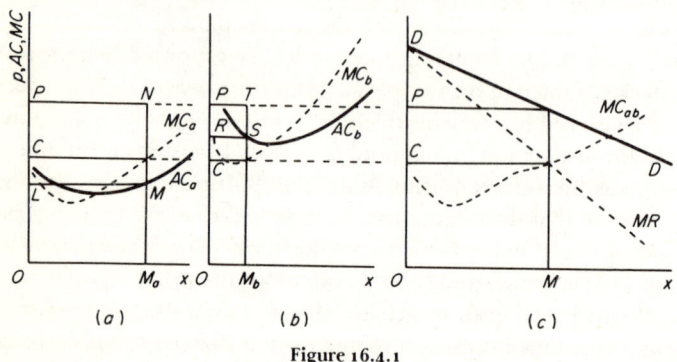

Figure 16.4.1

In Figure 16.4.1, we can discover geometrically the price of the product and the outputs of A and B at which these conditions will be fulfilled. The MC_{ab}-curve in diagram (c) is obtained by adding together laterally the MC_a- and MC_b-curves: thus, if OC is the marginal cost of the OM_a-th unit in A's plant and of the OM_b-th unit in B's, the coordinates of the corresponding point on the MC_{ab}-curve will be OC and OM_a plus OM_b ($= OM$). This MC_{ab}-curve shows the minimum addition to total costs that will be incurred by producing the last unit of any output, and this illustrates the second-condition mentioned above. The first condition is fulfilled when the total output of the product is OM per period and its price OP per unit, for at that output and price marginal revenue and the (minimum) addition to costs of production from producing the OM-th unit are the same. The duopolists will therefore plan to sell OM units of their product at a price of OP per unit, and A will produce OM_a and B, OM_b per period.[1] The output OM and the price OP are the 'monopoly' output and price respectively:

---

[1] Since the MC_{ab}-curve was obtained by adding together the outputs of A and B at each level of marginal cost, OM_a plus OM_b must together be equal to OM.

that is, they are those that would be produced and charged respectively were A and B to merge together to form a single firm that operated two plants in which the costs of production were as shown in diagrams (a) and (b) in Figure 16.4.1. For brevity's sake, we shall hereafter say that the price OP and the output OM (distributed between A and B in the proportion $OM_a : OM_b$) define the 'monopoly' solution.

The maximisation of their joint profits requires that A and B produce OM_a and OM_b per period respectively. This distribution of the 'monopoly' output OM implies a distribution of profits: A may expect to earn profits of $LMNP$ per period and B of $RSTP$ per period. The sum of $LMNP$ and $RSTP$ will be greater than the sum of the profits that A and B would earn with any distribution of output between them at any price other than OP, or with any other distribution of the output OM between them at the price OP. While the 'monopoly' solution promises the maximum joint profits to A and B, however, either might feel that he could command a larger profit[1] by acting independently of his rival. Thus, A might believe that, in the absence of any agreement, B's reactions to changes in his (A's) parameter(s) will promise him profits per period greater than $LMNP$. In these circumstances, A will not accept the distribution of output which the monopoly solution dictates unless some device is found for divorcing the profits which he receives during the period from the profits which he earns when producing his share of the monopoly output. Many such devices are possible: for example, A and B might pay the profits which they earn, when producing outputs of OM_a and OM_b respectively and selling them at a price of OP per unit, into a central pool or fund from which each then receives a sum which is not less than that which he believes (and which his rival agrees) he could earn by acting independently. A pooling agreement of this kind will always make it possible for A and B to maximise their joint profits, provided that the sum of the profits which they believe they can earn by independent action does not exceed the monopoly profits.[2] If the sum of the profits which each believes he can earn by acting independently of his rival exceeds the monopoly profits, then no agreement is possible, for the expectations

---

[1] That is, profits which are larger than the share of the 'monopoly' profits which he would earn when producing his share of the 'monopoly' output.

[2] This proposition can be interpreted in terms of Figure 16.2.5. If the sum of the profits which A expects to earn at L_a and which B expects to earn at L_b falls short of the monopoly profits there will be an overlap area between the iso-profit curves on which lie L_a and L_b respectively.

of A and B are inconsistent with one another.[1] In the ensuing periods, each duopolist will test his hypothesis about his rival's behaviour, and as its incorrectness becomes manifest will be forced to revise it. When the sum of the profits that each expects to earn if there is no agreement again falls short of the monopoly profits, then the 'monopoly' solution will again appear attractive.

Thus far we have confined our analysis to the model defined at the beginning of this section. We have so far assumed that the duopolists have different costs of production in producing the same product and that they have identical expectations about the behaviour of the demand for their product and the supplies of the inputs they employ during the period that lies ahead. The emergence of a unique and agreed 'monopoly' solution depends on this latter assumption. If A believes that the demand for the product will rise and that the prices of the productive services will fall, and if B expects demand to fall and costs to rise, then A will expect the monopoly profits (and his share of them) to be relatively large and B will expect them to be relatively small. In these circumstances, ignoring the possibility that either A or B might deem unacceptable his (earned) share of his estimate of the monopoly profits, there is little likelihood of agreement between them. Agreement may become the more likely as the gap between their expectations narrows as events confirm the estimates of A (or B), and thus lead B (or A) to revise his estimates of the future behaviour of demand and costs.

Our analysis and the conclusions it yields require little modification if the model is extended to reflect more accurately actual oligopolistic markets. Let us now suppose (*inter alia*) that (*a*) there are several firms in the oligopolistic industry; (*b*) each produces and sells a product that is a close substitute for that of each other; (*c*) each has the same expectations about the behaviour of the 'demand' for the product-group that they are producing and of the supplies of the productive services that they are using; and (*d*) they are considering the implications of an agreement that would promise the *maximum maximorum* of profits per period to all of them jointly. In this model, each firm will have many parameters of action: the present and future profits of firm A, for example, will depend on the relative values that he attaches to the price of his product, its quality, his techniques of production, and his advertising expenditure, and to his expenditure on the search for new

[1] In this case, in terms of Figure 16.2.5, the iso-profit curves on which L_a and L_b lie will not overlap with one another.

variants of the product, new methods of production, and new kinds and avenues of advertisement. There will still exist a 'monopoly' solution, however, in this more complex model, for there will be some set of values for the parameters of action of the oligopolists which promises them jointly the *maximum maximorum* of profits. As before, each firm might consider unsatisfactory the profits that it might expect to earn when its parameters had the values dictated by the 'monopoly' solution, and the chances of this happening become the greater the larger is the number of firms in the oligopolistic industry and the larger is the number of variables whose values lie within the control of each of them. In this, as in the simple model, a pooling agreement will still make possible the maximisation of the joint profits, provided that the sum of the minimum profits that each firm would demand from the pool is not greater than the 'monopoly' profits. When the parameters include research and development, and variations in product-quality and advertisement, however, it is probable that the sum of the expected profits from independent action will exceed the monopoly profits: for competition *via* variables other than price requires more skill (and perhaps more 'luck') than competition through price, and each firm may tend to over-estimate its proficiency in non-price competition and the good fortune that it expects to attend its efforts in that direction. If the oligopolists have different expectations about the future behaviour of demand and costs, each will have his own notion of what constitutes the monopoly solution, and some alternative though less profitable agreement must be sought.

We may conclude, then, that while the 'monopoly' solution promises the *maximum maximorum* of profits to the firms in an oligopolistic industry, it may not be reached for any one of three reasons: (*a*) because the oligopolists have different expectations about the future behaviour of demand and costs, and therefore about what constitutes the 'monopoly' solution; (*b*) because, while agreeing upon the monopoly solution, the sum of the profits that they expect from independent action exceeds the expected 'monopoly' profits; and (*c*) because, in the absence of reasons (*a*) and (*b*) above, the oligopolists will not accept (or are prevented from accepting) the pooling agreement which makes it possible for each to receive a share of the 'monopoly' profits that he deems satisfactory. If the oligopolists are deterred by any one of these reasons from effecting an agreement to maximise their joint profits, they need not necessarily eschew collusion of any kind. They may seek other agreements which are less comprehensive in that they do not cover all the variables whose values determine the distribution of profits between the firms, and which are potentially less profitable to the oligopolists taken as a group. We shall now examine briefly a few of these alternatives.

First, the oligopolists may agree to share the market. Let us again make the assumptions (a) to (g) that are listed at the beginning of this section, and let us consider the implications of an agreement between A and B to share the market for their product in the proportions 2 : 1. The market-shares that are agreed upon will be those that promise each duopolist a sum of profits per period that is not less than that which he believes he could earn either without any agreement or with any other kind of agreement. In Figure 16.4.2, the average and marginal costs of production of A are shown by AC_a and MC_a respectively in diagram (a); AC_b and MC_b in diagram (b) show the average and marginal costs respectively of B, and the DD-curve in diagram (c) is the market demand curve for the product. The D_aD_a and D_bD_b curves in diagrams (a) and (b) respectively are the market-share curves of A and B, and in our example, the permissible sales of A at any price on D_aD_a will be twice those of B at the same price on D_bD_b. Given the market-shares, A will plan to sell OM_a per period at OP_a per unit, for these plans promise him the maximum net revenue, and B will plan to sell OM_b at OP_b per unit. These plans cannot be simultaneously fulfilled, for since A and B produce the same product they must charge the same price. Having agreed to share the market, A and B must therefore agree upon a price for their product in the range OP_a to OP_b. The choice of a price and of actual values for the market-shares must be made simultaneously, for the profits that each duopolist can hope to earn if the agreement is effected will depend on both of these things.

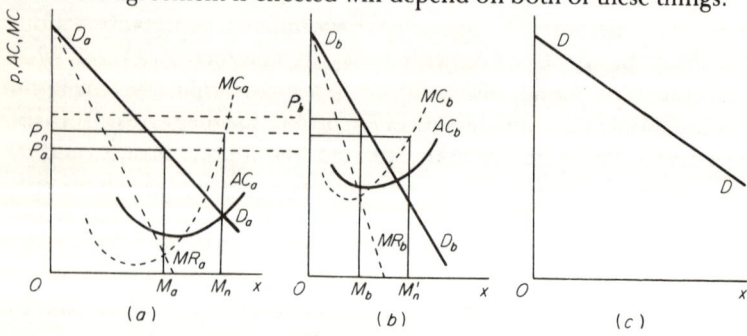

Figure 16.4.2

If the duopolists agree upon a price of OP_n per unit, it is clear from Figure 16.4.2 that each will be tempted to produce and sell more than his share of the market, for by doing so he will increase his profits or diminish his losses. Thus, at OP_n per unit, A's profits will be greatest when he is producing and selling OM_n per period, and B's when he (B) is selling OM'_n per period. If both firms succumb to this temptation, then both will accumulate stocks of the product, and these in turn may tempt one or other to dishonour the agreement by reducing his selling price. If one firm succumbs, and successfully sells more than his allotted share at the price OP_n, then the other firm's sales (and its share of the market) will be *pro tanto* reduced. In recognition of these temptations, the simple market-sharing agreement is normally fortified by a system of fines and compensations: firms that exceed their allotted quotas must pay a proportional or progressive tax on their excess sales, and the proceeds are used to compensate the firms that are thereby prevented from fulfilling their quotas.

A market-sharing agreement is perhaps most likely to occur when the oligopolists incur different costs of production in making the same product, and when a pooling agreement (without which the 'monopoly' solution would be unacceptable) is illegal. Once made, the agreement will persist for as long as the oligopolists are satisfied with the market- (and profit-) shares that it promises, and these shares depend on the profits that the oligopolists believe they can earn by the most attractive alternative agreement or with no agreement. Even when the oligopolists are producing the same product, over the long period each may spend money on research into new methods of production or new variants of the product, and as these efforts are attended by different degrees of success, the acceptable market- and profit-shares will alter. When this happens, the existing agreement will be terminated, and replaced by one in which the market- and profit-shares are different, or by an agreement of a different kind.

This simple model by which we have illustrated the market-sharing agreement may be extended to include other parameters of action. When the oligopolists are producing products that are close substitutes for one another, the profits that each can command over any span of future periods will depend on the relative values of his price, product-quality, techniques of production, advertisement, and expenditure on research. In these circumstances, there will exist some set of values for these variables that will distribute the 'market-demand' for the class of product that the firms are producing (and therefore profits) in any given proportions between them. This more inclusive market-sharing agreement will be subject to the same strains and stresses and will require the same safeguards in the way of penalties and compensations as the simple agreement that we have already examined. It is unlikely, however, that any such inclusive agreement will be reached, and for two reasons. First, the choice of a set of values for the relevant variables that is acceptable to all the participating firms may be impossible, for it rests not so much on ascertainable and measurable facts as on judgements about the future consequences of present changes in the relationship between prices, product-qualities, advertisements or research expenditures. Second, even if this choice is made, it may be impossible to devise a system of fines and compensations to safeguard the agreement, for changes in variables other than price are more easily concealed and their consequences are often less clear. For these reasons, when the number of variables is large, the oligopolists may agree on values for only one of them.

The variable that is most commonly the subject of agreement is price, for a reduction in price by one firm will usually have more immediate and marked effects on the sales of its rivals than an increase, for example, in its advertising or research expenditure. The price-agreement may specify the exact or minimum price that each oligopolist must charge for his product, or it may define the method by which the prices of the competing products must be fixed. The agreement may set out a uniform procedure that each firm must follow when fixing its price: thus there may be a table of 'standard', 'normal' or 'typical' costs and each oligopolist is obliged to base his price on these rather than on his own costs. Alternatively, if the oligopolistic industry consists of one large firm and several small firms whose costs are not very dissimilar, the choice of a price may tacitly be left to the former: the small firms might feel that it (the large firm) is the more likely to have a clear notion of the demand for the product or product-group and of costs of production than they have, and that it is therefore more likely to fix a price that approximates to the 'monopoly' level. In the price-leadership model in Section 16.2, we have described the choice of a price by the leader. In the kinked demand curve model (in Section 16.3) we have described one way in which a price-agreement might be maintained, without any explicit penalties or policing. A price-agreement is subject to the same stresses as any of the agreements that we have already examined: the agreement will generally disintegrate when one or more of the participants are convinced that he or they could command higher profits without it than within it.

In all models of collusive oligopoly that we have examined so far, we have supposed that whether or not a particular agreement is reached depends simply on whether or not it promises each oligopolist a higher rate of profit than that which he could earn without it. This assumption, though crude, was useful while our purpose was simply to catalogue some of the different kinds of agreement that might occur and to adumbrate the circumstances in which each was likely to appear. However, if we wish to explain how the spoils that any agreement promises are shared between the participants — that is, what determines the distribution of the 'monopoly' profits or the relative market-shares — then this assumption must be refined.

Let us return to the model that is defined at the beginning of this section. If there is no agreement, the profits per period that duopolist A might expect to earn will depend on the hypothesis which he makes about the expected reactions of his rival. For each hypothesis that he might make, there will be an expected rate of profit.[1] If A's objective is to earn the maximum profits per period, then he will only accept the agreement if his share of the 'monopoly' profits is not less than the maximum rate of profit that he believes he can earn without it. The share of the 'monopoly' profits that A will obtain, however, depends not only on his (A's) estimate of his prowess if no agreement is reached; it depends also on his rival B, for B will only enter the agreement if it promises him a higher rate of profit. If neither A nor B questions his rival's estimate of the rewards of independent action, and if the sum of these rewards is less than the expected 'monopoly' profits, then agreement is possible, and the precise terms of the agreement will depend on how the amount by which the 'monopoly' profits exceeds the sum of the minimum demands of A and B is divided between them. We shall define the 'relative strength' of an oligopolist as his power to command profits within an agreement, and we shall suppose that it is measured by the proportion of the joint profits which he obtains. We may then say that the outcome in our present example will reflect the relative strengths of the firms that participate in the agreement.

---

[1] Strictly, since A does not know how his rival will react there will be a range of probable values for his profits for each hypothesis about his rival's behaviour. For simplicity's sake, we shall assume that he reduces this range to a 'certainty-equivalent' or that he acts as if he does.

We have so far supposed that both duopolists accept the 'bargaining range' as defined by the maximum profits that each believes he could earn without the agreement. This is not likely to be generally true, for the agreement could be made potentially more profitable for either duopolist if he successfully lowered the bargaining limit of his rival. Thus, if the 'monopoly' profits are 100, the minimum demands of A and B 40 and 20 respectively, and their relative strengths in the proportion 3 : 1, then when each accepts the bargaining range, A will obtain 70 per period and B 30 per period; if B can lower A's estimate of the maximum profits that he (A) could earn without the agreement from 40 to 20, then, *ceteris paribus*, the agreement will promise A only 65 and B 35 per period; if A lowers B's minimum requirement to 10, then A will obtain $77\frac{1}{2}$ and B only $22\frac{1}{2}$ per period. Either duopolist can attempt to lower the bargaining limit of his rival by inducing him to revise the hypothesis on which his existing estimate is based: thus, in terms of Figure 16.2.5, A can lower B's bargaining limit by shifting the point L_b eastwards, southwards, or with any degree of southeastwardness in the figure, and he may seek to do so by propaganda and rumours whose purport is that for any given value of B's parameter he (A) will give a much higher value to his parameter than B now expects; similarly, B may make the agreement potentially more profitable to him by convincing A that L_a lies north, west, or northwest of the position in which A now believes it to be.

It is clear, then, that if agreement is possible, its terms will reflect the relative strengths of the oligopolists who are parties to it. The relative strength of a firm, as we have defined it, will depend on the size of the profits which it believes it could earn if no agreement is reached, and on its power to depress the bargaining limits of its rivals. The estimated profits from independent action will depend on certain objective and measurable characteristics of the firm and on the personality of the manager who guides it. Amongst the former, we must list the brute size of the firm, the nature of its liabilities and assets structures, and the shape and position of its cost function. If the firm is relatively large,[1] if a relatively large proportion of its assets is in the form of money or near-money, if the ratio of contractual liabilities (for example, debentures) to total liabilities is relatively low, and if its average total costs of production are relatively low and rise relatively slowly as its output is

---

[1] Where relative size is measured by the proportion of the total output of the oligopolistic industry that the firm would produce at any given price for the industry's product or any typical set of prices for the industry's products.

expanded, then, *ceteris paribus*, we would expect it to be able to command relatively large profits if no agreement is reached. Given all these facts, however, the actual profit-estimate on which the manager decides whether or not to enter an agreement will reflect his skill *qua* manager and his attitudes towards his rivals and the uncertainty that the future holds. These attitudes are in part inherited from his ancestors, and in part they are the consequence of the character of the development of his firm and of the history of its industry. There is little that can be said about a manager's ability to depress the bargaining limit of his rival(s), other than that it will reflect his skill as a manager and as a negotiator. Of all the determinants of relative strength that we have listed, it is probable that the objective factors and the manager's skill *qua* manager are the most important, for it is these that will shape the outcome if no agreement is reached. Negotiating skill and psychological attitudes can achieve more favourable results than the objective factors warrant only for so long as all the firms are unwilling to submit the hypotheses on which their bargaining limits are based to empirical testing.[1]

16.5 Game Theory and Oligopoly

In their *Theory of Games and Economic Behavior*, von Neumann and Morgenstern demonstrated the relevance of game theory to the description of economic behaviour.[2] Basically, a *game* involves a situation where the activities of one *player* affect the welfare, profits, sales, etc., of another player, and vice versa. Such games are either *co-operative* or *non-co-operative*. A co-operative game indicates that collusion between the two or more players will be mutually beneficial. Non-co-operative games indicate that a game can be played by one player to his own best advantage. The benefits received from playing a game are called 'pay-offs'. Clearly, the playing of games, co-operative and non-co-operative has, *prima facie*, a great deal to do with oligopoly where, as we have already seen, individual firms may gain by adopting particular *conflict strategies*, or, perhaps, all firms can gain mutually by adopting *co-operative strategies*.

---

[1] We have not so far considered oligopsony, nor shall we do so. For each of the models of an oligopolistic industry that we have examined in this chapter, we can construct a similar model of an oligopsonistic industry simply by substituting 'input' for 'product' and 'buyer' for 'seller' in each of the assumptions that define it.

[2] J. von Neumann and O. Morgenstern, *Theory of Games and Economic Behavior*, 1st ed. (Princeton University Press, Princeton, 1944; and Wiley, New York, 1964).

After much initial promise, it seems fair to say that the theory of games has cast some light on some oligopoly problems, but that, in general, its main achievement has been to restate the theorems that already exist but in a somewhat more attractive language. We indicate below the type of analysis and language adopted by game theory.

It is convenient to contain the discussion to a *two-person* situation – that is, to duopoly. The conflict, we shall assume, is about shares of the market. If A increases his share, B must reduce his. A game in which A's gains are B's losses is called a *zero-sum game*. Each firm is assumed to have variable strategies which it can adopt – packaging, advertising, pricing policy, and so on. These strategies can be listed for firm A and for firm B in the manner shown in Figure 16.5.1. The 'cells' in the table are filled with numbers indicating the pay-off to A. B's pay-off can be found by deducting A's pay-off from the total available pay-off, in this case the size of the total market. Thus, if A selects strategy 3, and B selects strategy 1, A's pay-off will be 9 units. Since we are considering market shares, we could take the figure to refer to the percentage of the market secured by A. Thus, in this case, A would secure 90 per cent of the market and B would secure 100–90 = 10 per cent. The table in Figure 16.5.1 is called a *pay-off matrix*.

	B's Strategies		
A's Strategies	$B1$	$B2$	$B3$
$A1$	50	30	10
$A2$	60	20	40
$A3$	90	80	30

Figure 16.5.1

If we assume that A and B know the relevant pay-offs, we can consider which strategy each player will choose. Thus, if A did choose strategy $A3$ it would be best for B to choose counter-strategy $B3$. The question is, of course, what A thinks B will do if he, A, selects a particular strategy. This will depend on A's general outlook. Suppose he assumes the worst – that is, that if he selects a strategy, B will countermove in such a way as to minimise A's gain. In terms of Figure 16.5.1 A would believe that his A_1 would be countered by B_3. A_2 would be met with B_2, and A_3 would be met by B_3. If A's highly cautious view determines how he plays, he must select his strategy by looking at the *row minima* we have noted. The best he can do is select the strategy which gives him the highest of these minima, the maximum of the minima – that is, strategy A_3, which, if the worst happens, will secure him 30 per cent of the market. Such a rule is called 'maximin'.

Now consider B. In his case the higher the number in the pay-off matrix cells, the worse off he is since numbers indicate A's gains. If he adopts a maximin strategy, he will proceed as follows. If he chooses B_1, he will assume A will select A_3. If B chooses B_2, he assumes A selects A_3, and if B chooses B_3 he assumes A will select A_2. In each case he assumes the worst. If he chooses between these strategies he selects, because of the way the table is presented, the lowest of the column maxima – that is he selects strategy B_3. His policy is called 'minimax'.

A's maximin strategy is A_3 and B's minimax strategy is B_3. But A's pay-off from A_3 is not what B *expects* A to gain if he, B, selects his minimax strategy B_3. On his minimax rule, B expects A to select A_2 if he, B, selects B_3. This lack of coincidence of expectations means there is no *equilibrium point*. What happens in this situation is uncertain. Both players may stick to their original strategies and tolerate whatever the outcome is: or they may switch strategies if they foresee the problem. One possibility is that the players will select *mixed strategies*. Basically what happens is that players select strategies at random, perhaps tossing a coin or a dice to see which strategy he will select. In our example, A may have a dice with A_1 marked on one side, A_2 on two sides, and A_3 on the remaining three sides. This would mean that A_1 has a probability of 1/6 of being selected, A_2 has a probability of 1/3, and A_3 a probability of 1/2. Without detailing the proof, it can be shown that the employment of these mixed strategies will lead to an equilibrium. Since two person zero-sum games that do not require mixed strategies have an equilibrium point, all two-person zero-sum games have an equilibrium.

To illustrate the idea of an equilibrium, consider Figure 16.5.2. A pay-off matrix is shown there in which there is an equilibrium. A's procedure is as follows: A_3 is assumed to be countered by B_3; A_2 by B_3; and A_3 by B_3. Hence maximin requires that A selects A_3. Now consider B's strategy. $B1$ will, B assumes, be countered by $A3$; $B2$ by $A3$ and $B3$ by $A3$. B must therefore select the minimax, which is $B3$. In this case, A's maximin and B's minimax converge on $A3$, $B3$. Hence there is an equilibrium point, or, as it is frequently called, a *saddle point*.

	B's Strategies		
A's Strategies	$B1$	$B2$	$B3$
$A1$	50	30	10
$A2$	60	40	20
$A3$	90	80	70

Figure 16.5.2

Notice that a zero-sum game contains no incentive to co-operation between players, simply because A's gain is B's loss. Indeed, such games are sometimes called *non-co-operative* games. We can indicate the gains from co-operation is a non-zero-sum game by looking at Figure 16.5.3. To make things simple we assume only two strategies for A and B. Since the game is non-zero-sum we must also indicate B's gains explicitly. This is done by showing the gains to A first and then the gains to B, in each cell, so that cell $A1$, $B1$ means that this combination of strategies yields A a return of 3 and B a return of 5. It is not a zero-sum game since the paired elements in each cell do not add up to the same total. Now, A is certain to select $A2$ since it yields him 6 if B selects $B1$ and 1 if B selects $B2$. This is better than the outcome if A selects $A1$. B selects $B2$ because it promises maximum gains whatever strategy A selects. Hence, acting independently, the players choose $A2$, $B2$, giving combined gains of 3 units. Obviously this is not a satisfactory solution from any point of view. $A1$, $B1$ promises maximum joint gains *and* an improvement in the situation of each player compared to $A2$, $B2$. What is required is co-operation. A coalition between A and B would move them to $A1$, $B1$ so that both are better off.

This example, simple though it is, reflects a basic characteristic of economic activity. Acting in their own self-interest, individuals will frequently bring about a situation which, while possibly 'satisfactory' to each individual, is not the best that can be achieved. If this is correct it has fundamental implications for the operation of economies: a free market system, for example, rests upon the idea that self-interest should be permitted to regulate the economic system. But it is clearly conceivable that such a system will not maximise economic welfare: further gains can be secured by co-operation, trust, mutual agreement and understanding. Of course, co-operation will not be voluntary in a world of self-interested individuals unless each can be sure that co-operation will secure higher *private* gains than by non-co-operation.

	B's Strategies	
	B1	B2
A1	3,5	0,6
A2	6,0	1,2

A's Strategies

Figure 16.5.3

In Figure 16.5.3 higher personal gains are secured by each player by moving to A_1, B_1. In fact, the joint gain there is 8 units compared to only 3 units in the initial 'equilibrium'. These 8 units could be shared equally, 4 and 4, or in some other way, in order to secure the move. Thus, if the shares remain as shown in the first cell, A would gain 2 units (3−1) and B would gain 3 units (5−2). To induce A to move, B may have to offer a little more than the 2 units A will gain, even though A starts at a lower total. Perhaps A will argue that it is 'unfair' if the move secures 2 for him but 3 for B. It is still to B's advantage to offer A a bribe in addition to A's automatic gains. If he gives him one-half of one unit for example, the result will be $A = 3\frac{1}{2}$, $B = 4\frac{1}{2}$. The precise outcome will depend on bargaining strength and the type of rule adopted (equal gains, parity in the final total, improvement of relative position of one party to another, and so on). Various attempts have been made to derive 'fair' solutions, but their detail is beyond the scope of this book.[1]

[1] See J. F. Nash, 'The Bargaining Problem', *Econometrica,* Apr. 1950; and the same author's 'Two-Person Co-operative Games', *Econometrica,* Jan. 1963.

17

Bilateral Monopoly

17.0 Price-Taker Context

Bilateral monopoly exists when one buyer faces one seller. We shall take barter between two parties as our prototype of this market structure. Let us suppose that (a) '*A* has ... a basket of apples, *B* a basket of nuts', and that '*A* wants some nuts, *B* wants some apples';[1] (b) all *A*'s apples, and all *B*'s nuts, are homogeneous; (c) we are given the indifference maps of *A* and *B*; and (d) each party seeks to maximise his satisfaction. The consequences of these assumptions are illustrated in Figure 17.0.1. *A*'s indifference map is drawn in diagram (a) and this

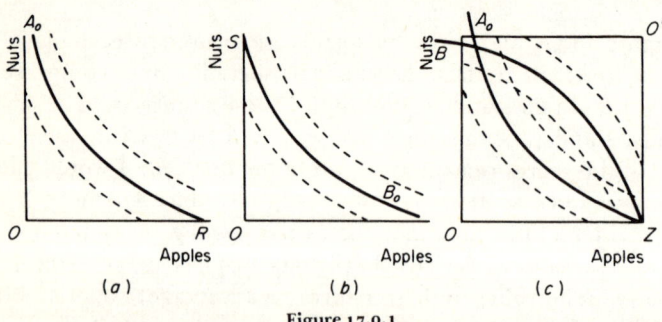

Figure 17.0.1

shows *A*'s tastes for apples and nuts and his preferences as between different combinations of them. *A*'s basket contains OR apples, and the indifference curve A_0 on which R lies divides all combinations of nuts and apples which *A* would prefer to OR apples from those he would deem less attractive. Similarly, the indifference curve B_0 in diagram (b) illustrates *B*'s bargaining limit, for he will not trade with *A* unless it leads to a combination of nuts and apples which he prefers to any com-

[1] A. Marshall, *Principles of Economics*, 8th ed. (Macmillan, London, 1947) App. F, p. 791.

Bilateral Monopoly

bination lying on B_0. In diagram (c), B's indifference map, after having been rotated anti-clockwise through 180°, is superimposed on A's; OZ (= OR) shows the number of apples in A's basket and $O'Z$ (= OS) the number of nuts in B's basket. A and B will only be willing to trade with one another if as a result of trade each is left with a combination of nuts and apples that lies within the area bounded by A_0 and B_0 in diagram (c).

The assumptions that we have made so far are not sufficient to enable us to decide what quantities of nuts and apples will be exchanged.[1] They merely tell us that the point denoting these quantities must lie within the area enclosed by A_0 and B_0 in diagram (c). If we wish to narrow the range of possible outcomes in this example of barter exchange, we must make some assumption about the market behaviour of A and B. We shall suppose initially that A and B do not enter into explicit negotiations with each other in pursuit of a mutually acceptable solution. In this section we shall explore the consequences of assuming that both A and B are price-takers. In Section 17.1 we consider the effects when A (or B) is a price-maker and B (or A) a price-taker; and then what happens when both A and B try to be price-makers. When that has been done, we shall illustrate the process of negotiation and describe its probable consequences.

The assumption that A and B are price-takers may be stated in other words: we may say that each is a quantity-adjuster, or that each behaves as if he were a pure competitor. The consequences of this assumption are illustrated in Figure 17.0.2. The indifference map of A is drawn in diagram (a). The slope of the straight lines radiating from R illustrate alternative prices for apples in terms of nuts: it is in fact the *terms of trade* between apples and nuts. If A could buy OL/OR nuts for each apple, he would maximise his satisfaction by selling CR apples for OD nuts and thus acquiring the combination of apples and nuts denoted by the point P at which the price-line RL is a tangent to one of his indifference curves. When all points such as P are joined together, we have the curve RR', which is A's price-consumption or *offer curve*. The RR'-curve shows us the quantity of apples that A would be willing to sell at each rate of exchange between nuts and apples. The SS'-curve

[1] Once the quantities are known, the price of apples in terms of nuts, or of nuts in terms of apples, is known also. The price of apples in terms of nuts will be the number of nuts that will be exchanged for one apple, and this will be equal to the quantity of nuts that B sells (A buys) divided by the number of apples that B buys (A sells). Similarly, the price of nuts in terms of apples will be equal to the quantity of apples divided by the quantity of nuts.

in diagram (b) is derived in a similar way, and has a similar meaning. In diagram (c), (a) and (b) have been superimposed on one another. The quantities of nuts and apples that will be exchanged and the rate at which they will be exchanged are implicit in the point V where the offer curves intersect: the price of apples in terms of nuts is shown by the slope of ZV, and at this price A will sell ZE apples for OF nuts, and B will sell ZH nuts for $O'G$ apples. This represents an equilibrium position, for $OF = ZH$ and $ZE = O'G$ – that is, the planned purchases and sales of each commodity are the same. This model of bilateral monopoly is analogous to the simple Cournot model of oligopoly which we described in Section 16.1: the offer curves are the analogues of the reaction curves, and our model enjoys the same advantages and suffers from the same defects as the Cournot model.

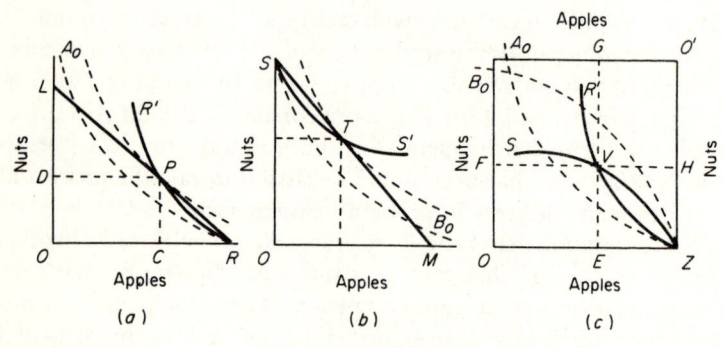

Figure 17.0.2

The equilibrium denoted by V in diagram (c) of Figure 17.0.2 can be illustrated in terms of demand and supply analysis. In Figure 17.0.3, we measure the rate of exchange between nuts and apples on the vertical axis, and the quantity of apples demanded and supplied on the horizontal axis. Implicit in the RR'-curve in Figure 17.0.2, there is a relationship between the rate of exchange and the number of apples that A would be willing to supply, and this relationship is shown explicitly by the SS-curve in Figure 17.0.3. Similarly, DD is the demand curve for apples and it is derived from the SS'-curve in Figure 17.0.2. The price of apples in terms of nuts will tend towards OP (= the slope of ZV in Figure 17.0.2), and the quantity of apples that will be demanded and supplied at this price will be OQ (= ZE or $O'G$ in Figure 17.0.2).

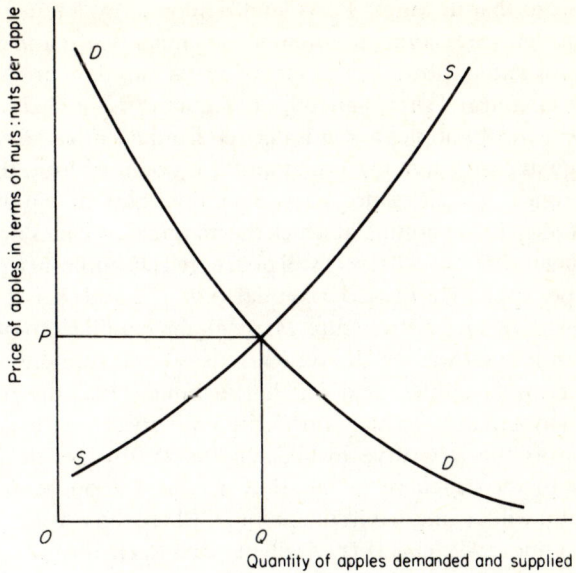

Figure 17.0.3

17.1 Price-Maker context

We shall next suppose that A is a price-maker and B a price-taker: that is, that A behaves as if he were a monopolist for apples and a monopsonist for nuts and B as if he were a pure competitor, or that A acts 'conjecturally' and B 'autonomously'. The consequences of this assumption are illustrated in Figure 17.1.1. The ZA_0 and ZB_0 curves have the same meaning as in the preceding figures, and ZS' is B's offer curve. If A knows the quantity of nuts that B will sell (or the quantity of apples that B will demand) at each rate of exchange which he (A) might fix,[1] he will choose that exchange rate which promises him maximum utility. This is shown in the figure by the slope of the line ZL_a, where L_a is the point at which B's offer curve is tangential to one of A's indifference curves. The equilibrium price of apples in terms of nuts will be UL_a/UZ, and at this price A, the monopolist, will plan to sell UZ apples; alternatively, we may say that the equilibrium price of nuts in terms of apples will be UZ/UL_a, and that at this price A, the monopsonist, will plan to buy OJ nuts. It is apparent that this model is

[1] That is, if A knows B's offer curve.

analogous to that in which A acts (and is allowed by B to act) as the output-leader (see Section 16.2), and it has similar merits and defects.

The information portrayed in Figure 17.1.1 can be represented in terms of demand and supply analysis. In Figure 17.1.2(a), DD is B's demand curve for A's apples and it is derived from B's offer curve; SS is A's 'marginal cost' curve for apples and it is obtained from the ZR'-curve in Figure 17.0.2(c). Since A acts as a monopolist, his equilibrium will be implicit in the point E at which the marginal revenue curve corresponding to DD cuts SS – i.e. A will plan to sell OC apples at a price of OD nuts per apple. The price OD is equal to UL_a/UZ and OC is the same as UZ in Figure 17.1.1. In Figure 17.1.2(b), the equilibrium of A qua monopsonist is shown: on the vertical axis, we measure the price of nuts in terms of apples, and on the horizontal axis, the planned purchases by A of nuts. In diagram (b), the $S'S'$-curve gives the same information as the DD-curve in (a), and the $D'D'$-curve in (b) corresponds to the SS-curve in (a). If A acts as a monopsonist, his equilibrium will be implicit in the point H, where the marginal curve corresponding to $S'S'$ cuts $D'D'$. A will plan to buy OF nuts at a price of OG per nut.

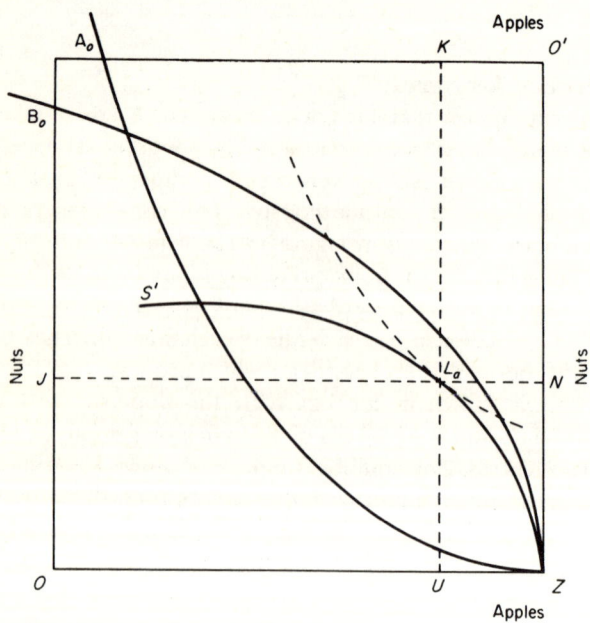

Figure 17.1.1

Bilateral Monopoly

OG is equal to UZ/UL_a in Figure 17.2.1 and to $1/OD$ in Figure 17.1.2(a) and OF is the same as OJ (or ZN) in Figure 17.1.1. Next, we shall assume that both A and B try to be price-makers: that is, that A acts as a monopolist for apples and as a monopsonist for nuts, and that B acts as a monopolist for nuts and as a monopsonist for apples, or that A behaves conjecturally believing that B will act autonomously, and that

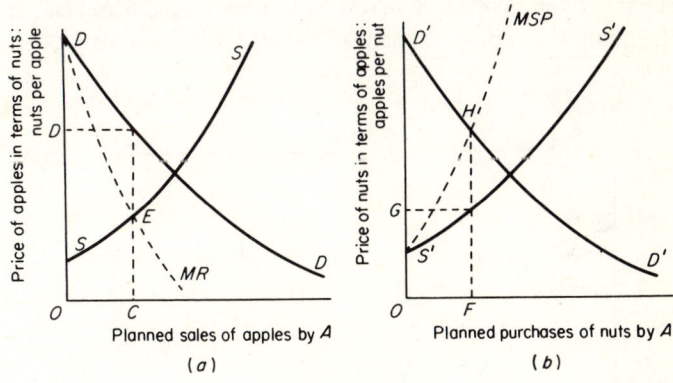

Figure 17.1.2

B behaves conjecturally believing that A will act autonomously. The consequences of this assumption are portrayed in Figure 17.1.3. ZR' and ZS' are the offer curves of A and B respectively. Knowing B's offer curve, A will plan to exchange the quantities implicit in L_a (where ZS' touches one of A's indifference curves) by fixing the rate of exchange at UL_a/UZ; knowing A's offer curve, B will plan to exchange the quantities implicit in L_b (at which ZR' is tangential to one of B's indifference curves) by fixing the rate of exchange at $U'L_b/U'Z$. In this model, it is clear that no equilibrium will be reached. The hypothesis that A (or B) makes about B's (or A's) behaviour will be proved wrong as soon as it is tested, and the assumptions by which our model is defined do not help us to identify what new hypothesis each party to the barter exchange will choose. The analogy between this model and the model of duopoly in which each firm aspires to output-leadership (see Section 16.2) is apparent.

The information contained in Figure 17.1.3 may be represented with the aid of demand and supply curves and their derivatives. In Figure 17.1.4, the DD- and SS-curves have the same meaning as in Figure 17.1.2(a). The expected marginal revenue curve of A, the monopolist for apples, is shown by MR; we shall call the MSP-curve, which is the marginal curve corresponding to SS, the marginal supply price curve of B, the monopsonist for apples. The monopolist A will plan to sell OD apples at a price of OC nuts per apple; OD is equal to UZ in Figure 17.1.3, and OC to UL_a/UZ. The monopsonist B will plan to buy OF apples at a price of OE nuts per apple; OF is the same as $U'Z$ in Figure 17.1.3 and OE is equal to $U'L_b/U'Z$. We can say no more than that the rate of exchange will lie somewhere between OE and OC, and that the quantity of apples exchanged for nuts will lie between OF and OD.

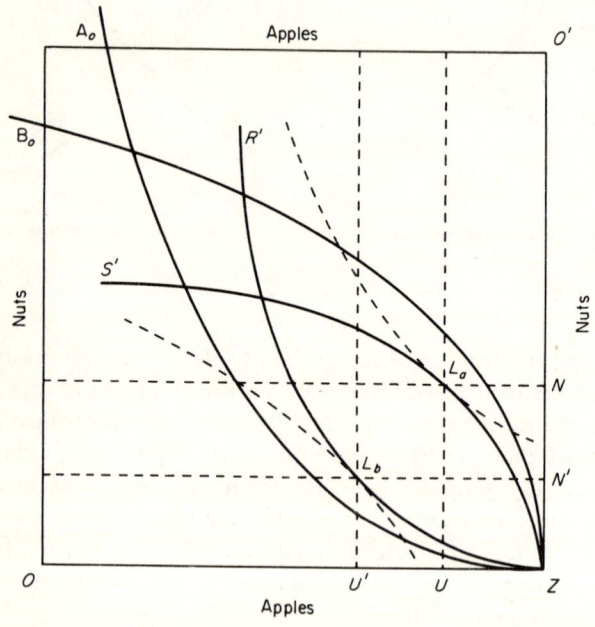

Figure 17.1.3

Finally, we shall assume that A and B have decided to agree upon a rate of exchange by negotiating with one another. Let us suppose that each party knows the indifference map of the other, so that each is aware that the quantities exchanged must be denoted by a point lying within the area bounded by ZA_o and ZB_o in Figure 17.1.5. Let us further suppose that A opens the negotiations by offering to sell B LZ apples in return for LP_1 nuts. It will be clear to both A and B that each of them can increase his satisfaction by moving north-westwards from P_1 within the envelope created by the indifference curves that cut one another at P_1. If they move to P_2, for example, each will still be able to enhance his satisfaction by moving north-westwards within the envelope created by the indifference curves that have one of their points of intersection at P_2. And so on, for if they start from any point

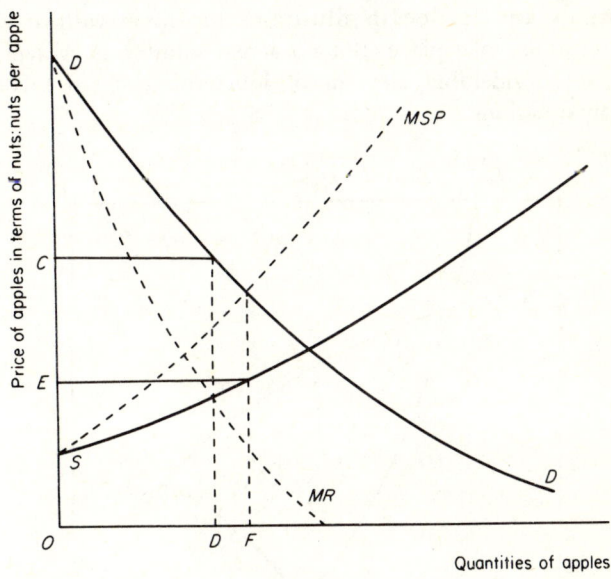

Figure 17.1.4

near $Z(Q)$, it will always pay A and B to increase (decrease) the quantities of apples and nuts that they exchange until some such point as C is reached, at which one of A's indifference curves is tangential to one of B's. The point C denotes a possible equilibrium position, for once it is reached, any movement away from it in any direction will reduce the satisfaction that is enjoyed by at least one of the parties. There will, however, be an infinite number of points such as C, and the one which is actually reached will depend on the point from which the negotiations begin and on the precise direction in which A and B move from it as the negotiations proceed. All these points will lie on the curve XY, which is called the *contract curve*. If we start from any point on the contract curve, a movement away from the curve in any direction will reduce the utility of both A and B, and a movement along XY will increase the satisfaction of A (or B) and reduce that of B (or A). Of all the solutions that lie on XY, A will prefer that denoted by Y, for that promises him the *maximum maximorum* of utility, and he will not accept any solution lower than that shown by X; B will prefer that denoted by X, and he will not be willing to trade if the quantities of nuts and apples that are to be exchanged both fall short of the quantities denoted by Y. The contract curve is thus the locus of all possible outcomes of the negotiations and its length illustrates the *range* within which bargaining must take place. But no actual solution is evident, indicating a considerable element of indeterminancy in bilateral-monopoly situations.

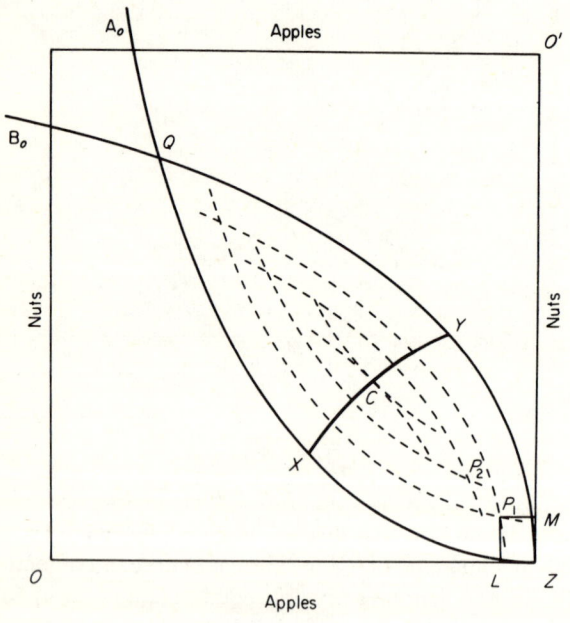

Figure 17.1.5

We add little of substance to either our analyses or the conclusions we have drawn from them if we take other examples of bilateral monopoly. If we suppose, for example, that A is an employers' federation and B a trade union, we can develop a succession of models similar to those we have examined above, and we shall find that each yields the same kind of solution. If there is collective bargaining between A and B to help to determine the wage-rate, then, as in the previous paragraph, we can narrow the range of possible outcomes to those lying on some such line as XY; and the extent of the range will depend on the positions of X and Y – that is, the minimum acceptable solutions of A and B respectively – and these will depend on who or what A and B represent. We may say that the precise terms of the agreement will reflect the relative strengths of the negotiators.

18

Normative Price Theory

18.0 Introduction

It should be clear from the previous chapters that the resources of an economy can be allocated in a near-infinite number of ways. Strictly, 'positive' economics concerns itself only with factual statements about the effects of one allocation rather than another. It makes no attempt to *evaluate* different allocations in terms of criteria of what is good or bad. The function of evaluating allocations is reserved for 'normative' economics, more popularly called *welfare economics*.

Now, clearly, what constitutes a good or bad allocation of resources depends on our selected criteria for goodness or badness. A good allocation might be one which makes people in a certain class or income group feel happier regardless of whether people outside that group feel happy with the allocation or not. Or it might be an allocation which improves the happiness of at least some people and does not deteriorate the happiness of anyone else. Various rules can be proposed. These rules are built into a *social objective function*, or, as it is more commonly called, a *social welfare function*. It must be made absolutely clear that no one social welfare function is better than any other unless we all have some agreed criteria by which to choose between such functions. Since people do disagree about what constitutes good and bad, the social welfare function used in practice is most likely to be some compromise between competing groups, containing large elements of 'social contract' whereby A inhibits some of his desires (because they are harmful to B) provided B does the same. At the very worst, there might be as many social welfare functions as there are individuals in society, each one with his or her particular view of how resources are 'best' allocated.[1]

---

[1] For this approach see I. M. D. Little, 'Social Choice and Individual Values', *Journal of Political Economy*, Oct. 1952.

Normative Price Theory

Having denied the strict possibility of a unique social welfare function, the remainder of this chapter is none the less concerned with a specific approach to normative economics. This approach is usually termed 'Paretian' because its origins stem from some of the writings of Vilfredo Pareto. The prefix is somewhat ill-advised now, since, in the first place, only some of Pareto's views are implicit in the approach currently widely used, and, second, those views have been substantially modified in an attempt to overcome an obvious difficulty in the initial approach. However, Paretian welfare economics tends to underlie not just the theory of normative resource allocation, but also its practice. Here, then, is one very good reason for looking at the underpinnings of Paretian welfare theory – it is actually used (its current guise is called *cost-benefit analysis*[1]) and we should understand how it influences decisions. Our immediate task is to introduce a number of concepts and then show how they are combined to make up the theory of welfare economics as it is conventionally understood.

18.1 Consumer's Surplus: The Concept

The first concept we shall need is that of *consumer's surplus*. The general idea of consumer's surplus (CS) is easily conceived. If we look at the normal demand curves derived in Chapter 2 we see that they slope down from left to right. The forces of supply and demand will generate some equilibrium price for the commodity in question, call it $\bar{p}$. Now if price was below $\bar{p}$, the consumer would purchase more of the commodity. This is what the demand curve tells us. If the price is above $\bar{p}$ the consumer would still buy some of the commodity, however. Therefore, for these initial units we can conclude that the consumer was *willing to pay* more than the ruling market price. There is a sense then in which he gets something for nothing – he is paying less than he is willing to pay. The last unit he buys also costs him $\bar{p}$ but it is only just valued at this amount by the consumer. He buys no more because $\bar{p}$ is too high a price for the extra units when compared to his personal valuation.

Now, if we look at the consumer's purchases in terms of the costs and benefits to him we observe the following. First, he has paid out some sum of money $\bar{p} \cdot \bar{x}$ where $\bar{x}$ is the quantity purchased at price $\bar{p}$. We can think of this as a loss to the consumer. Second, he must value

---

[1] See A. Dasgupta and D. W. Pearce, *Cost-Benefit Analysis: Theory and Practice* (Macmillan, London, 1972).

the quantity he purchases *at least* at $\bar{p}$. $\bar{x}$ since we know that the last unit he buys is worth just $\bar{p}$ to him. We can argue, therefore, that his benefits from consumption at least offset his costs. (Indeed, if they did not our consumer would not be 'rational' in the sense described in Chapter 1. Our conclusion so far should not, therefore, be at all surprising.) Third, we know that the initial units purchased by the consumer were valued more highly than the price actually paid. Thus, there is some excess benefit, which we have called 'consumer's surplus', which we need to add in if we are calculating the individual cost-benefit picture for the consumer. What we have now shown is that consumer's surplus, if it can be measured, provides an indicator of the *net benefits* to the consumer of purchasing the quantity he does purchase.

If we can sustain this argument, it is obviously going to have important implications. Suppose, for example, that we can calculate the change in consumer's surplus arising from some policy change – say the withdrawal or introduction of some good, or a price change in a good due to a tariff, or a tax, or an expansion of supply. Then our simple analysis so far would suggest that we can calculate the net benefits to individual consumers of such policy changes. Such an approach would indeed provide a clear-cut indicator of the 'worth' of any policy as far as each individual consumer is concerned. If, as a next step, we could find some way of adding up these individual net benefits (or losses) we would have an indicator of *social net benefits*.

We have effectively prejudged the issue because so-called 'Paretian' welfare economics does in fact do exactly what we have suggested above – it attempts to measure CS and to aggregate gains and losses in CS to provide, at best, a unique indicator of the social net benefits arising from a policy change. Obviously then, we need to investigate the concept of consumer's surplus and the way in which aggregation is suggested.

18.2 Consumer's Surplus: The Marshallian Approach

First, we return to the equation of equilibrium for the individual consumer. This was given in Chapter 1 as

$$PRS_{x_1, x_2} = \frac{p_1}{p_2}$$

and this can be rewritten

$$PRS_{x_1, x_2} = \frac{p_1}{p_2} = -\frac{\Delta x_2}{\Delta x_1} \tag{1}$$

since $-\Delta x_2/\Delta x_1$ is the slope of the indifference curve. Now points on the same indifference curve are of equal utility, by definition. In Figure 18.2.1 this means that utility levels at points A and B are equal.

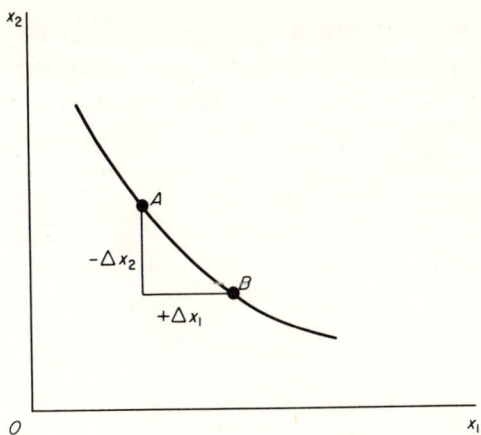

Figure 18.2.1

The move from A to B is made up of a loss of x_2 and a gain in x_1 so that we can write

$$-\Delta x_2 \cdot dU_2 + \Delta x_1 \cdot dU_1 = 0$$

or
$$\Delta x_2 \cdot dU_2 = \Delta x_1 \cdot dU_1 \tag{2}$$

where dU refers to the change in utility that occurs. All that equation (2) says is that the utility change due to the small change in x_2 must equal the utility change due to a small change in x_1, and this is self-evident when we remember that points A and B are on the same indifference curve.

Upon substitution of equation (2) in equation (1) we obtain:

$$-p_1 \cdot dU_2 = p_2 \cdot dU_1.$$

Further rearrangement gives

$$-\frac{p_1}{dU_1} = \frac{p_2}{dU_2}. \tag{3}$$

Now suppose we make good 2 'all other goods' (i.e. income). We shall find this a useful manoeuvre since it will eventually enable us to define consumer's surplus in terms of money income. Instead of p_2 and

dU_2 we now write p_Y and dU_Y and equation (3) becomes

$$-\frac{p_1}{dU_1} = \frac{p_Y}{dU_Y}. \tag{4}$$

The notation p_Y means, effectively, 'the price of income' or 'the price of money'. But Y is in fact the *numéraire*: it is the 'commodity' whose price is set equal to unity such that all other prices (p_1 in this case) are expressed in terms of it. Consequently we have $p_Y = 1$. Equation (4) is now considerably simplified to

$$-\frac{p_1}{dU_1} = \frac{1}{dU_Y}$$

or
$$-dU_1 = p_1 \cdot dU_Y \tag{5}$$

or
$$-\frac{dU_1}{dU_Y} = p_1 \tag{5a}$$

The notation dU_Y needs a little explanation. Just as dU_1 refers to the extra utility gained from a small increment in the amount of good 1 – the marginal utility of good 1 – so dU_Y is the *marginal utility of income*.

We can now begin to relate equation (5) to the measurement of consumer's surplus. The implication of equation (5) is that the extra utility gained by the consumer from increasing the amount of a good is related directly to its price. In Figure 18.2.2 this would imply that *the*

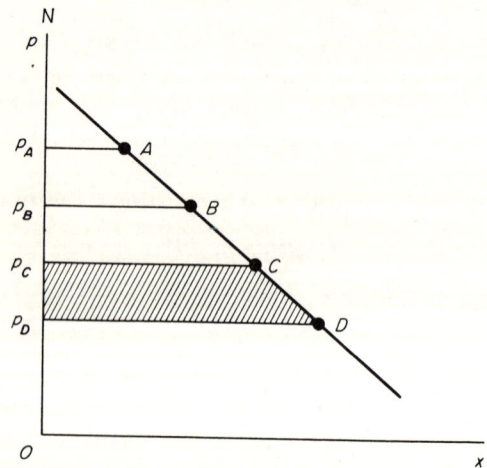

Figure 18.2.2

points on the demand curve are some sort of indicator of utility. Thus at A we could conclude that the consumer's marginal utility of the A-th unit of the good in question is related in some way to the price p_A. Similarly, p_B would be some sort of indicator (we have not yet said whether it will be accurate) of the marginal utility of the B-th unit, and so on. If the consumer settles at C because p_C is the market price, it follows that his net benefits (his consumer's surplus) are related in some way to the area NCP_C. Similarly, if the price fell to p_D we could say that the extra consumer's surplus is related to the 'arrow-head' area $p_C p_D DC$.

However, we have said nothing about the marginal utility of income. If equation (5) showed an *equivalence* between dU_1 and p_1, our preceding remarks about the relationship between the areas under the demand curve and net benefits to the consumer could have been interpreted more rigorously. *We could in fact have equated net benefits (consumer's surplus) with areas under the demand curve.*

But as we move down the demand curve in Figure 18.2.2, the consumer's real income changes because of the income effect of the price change. Or, at least, it will do as long as our demand curve is of the general 'Marshallian' type derived in Chapter 2. It will be remembered that the significant factor about that curve was that it incorporated both the substitution and income effects of a price change. But if real income changes as we move down the demand curve, dU_Y, the marginal utility of income will also change. And this introduces a variable element into our attempt to measure consumer's surplus by areas under the demand curve. We can offer the interim conclusion then that areas under Marshallian demand curves do not measure consumer's surplus, at least not accurately. In practical work we might be prepared to accept that some error is involved and that the error is not substantial, but this would be a matter of judgement.

Or, if the marginal utility of income was constant regardless of the amount of x_1 bought, we would have a proportional relationship between price and dU_1 such that areas under demand curves would be proportionally related to consumer's surplus in terms of utility.

Having stated the problem, the escapes from it should be fairly self-evident. The trouble arises because of the fact that an income effect is incorporated into the Marshallian demand curve. The simple solution is to eliminate the income effect, which has the effect of making the marginal utility of income constant. Marshall's own approach was to eliminate the income effect by assuming vertically parallel indifference curves (see Section 2.8). The Marshallian measure of consumer's surplus in a context of vertically parallel indifference curves is shown below in Figure 18.2.3.

By drawing the indifference curves vertically parallel we establish that $PRS_{x_1,Y}$ at A is equal to $PRS_{x_1,Y}$ at B. (Figure 18.2.3 can be compared to Figure 2.8.2 where the vertical axis is x_2 and the indifference

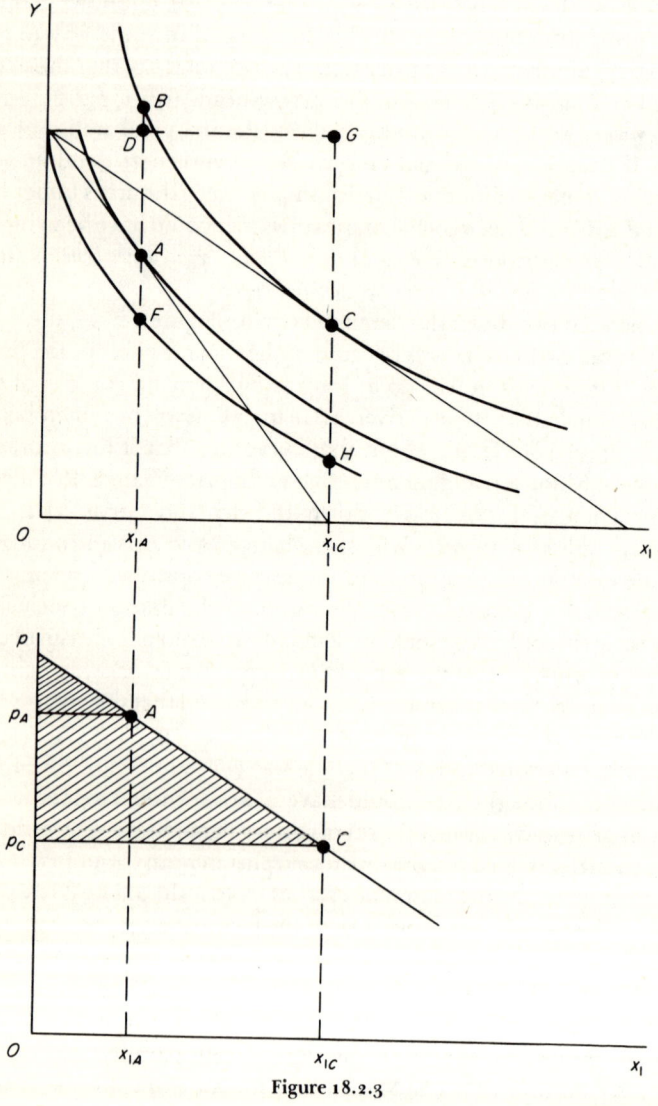

Figure 18.2.3

Normative Price Theory

curves are vertically parallel.) Any increase in money-income in Figure 18.2.3 shifts the consumer's position in such a way that more Y is consumed but the same amount of x_1 is consumed. A change in the price of x_1 will alter the amounts of both Y and x_1 consumed. Thus a change in the price of x_1 may move the consumer from A to C in Figure 18.2.3. Note that the slope of the budget line in this particular case *is* the price of x_1. This is because p_Y has, by definition, been set equal to unity.[1]

So far then, we have an initial consumer equilibrium at A, and a new equilibrium at C after a price fall in good 1. At A the consumer buys an amount x_1 at a price given by the distance AD.[2] To calculate the consumer's surplus attached to situation A we need to know what the maximum amount is that the consumer would be willing to pay in order to avoid going without good 1 altogether. We assume in this respect that the consumer is *able* to go without good 1.[3] Given the budget line through A, going without good 1 would mean moving to situation E which is on a lower indifference curve. Hence we can rephrase our question as: 'what sum of money is the consumer willing to pay to remain at A rather than move to situation E?' Now E is indifferent to F at which the same amount of x_1 as at A is bought. Accordingly, the consumer should be willing to pay any amount up to, but no greater than, DF in order to stay at A. We now have all we need to measure consumer's surplus in this context.

DF is the maximum sum the consumer is willing to pay to stay at A.
DA is the sum he actually pays to secure A.
Hence $DF - DA = AF$ is his consumer's surplus.

We can relate the measure AF to an area beneath the demand curve

---

[1] If the indifference curves are vertically parallel, $PRS_{x_1, Y}$ at $A = PRS_{x_1, Y}$ at B, by definition. Hence $dU_1/p_1 = dU_Y/p_Y$ at both A and B. But we know that $p_Y = 1$, dU_1 is the same at A and B (since B lies directly above A and the quantity of x_1 has not therefore changed), and p_1 is also the same at A and B. Hence dU_Y must be the same at B as it is at A.

[2] Remember that the slope of the budget line is given by the price of good 1. If we treat Ox_{1A} as one unit, the slope of the budget line tangential to A is $AD/FD = AD/1 = AD$, and hence the price of good 1 is given by the distance AD.

[3] Which in turn means that there will be some combination of Y and x_1 which includes a zero amount of x_1. This obviously means that our indifference curves cut the vertical axis, thus violating the strict convexity axiom. Where a good is a *necessity*, indifference curves will not cut the axes and the above analysis does not apply. The reader should not assume that indispensable goods are insignificant – what one person can do without others cannot. Since consumer surplus analysis is often applied to situations where people are required or asked to forgo their homes, their community, or some deeply personal commodity, it is very proper to question whether the analysis is even *prima facie* applicable in many situations.

derived from the indifference map in Figure 18.2.3. The demand curve shown is derived directly from the slopes of the budget lines in the upper part of the figure because, as we saw, these slopes were definitionally equal to the price of good 1. The distance AD in the upper diagram is therefore equal to $Op_A AX_{1A}$ in the lower diagram. Similarly, $CG = Op_C Cx_{1C}$. The surplus at A is AF in the upper diagram, equal to the dark shaded area in the lower diagram. The surplus at C is CH, equal to the dark plus light shaded areas in the lower diagram. The change in consumer surplus is the light shaded area in the lower diagram, equal to $CH - AF$ in the upper diagram.[1]

To sum up so far, we have established two propositions:
(i) the measurement of consumer's surplus is ambiguous if the demand curve is 'Marshallian' in the sense of including both income and substitution effects;
(ii) the area under a (true) 'Marshallian' demand curve is an unambiguous measure of consumer's surplus, where the demand curve is derived from an indifference map containing vertically parallel indifference curves.

Marshall's case, as we have shown it, requires the marginal utility of income to be held constant. As the demand curve derived from the vertically parallel set of indifference curves shows, this is implied by holding real income constant.

18.3 Hicks's Four Measures of Consumer's Surplus

The last section concluded that the Marshallian measure of consumer's surplus was unambiguous only if the indifference map contained the unlikely property of being vertically parallel. We now need to consider what the measure of consumer's surplus might be if the PRS between Y and x_1 changes as we move up the line $ABCD$ in Figure 18.2.2. In other words, we need a measure of consumer's surplus in the more likely case of indifference curves not being vertically parallel.

In a seminal article, Hicks reformulated the concept of consumer's surplus.[2] Figure 18.3.1 shows the familiar indifference map of the con-

---

[1] Proofs of these equivalences are tedious. The interested reader can consult D. M. Winch, *Analytical Welfare Economics* (Penguin, 1972) ch. 8, for the methodology.

[2] The student is best advised to begin with J. R. Hicks, 'The Four Consumers' Surpluses', *Review of Economic Studies*, 1944, although even this article is a reply to some criticism made by A. M. Henderson of Hicks's original treatment in the first edition of his *Value and Capital*. Alternatively, to avoid the arguments and counter-arguments, interesting though these are, the student should consult J. R. Hicks, *Revision of Demand Theory* (O.U.P., London, 1956) ch. 8.

sumer. A move in the budget line from H_1 to H_2 indicates a fall in the price of x_1. H_3 is drawn parallel to H_2 and H_4 is drawn parallel to H_1. The consumer is initially in equilibrium at X. His new equilibrium is Y. Utility has increased and we need a measure of this increased net benefit to the consumer. Hicks first defined a *compensating variation* (CV) as a sum of money which when paid or received would leave the consumer in his *initial* welfare situation. In Figure 18.3.1, for example, the consumer benefits by moving from X to Y. We can then argue that the consumer should be willing to pay some sum of money to secure the benefits of buying at the lower price of x_1. In Figure 18.3.1 this sum of

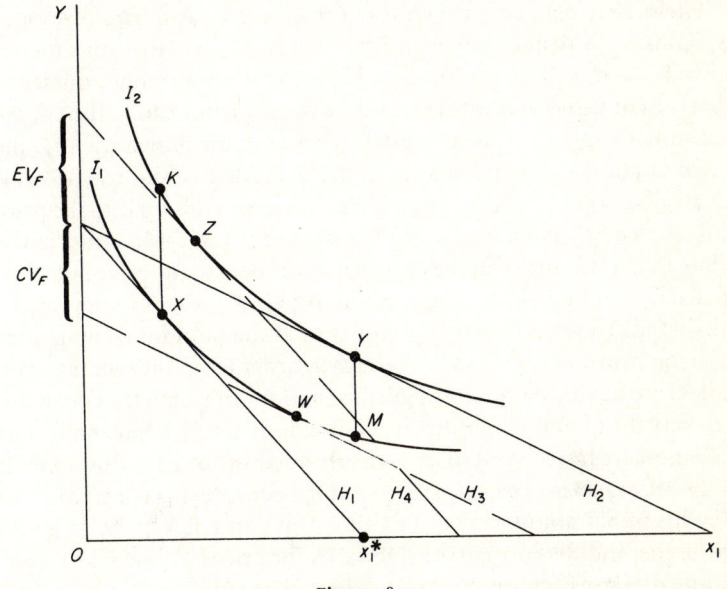

Figure 18.3.1

money will be given by CV_F (the subscript F reminds us that we are analysing it in terms of a price fall, of convenience). CV_F is the maximum sum of money which the consumer would be willing to pay to get to position Y. This is because, if he reaches Y, payment of CV_F would put him on the lower budget line H_3 and at position W where he is as well off as he was at X. Notice that the consumer is free to change the quantity that he buys in the sense that he moves from Y to W by making the compensating payment. We shall need a different measure if the consumer is constrained to buy at the new position Y. Accordingly, we distinguish two types of CV_F. First, we have $CV_{F,P}$ which is the *price compensating variation*, which measures the payment the consumer would make to secure the price fall assuming he can choose the quantity he buys. Second, we have $CV_{F,Q}$ which is the *quantity compensating variation*. In this latter case, the consumer is constrained to buy x_1^*, the amount of x_1 at Y, and the amount he would have bought in light of the price fall and if no compensating payments were made. The relevant measure in this case is YM, for at Y he can pay YM, still consume x_1^*, and return to his old indifference curve. That is, the consumer should be willing to pay YM to secure the price fall if he is constrained to buy the amount of x_1 relevant to Y.

Hicks next defined an *equivalent variation* (EV) as a sum of money which is equivalent to the price fall and which leaves the consumer in his *subsequent* welfare position. In Figure 18.3.1 we remind ourselves that the consumer increases his utility by going from X to Y. If, at X, the consumer's income was increased by an amount shown by EV_F, the price of good 1 remaining as at X, the consumer would reach Z. Z is clearly as good as Y which is where the consumer ends up with the price fall. Hence EV_F is a measure of the consumer's increased utility in the sense that it is a sum of money which is equivalent to the price fall. Now Z is achieved only if (a) compensation is paid; (b) the price level stays unaltered. Hence EV_F can be thought of as the minimum compensation the consumer is willing to receive in order to go without the price fall. Once again, we can distinguish situations in which the consumer can vary the quantities he buys from situations in which he cannot. The EV_F measure introduced so far is clearly unconstrained in this sense. It is the *price equivalent variation* $(EV_{F,P})$. If the consumer is constrained to buy his initial amount of x_1, he will require an amount XK to get to the higher indifference curve achieved by the price fall, and if he is constrained to consume his initial quantities, the consumer would require XK in compensation. $EV_{F,Q}$ is therefore the *quantity equivalent variation*.

In terms of Figure 18.3.1 we have four measures of consumer's surplus for a *price fall*. These are:

$CV_{F,P}$ = price compensating variation;
$CV_{F,Q}$ = quantity compensating variation = distance YM;
$EV_{F,P}$ = price equivalent variation;
$EV_{F,Q}$ = quantity equivalent variation = distance XK.

We can easily reverse the picture and consider a *price rise*. Consider the move from H_2 to H_1 in Figure 18.3.1. This is a move from Y to X. Suppose we look for just the price compensating variation. This will be a sum of money required by the consumer to compensate him for suffering the effects of the price rise, which sum, if received, would put him back on his initially higher indifference curve. In Figure 18.3.1 this will be the sum of money shown by EV_F since this will return the consumer to the higher indifference curve, though at Z instead of Y. Consequently we have the equation

$$EV_{F,P} = CV_{R,P}$$

that is, the price equivalent variation for a price fall is equal to the price compensating variation for a price rise.

Similar analysis would show that

$$EV_{R,P} = CV_{F,P}$$
$$EV_{R,Q} = CV_{F,Q}$$
$$EV_{F,Q} = CV_{R,Q}.$$

It follows that, although there are four measures of surplus for a price fall and four for a price rise, these equivalences reduce the total number of surpluses to four over all.

Figure 18.3.2 illustrates these four measures and the ordinary Marshallian measure on one figure. Curve D_H^0 is the Hicksian compensated demand curve derived from looking at the substitution effects on the *lower* indifference curve in Figure 18.3.1. It is, in fact, the Hicksian compensated demand curve we introduced in Chapter 2. D_H^1, on the other hand, is the Hicksian compensated demand curve derived from looking at the substitution effects on the *upper* indifference curve in Figure 18.3.1 – e.g. by looking at moves such as that from Z to Y. The reasoning is entirely analogous to that used for the previously analysed compensated demand curve. D_M is the ordinary Marshallian demand curve including both income and substitution effects.

The relevant correspondences are then

(a) $CV_{F,P} = P_1 . P_2 . D . B .$ – that is, the change in the price compensating variation because of the price fall is measured by the change in the area under the Hicksian compensated demand curve D_H^0.

(b) $EV_{F,P} = P_1 . P_2 . E . C .$ – that is, the change in the price equivalent variation because of the price fall is measured by the change in the area under the Hicksian compensated demand curve D_H^1.

(c) Area $P_1 . P_2 . E . B . =$ the change in the area under the 'Marshallian' demand curve and this is the ambiguous measure of

consumer's surplus introduced earlier.
  (d) $CV_{F,Q} = P_1 . P_2 . D . B - DEF = CV_{F,P} - DEF$.
  (e) $EV_{F,Q} = P_1 . P_2 . E . C . + ABC = EV_{F,P} + ABC$.

These results suggest that, first, EV will be greater than CV for a price fall (and vice versa for a price rise). Second, the Marshallian measure will not coincide with any of Hicks's four measures unless there is a zero income effect (vertically parallel indifference curves), in which case all the three demand curves in Figure 18.3.2 will coincide and the

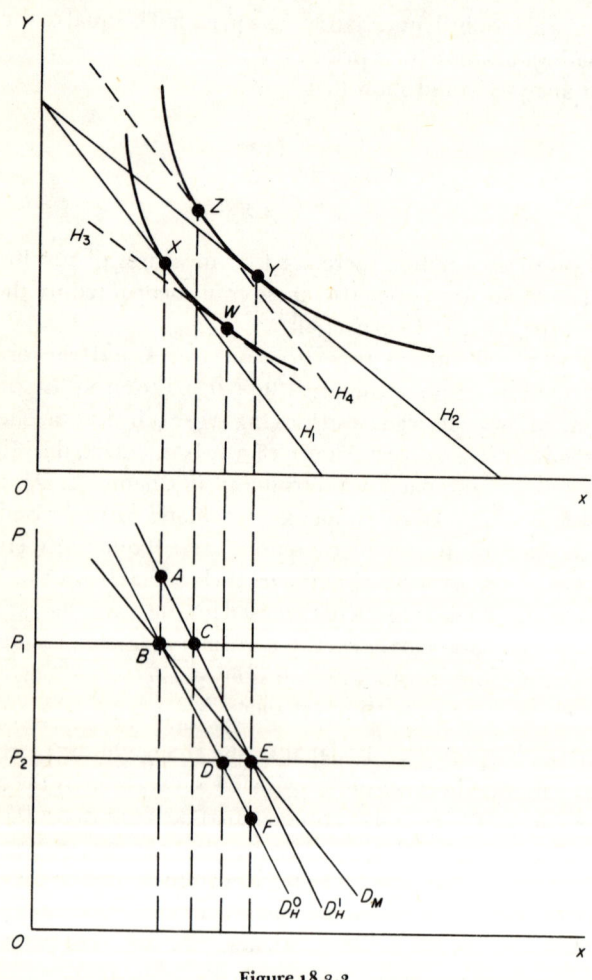

Figure 18.3.2

Marshallian measure will be unambiguous. Third, the quantity compensating variation will be less than the price compensating variation for a price fall. Fourth, the price equivalent variation will be less than the quantity equivalent variation for a price fall.

Notice that all the preceding analysis in this section has been in terms of a price change. Clearly, practical examples will exist in which consumers have to forgo or be introduced to a commodity. That is, we should analyse the situation for introduction or removal of a commodity. Figure 18.3.3 shows how this is done. The new commodity, or the commodity to be removed, is measured on the horizontal axis. The vertical axis is again income. The consumer is assumed initially to be at A where he consumes some money income but none of x_1.[1] He is on indifference curve 1. Then the commodity is introduced and he moves to B, on a higher indifference curve.

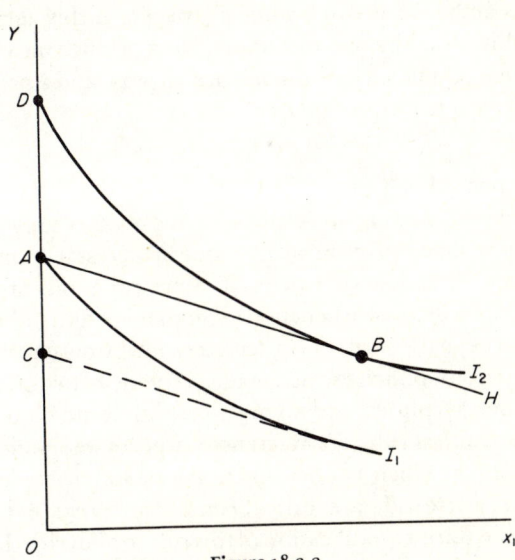

Figure 18.3.3

His price-compensating variation is given by the distance AC, and his price-equivalent variation by the distance AD. If we now assume the commodity is to be removed, we begin at B and move to A. By our previous definitions, his CV_p will be AD and his EV_p will be AC.

In practical work it is often the Marshallian measure which is used. The quantity variation measures are not generally thought to be

[1] Since x_1 does not exist yet, he cannot be to the right of A.

applicable since consumers are not widely constrained in the manner these measures imply. Although the Marshallian measure is ambiguous, it is usually argued that the income effects of the projects in question are not sufficiently large for the practitioner to worry about the fine differences between the Hicksian measures and the Marshallian measures. Indeed, since there is also some dispute about the relative merits of CV_p and EV_p the Marshallian measure might even be thought of as some compromise (since it can be thought of as an average of the two – see Figure 18.3.2). Most important, however, is the fact that, if any demand curve at all can be estimated, it is often only the Marshallian curve, although other examples of practical work can be found in which compensated demand curves are estimated.

For policy purposes it is obviously not very useful to have measures of consumers' surplus for each individual unless those surpluses can be added together to provide some aggregate. If this aggregate was meaningful it would be possible to say that a positive measure would indicate a net gain to society, on balance anyway, and a negative total would indicate a net loss to society.

18.4 Compensation Tests

The problem with adding up surpluses in the manner suggested in the last section is that policy measures almost necessarily make some people better off and some worse off. Since no goods are free, any policy measure will involve benefits to some and costs to others, even if the costs accrue in the form of higher taxes only. Consequently, a rule which approved of policies which made everyone better off (increased their consumer surpluses) and no one worse off would be an unexceptionable but fruitless rule. For reference purposes we should note that such situations, in which a policy makes at least some people better off and no one worse off, are called *Pareto Improvements*. Obviously, however, we require a modification of this rule to allow for the fact that there are always losers.

The modification proposed by neoclassical welfare economics is the *compensation test*. Essentially, it is very simple. If we add up the consumers' surpluses of those who gain and add up the lost consumers' surpluses of those who lose, we shall have one of three situations:

(a) The sum of gainers' CS exceeds the sum of losers' CS.
(b) The sum of gainers' CS is less than the sum of losers' CS.
(c) The two sums are equal.

If (a) occurs, we could argue that the gainers could transfer money to the losers in such a way as to make the losers no worse off than they were before. The amount transferred would be less than the gainers have gained so that they would still have something left over. Hence the gainers still gain (but not so much compared to their gains if they did not pay the compensation) and the losers stay at the same utility level as before. The transfer enables us to determine that such a situation would be a Pareto improvement in the sense defined above. Similar reasoning would show that situation (b) would be a Pareto deterioration, and situation (c) would imply a policy which offered neither improvement nor worsening of the present situation.

The idea that policies can be judged in terms of the feasibility of compensation originates with articles by Kaldor and Hicks.[1] Hence, a policy is said to meet the *Kaldor–Hicks* test if the sum of gainers' consumers' surplus exceeds the sum of the losers' consumers' surplus. The test is not met if the situation is as in (b) or (c) above, and the policy would be judged not worthwhile. A complication with the criterion, however, is that it is not suggested that compensation *should* be paid. It is argued that it is only necessary for compensation to be payable in principle. That is, a policy will be judged worthwhile if case (a) above is met, but no compensation is paid, so that the losers remain losers and the gainers actually secure their initial gains. Obviously, a rule which does not require payment of compensation will be a much stronger rule since universal transfers of the kind that would be required would involve a complexity of organisation that no economy is likely to manage.

Consider a policy which entails a price fall benefiting some people and a price rise incurring losses for others. We can say that $CV_{F,p}$ will reflect the maximum compensation which the gainers would be willing to pay. Similarly, $CV_{R,p}$ will measure the minimum that the losers would accept. The Kaldor–Hicks test would *not* be met – that is, the policy would not be worth undertaking – if

$$\sum_{G} CV < \sum_{L} CV$$

where the subscripts G and L remind us that there are two groups, gainers and losers. Now consider the possibility of the losers paying

---

[1] Strictly, the Kaldor–Hicks tests as originally proposed were different. The current tendency is to lump them together, as we have done here. For the original articles see N. Kaldor, 'Welfare Propositions and Interpersonal Comparisons of Utility', *Economic Journal*, 1939; and J. R. Hicks, 'The Valuation of Social Income', *Economica*, 1940.

the gainers to forgo the change. Since the (potential) gainers are now to go without a benefit, they will require some equivalent compensation – measured by their EVs. Equally, the maximum sum that the potential losers will be willing to pay is their EV. Clearly, the potential losers will succeed in preventing the change if

$$\sum_G EV < \sum_L EV$$

but they will *fail* to prevent the change if

$$\sum_G EV < \sum_L EV$$

Consequently, a contradiction could arise if gainers' CVs were less than losers' CVs, *and* if gainers' EVs were greater than losers' EVs. We wish to know if

$$\sum_G CV < \sum_L CV \quad (1)$$

$$\sum_G EV > \sum_L EV \quad (2)$$

can both be true. In addition, we have to remember that

$$\sum_G EV > \sum_G CV \quad (3)$$

$$\sum_L CV > \sum_L EV \quad (4)$$

If inequalities (1) – (4) can be satisfied simultaneously, we shall have shown that (*a*) a policy is not worth undertaking on the Kaldor–Hicks test, but (*b*), if undertaken, could not be repealed by using the test. In short, the test would not justify the policy, but nor would it justify the repeal of the policy if it were undertaken, which would be odd.

Some arbitrary numbers will demonstrate that (1) – (4) can be simultaneously satisfied. Let $CV_L = 6$, $CV_G = 2$, $EV_G = 4$ and $EV_L = 3$. Then, on substitution in (1) – (4), all equations are seen to be satisfied. The possibility of this 'paradox' was first noted by Scitovsky.[1] The paradox may also arise for the case where the policy move is justified by the Kaldor–Hicks test, but the move back is also justified. This happens when either $EV_G < CV_G$ (the opposite of condition (3) above) or $EV_L > CV_L$ (negating condition (4)), or both. This can only arise if one of the goods has a negative income effect – that is, is an inferior good.

[1] T. Scitovsky, 'A Note on Welfare Propositions in Economics', *Review of Economic Studies*, 1941–2.

18.5 Pareto-Optimal Allocations

The previous sections have suggested that the concept of consumer's surplus, allied with the Kaldor–Hicks compensation test, provide a foundation for a normative economics. How far the foundation is a satisfactory one is very debatable, not least because the use of a compensation test which does not require compensation to be paid will, of course, lead to substantial changes in the distribution of welfare between individuals. For any one policy the change may be slight. For all policies it must be significant unless those policies are executed in such a way as to provide gains to specific sections of the population which are later offset by losses, and vice versa. Failure to incorporate distributional effects into policy judgements is tantamount to recommending the distribution of welfare that follows a policy change. It is not therefore an issue of *extra* value judgements entering the picture when distributional effects are incorporated, since a tacit value judgement has already been made by arguing that they should be excluded. However, this is an issue which the reader can follow up in texts on public economics. We now wish to consider the Pareto rule in a general equilibrium context.

In fact, the relationship between our surplus rules and the requirements of Pareto optimality is a direct one. A Pareto improvement was defined in Section 18.4 as a move which made at least some people better off and no one worse off. From this definition we can easily derive a definition of a Pareto optimum: it must be a state in which no change could be made which would effect a Pareto improvement. In a Pareto optimum we would certainly be able to make some people better off but only at the expense of making others worse off. We can immediately relate this to consumer's surplus. A Pareto optimum will exist if we cannot improve some people's surplus without decreasing that of others.

We can illustrate the idea of a Pareto optimum by looking at an economy in which we assume there are only two people, A and B. Figure 18.5.1 shows A's indifference map in the normal way. But we have superimposed B's indifference map on the figure as well. This is done by turning B's map upside down and beginning at point O'. The resulting 'box' figure is then easily interpreted.[1] The size of the 'box' is set by the available quantities of x_1 and x_2 in our simple economy. We shall return to the issue of how these amounts are determined: for the

---

[1] If in doubt, turn the page upside down and think of O' as the normal origin for B's indifference map.

moment we take them as given. So far then we have (a) some given amounts of two goods, (b) utility functions for individuals A and B.

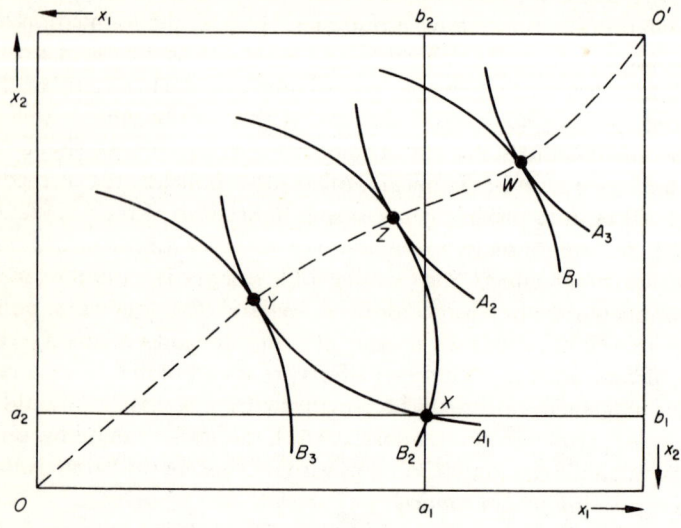

Figure 18.5.1

Suppose we allocate goods so as to achieve point X in Figure 18.5.1. Then A will have Oa_1 of good 1, and Oa_2 of good 2. B must then have the rest – that is, $O'b_1$ of good 2, and $O'b_2$ of good 1. The question we need to answer is whether this allocation at X is optimal. It is easy to see that it is not. Suppose we reallocate goods so as to move along the section XZ of B_2 – one of B's indifference curves. By definition B is indifferent betwen X and Z. Hence he is no worse off by such a move. But A's utility increases because we take him off indifference curve A_1 and move him to A_2. The move from X to Z must therefore be a Pareto improvement. Similarly, a move from X to Y would be an improvement. If the exercise is repeated, it will be seen that a move from *any* point *off* the line through YZW to a point *on* that line will be a Pareto improvement. But a move from, say, Y to Z is one we cannot evaluate on the simple rule advanced so far, for it involves an improvement for A but a deterioration in utility for B. The line YZW is the *contract curve*: it shows all the combinations of goods that will give rise to a Pareto optimum. But, as we have seen, there are many optima, each corresponding to a different combination of abilities to buy the goods in question – that is, to differing distributions of income. If we persist in the view that we should not make judgements about the desirable distribution of income, it is obvious that we shall have nothing to say about which point on the contract curve is best. If, on the other hand, we do permit such judgements, we shall be able to pinpoint an *optimum optimorum*.

If we look at the optima in Figure 18.5.1, we see that they all occur where indifference curves are tangential to each other. Such a tangency means that the *PRS*s of *A* and *B* between the two goods must be equal. That is, we can write that an optimum requires

$$PRS^A_{x_1,x_2} = PRS^B_{x_1,x_2}$$

and this equation can be generalised for any number of individuals. Note too that this equation relates back to our measures of consumer's surplus. The move from *X* to *Z*, for example, was a move which enabled *A*'s surplus to increase and *B*'s to stay the same.

We have said nothing so far about the production side – that is, about what determines the size of the box in Figure 18.5.1 and its particular dimensions. In fact, we can illustrate this fairly easily by use of a similar box figure. In Figure 18.5.2 the axes are now capital (*K*) and labour (*L*) and instead of two consumers we consider two products, 1

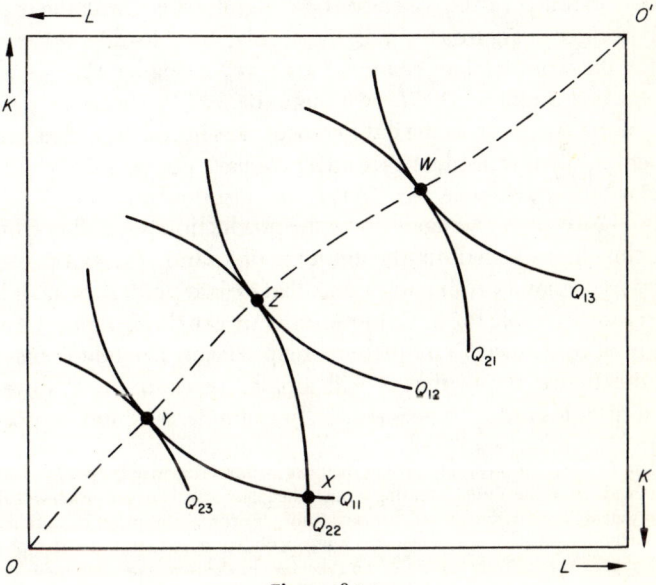

Figure 18.5.2

and 2, with the production function of good 1 being 'viewed' from origin O, and good 2 from origin O'. The production isoquants are shown as Q_{11}, Q_{12}, Q_{13} for good 1 and Q_{21}, Q_{22}, Q_{23} for good 2. Consideration of a point such as X will show that it is inefficient in the sense that we can move to Z and increase the output of good 1 without decreasing the output of good 2. Unless good 1 is undesirable, our axiom of dominance (see Chapter 1) will ensure that this results in an increase in utility. Hence Z must be preferred to X. If the analysis is repeated it will be found that *any* point *off* the locus $OYZWO'$ is inefficient in this sense.

Now the efficiency locus in Figure 18.5.2 shows different combinations of inputs, but it also shows us the different combinations of outputs which are efficient. We can therefore plot these output combinations in Figure 18.5.3 as a *production possibility frontier* or *transformation curve*. Note that, since production isoquants in Figure 18.5.2 are tangential on the efficiency locus, we have

$$MRTS^1_{K,L} = MRTS^2_{K,L}$$

that is, marginal rates of technical substitution are equal along the production possibility frontier in Figure 18.5.3. Points inside the frontier correspond to points off the efficiency locus in Figure 18.5.2.[1]

We can integrate the consumer box (Figure 18.5.1) with the production frontier in Figure 18.5.3. Quite simply, the consumer box must fit inside the frontier. Two examples are given in Figure 18.5.3 – a particular box might be $OABE$ or it might be $OFCD$. Figure 18.5.4 takes one of these and shows the indifference maps inside the consumer box which, in turn, is inside the frontier. We have not yet said how a particular box is to be selected. To this we must now turn.

In Figure 18.5.5 we again show the production possibility frontier. But this time we shall fix the amounts of x_1 and x_2 that A possesses. Suppose he has a combination such that he is at point A. What is left is therefore available for B. Consequently, we can think of point A as the origin of consumer B's indifference map. Placing his indifference map on the figure shows that B will aim to reach point K since this maximises his utility. If he was at Z, for example, he could improve his

---

[1] The production possibility frontier shown assumes decreasing returns to scale in both products. If there are increasing returns the frontier will be concave. It will also be noted that we have assumed well-behaved utility functions and production functions. The reader may wish to experiment with linear production isoquants, for example. The result will be that optima will occur on the edges of the box – we shall have 'corner' solutions.

utility level by moving to K without in any way affecting A. Such a move would, by definition, be a Pareto improvement. We could switch consumers, making A the origin for A's indifference map, and the same conclusion would follow. But we already know that the personal rates

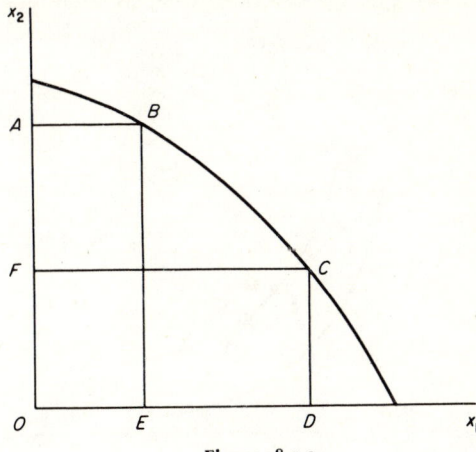

Figure 18.5.3

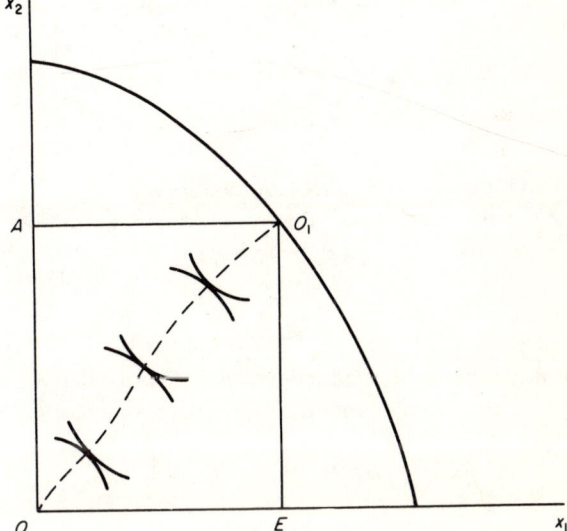

Figure 18.5.4

of substitution must be equal for there to be a Pareto optimum. Figure 18.5.5 suggests that each individual's *PRS* should also be equal to the marginal rate of product transformation shown by the slope of the production possibility frontier. In short, we shall not reach a Pareto optimum unless we meet the following total condition:

$$PRS^A_{x_1,x_2} = PRS^B_{x_1,x_2} = MRT_{x_1,x_2}$$

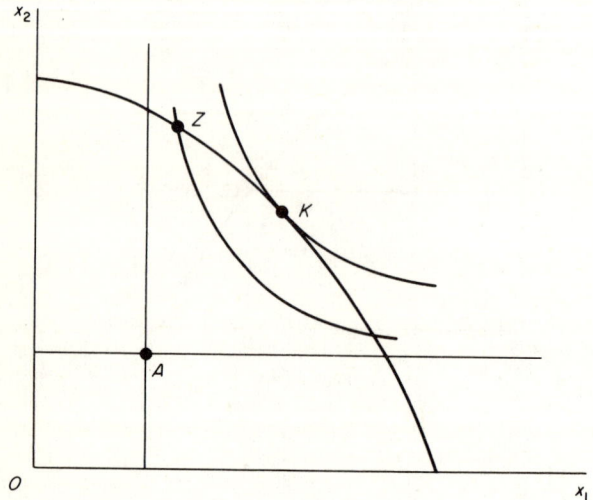

Figure 18.5.5

18.6 The Optimality of Perfect Competition

From the equation for overall Pareto optimality we can derive some interesting results. MRT_{x_1,x_2} can be written as

$$\frac{dx_1}{dx_2}$$

since it is the slope of the production possibility frontier. But dx_1 is the change in the output of x_1 and must be equal to

$$dx_1 = -[dL \cdot MP_L(x_1) + dK \cdot MP_K(x_1)].$$

Similarly,

$$dx_2 = -[dL \cdot MP_L(x_2) + dK \cdot MP_K(x_2)]$$

so that
$$MRT_{x_1,x_2} = \frac{dx_1}{dx_2} = -\frac{MP_L(x_1)}{MP_L(x_2)} = -\frac{MP_K(x_1)}{MP_K(x_2)}.$$

Now, for any firm we know that
$$MC = \frac{W}{MP_L} = \frac{R}{MP_K}$$

where W is the price of labour, R the price of capital (rate of interest), and MC is the marginal (product) cost. Hence
$$MP_L = \frac{W}{MC} = \frac{R}{MC}.$$

We also know that
$$MRS_{x_1,x_2} = \frac{MU_{x_2}}{MU_{x_1}} = \frac{p_{x_2}}{p_{x_1}}$$

for any consumer in equilibrium. Hence
$$\frac{p^A_{x_2}}{p^A_{x_1}} = \frac{p^B_{x_2}}{p^B_{x_1}} = \frac{W_1 \cdot MC_{x_2}}{W_2 \cdot MC_{x_1}}$$

which tells us that the ratio of prices faced by each consumer, A and B, must be equal to the ratio of wage rates in the industries multiplied by the ratio of marginal costs for there to be Pareto optimality.

Now, under perfect competition, price discrimination cannot be practised so that
$$p^A_{x_1} = p^B_{x_1}$$
and
$$W_1 = W_2.$$

Substituting back gives
$$\frac{p_{x_2}}{p_{x_1}} = \frac{MC_{x_2}}{MC_{x_1}},$$

Now we consider the supply of labour. In balancing the claims of leisure and work on his time the consumer will meet the following condition
$$MRS_{D,x} = MRT_{D,x}$$

where D is leisure and x is a good bought by the consumer. But the $MRT_{D,x}$ must be the output which would be produced if leisure time was used as work, so that

$$\frac{dx}{dD} = MP_L(x).$$

Also, $MRS_{D,x}$ must equal a ratio of prices. But the price of leisure is the wage forgone, W. Hence

$$MRS_{D,x} = W/P_x.$$

Hence we have

$$MRS_{D,x} = MRT_{D,x} = \frac{W}{P_x} = MP_L(x) = \frac{W}{MC_x}.$$

But the last equation will hold true only if

$$P_x = MC_x.$$

We establish, then, that a Pareto optimum will exist if prices everywhere are set equal to marginal cost. But under perfect competition, prices are equal to marginal cost since this condition maximises profits for firms. Hence, on the heroic assumption that our analysis has not omitted major qualifications, we establish that perfect competition maximises welfare in the sense that it secures a Pareto optimum.

18.7 The Problem of Second Best

There are in fact many serious qualifications to be made to the conclusion of the previous section. We know that factor and product markets are not perfect, that economies of scale exist, that marginal private cost does not reflect the true cost of production to society (because of the many uncompensated social costs that exist), and so on. In this section we shall look at just one modification.

Suppose we have an economy in which some products are not priced equal to marginal cost, and that we have no way of altering this situation. We shall not be able to secure a Pareto optimum in the sense of setting price equal to marginal cost everywhere – a 'first best' is not available to us. It is tempting to think that we shall do the best we can – that is, secure a 'second best' – if we aim to set as many prices as possible equal to marginal cost. In fact, however, it can be demonstrated that observance of the 'first best' rules by those firms that can be subjected to direction will not even secure a 'second best'. The most

Normative Price Theory

explicit formulation of this 'theorem of the second best' is due to Lipsey and Lancaster.[1]

The Lipsey–Lancaster conclusions can be stated as:

(i) If at least one of the Paretian first-best conditions is not met, second-best optima can only be achieved by departing from *all* other Paretian first-best conditions.

(ii) While it is tempting to think that it will improve things to minimise the number of 'failures' to observe first-best conditions, provided at least one first-best condition remains unmet we *cannot* say whether welfare will be improved or not by such a procedure.

To make this is a little easier, imagine a list of first-best conditions, shown in Figure 18.7.1. Suppose we are at point X, with all the conditions from O to X met, but those from X to Z not met. Statement (ii) above says that moving from X to Y may or may not improve welfare, we cannot say without what is in effect a full general equilibrium analysis. A move from X to Z would, of course, achieve first best.

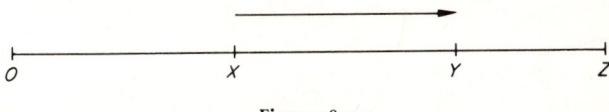

Figure 18.7.1

Similarly, if we imagine the same lines applied to two sectors (public and private perhaps), reaching Z in one sector and staying at X in the other will *not* achieve a second best (statement (i) above). It will be necessary to operate at, say, X in both sectors, but the rules are not obvious.

Figure 18.7.2 illustrates the theorem. Suppose there are two firms X and Y, each producing goods 1 and 2, quantities of which are denoted by X_1 and X_2. TT' is the transformation function *for each firm*, assumed identical. The economy's production frontier is therefore $STST'$. Now suppose firm X is constrained to produce at B on TT', whereas Y can produce anywhere on his transformation function. To construct the constrained ST function, suppose Y also produces at B on his TT'. Then point C denotes one point on the constrained ST function. Now suppose Y produces at T, and X is of course still constrained to produce

---

[1] R. G. Lipsey and K. Lancaster, 'The General Theory of Second Best', *Review of Economic Studies*, 1956–7.

at B. Social output is now the combination of X_1 and X_2 given at B, *plus* OT of X_2, giving point D as a point on the constrained function. If Y selects T' as his production point, similar analysis will give E as the constrained point.

Thus, whereas $STST'$ is the unconstrained ST function, the ST function when X is constrained to produce at B is given by DCE. If it were possible to think of some function reflecting *social* welfare, we could superimpose the welfare function (W_0, W_1, W_2). We see that point G is the *unconstrained* social optimum. At G, rates of product transformation are equal for both firms and are also equal to rates of social substitution. We have a Pareto optimum.

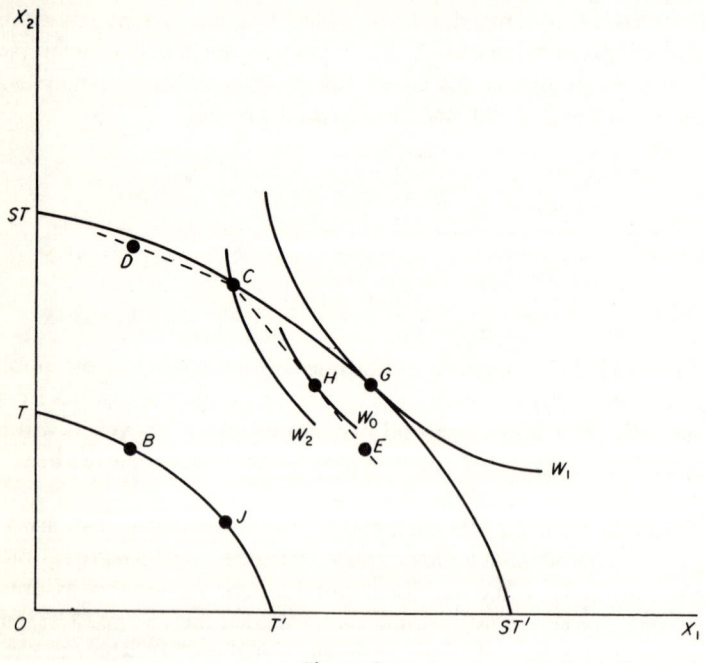

Figure 18.7.2

But in the constrained case, X produces at B. If firm Y is made to produce at B as well, social welfare is not maximised ($W_2 < W_0$). The second-best solution is in fact at H. But H corresponds to a situation where X is producing at B and Y is producing at a point like J – that is, rates of product transformation are not equalised across firms.

18.8 Public Goods

The efficient allocation conditions derived in Section 18.5 will also be incorrect if, as is almost certainly the case in real economies, the economy contains *public goods*. Throughout this book we have been concerned with *private goods*. Private goods have two features. First, they are *excludable* – there exists some mechanism whereby the good can be priced or rationed so as to prevent other people from enjoying the benefits of the good. Second, private goods are *rival* – consumption of the good by one person precludes its simultaneous consumption by another person. But a public good has exactly the opposite features – it is *non-rival* in the sense that its provision to individual A entails its provision to individual B, whether he wants it or not. The most obvious example is national defence. In addition, it is *non-excludable* in that we cannot prevent individual B securing the benefits (if they exist) of the good. If such a good exists, then it follows that each individual consumes the same amount of it. Its provision to one person entails its provision to everyone else.

To underline this distinction, we can write the amount available of a *private* good (x_{PR}) as the sum of the amounts consumed by the individuals (A, B etc.) in the community. We have

$$x_{PR} = x_{PR}^A + x_{PR}^B + x_{PR}^C + \ldots x_{PR}^N$$

whereas for the public good (x_{PU}) we shall have to write

$$x_{PU} = x_{PU}^A = x_{PU}^B = x_{PU}^C = \ldots x_{PU}^N.$$

How does the existence of public goods affect the marginal equivalences established in Section 18.5? We can deal with the marginal rate of transformation, MRT, straight away. A public good has to be produced just like any other good, so that the equivalence between $MRTS$s is not affected. We can therefore think of a transformation function between public and private goods just like the transformation function between two private goods. It is the marginal rate of substitution side that causes the problem.

If we increase the amount of the public good by some small amount Δx the extra utility to any one consumer, i, will be

$$\frac{dU^i}{dx} \cdot \Delta x.$$

But in increasing the supply of x to consumer i we have, *ex hypothesi*, increased it for j, k, l, m and so on. The total 'social' increase in utility

(ΔSU) must therefore be

$$\Delta SU_{PU} = \frac{dU^i}{dx} \cdot \Delta x + \frac{dU^j}{dx} \cdot \Delta x + \frac{dU^k}{dx} \cdot \Delta x + \text{etc.} \qquad (1)$$

$$= \Delta x \cdot \left[\frac{dU^i}{dx} + \frac{dU^i}{dx} + \frac{dU^k}{dx} + \ldots \right]$$

$$= \Delta x \sum_i^m \frac{dU}{dx}$$

where m is the number of consumers involved. Now the marginal rate of substitution, $MRS_{PU,PR}$ for any one individual i is in fact

$$MRS^i_{PU,PR} = \frac{MU^i_{PU}}{MU^i_{PR}}.$$

Hence we can rewrite (1) as

$$\frac{\Delta SU_{PU}}{\Delta x \cdot \Delta SU_{PR}} = \sum_i^m \left(\frac{dU_{PU}}{dx} \bigg/ \frac{dU_{PR}}{dx} \right) = \sum_i^m MRS_{PU,PR}.$$

That is, the social rate of marginal substitution between the public and private good is equal to the *sum* of the individual marginal rates of substitution. It is this sum that must be equated with the MRT to obtain a Pareto optimum in an economy containing public and private goods. In other words, the condition for optimality becomes:

$$MRS^A_{PU,PR} + MRS^B_{PU,PR} + MRS^C_{PU,PR} \text{ etc.} = MRT_{PU,Pr}.$$

Note that this differs from the condition for an economy containing private goods alone in that it requires the sum of the MRSs to equal MRT, whereas the 'private-goods-only' economy required the MRSs to be equal to each other and also equal to the MRT.

Figure 18.8.1 shows the implications of this equivalence. MC_{PU} is the marginal cost of providing the public good, assumed to rise as more is provided.[1] To avoid complicating the figure we have shown *marginal evaluation* curves. These curves show the consumer's valuation of a commodity in terms of the commodity he forgoes in order to have one more unit of the good in question. In other words, it is measured

---

[1] Notice that this is the marginal cost of increasing the physical quantity supplied. The marginal cost of adding one consumer – that is, of increasing consumption as opposed to availability – is of course zero for a pure public good. Indeed, this equivalence is often used to define public goods.

Normative Price Theory

by the slope of the individual's indifference curve. Now MV_1 is the marginal valuation curve for individual 1, and MV_2 is that for individual 2. Since MV measures MRS we can relate the figure directly to the condition for optimality derived above. For we require the *summation* of MVs to be equal to MRT, where MRT in this case is shown in terms of marginal cost.[1]

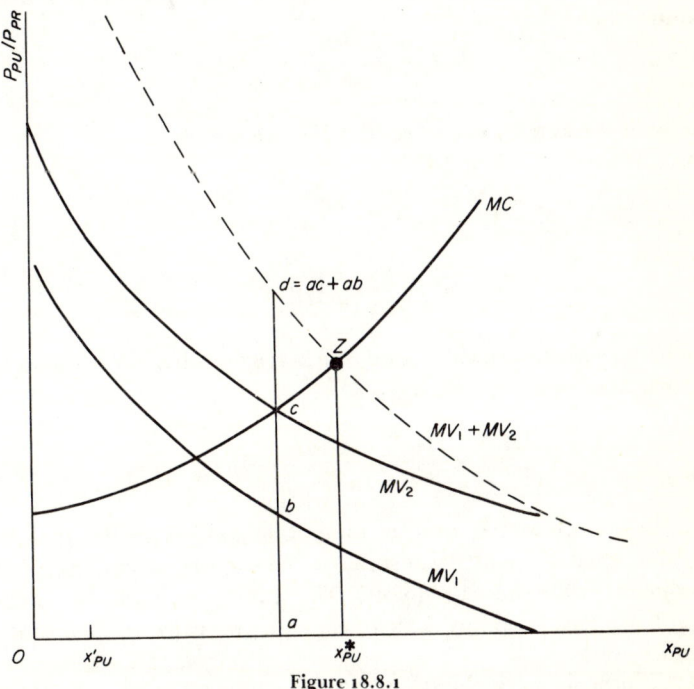

Figure 18.8.1

But instead of deriving an aggregate marginal valuation curve by summing the MVs horizontally (in analogous fashion to the horizontal summation of demand curves to obtain a market demand curve) we must sum them *vertically*. We must do this because each unit of the public good is consumed by each consumer. The individual marginal valuation curves allow for the fact that consumers will value these units differently, but the fact remains that each unit of the good – for example, Ox_{PU}^1 in Figure 18.8.1 – is consumed by each individual. It follows that the optimal provision of the public good is at Z, with quantity x_{PU}^*.

[1] That is, as MC_{PU}/MC_{PR}. The reader should check that this interpretation is correct by looking at the marginal equivalences in Section 18.5.

One very important corollary follows from this analysis.[1] Section 18.6 argued that, under certain highly restrictive conditions, a perfectly competitive economy would automatically secure Pareto optimality. In the presence of public goods – which, notice, do not derive from institutional features but are as 'natural' as private goods – this theorem no longer holds. The demonstration of this is simple, given our condition for optimality with public goods. On the production side we require

$$MRT_{PU,PR} = \frac{MC_{PU}}{MC_{PR}} = \frac{P_{PU}}{P_{PR}}.$$

For each consumer to be in equilibrium we require

$$\frac{MU_{PU}^A}{MU_{PR}^A} = \frac{P_{PU}}{P_{PR}}$$

and

$$\frac{MU_{PU}^B}{MU_{PR}^B} = \frac{P_{PU}}{P_{PR}}.$$

But because we have public goods the overall result of these equations for *individual* optimisation is

$$\frac{MU_{PU}^A}{MU_{PR}^A} + \frac{MU_{PU}^B}{MU_{PR}^B} = \frac{2 \cdot P_{PU}}{P_{PR}} > MRT_{PU,PR}.$$

That is, the optimal amount of the public good is greater than the amount actually provided by producers (consumers' valuations exceed producers' willingness to supply). The public good will be undersupplied in an economy which relies on the price mechanism to allocate goods.

Of course, if marginal valuations were fully revealed – if, that is, some clear-cut mechanism existed whereby people could and would record their valuations – then, no doubt, some slightly modified competitive economy would be optimal in the presence of public goods. But it should be clear that there is no *incentive* on the part of individuals to reveal their preferences if the method of financing the public good is one which relies on contributions from individuals. For if one individual knows that he will receive the benefits anyway, why should he

---

[1] It should be stressed that we have taken the example of a 'pure' public good. In reality the classification of goods according to their degree of 'publicness' is extremely difficult, though important. On some of the problems see M. Peston, *Public Goods and the Public Sector* (Macmillan, London, 1972).

bother to contribute to the finance of the product? He will receive the benefits because he cannot be prevented from doing so – the product is non-excludable. This is the problem of the so-called 'free rider'.

18.9 External Effects

In the discussion of public goods it was pointed out that the provision of such a good to one person entailed its automatic provision to another. In addition, this automatic provision could not be corrected in such a way as to discriminate between consumers because of the impossibility of devising an excludable pricing system. Another way of looking at the automatic provision aspect is to say that the good possesses *external benefits*: that is, my consumption of the good 'spills over', in a beneficial way, to you. In addition, you do not pay for the benefit – it goes *unappropriated*. Consequently, we can say that a feature of such goods is that they have external benefits, or, to note some of the many titles now given to such goods, *positive externality*, or *positive external effect*, or *positive spillover*.

Equally, a good may yield pleasure to its consumer but be a nuisance to someone else. Such a good would be said to possess *negative externality*, *negative external effect*, *external cost*, or *negative spillover*. This externality aspect may arise because of the inputs used, or because the act of consumption itself is a nuisance. In the former case we can think of pollution due to the use of chemicals as inputs; in the latter case we can think of offensive behaviour, lighting bonfires, unsightly landscape, and so on.

The essence of an externality, then, is that it involves (*a*) an interdependence between two or more economic agents, and (*b*) a failure to price that interdependence. The interdependence could be between consumers, between producers, or between producers and consumers. It is also the case that the existence of externalities will mean that Pareto optimality cannot be achieved unless the price mechanism contains some automatic adjustment procedures whereby externalities are 'corrected'. The first proposition can be demonstrated as follows.

Suppose we have two firms producing, respectively, outputs x_1 and x_2. Then we could write

$$\frac{dx_1}{dL_1} = MP_{L,1} \tag{1}$$

and

$$\frac{dx_2}{dL_2} = MP_{L,2} \tag{2}$$

where dx simply refers to the change in output, dL to the change in the input labour (we assume one variable input for convenience) and $MP_{L,1}$ means the marginal product of labour in producing x_1. This much is self-evident since all we have done is define marginal products. Now suppose that the output of x_2 is affected by the level of production in firm 1: the production function in firm 2 will involve the dependence of output not just on the labour input in firm 2 but also on the output of firm 1. This establishes that there is an interdependence. We shall further assume that it is 'untraded' – no price is paid for this interdependence. Hence we have an externality.

With this interdependence we shall need to redefine marginal product. Equations (1) and (2) above stand as definitions of *private* marginal product. But they do not express *social* marginal product. If the externality is negative – firm 1 imposes costs on firm 2 and does not compensate firm 2 – we shall have to write

$$SMP_{L,1} = \frac{dx_1}{dL_1} - \frac{dx_2}{dL_1} \tag{3}$$

$$SMP_{L,2} = \frac{dx_2}{dL_2}. \tag{4}$$

Equation (3) is the important one. For from private marginal product we have subtracted an expression dx_2/dL_1: this is the change in the output of x_2 due to a change in the input labour in producing good 1. (Notice that we have expressed it in terms of output changes with respect to labour inputs – this allows for the fact that output of good 2 varies with the output of good 1 which in turn varies with the input of labour to good 1.)

Now, if we have perfect competition and firms are all profit maximisers, we shall have

$$W \bigg/ \frac{dx_1}{dL_1} = MC_1 = p_1$$

and

$$W \bigg/ \frac{dx_2}{dL_2} = MC_2 = p_2$$

which in turn, under perfect competition, implies

$$\frac{dx_1}{dL_1} = \frac{dx_2}{dL_2}.$$

That is, the self-interested behaviour of firms under perfect competition will lead to the equality of (real) marginal products. But it is *private* marginal products that are equated, not social marginal products. For if it was the latter we would require, in our example,

$$\frac{dx_1}{dL_1} - \frac{dx_2}{dL_1} = \frac{dx_1}{dL_1}.$$

In other words, Pareto optimality would require the equivalence of social marginal products. But our competitive state secures only the equivalence of private marginal products. Hence externalities entail non-optimality. If the externality is negative, the output of the 'offending' activity will be too large. If the externality is positive, the output will be too small.

We can finally illustrate external effects by looking at the familiar figure for the firm's equilibrium under perfect competition. In Figure 18.9.1 the curve *PMC* measures private marginal cost. The curve *SMC* measures social marginal cost and is shown lying above *PMC* because a negative externality is assumed to exist (social marginal product is less than private marginal product: hence social marginal cost is above private marginal cost). The optimal output is seen to be x_s and not x_p which is the private profit-maximising solution. In fact the amount of externality that is undesirable is shown by the shaded area in the figure. This is sometimes called the 'Pareto-relevant' externality. Notice that at

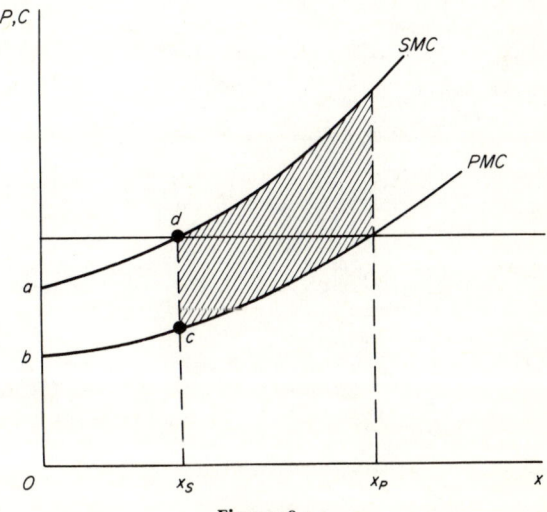

Figure 18.9.1

x_s some social loss remains, and we could measure this by the area $abcd$. In this way we can derive the following general propositions:

(i) A negative externality implies that the output of the 'offending' activity is too large. Vice versa for a positive externality.

(ii) A negative externality should not be removed altogether. Instead, the aim should be to secure the *optimal amount of externality*.

It is left to the reader to consult texts in public economics on the best way to secure optimal externality. The interested reader might also repeat the exercise of this section for imperfect competition, since there are added difficulties.

Index

advertising 266
  monopolist 285–7, 288, 292
analysis, general 249–51
  partial and 247–8
Andrews, P. W. S. 298 n.
Armstrong, W. 5 n.
attainable set 8–9, 19
autonomous behaviour 314–16, 318

bandgwagon effect on demand 67
bargaining
  collective 220–2, 352–3
  oligopolistic 319, 321–2, 338
  power, firm's 338–9
barter 344–52
Baumol, W. J. 281 n.
Bertrand model of oligopoly 316
bonds
  demand curve 207–9, 234–6, 239, 245
  interest 205–7, 209, 233–4, 245
  prices 233
  savings in 204–9
  supply curve 207–8, 234–5
Brems, Hans 319
budget lines 19–21, 27, 39, 47, 49, 58, 361–2
budget set, consumer's 19–21
business saving 200–1

capital
  fixed 93, 115, 139
  gains 205–6, 209
  human 226–8
  working 237
capital/labour ratio 76, 80–4, 90–1
Chamberlin, E. H. 275, 297 n., 298 n.
choice

consistent 59
  see also preferences
classification 133
  inputs 226–7
  markets 272–5
Cobb, C. W. 112 n.
Cobb–Douglas production function 112–13
cobweb theorem 130, 167
collective bargaining 220–2, 352–3
collusive oligopoly 307, 329–39, 343
commodity 2–3, 6–7, 12–13
  prices, labour supply and 173–5
  space 5–7, 13–14, 17
  substitution rate 14
  see also goods; product
company, *see* firms
compensated demand curves 54, 365–7
compensating variation 363
compensation tests 368–70
competition
  discouraging 287–9, 292–3
  free 265
  imperfect 100, 260, 388
  monopsonistic 304–6
  monopsonistic 304–6
  non-price 333
  perfect 100, 102, 118, 155, 246, 260, 275, 280, 289–90, 294
    conditions for 264–73
    optimality of 376–8, 384
  pure 261–4, 271, 273, 275, 345
competitive output 313–16
complements
  goods 56–8
  inputs 80, 163
  perfect 24
  processes 80–2

completeness, axiom of 8, 16
concavity 22
conformity, consumer preferences and 67
conjectural behaviour 315, 322–4
conjectural demand or sales curve 326
consume, propensity to 196–8
consumer
  budget set 19–21
  equilibrium 20–1, 27, 361
    preferences and 1–30
  expenditure 31–2, 151–2
  household as 1–2
  income, determination of 172–4
  landowners 186–7
  market period 151–2
  selection 8–9, 21
  sovereignty 2 n.
  surplus 355–6
    compensation tests 368–70
    demand curve and 359–62, 365–8
    Hick's four measures of 362–8
    income changes and 359–61
    Marshallian approach 356–62, 368
    see also under indifference; preferences; sales plan
consumption
  income relationship with 69–74
  planning 124–5, 127–9, 138
  price relationship with 36–8, 142, 151–2
  quantities, optimal 41
  saving and 197–8
    choice between 188–91, 200
  time, work time and 172–4, 176–80
consumption-saving plan 197–9
contract curve 351–2, 372
convexity
  consumer preference curves 14–17, 79
  isoproduct curves 79–32
  strict 16–17, 79
  weak 17, 21–2
cost–benefit analysis 355–6
costing margin 298–300
cost(s)
  average 169, 296, 298–301
  curves 95–7, 116–18, 122, 271–2
    production isoquants and 89–91, 95–8
    supply curves and 104–5
  decreasing 289–90
  durable goods 168–71

fixed 72–3, 93, 107–8, 160, 298
  and variable 94
functions 92–7
  long-run 116–18, 120, 122
  short-run 88–108
indirect 298–9
labour 98, 150, 156–8
long-run 145, 169, 296, 289–90
marginal 94–5, 102, 278, 296
  prices equal to 378
  private and social 387
  minimising 71–2, 77–8, 88–9, 91, 114, 116
  opportunity 230 n.
  output and 97–104, 118
  prices 251, 378
  production below 103–4, 135
  substitution effect on 97–8
  theory of price 298–301
  see also inputs
coupon yield 205
Cournot, A. 247 n., 308 n.
  model of oligopoly 308–16, 346

Dasgupta, A. 355 n.
Debreu, G. 25 n., 80 n.
demand
  advertising and 285–6
  cross elasticity of 56–8
  curves 38–42, 52–6, 125, 127, 130–1, 244–5
  see also elasticity; inputs; labour
    bonds and money 207–9, 234–6, 239, 245
    compensated 54, 365–7
    competition, pure or perfect 271
    conjectural 326
    consumer surplus and 359–62, 365–8
    discontinous 63–4, 327
    Hicksian 53–4, 365
    kinked
      monopolist 289
      oligopolistic 325–9, 336
    monopolistic competition, under 294–5
    pathological 62–5
    price-maker and price-taker 100–2, 155
    total 65–6, 123
  durable goods 168–71, 222–3
  effort 180–3
  functions 31–69

Index

demand (*contd.*)
  functions (*contd.*)
    inverse   42
    partial   41
    price   38–42, 251
  government bonds, for   206–7
  market   65–6, 123
    aggregation problems   66–9
    price mapping of   40–1
    short-run and long-run   150–3
  supply and   123–32, 139
    long-run analysis   144–8, 152–3
    short-run analysis   132–9
destruction of goods   136
diminishing returns, law of   82–6, 95, 113–14, 122, 158–9
diseconomies   140–1, 150
dispreference   3
dominance, axiom of   9–12, 16
  relaxing   23–5
Douglas, Paul   112 n.
duopoly   308–15. *See also* monopoly, bilateral
durable goods
  demand for   168–71, 222–3
  pricing   222–5

education as investment   227–8
effort
  demand for labour   180–3
  price   180–2
  supply   172–88
elasticity   34
  cross   56–8
  demand of
    income   34–6, 41, 46–51
    inputs   163–4, 167–9, 171
    price   42–6, 62–5, 126, 137, 158–9, 167–8, 284–6, 327–8
    total revenue and   44–6, 284
    under monopolistic competition   295
  input substitution   98–9
  measurement of   34–5
  supply   125, 129, 140–1, 143, 150
    conditions for long-run   265–70
    inputs   266–70
    labour   185–6, 266–8
    price   106–7, 137
Engel, Ernst   36 n.
Engel curves   33, 35
entrants to industry, new   265–6
  monopolistic competition,
    under   296–7
monopoly and   287–9
monopsonistic competition, under   305
equilibrium
  consumer   20–1, 27, 361
    preferences and   1–30
  cost functions and   91–108
  duopolist   313–16
  firm's   99–105, 157–8
  general, Pareto optimum and   371
  interest rates and   240–5
  leadership   317–18
  market   129, 262–3
  monopolist   276–80, 290
    bilateral   346, 348, 351
  monopolistic competition, under   295–8
  monopsonistic   303–6
  oligopolist   314, 316
  pay-off   341–2
  price, *see under* prices
  profit-maximising   278, 290
equipment, *see also* durable goods
  specialised   148–9
equivalence relations   5, 10 n.
equivalent variation   364–5, 367
evaluation curves, marginal   382–3
expansion path, firm's
  cost-minimising   89, 91, 114, 116
  long-run   110, 114, 118, 122
  short-run   92–4, 108, 163
  supply curve   107
expenditure–consumption curve   31–2
external economies   149–50
external effects of public goods   385–8
externality   387–8

feasible set   8–9, 19
Fellner, W.   316 n., 329 n.
firm   70
  bargaining power   338–9
  equilibrium   99–105, 157–8
  limited liability   200
  multiproduct   131–2, 148, 301
  objectives of   71–2, 108, 159
  profits of   200
  restricting entry to industry, 266 (*see also* entrants to industry)
  see also expansion path; purchase plan; sales plan
free disposal, axiom of   80
Friedman, M.   259 n.

games theory and oligopoly 339–43
Giffen, Sir Robert 38 n.
Giffen goods 38, 51–2, 62, 66
goods
    complementary 56–8
    destruction of 136
    Giffen 38, 51–2, 62, 66
    indispensable 361 n.
    inferior 32–3, 51–2, 370
    normal 51–2
    private 381
    public 381–5
        external benefits of 385–8
    see also commodity; durable goods; product
government
    monopolies and 291–2
    output restriction by 136
    stock 205–6
Green, H. A. J. 15 n.

Hall, R. L. 326 n.
Hayek, F. A. 263 n.
Heathfield, D. F. 113 n.
Henderson, J. 15 n.
Hicks, J. R. 15 n., 47–50 n., 57 n., 362 n., 369
    demand curve 53–4, 365
    four measures of consumer surplus 362–8
Hitch, C. J. 326 n.
homogeneity 111 n., 261–2, 273
household as consumer 1–2
human capital 226–8

import taxes 292
income
    changes in 41
        consumer surplus and 359–61
    consumer's, determination of 172–4
    consumption relationship with 36–8, 69–34, 142, 151–2, 198
    consumption time and 172–4, 176–80
    distribution 250–1, 373
    effort price of 180–2
    elasticity of demand 34–6, 41, 46–51
    interdependence 67
    investment and 243
    leisure and 173, 182
    marginal utility 359, 362
    real 32–3, 174
        constant 47–50, 54, 57

saving and 195, 198, 204
subsistence level 177
substitution effects and 46–52, 54–7, 62, 178–80, 182
total 240
indifference
    consumer 2–5
        curve 12–13, 17–19, 21
            barter 344–6, 351
            budget lines and 21, 27
            concave 22
            convex 14–17, 21, 189
            convex–concave 63–5
            dominance axiom 9–12
                relaxing 23–5
            leisure-income 173, 182
            linear 22
            parallel 54, 56, 359–61
            Pareto optimum and 371–5, 383
            satiation and 25–7
            saving 189
            utility function and 28–30
        map 9–12, 17, 26, 46–7, 52–3, 173, 178
        preference and 3–5, 7–12
    investor's 211–14
    producer curve 76
    profit curve 311–12, 316–18, 320–2
    relationships 5
indivisibilities 6–7, 113–14, 269–71, 292
inferior goods 32–3, 51–2, 370
inferior inputs 98
innovation 120, 144, 147, 292
inputs
    classification 226–7
    complementary 80, 163
    demand for 154, 252
    curves
        labour 216–19
        long-run 164–5, 218–19, 221–2
        short-run 155–6, 161–4, 216–18, 220
        total 165–8
    durable goods 168–71, 222–3
    interest rates and 171, 241
    long-run. 164–5, 218–19, 221–2, 268
    parameter changes and 159–60
    price elasticity 163–4, 167–9, 171
    production possibilities and 159–61

Index

inputs (contd.)
  demand for (contd.)
    selling price relation with   159–60, 165–8
      short-run   216–18, 220
        one variable   154–8
        two variables   160–4
    diminishing returns from   82–6, 158–9
    efficiency of   228–30
    fixed   113, 115–17, 139, 160, 165
    inferior   98
    indivisible   113–14, 269–71, 292
    maringal product of   81–3, 86, 170
      market, pure competition   264
    mobility of   266–8
    monopsonist   304
    planning curve   164, 169
    prices
    see also cost(s); labour
      changes in   89–99, 108, 147–50, 157–8, 249, 268
      elasticity of   158–9
      determining, firm's role in. 165, 171, 216
      marginal revenue product equal to   170–1
      relative   89–99
        determination of   216–45
        durable goods   222–4
        interest and   233–45
        labour   216–22, 226–30
        rent   224–5, 230–3
    purchase planning   71–2, 154–71
    redundant   80
    rising   110–12
    substitute   80, 83, 92, 98–9, 163, 165
    supply   172, 252
      curve, labour   216–22
      elasticity   266–70
      units   114, 266–8
interdependence   249–50
  consumer preferences   67
  incomes   67
  oligopolistic   316
  price-supply   246–7, 261
  unpriced   385–6
interest
  bonds   205–7, 209, 233–4, 245
  calculation of   169 n.
  price element   226
  rate   233
    changes in   239–40, 243

    saving and   191–5, 201–2
    consumer preference changes and   244
    determination of   233–45
    input–demand relation with   171, 241
    long-run equilibrium   240–5
    market   238–43
investment
  human capital   277–8
  income relationship with   243
  indifference curve   211–14
  interest rate and   244
  savings plan   204–15
  uncertainty and   268
  variance calculation   211, 213–14
  yield   205–6, 210–11, 215
  see also inputs; savings
investment–saving equilibrium   241–3
isocost lines   89–91, 118
isoproduct curves   75–6, 86
  convexity of   79–82
isoquants, production   75–80, 82, 110, 112, 115, 374
  convexity   79–82, 98, 374–5
  cost curves and   88–91, 95–8
  linearity   86–7, 98, 374 n.
iso-utility curve   28

Johnston, J.   300 n.

Kaldor, N.   369
Kaldor–Hicks tests   369–70
kinked demand curve
  monopolistic   289
  oligopolistic   325–9, 336
Knopf, A. A.   316 n.

labour/capital ratio 76, 80–4, 90–1
labour
  costs   98, 150, 156–8
  demand
    curves   216–19
    effort   180–3
    elasticity   158
  efficiency   228–30
  human capital   226–8
  market   174
  mobility   266–8
  supply   172–4
    curve   175–8
      long-run   183–6, 218–19, 221–2, 231

labour (*contd.*)
  supply (*contd.*)
    curve (*contd.*)
      short-run 216–18, 220
      total 173
      elasticity 185–6, 266–8
    see also wages
Lancaster, K. 379 n.
land
  change of use 187
  services, prices of 202, 224–5
  supply 186–7
  taxation 233
leadership models 316–25, 349
Leibenstein, H. 67, 68 n.
leisure-income preferences 172–5, 182
Lipsey, R. G. 379 n.
Little, I. M. D. 354 n.
loans 201–2

machines
  demand for 168–71
  marginal revenue productivity of 170–1
Majumdar, T. 5 n.
management
  ability of 113, 141, 298, 339
  large-scale 140–1
  utility, maximising 71
manager
  knowledge 267
  uncertainty and 268–9
mapping
  indifference 9–12, 17, 26, 46–7, 52–3, 173, 178
  price-demand 40–1
market
  behaviour 261–75
    assumptions 259–63, 265–70, 273
    monopoly 276, 282
    oligopoly 308, 313–14, 316, 318–20, 324–5, 329, 332
  classification 272–5
  demand 65–6, 123
    aggregation problems 66–9
  division of 284–5, 304
  equilibrium 129, 262–3
  inputs 264
  interest rate 238–43
  knowledge of 262–3
  labour 174
  methodology 259–60
  monopoly 276

  period 251–2
  price 205–7, 259
  sharing agreement 334–6
  supply 105–6, 123
  see also competition; monopoly; monopsony; oligopoly
Marshall, A. 344 n.
Marshallian demand curve 38, 53–4
mergers 292
monetary authorities' purchase and sale of bonds 236, 239
money
  demand for 208–9, 236–8, 245
  medium of exchange 236–7
  savings in 204, 208–10
  supply 208, 236, 243
monopolistic competition 275, 280, 294–31
monopoly 276–93
  advertising 285–7, 288, 292
  bilateral 275, 344–53 (*see also* duopoly)
  demand curve, kinked 289
  discouraging competitors 287–9, 292–3
  equilibrium 276–80, 290
  genesis and maintenance of 290–3
  natural 291
  nature of 274, 276
  objectives of 280–2
  output and price 330–1
  price determination 276–82
  price discrimination 282–5
  profit-maximising 278, 282, 286, 289–90, 295, 331
monopsonistic markets 302–3
monopsony 274, 302–4, 348–9
  competition under 304–6
monotonicity 10
Morgenstern, O. 339 n.
multiproduct firm 121–2, 148, 301

Nash, J. F. 343 n.
negative externality 385–8
Neumann, J. von 339 n.
Newman, Peter 15 n., 58 n., 61
nonsatiation 10
normative price theory 354–88. *See also* consumer surplus

offer curve 36
oligopoly 274, 307–43
  bargaining under 319, 321–2, 338

oligopoly (contd.)
  collusive 307, 329–39, 343
  Cournot model 308–16, 346
  demand curve, kinked 325–9, 336
  game theory and 339–43
  leadership models 316–25, 349
  nature of 307–8
  reaction curve 312–13, 315, 317–18, 323
oligopsony 274, 339 n.
optimal externality 338
optimality, Pareto 371–8, 380, 383
  individual 384
  perfect competition 376–8, 384
  public–private goods 382–4
output
  competitive 313–16
  costs and 97–104, 118
  government restriction of 136
  leadership 316–18, 349
  monopoly 330–1
  subsidies and 145–6
  wage rates and 228–30
  see also production; sales plan
overcompensation effect 62

Pareto, V. 355
  improvements 368–9, 372, 375
  see also optimality
Pareto-relevant externality 387
patents 266, 292
pay-off equilibrium 341–2
Pearce, D. W. 355 n.
Peston, M. 384
Pigou, A. C. 199
planning
  consumption and supply 124–5, 127–9
  curve 139–41, 148–9
    inputs 164, 169
  new techniques 147–8
  periods 72–3
    saving and 188–9, 192
  production and sales 138, 171
  purchases and consumption 138
  saving 188–204
  supply 124–5, 127–9
  see also sales plan
pollution 385
portfolio, investor's 204, 207
  mixed 210
  variance calculation 211, 213–14
positive externality 385, 387–8

positivists 260
prediction, economic 133–4, 146–7
preferences, consumer 2–3
  advertising and 285
  axioms of 7–17
    relaxing 23–5
  change in 67, 191, 244
    price equilibrium and 248–9, 251
  continuity of 13–14
  curve 14–17, 19
  equilibrium and 1–30
  indifference and 3–5, 7–12. *See also* indifference curve
  indirect 61
  individual and household 1–2
  interdependent 67
  interest rates and 244
  lexicographic ordering of 12–14
  production pattern influenced by 250
  revealed 58–62
  switching 11
  time 189–90
  wage rates and 219
  work and leisure 172–5
price
  discrimination 282–5
  effect 48–9, 52, 54
  leadership 324–5, 329, 336
  line 19
  mapping of demand 40–1
  -makers
    bilateral monopoly, in 347–53
    demand curves 100–2, 155
    independent and interdependent 274
    land services and 202, 224–5
    monopolist 284
    price-takers and 100–2, 155, 259, 264
  -takers, bilateral monopoly 290, 344–6
prices
  agreements on 325, 329–30, 334–6
  analysis of, general 249–54
    and partial 246–8
  change in 128–30, 150–3
    consumer-surplus and 362–70
    relative 126–7, 133, 144–5, 249
    sales plan's response to 104–8, 118, 151
    saving-consumption plan and 198, 249

prices (contd.)
    change in (contd.)
        time path 264–5
        variable factors in 273–4
    commodity, labour supply and 173–5
    compensating variation 364, 365, 367
    consumption relationship with 36–8, 142, 151–2
    control of 132–6
    costs and 251, 378
    demand as function of 38–42, 251
    determination of 123–4, 150–3
        average-cost 298–300
        durable goods 222–5
        general equilibrium 246–58
        long-run 139–50
        monopoly 276–85, 330–1
        monopsonist 302–6
        short-run 124–39
    effort 180–2
    entry-forestalling 288
    equilibrium 125, 127, 129, 131, 264
        general 247, 251–9
        consumer preference changes and 248–9, 251
        formal approach 251–4
        partial analysis of 247–8
        stability of 256–8
        long-run 139–40, 142–3, 150
    equivalent variation 364, 365, 367
    falling 47, 51, 142, 144–5
        firm's revenue and 100–1
    fluctuating 129–30, 143
    interdependence with supply 246–7, 261
    interest, rent and wages in 226
    market 259, 205–7
    market-sharing 334
    production pattern determined by 250
    quality and 67–8
    relative 123–53, 246–58
    selling 106, 159–60, 165
    storage and 138
    subsidy's effect on 145–6
    taxation effect on 137–8
    see also under elasticity; inputs; product
private goods 381
processes 76
    changed, supply and 107
    combination of 77–9, 81

complementary 80–2
substitution of 80–2
producer-indifference curves 76
product
    curves 115–16, 154–5. See also isoproduct curves
        cost curves and 95–7
        linearity and 86–7
    differentiation 287, 297–8
    homogeneous 261–2, 273
    marginal 81–4, 86–7, 155, 170–1, 386–7
    prices
        changes in, supply curve 104–5, 118, 128–30, 139–45, 152–3
        constant 155
        input demand and 159–60, 165–8
        relative, determination of 123–4, 150–3
        long-run 139–50
        short-run 124–39
    sales plan and 104–8, 118, 151
    transformation
        curve 374, 376, 379–80
        function, public–private 381
        rate 121–2
    variants 287
    see also commodity; goods
production 70
    below cost 103–4, 135
    function 73–5
        homogeneous 111–13
        linear case 75–8
        sales plan 110–16, 121–2
        short-run 70–87, 109
        smooth case 79–82, 93, 95, 112
    pattern determined by prices 250
    planning 138, 171
    possibilities
        frontier curve 374, 376, 379
        input demand and 159–61
        intermediate period 120
        long-run 114–16
    sales and 138, 171
    set 77
    see also isoquants; output
profit(s)
    increasing with demand 270
    indifference curve 311–12, 316–18, 320–2
    maximising 71–2, 102–5, 118, 139, 142, 145
        agreement on 329–33, 337–8

Index

profit(s) (*contd.*)
  maximising (*contd.*)
    average-cost theory and   300–1
    duopolist   311–12
    monopoly   278, 282, 286, 289–90, 295, 331
    minimum necessary   281–2
    pooling agreement   331, 333
    possibilities   308–13, 318–19, 321
    restriction of   289
    sharing, oligopolistic   335, 337
    undistributed   200–1
    use of   200–1
public goods   381–5
  external benefits of   385–8
purchase plan   138
  firm's   71–2, 154–71

quality and price   67–8
Quandt, R.   15 n.
quantity variation   364
quasi-substitution effect   62

rationing   134–5
reaction curve, oligopolist   312–13, 315, 317–18, 323
reflexiveness, consumer indifference   5
rent   224–6, 230–3
research planning   147–8
returns
  diminishing   82–6, 95, 113–14, 122, 158–9
  non-proportional   82–6, 113, 154
  to scale   110–12, 116, 118
    increasing   289–90
revenue
  curves   99–104, 122, 154–5
    monopolist   277, 283–4, 296
    marginal   155, 170–1, 278, 283, 296, 348, 350
    maximising   281, 283
    total, price elasticity of demand and   44–6, 284
risk-bearing   211, 214, 245
Robinson, J.   229 n., 284 n.
Rothenberg, J.   5 n.
Rowan, D. C.   240 n.

sales
  curve, conjectural   326
  maximising   71
  see also prices
sales plan, consumer

land services   186–7
saving and savings   188–215
supply of effort and   172–88
sales plan, firm's   70–1
  cost function   116–18, 120
    equilibrium and   88–108
  intermediate period   119–21
  long-run   109–22, 142
  production function   70–87, 109–16, 121–2
  response to price changes   104–8, 118, 151
  revision of   120, 265
  short-run   70–109
sales
  production and   138, 171
  tax   136–8
Samuelson, P. A.   58, 243 n.
satiation, commodity   25–7
save, propensity to   196–8, 201–4
saving
  business   200–1
  consumption and   191, 197–9, 204
    choice between   188–91, 200
  income changes and   195, 198
  indifference curve   189
  interest rates and   191–5, 201–2
  plan   188–204
  price changes and   249
  supply of   201–3
saving-consumption plan   197–9
saving-investment equilibrium   241–3
savings   188
  consumer   10 n.
  firm's   200
  money   204, 208–10
  plan, investment and   204–15
Scitovsky, T.   370
selection, consumer   8–9, 21
selfishness axiom   67
selling price   106, 159–60, 165. *See also* product price
shares, savings in   204
Slutsky, E.   47–51, 53–4
snob effect   68
social benefits, net   356
social welfare functions   354, 380. *See also* welfare
speculation   239–42
spillover   385
Sraffa, P.   290 n.
stock, savings in   204–6. *See also* bonds

stocks, government accumulation of 136
subsidies 145–6
subsistence level incomes 177
substitute
  goods 56–8, 248–9
  perfect 22, 261, 294, 297
  processes 80–2
substitution
  effects
    cost 97–8
    income 46–52, 54–7, 62, 178–80, 182
      Hicks's approach 47–50, 57
      Slutsky approach 47, 49–51
  input 80, 84, 92, 98–9, 163, 165
  rate
    commodity 14
    marginal 15, 264
      future/present goods 189–90
      public-private 381–2
      technical 82, 91, 98, 264, 374
    personal 14–15, 21–2, 54–5, 375–6
supply
  changes in 107, 126
  curve 105–6, 123, 126, 128, 131, 140–4, 148, 208, 236, 243
    bonds 207–8, 234–5
    cost curve and 104–5
    firm's expansion path 107
    product price changes and 104–5, 118, 128–30, 139–45, 152–3
    subsidies and 146
    total 124, 167
  demand and 123–32, 139
    long-run analysis 144–8, 152–3
    short-run analysis 132–69
  effort 172–88
  inputs
    elasticity 266–70
    price 230, 232, 265–7
  land 186–7
  market 105–6, 123
  money 208, 236, 243
  planning 124–5, 127–9
  prices interdependence with 246–7, 261
  saving 201–3
  see also under elasticity; labour
surplus, consumer
  economic rent as 233
  see also under consumer
Sweezy, P. M. 326 n.

symmetry, consumer indifference 5

tariffs 292
taxation 136–9, 233
technological progress 147–8
terms of trade 345
time
  constraint line 174–5, 179
  consumption and work 172–4, 176–80
  optimal allocation of 173–4
  path, price-change 264–5
  preference, marginal rate of 190
  work and leisure 172–4
trade unions 185
  collective bargaining 220–2
  monopoly power 292
training 227, 267
transaction balance 237
transfer earnings 230 n.
transitivity 5, 8, 16, 61

uncertainty 267–9
utility
  constant 50–1, 56
  function 29–30
  income 359–62
  managerial 71
  marginal 358–9
  maximising 9, 30, 71, 264, 352

valuations, marginal 382–4
variable proportions, law of 300
variance calculation, investment 211, 213–14
variation
  compensating 363
  equivalent 364–5, 367
Veblen, Thorsten 68

wage rates 156–8
  changes in 174–9, 182–3, 185, 219, 270
  consumer preferences and 219
  firm's equilibrium and 157–8
  output and 228–30
  relative, determination of 202, 216–22
wages 172
  economic rent in 230–2
  price element in 226
Walras, Leon 247, 258
wealth constraint 19

welfare
- economics 354 (*see also* consumer surplus)
- games theory and 343
  - Paretian 355, 371–8, 380
  - price system and 262
- maximised in perfect competition 378, 386–7
- Pareto optimum 371–8, 380
- second-best theorem 378–80

Winch, D. M. 362 n.

work time, consumption time and 172–4, 176–80

working hours and wage rates 180–3

yield, investment 205–7, 210–11, 215